S0-BHS-391

THE COMMUNITARIAN CHALLENGE
TO LIBERALISM

THE COMMUNITARIAN CHALLENGE
TO LIBERALISM

Edited by

**Ellen Frankel Paul, Fred D. Miller, Jr.,
and Jeffrey Paul**

JC
574
C65
1996

Regis College Library
15 ST. MARY STREET
TORONTO, ONTARIO, CANADA
M4Y 2R5

WITHDRAWN

CAMBRIDGE
UNIVERSITY PRESS

Published by the Press Syndicate of the University of Cambridge
The Pitt Building, Trumpington Street, Cambridge CB2 1RP, England
40 West 20th Street, New York, NY 10011, USA
10 Stamford Road, Oakleigh, Melbourne, Victoria 3166, Australia

Copyright © 1996 Social Philosophy and Policy Foundation

First published 1996

Printed in the United States of America

Library of Congress Cataloging-in-Publication Data

The communitarian challenge to liberalism / edited by Ellen Frankel Paul,
Fred D. Miller, Jr., and Jeffrey Paul.   p.   cm.
Includes bibliographical references and index.
ISBN 0-521-56742-4
1. Liberalism.   2. Community.   I. Paul, Ellen Frankel.   II. Miller,
Fred Dycus, 1944–   III. Paul, Jeffrey.
JC574.C65   1996
320.5'1–dc20   95-40055
CIP

ISBN 0-521-56742-4 paperback

The essays in this book have also been published,
without introduction and index, in the semiannual journal
Social Philosophy & Policy, Volume 13, Number 1,
which is available by subscription.

CONTENTS

INTRODUCTION

Over the past two decades, a debate has raged within political theory between liberals, with their emphasis on protecting individual rights, and their communitarian challengers, who stress the overriding importance of community values and interests. Several questions are at the heart of this debate: Should group rights trump individual rights? Should the common good prevail over individuals' self-interest? What role do communities play in shaping the values of their members, and what obligations, if any, do individuals owe to their communities? Does government have any legitimate part to play in promoting community values, and how should government respond when individuals and communities come into conflict?

The essays in this volume—written from a range of perspectives by philosophers and political and legal theorists—address these questions and explore related issues. Some discuss disagreements between liberals and communitarians over the nature of moral agency and the proper functions of government. Some examine alternative ways of conceiving liberalism or community, or challenge widely held beliefs about the harmful effects of capitalism on community, or about the value of traditional practices as guides to judicial reasoning. Other essays seek to determine whether it makes sense to think of societies as having and pursuing a common good, or whether culturally diverse societies can ever hope to achieve social unity. Still others examine the role of states in promoting their citizens' civic education and their participation in the voluntary associations and institutions of civil society.

In the opening essay, "Moral Agency, Commitment, and Impartiality," Neera K. Badhwar contrasts liberal and communitarian views of moral agency. Badhwar notes that the liberal tradition holds that individuals are able to take up an impartial, universal viewpoint when they evaluate their own projects and conceptions of the good and those of others. Communitarians reject the impartial, universal viewpoint of liberal morality, holding instead that an individual's conception of the good is extensively shaped (or even determined) by the communities of which he is a part— especially his political community. Badhwar argues that the communitarian's emphasis on the centrality of political community raises important questions about the treatment of outsiders and of dissenters within the community itself: When members of a community act to pursue their common good, are there objective limits on what they may do to dissidents or members of other communities, or are they limited only by the accepted traditions and practices of their own community? Moreover, to what extent may an individual question the traditions and practices of his own community, and to what extent may a community exercise its authority over those who challenge its preeminence? Badhwar contends that the liberal's conception of moral agency is better able to deal with these troubling issues: by taking up an impartial, universal standpoint, one can step back and evaluate one's traditions and the traditions of others. She maintains, further, that our individual commitments to particular persons and projects can only be understood in light of the liberal's belief that it is possible for individuals to make moral assessments from an impartial, universal standpoint. In forming such commitments, she argues, we must recognize both ourselves and others as equal bearers of rights to our own (compossible) values and pursuits.

Like Badhwar, Martha Nussbaum is concerned with the question of how individuals should interact as moral agents. Nussbaum's "Compassion: The Basic Social Emotion" examines the role of compassion or pity in linking individuals to their communities and to one another. In light of liberalism's emphasis on justifying moral and political principles through reason, some communitarian critics question whether liberal theory can accommodate sentiments such as compassion; but Nussbaum believes that a crude contrast between "reason" and "emotion" has obscured our understanding of the function that compassion might play in our public life. Drawing on Aristotle's analysis in his *Rhetoric*, she characterizes compassion as "a painful emotion directed at another person's misfortune or suffering" which is inspired by a belief that the suffering is serious, that it was not brought on by the sufferer's own actions, and that one might suffer a similar misfortune oneself. Compassion is rational, then, in the sense that it is based upon and constituted by beliefs or judgments about the well-being of others. Nussbaum defends this account and discusses how narrative literature, and especially tragic drama, can help foster and develop compassion by allowing people to understand and identify with the suffering of others. She concludes by examining the implications of her account for moral and civic education, the selection of political leaders, the promotion of economic development, the evaluation of judicial reasoning, and the design of public institutions.

While Nussbaum attempts to show how compassion can draw people together, John Haldane explores the role of fellowship in the formation of community. In "The Individual, the State, and the Common Good," Haldane draws on Augustine's definition of a people as "a gathering of rational beings united in fellowship by a common agreement about the object of its love"—an agreement, that is, about the common good. He believes that such fellowship can indeed be the basis of valuable forms of community, but argues that modern political communities generally lack the requisite commonality of history, traditions, and interests. Haldane thus rejects the communitarian ideal of a state in which citizens are united in their pursuit of a common good; in this, he agrees with John Rawls and other liberal theorists who deny the possibility of a society in which citizens all share the same comprehensive political doctrine and conception of the good. Nevertheless, Haldane criticizes Rawls's attempt to ground his liberal theory in an "overlapping consensus" about principles of justice that are said to be neutral with respect to persons' conceptions of the good. When fundamental disagreements about important issues arise, he argues, Rawls is forced to retreat to his own, nonneutral individualist doctrine. Rawls's overlapping consensus, Haldane concludes, is no more stable than a political *modus vivendi*, a political system of the kind that exists in Great Britain, comprised of institutions developed over time to address specific needs and serve specific purposes.

Chandran Kukathas's contribution to this volume is also concerned with the tension between the communitarian's emphasis on pursuit of the common good and the liberal's emphasis on the individual's pursuit of his own interests. In "Liberalism, Communitarianism, and Political Community," Kukathas examines the communitarian critique of liberalism and the liberal response, focusing on the account of political community implicit in both stances. He defines a community as "an association of individuals who share an understanding of what is public and what is private within that association"; members of a political community, on this view, have a common understanding about what issues are open to political resolution and what practices are subject to political control. Kukathas argues that we can acknowledge the existence of this sort of political community while at the same time recognizing that political community need not play the central role in shaping individuals' lives that some communitarians would have it play. Indeed, he argues that both communitarianism and contemporary liberalism exaggerate the value of political community. Communitarians fail to fully appreciate the extent to which individuals belong to a wide range of "partial" communities and associations whose values may conflict with those of the political community (and with those of other associations). Contemporary liberals, while stressing the importance of individual rights and liberties, nevertheless, tend to assume that the fundamental questions of social order must be addressed by the institutions of the political society. Kukathas concludes that the subordination of partial communities (such as religious or cultural groups) to the political community involves a centralization of legal power and a potential for cultural imperialism that may well be destructive of the kind of pluralism that liberalism is supposed to respect.

Will Kymlicka's "Social Unity in a Liberal State" focuses on a specific category of "partial" communities — ethnic minorities — and their relationship to the larger political community. Kymlicka notes the instability of multiethnic countries around the world and sets out to explore the possible bases of social unity in states that contain significant ethnic divisions and rivalries. He distinguishes two sources of ethnocultural diversity and argues that they have profoundly different implications for political stability. The first source is the admission of voluntary immigrants; the second is the incorporation, through conquest, colonization, or federation, of preexisting culturally distinct societies. Kymlicka argues that while voluntary immigrant groups pose few if any threats to the stability of a liberal-democratic order, the existence of incorporated societies can be much more destabilizing. Such groups tend to see themselves as distinct "peoples" or "nations"; they tend to demand rights of self-government and may even contemplate secession. In attempting to discover what can hold such "multination" states together, Kymlicka considers some recent liberal and communitarian approaches, and concludes that none provides a plausible account of social unity in multination states.

Another source of instability in modern states is the sharp increase in family breakdown and crime that has occurred in recent decades, particularly in the advanced societies of the West. In "Capitalism and Community," David Conway acknowledges that this trend suggests that there is some feature of these societies that makes them unconducive to valuable forms of human community, but he rejects the claim, made by many philosophers and social theorists, that these societies are inimical to community because they are capitalist in form. Conway maintains, instead, that the principal enemy of worthwhile forms of human community in present-day societies is overextended government. After setting out four kinds of communal attachment that human beings may feel toward one another—family, neighborhood, national, and political community—Conway examines and responds to communitarian arguments designed to show capitalism's deleterious effects on these forms of community. He challenges communitarian claims that capitalism encourages a destructively individualistic mentality and demands a degree of labor mobility which is disruptive of families, that capitalist urban development undermines neighborhoods, that freedom of immigration damages distinct national cultures, and that the form of representative democracy adopted by most capitalist countries precludes the formation of a common will among citizens. He argues that government welfare programs have contributed to the breakdown of the family and the decay of urban neighborhoods, and that government interference in the sphere of education has undermined the kind of educational pluralism that could foster community among members of various national groups. He concludes, finally, that the breakdown of these other forms of community, together with growing resentment of costly and invasive government, has led to the erosion of patriotism and political community.

The next two essays address the liberal-communitarian debate by exploring new ways of thinking about liberalism. In "The Postmodern Self and the Politics of Liberal Education," Steven Kautz analyzes the postmodern liberalism of Richard Rorty. Rorty's postmodern liberal "ironist," unlike the classical liberal rationalist, "faces up to the contingency of his or her own most central beliefs and desires," recognizing that those beliefs and desires are shaped by cultural influences and historical accidents over which he or she has no control. Kautz examines the psychological consequences of conceiving of liberalism, and of the relationship between individual and community, in this new way, attempting to discover what sorts of human beings will emerge as we learn to "face up to our contingency." Since Rorty suggests that his new way of thinking about liberalism entails a new approach to liberal education, Kautz asks whether Rorty's postmodernist strategy for defending liberalism works in the particular case of liberal education. In the course of his discussion, Kautz explores the tension between the conservative and radical dimensions of education, between the need to educate students in the history and traditions of their society, so that they may take their place as citizens, and the need to teach students to think critically about their society's values. He shows how Rorty's liberal ironism would redirect the mission of education — promoting an "exaltation of democracy for its own sake" and encouraging students to engage in "self-creation." Kautz concludes by describing some potential negative effects of the postmodern approach, arguing that the postmodern emphasis on the contingency of one's beliefs and desires can lead students to become uncritically self-satisfied, apathetic, and complacent.

In "What Liberalism Means," Ronald Beiner attempts to reorient the liberal-communitarian debate by asking whether either the leading defenders of contemporary liberalism or their communitarian critics live up to a sufficiently robust standard of social criticism. Beiner argues that liberalism should be defined not merely in terms of its preferred economic and political institutions, or its position on the limits of state power, but, more ambitiously, in terms of the encompassing "philosophy of life" that it articulates. On the basis of this broader definition, he argues that what is ultimately at issue between leading liberals and their critics has to do with cultural judgments concerning the adequacy of a characteristically modern way of life — a way of life marked by hyper-individualism, mindless consumerism, the failure of civic solidarity, and the erosion of basic social institutions like the family. On this view, liberals are marked not merely by their insistence that individuals should have the freedom to make their own choices and shape their own lives, but also by their reluctance to question the decisions that individuals make and the kinds of lives they choose to lead. As a result of this reluctance, Beiner argues, contemporary liberals are reduced to tinkering with the political and economic institutions of modern societies and ignoring crucial questions about the quality of life that such societies promote. He calls for a return to a richer and more radical form of social criticism, of the kind practiced by such theorists as Plato, Rousseau, Tocqueville, and Nietzsche.

Cass R. Sunstein's contribution to this volume focuses on an issue touched upon by both Kautz and Beiner: the extent to which theorists should question the traditions of their society. In "Against Tradition," Sunstein notes that many communitarians are (at least implicitly) traditionalists, in that they reject the rights-based approach of liberal political thought as insufficiently respectful of the long-standing customs and practices of communities. Focusing on the role of tradition in constitutional interpretation, Sunstein agrees with traditionalists that people (and especially judges) should proceed with caution when considering whether to reject time-honored practices, but he argues that appeal to tradition is not the best method for defining and interpreting constitutional rights. Reliance on tradition is problematic, Sunstein contends, since traditions do not come "prepackaged" for easy identification: any identification of tradition involves historical interpretation and must be to some extent evaluative. He illustrates his points with discussions of key legal cases involving sexual privacy and abortion, arguing that these cases should be resolved not by appeals to tradition, but by appeals to equality and procedural fairness: restrictions on the sale of contraceptives, for example, should be rejected on the grounds that they discriminate against women, while statutes outlawing certain sexual practices should be considered unconstitutional because they are only rarely and selectively enforced. In the end, Sunstein concludes, traditions must be evaluated on their merits, and, indeed, this is one of the most important functions of our public political institutions.

A central element of the Western tradition is its emphasis on tolerance as a way of accommodating the diverse values and practices of people living in pluralistic communities, and this is the subject of George P. Fletcher's contribution to this collection, "The Case for Tolerance." Fletcher sets out a defense of tolerance that involves three elements: he argues against intolerance of the beliefs and practices of others, against the moral failing of indifference toward them, and against the practice of extending an uncritical respect toward everyone. He discusses the difference between general intolerance of others and specific intolerance of particular people and actions, and between private intolerance and that which is sanctioned by government; and he analyzes examples involving political correctness, the anti-smoking movement, and efforts by the French to defend their language against corruption by outside influences. Placing the subject of religious intolerance in its historical context, Fletcher observes that it was often motivated by concern for one's neighbor's salvation, and he shows how greater tolerance can also bring with it indifference to the well-being of others. He argues that the richest form of tolerance involves an element of suffering and regret: one wants to intervene in another's life for the other's own good, but one recognizes that there are some values that cannot be imposed from the outside. Fletcher concludes by distinguishing tolerance from respect, and expressing doubts about whether the former need involve the latter, especially when one practices tolerance in spite of one's moral disapproval of another's actions.

The remaining three essays in this volume examine ways of strengthening the ties between individuals and their communities. In "Community, Diversity, and Civic Education: Toward a Liberal Political Science of Group Life," Stephen Macedo begins with the observation that local community life can make vital contributions to the moral development of citizens of modern mass societies. Macedo draws on the work of Adam Smith and others to explore the ways that statecraft can help to gently shape and encourage those patterns of associative life that generate liberal civic virtues such as trust, cooperativeness, self-control, and reciprocity. A liberal science of group life, he contends, can provide liberal states with indirect but vital tools of civic education: it can show how people may be encouraged to use their freedom in ways that produce educative side-effects. Macedo sketches Smith's views on civic education, on religious freedom, on the limits of religious morality, and, perhaps most importantly, on the value of small-scale associations in giving people motives for acting morally. By participating in such associations, individuals gain social visibility; concern for their own status and reputation gives individuals an incentive to regulate their conduct. Moreover, as Alexis de Tocqueville argued, participation in small associations can itself be instructive: as participants gain experience, they are able to move on to new levels of cooperation. Macedo discusses a number of examples of such associations, including rotating credit associations and mutual aid societies designed to provide health care and social-welfare assistance to their members. The proper role of government, Macedo argues, is to encourage participation in associations without undermining them through excessive centralization.

Benjamin R. Barber's contribution to this volume is similarly concerned with the part that associations can play in giving individuals a voice and a stake in their society. His essay, "An American Civic Forum: Civil Society between Market Individuals and the Political Community," explores the prospects for a revitalization of civil society, a set of intermediate institutions that are private and voluntary, yet engaged in public discussion of issues and policy proposals. Barber envisions civil society — made up of religious organizations, community-service and charitable foundations, parent-teacher associations, and other public-interest groups — as a private realm devoted to public goods. Such a realm, he argues, should give rise to a public voice, a public conversation about crucial and often divisive issues. This public voice would be marked by inclusiveness, a search for common ground, a willingness on the part of participants to listen, to engage in genuine deliberation, to admit mistakes and revise their beliefs. Barber contrasts this voice with the kinds of voices one hears in the mass media, which are often reduced to endless arguments in which each party holds to an unchanging and unchallengeable position. He also distinguishes the kind of "lateral" exchange among citizens that he proposes from the "vertical" conversations that often take place between political leaders and their followers, and between special-interest groups and the legislators they attempt to influence. In order to foster worthwhile forms of lateral exchange, Barber proposes a "civic forum" that would bring people together through local assemblies, national-service organizations, and innovative uses of new technology, such as video-linked town meetings. The aim of such a forum, he suggests, would be not to create an alternative government, but to allow citizens to find a common voice with which to speak both to their government and to the private-sector institutions of their society.

The final essay, James S. Coleman's "Distributional Problems: The Household and the State," proposes a way of overcoming income-distribution problems that arise in contemporary societies. Coleman notes that while family households have, in modern times, declined in importance as units of economic production, they have nevertheless still been seen as the appropriate units of income distribution. Wage earners are expected to provide for members of their families who do not produce income, and where they do not, the welfare state steps in to perform this function. Whenever consumption is not directly tied to production, Coleman observes, free-rider problems develop; and in earlier times households developed ways of overcoming these problems, by awarding status within the family to those who were productive, and, where appropriate, by stigmatizing those who were not. Coleman argues that the breakdown of families makes it difficult for these kinds of incentives to operate, and that some alternative method of distribution must be devised. He proposes a constitutional reform which would give individuals transferable rights to participate in collective decisions within the political system. These rights would have economic value, and citizens would be able to realize their value through exchange (unlike our current system, in which citizens are unable to realize any direct economic gains from their votes). Corporations and trade associations would influence political decisions which affect their activities by purchasing these decision-rights from citizens, and would include the price of these rights among their costs of production. Coleman contends that such a system, if carefully designed to maintain competition between corporations and incentives for productive labor, would help solve the distributional problems that modern societies face.

The proper relationship between individual and community is the subject of one of the central debates among political theorists. The thirteen essays in this volume offer diverse approaches to this debate over the ways in which government can protect individual rights even while encouraging the flourishing of valuable forms of community.

ACKNOWLEDGMENTS

The editors wish to acknowledge several individuals at the Social Philosophy and Policy Center, Bowling Green State University, who provided invaluable assistance in the preparation of this volume. They include Mary Dilsaver, Terrie Weaver, and Pamela Phillips.

The editors would like to extend special thanks to Executive Manager Kory Swanson, for offering invaluable administrative support; to Publication Specialist Tamara Sharp, for attending to innumerable day-to-day details of the book's preparation; and to Managing Editor Harry Dolan, for providing dedicated assistance throughout the editorial and production processes.

CONTRIBUTORS

Neera K. Badhwar is Associate Professor of Philosophy at the University of Oklahoma, where she has taught since 1987. She received her Ph.D. from the University of Toronto in 1986, and was a Killam Postdoctoral Fellow at Dalhousie University in 1986-87. She has written on friendship, self-interest and altruism, virtue, communitarianism and liberalism, consequentialism, and Kantianism, in such journals as *Ethics*, *American Philosophical Quarterly*, *Social Philosophy and Policy*, *Philosophy and Phenomenological Research*, and the *Journal of Political Philosophy*. Her anthology *Friendship: A Philosophical Reader* was published by Cornell University Press in 1993.

Martha Nussbaum is Professor of Law and Ethics at the University of Chicago Law School. She has taught previously at Brown University and is the author of *Aristotle's De Motu Animalium* (1978), *The Fragility of Goodness: Luck and Ethics in Greek Tragedy and Philosophy* (1986), *Love's Knowledge: Essays on Philosophy and Literature* (1990), *The Therapy of Desire: Theory and Practice in Hellenistic Ethics* (1994), and *Poetic Justice: The Literary Imagination in Public Life* (1996).

John Haldane is Professor of Philosophy at the University of St. Andrews in Scotland, where he is also Director of the Centre for Philosophy and Public Affairs. He has published widely in aesthetics, the history of philosophy, metaphysics and philosophy of mind, and political and social philosophy. He is coeditor, with Crispin Wright, of *Reality, Representation, and Projection* (1993), and is coauthor, with J. J. C. Smart, of *Atheism and Theism* in the Great Debates in Philosophy series (1995).

Chandran Kukathas is Senior Lecturer in Politics at the University of New South Wales (Australian Defence Force Academy). He is the author of *Hayek and Modern Liberalism* (1989), *The Theory of Politics: An Australian Perspective* (with David Lovell and William Maley, 1990), and *Rawls: A Theory of Justice and Its Critics* (with Philip Pettit, 1990), and is the editor of *Multicultural Citizens: The Philosophy and Politics of Identity* (1993). He is coeditor of the *Journal of Political Philosophy*.

Will Kymlicka is Research Director of the Canadian Centre for Philosophy and Public Policy in the Department of Philosophy, University of Ottawa, and Visiting Professor in the Department of Philosophy, Carleton University. He is the author of *Liberalism, Community, and Culture* (1989),

Contemporary Political Philosophy (1990), and *Multicultural Citizenship: A Liberal Theory of Minority Rights* (1995). He is also the editor of *The Rights of Minority Cultures* (1995), and *Justice in Political Philosophy* (1992).

David Conway is Professor of Philosophy at Middlesex University, where he is Head of the School of Philosophy and Religious Studies. He was educated at the Universities of Cambridge and London. He is the author of *A Farewell to Marx* (1987) and *Classical Liberalism: The Unvanquished Ideal* (1996). He has also written on equal opportunity, killing and letting die, and nuclear deterrence. His main current research interests lie in the fields of moral and political philosophy.

Steven Kautz is Associate Professor of Political Science at Emory University. He was educated at Michigan State University and at the University of Chicago, where he received his Ph.D. from the Committee on Social Thought in 1989. His book *Liberalism and Community* was published by Cornell University Press in 1995.

Ronald Beiner is Professor of Political Science at the University of Toronto. He is the author of *Political Judgment* (1983), and the editor of Hannah Arendt's *Lectures on Kant's Political Philosophy* (1982) and of *Theorizing Citizenship* (1995). He is the coeditor of *Democratic Theory and Technological Society* (1988) and *Kant and Political Philosophy: The Contemporary Legacy* (1993). He was awarded the Canadian Political Science Association's 1994 Macpherson Prize for his book *What's the Matter with Liberalism?* (1992).

Cass R. Sunstein is Karl N. Llewellyn Professor of Jurisprudence at the University of Chicago Law School. He is the author of *After the Rights Revolution* (1990), *The Partial Constitution* (1993), *Democracy and the Problem of Free Speech* (1993), and *Political Conflict and Legal Judgment* (forthcoming).

George P. Fletcher is Cardozo Professor of Jurisprudence at the Columbia University School of Law. He is the author of *With Justice for Some: Victims' Rights in Criminal Trials* (1995), *Loyalty: An Essay on the Morality of Relationships* (1993), *A Crime of Self-Defense: Bernhard Goetz and the Law on Trial* (1988), and *Rethinking Criminal Law* (1978). In addition, he has published over sixty scholarly articles in professional journals, and has written numerous shorter commentaries on criminal justice and public policy in *The New York Times*, *The Los Angeles Times*, and *The New York Review of Books*.

Stephen Macedo is Michael O. Sawyer Professor of Constitutional Law and Politics at the Maxwell School of Citizenship and Public Affairs, Syracuse University. He is the author of *Liberal Virtues: Citizenship, Virtue, and Community in Liberal Constitutionalism* (1990) and *The New Right v. The*

Constitution (1987). He is currently completing a book to be titled *Diversity and Distrust: American Public Schooling and Liberal Civic Education.*

Benjamin R. Barber is Walt Whitman Professor of Political Science at Rutgers University and Director of the Whitman Center for the Culture and Politics of Democracy. Among his books are *Strong Democracy* (1984), *The Conquest of Politics* (1988), *An Aristocracy of Everyone* (1992), and *Jihad versus McWorld* (1995). His essays have appeared in a broad range of scholarly and popular journals and magazines, including *Harper's*, *The Atlantic*, *The New York Times*, *Dissent*, *The New Republic*, the *London Review of Books*, *Ethics*, and the *American Political Science Review.*

James S. Coleman served as University Professor of Sociology at the University of Chicago. His books include *Adolescents and the Schools* (1965), *Equality of Educational Opportunity* (1966), *Individual Interests and Collective Action* (1986), *Foundations of Social Theory* (1990), and *Parental Involvement in Education* (1991).

The editors note with deep regret the death of James S. Coleman on March 25, 1995. This volume is dedicated to his memory.

MORAL AGENCY, COMMITMENT, AND IMPARTIALITY*

By Neera K. Badhwar

I. Introduction

Liberal political philosophy presupposes a moral theory according to which the ability to assess and choose conceptions of the good from a universal and impartial moral standpoint is central to the individual's moral identity. This viewpoint is standardly understood by liberals as that of a rational *human* (not *transcendental*) agent. Such an agent is able to reflect on her ends and pursuits, including those she strongly identifies with, and to understand and take into account the basic interests of others. From the perspective of liberalism as a political morality, the most important of these interests is the interest in maximum, equal liberty for each individual, and thus the most important moral principles are the principles of justice that protect individuals' rights to life and liberty.[1]

According to the communitarian critics of liberalism, however, the liberal picture of moral agency is unrealistically abstract. Communitarians object that moral agents in the real world neither choose their conceptions of the good nor occupy a universalistically impartial moral standpoint. Rather, their conceptions of the good are determined chiefly by the communities in which they find themselves, and these conceptions are largely "constitutive" of their particular moral identities. Moral agency is thus "situated" and "particularistic," and an impartial reflection on the conception of the good that constitutes it is undesirable, if not impossible. Further, communitarians contend, the good is "prior" to the right in the sense that moral norms are derived from, and justified in terms of, the good. An adequate moral and political theory must reflect these facts about moral agency and moral norms.

The idea that our moral identities are constituted by communally determined conceptions of the good and the right, and that an impartial reflection on these conceptions is impossible or undesirable, is essential to what I will call "communitarian morality." This view has been defended by Alasdair MacIntyre, Michael Sandel, and Michael Walzer, and something

---

*I would like to thank Chris Swoyer, the other contributors to this volume, and its editors, for their helpful comments.

[1] Thus, liberalism as a political philosophy obligates the state to enforce, and the individual qua citizen to respect, primarily (or only) these "negative" rights and other principles of justice. The wider moral theory from which liberalism draws its picture of the moral agent and moral viewpoint does, of course, recognize other sorts of moral duties and virtues of individuals.

© 1996 Social Philosophy and Policy Foundation. Printed in the USA.

close to it has often been defended by Charles Taylor and others. There are some important differences between Walzer's defense of "democratic communitarianism," on the one hand, and MacIntyre's and Sandel's defenses of "republican communitarianism," on the other.[2] Nevertheless, all three see communitarian morality, in contrast to liberal morality, as being respectful of the shared understandings and particularities of different communities; and all three see the only valid, efficacious, or even possible, moral criticism as criticism that is internal to a community's history and traditions. Internal criticism, they contend, is capable both of respecting a community's particular understandings, and of condemning any reprehensible practices it might engage in, such as slavery.

Liberals have challenged the communitarian view about the nature of moral identity and the moral point of view, as well as the claim that internal criticism is capable of distinguishing between good and bad communal practices. Liberals have also questioned communitarians' emphasis on political participation as a prerequisite of a good polity.[3] I will not repeat these criticisms here. Instead, I will concentrate on an issue that has gone almost unremarked by liberals, namely, the centrality of the political community to communitarian morality and the implications of this centrality for partial communities such as family or friends, as well as for other political communities.[4]

My first aim in this essay is to show that the communitarians' rejection of the impartial, universal viewpoint in favor of the situated viewpoint of the political community is incompatible with concern for the particularities of people's lives in partial communities as well as in other political communities.[5] Further, the communitarians' adoption of the political

---

[2] I will note these differences as and when they become relevant. Charles Taylor is generally regarded as a republican communitarian, although both he and Walzer seem recently to have distanced themselves from communitarianism. Even MacIntyre has declared that he is not and "never" has been a communitarian, but all he means by this is that he does not believe that a "systematically" communitarian society is any longer possible, not that communitarianism is not an ideal. In any case, all these writers continue to use the label "communitarian" for others who defend, or have defended, the view I have identified as communitarian morality, or similar views. See Daniel Bell, *Communitarianism and Its Critics* (Oxford: Clarendon Press, 1993), p. 17 n. 14. (Bell may be the only communitarian theorist who calls himself a communitarian.)

[3] On these points, see, for example, Amy Gutmann, "Communitarian Critics of Liberalism," *Philosophy and Public Affairs*, vol. 14, no. 3 (Summer 1985), pp. 308–22; and Allen E. Buchanan, "Assessing the Communitarian Critique of Liberalism," *Ethics*, vol. 99, no. 4 (July 1989), pp. 852–82.

[4] A major exception to the first part of my claim is Stephen Holmes, "The Permanent Structure of Antiliberal Thought," in Nancy L. Rosenblum, ed., *Liberalism and the Moral Life* (Cambridge: Harvard University Press, 1989), pp. 227–53. However, Holmes does not discuss the implications of the centrality of political community for other communities; rather, his concern is to point out the "unbroken continuity" of antiliberal thought since the Counter-Enlightenment of the late eighteenth and early nineteenth centuries, including the similarities between European fascism and republican communitarianism (p. 227).

[5] It is important to note that the rejection of the universal viewpoint is not simply a rejection of liberal political morality, as communitarian criticisms typically suggest, but a rejection of all ethical systems whose fundamental principles include norms of respect or concern,

community as the preeminent moral community is unjustified even if the general thesis about the situated nature of moral agents and the moral standpoint is granted. Indeed, I argue, on any plausible construal of this thesis, it is incompatible with the centrality of political community in communitarian morality.

My second aim is to show that there is an important sense in which the impartial, universal standpoint is internal to the standpoint we take in committing ourselves to particular persons or projects that have an intrinsic human importance. The impartial standpoint commits the liberal agent to treat all persons as equally real, as equally bearers of rights to their own (compossible) values and pursuits, by virtue of their common humanity. The ability to do this, I will argue, is inherent in the ability to commit oneself to particular goods that have, and are valued as having, an intrinsic human importance. Hence, insofar as such commitment is constitutive of an individual's or a community's identity, the impartial, universal standpoint is also constitutive of that identity, whether or not the individual or the community understands this explicitly or acts accordingly. To the extent that individuals or communities fail to act accordingly, they fail to act consistently with their own particular commitments and identity. An "internal" criticism of individuals or communities committed to goods with an intrinsic human importance, then, is certainly possible, but what it is internal to is not necessarily their practices or explicit self-understandings (which may be inconsistent with their commitment), but rather, the nature of their commitment to these goods.

II. The Political Morality of the Common Good

According to communitarians, our good as individuals is to be found primarily in our relationships to particular people (e.g., in family or friendship), in our various social roles (e.g., as doctor or farmer), in our membership in certain voluntary associations (e.g., tribe or church), and in the community which contains all these partial communities, namely, our political community or society. The most important goods we find in

---

however understood, for all human beings. These systems include not only secular humanism and Christianity but also (though some communitarians might deny it) Aristotle's ethics. For, despite his parochialism, and his endorsement of the idea that only free males, in contrast to "natural slaves" and to women, were capable of full human rationality, Aristotle regards justice and the other virtues as based on universal features of human nature and, therefore, as applicable to all human beings. Thus, justice is possible not only between men and women, but also between masters and slaves, and between Greeks and all other human beings: "every human being seems to have some relations of justice with everyone who is capable of community in law and agreement," including slaves; and, since justice, community, and friendship are coextensive, there is friendship even with a slave "to the extent that a slave is a human being" (Aristotle, *Nicomachean Ethics*, trans. Terence Irwin [Hackett Publishing Co., 1985], 1161b6; see also 1097b9–11, 1155a17–22, 1159b25–30; and *Eudemian Ethics*, 1245b18–19).

any of these communities are joint or common goods — goods that exist and can be realized only in these communities, and that, when realized, devolve jointly on the participants. A shared understanding of the common good of a community is, indeed, the primary bond of its members. Our moral norms or virtues are defined and justified in terms of these goods, and our moral selves are constituted by our commitment to these goods and norms.

But all of us are members of a variety of communities, each with its own goods and meanings. In case of moral disagreement, which of these is primary? The primary moral community for any of us, according to communitarians, is the political community, the community of citizens. As Walzer observes, "the political community is probably the closest we can come to a world of common meanings," and "in matters of morality, argument simply is the appeal to common meanings."[6] Walzer's claim that the political community is "a world of common meanings" rests on the assumption that the political community is also, typically, a historical community with a common language and culture, and shared "sensibilities and intuitions."[7] The common understandings of this political-historical community shape all our categories and commitments, including our view of the proper distribution of goods in different distributive spheres (e.g., education or employment) and of the proper use of political power in enforcing these distributions.[8] It is possible, of course, for those with political power to misunderstand the common meanings of some sphere, or deliberately to override them, but that is "the unavoidable risk" of a communitarian democracy.[9] Moreover, the only "plausible alternative to the political community is humanity itself, the society of nations," but an international community with a set of common meanings does not yet exist.[10]

Since "we exist as the moral beings we are" only by virtue of our political community, this community is also "authoritative for us" vis-à-vis any universalist morality.[11] There is, according to Walzer, a universal moral code prohibiting such things as murder or deception, a code which provides the framework for a moral life — but it is no more than a framework.

[6] Michael Walzer, *Spheres of Justice* (New York: Basic Books, Inc., 1983), pp. 28, 29. I will follow communitarian practice in using "society," "nation," "state," and "political community" interchangeably.

[7] *Ibid.*, p. 28. However, even when by his own admission it is *not* the case that the political and historical communities are identical, Walzer continues to describe the political community as the community of "common meanings" (p. 29).

[8] Michael Walzer, *Interpretation and Social Criticism* (Cambridge: Harvard University Press, 1987), p. 21; Walzer, *Spheres of Justice*, pp. 15n, 29.

[9] Michael Walzer, "Liberalism and the Art of Separation," *Political Theory*, vol. 12, no. 3 (August 1984), p. 328; cited in William Galston, "Community, Democracy, Philosophy: The Political Thought of Michael Walzer," *Political Theory*, vol. 17, no. 1 (February 1989), p. 130.

[10] Walzer, *Spheres of Justice*, pp. 29–30.

[11] Walzer, *Interpretation and Social Criticism*, p. 21.

All the "substantive details," necessary for answering substantive moral and legal questions about the good or the right, need to be filled in by our political community.[12] The morality of a society consists of the detailed social meanings inherent in the interactions and shared understandings of its members, and it is these meanings that the law enforces (or ought to enforce). Hence, we cannot compare and evaluate different societies with respect to their moral or legal codes.[13]

MacIntyre and Sandel present the same basic picture of morality as Walzer in their republican communitarianism, differing from Walzer chiefly in placing a greater emphasis on social unity and in seeing their accounts as offering an objective theory of the good.

Thus, MacIntyre sees the ideal political community as transcending the potentially conflicting goods of the other (partial) communities by uniting all its members in a shared vision and pursuit of the common good, which includes both "the good for man" and "the good of that community."[14] The political community thereby provides what MacIntyre regards as the only adequate context for ordering and evaluating partial goods and defining moral norms and virtues.[15] In doing so, it provides, according to him, an "objective" standard for making choices between goods. Without this objective standard, individuals would have to choose on the basis of their own preferences, and thus their choices would be "criterionless" and the moral life would be marked by a "subversive arbitrariness."

Sandel's endorsement of a "politics of the common good" over a "politics of rights" is based on the same basic understanding of the role of the political community in our moral lives.[16] In a politics of the common good, "the nation" would serve "as a formative community" for a common life, and not, as in a politics of rights, "as a neutral framework for the play of competing interests."[17] Only in such a community of common purposes could we find "moral ties antecedent to choice," and only with such antecedent moral ties could we make sense of our moral and political lives.[18]

---

[12] *Ibid.*, pp. 24–25.

[13] Walzer, *Spheres of Justice*, p. 314.

[14] Alasdair MacIntyre, *After Virtue: A Study in Moral Theory* (Notre Dame: University of Notre Dame Press, 1981), p. 233; see also pp. 146, 188–89, 204–5.

[15] *Ibid.*, pp. 188–89. MacIntyre defines justice in terms of desert, and desert in terms of contribution to the common good (p. 188). This conception of justice, he adds, is possible only in the kind of community described above, and thus the conception of justice as desert is alien to liberal society, where "there is a limit to the bonds between us, a limit set by our private and competing interests" (p. 233).

[16] Michael Sandel, "The Procedural Republic and the Unencumbered Self," *Political Theory*, vol. 12, no. 1 (February 1984), pp. 81–96; and Sandel, "Morality and the Liberal Ideal," *New Republic*, May 7, 1984, pp. 15–17.

[17] Sandel, "The Procedural Republic," p. 93.

[18] *Ibid.*, p. 87.

Thus, Sandel and MacIntyre agree, our very personhood is inconceivable "without reference to our role as citizens"; the moral community just *is* the community of citizens.[19] The goods and norms of partial communities — personal relationships, social roles, religious or ethnic affiliations — derive their moral worth from the extent of their contribution to the (politically defined) common good, or, at least, their compatibility with it. Indeed, in the ideal political community there is no real difference between individuals' interests as members of these partial communities and their interests as citizens. For in such a community their basic interests are shaped by their commitment to the common good, such that, under certain circumstances, they are best described as possessing an "intersubjective self."[20]

The expectations, obligations, and responsibilities we inherit from our political affiliations — and our affiliations to those partial communities that are compatible with our political affiliations — provide us with our historical and moral identity.[21] Accepting this identity implies accepting the shared understandings of our own society as the standard for judgments of justice or generosity, or of our individual, communal, or human good.[22] It also implies recognizing, as Sandel argues, that our inherited

[19] Michael Sandel, *Liberalism and Its Critics* (New York: New York University Press, 1984), p. 5; MacIntyre, *After Virtue*, pp. 236–37.

[20] Sandel, *Liberalism and the Limits of Justice* (Cambridge: Cambridge University Press, 1982), pp. 62–63, 143–44, 150. See also MacIntyre, *After Virtue*, p. 233.

[21] MacIntyre, *After Virtue*, pp. 205–6. See also Alasdair MacIntyre, "Is Patriotism a Virtue?" The Lindley Lecture, University of Kansas (March 26, 1984), pp. 3–20; excerpted in *Morality and Moral Controversies*, 3d ed., ed. John Arthur (Englewood Cliffs, NJ: Prentice Hall, 1993), pp. 424–31. It has been suggested to me that in this essay MacIntyre is not *defending* the morality of patriotism, but merely trying to show its incompatibility with the morality of liberalism. This may, indeed, be MacIntyre's formal task here. However, since MacIntyre defends patriotism in *After Virtue*, and criticizes liberalism in it and several later works (cited below), it is safe to conclude that in showing the incompatibility of patriotism with liberalism, MacIntyre thinks that we ought to opt for the former.

For a similar view of identity, see Charles Taylor, "Atomism," in *Philosophy and the Human Sciences, Philosophical Papers 2* (Cambridge: Cambridge University Press, 1985), pp. 188–89, 208–9. Taylor does not subscribe to the view that morality just *is*, first and foremost, the morality of the political community we happen to find ourselves in; but he does believe, contrary to liberals, that we have a "natural," fundamental, and unconditional "obligation to belong" to a political community, to "obey authority," because we need such a community to realize our human powers and achieve our full human identity as autonomous beings.

[22] MacIntyre, *After Virtue*, pp. 204–5, 233. In "Is Patriotism a Virtue?" MacIntyre argues that this kind of loyalty to one's moral-political community is part of the virtue of patriotism (p. 5). Patriotism, a central virtue for communitarian morality, "requires me to regard such contingent social facts as where I was born and what government ruled over that place at that time . . . as deciding for me the question of what virtuous action is . . ." (p. 5).

For a more liberalized understanding of patriotism, see Charles Taylor, "Cross-Purposes: The Liberal-Communitarian Debate," in Rosenblum, ed., *Liberalism and the Moral Life*, pp. 172–80. Here Taylor acknowledges the possibility of a common good defined in terms of the rule of right, and the possibility of a patriotism that consists of loyalty to this common good, but expresses reservations about the continuing viability of a regime in which participatory self-rule is marginalized.

loyalties and allegiances go "beyond the obligations [we] voluntarily incur and the 'natural duties' [we] owe to human beings as such."[23]

Nor can any part of this account of the moral self or moral community be legitimately criticized from a universal, impartial standpoint, the standpoint of a rational person as such, detached from his particular moral community. For there is no reason, according to communitarians, why we should — even if we could — adopt this standpoint. Attempts to discover or invent a morality from this "transcendental" standpoint will succeed either in delivering only "disguised interpretations" of the already existing morality, or in delivering a theory that, although new, is neither plausible nor effective.[24] Moreover, adopting this "artificial" viewpoint toward our deepest aims and attachments — as liberal morality demands we do — requires us to be shallow, characterless persons. For adopting the rational standpoint implies evaluating and, possibly, revising and rejecting even those attachments that are constitutive of our very identities. But no one who has such attachments, i.e., no one with character, can do this without profound damage to his "loyalties and convictions" and, thus, to his self-understanding.[25]

In short, according to communitarian morality, the communal loyalties and convictions that make us the persons we are, not only determine to a large extent what we happen to find meaningful or important, right or wrong, they also determine what truly *is* important in our lives, what truly *is* right or wrong. And so the liberal ideal of the impartial moral agent is both psychologically implausible and morally unappealing.

III. ANTI-UNIVERSALISM AND OUTSIDERS

The obvious question that communitarian morality must raise for anyone who believes in universal rights (or any universal norms of justice or goodness) is: What if the common good of a community requires it to harm strangers who have done the community no harm? Do the interests of outsiders impose no limits on a community's pursuit of the common

---

[23] Sandel, *Liberalism and the Limits of Justice*, p. 62.

[24] Walzer, *Interpretation and Social Criticism*, pp. 20–21; Walzer, *Spheres of Justice*, p. xiv. See also Sandel, *Liberalism and the Limits of Justice*, p. 7; Sandel, *Liberalism and Its Critics*, pp. 5–6, 9; MacIntyre, *After Virtue*, pp. 119, 205; MacIntyre, "Patriotism," p. 12; and MacIntyre, "Moral Rationality, Tradition, and Aristotle: A Reply to Onora O'Neill, Raimond Gaita, and Stephen R. L. Clark," *Inquiry*, vol. 26 (1983), pp. 447–66. In "Moral Rationality," MacIntyre describes the liberal moral agent, "the individual *qua* rational person . . . characterizable independently of his or her social role and situation," as belonging to the same realm as "unicorns, glass mountains, and squared circles" (p. 454).

[25] Sandel, *Liberalism and the Limits of Justice*, p. 179. See also MacIntyre's *After Virtue*, according to which a person's attempt to reject his past by rejecting his "inherited" obligations and responsibilities "in the individualist mode, is to deform . . . [his] present relationships" as well as to lose his self-understanding and disrupt his identity (pp. 205–7).

good? And if they don't, then how should the reader understand the universalist-sounding talk that sometimes appears in the communitarian literature? For as we have seen above, Sandel talks of " 'natural duties' " to all human beings as human beings, and MacIntyre describes the political community as having the shared aim of realizing the "good *for man*," which he proceeds to characterize as "the life spent in seeking for the good life *for man*."[26] Walzer goes even further by explicitly affirming universal rights to life and liberty as based on "our common humanity" — rights that ground his theory of just war and his view that there is "universal value in opposing oppression. . . ."[27] How can these claims be reconciled with the fundamental tenet of communitarian morality that the good, the right, and the moral self are to be defined in terms of the (communally understood) common good?

Sandel and MacIntyre reconcile them by making the universalist claims secondary to the requirements of the communal good. According to Sandel, our natural duties are secondary to our communal obligations, which may "allow" us to give to those individuals, groups, and institutions with whom we share our communal heritage more than justice "even permits."[28] Since the conception of justice Sandel is discussing in these passages — that of John Rawls — primarily requires respect for the negative rights of all individuals, it follows, from Sandel's claim, that our communal obligations may even allow us to give to members of our community more than is permitted by respect for the negative rights of those outside our community. In other words, our communal obligations may even allow us to violate the rights to life and liberty of those outside our community.

MacIntyre is explicit on this point. He argues that the virtue of patriotism requires "unconditional" loyalty to the nation, seen as a project to pursue the common good. Such loyalty implies that the nation be "permanently exempted from criticism" and, indeed, supported in all enterprises "crucial to its overall project," even when their success would be contrary to the best interests of mankind impartially understood.[29] Hence, if the nation's conception of the good life includes raiding the territories of traditional enemies, including peaceful, nonthreatening agricultural communities, republican virtue demands loyalty to this project and, consequently, a (righteous) violation of what an impartialist morality sees as the rights of outsiders.[30] The claim that the search for the

[26] Sandel, *Liberalism and the Limits of Justice*, p. 62; MacIntyre, *After Virtue*, pp. 146, 204 (italics mine).

[27] Michael Walzer, *Just and Unjust Wars: A Moral Argument with Historical Illustrations* (New York: Basic Books, 1977); Walzer, *Spheres of Justice*, p. xv; Walzer, *The Company of Critics* (New York: Basic Books, 1988), p. 227.

[28] Sandel, *Liberalism and the Limits of Justice*, p. 179.

[29] MacIntyre, "Is Patriotism a Virtue?" pp. 13–14.

[30] *Ibid.*, p. 7.

human good is part of the community's common good does not, after all, imply that the good of outsiders may not be sacrificed to the cause of protecting the community's ability to keep searching.

Sandel's and MacIntyre's references to our "natural duties" to all human beings and to "the human good," then, turn out to be mere formalities, with no moral leverage in their theories. This is not surprising, however, since these concepts seem equally to be without foundation in their theories.

By contrast, Walzer's affirmation of our common humanity does have leverage insofar as he sees it as justifying a condemnation of oppression anywhere. But can this affirmation be squared with his view that justice "is relative to social meanings," that a society is just so long as it is "faithful to the shared understandings of the members"?[31] Does not this relativistic view of justice imply that a community acts justly in violating universal rights if its members share the understanding that doing so is justified? Walzer might reply that his theory of justice as relative to shared understandings requires that we respect *all* societies' shared understandings, and since we may safely assume that every society shares the understanding that it has a right not to be invaded, invasive societies are necessarily unjust. This entails, however, that the shared understandings of invasive societies — societies that do *not* regard themselves as bound to respect the shared understandings of other societies — are unjust, contrary to the view that justice must be defined simply as living according to the shared understandings of one's society.[32]

Perhaps Walzer would point out that his relativism about justice is limited to distributive justice, that justice in matters of life and liberty is universal and, therefore, independent of shared understandings. But there is no principled way to draw such a line between (relativistic) distributive justice and (universalistic) rights-based justice. For, as MacIntyre's example of raiding societies suggests, a society that invades another for its wealth may simply be acting on its conception of distributive justice. To save his view that justice must be defined simply as living according to shared understandings, Walzer must bite the bullet and agree with Sandel and MacIntyre that an invasive society acts justly in trampling on the lives and liberties of others, so long as doing so is part of, or a means to, its conception of the common good.[33]

[31] Walzer, *Spheres of Justice*, pp. 312, 313. The notion of morality, including justice, as grounded in shared understandings is retained in *The Company of Critics*, where Walzer argues that the good critic "gives expression to his people's deepest sense of how they ought to live . . ." (p. 232). More recently, however, Walzer might have changed his view of justice. In "The Communitarian Critique of Liberalism," *Political Theory*, vol. 18, no. 1 (February 1990), pp. 6–23, he rhetorically asks how, "if we really are a community of strangers," as Sandel claims, we can do anything "but put [liberal] justice first" (p. 9).

[32] Cf. Galston, "Community, Democracy, Philosophy" (*supra* note 9), p. 123.

[33] Is it open to Walzer to argue that respect for universal rights sets a *limit* on the view that distributive justice is a matter of shared understandings? I think not. For if there is no

Communitarian morality thus justifies a total nonconcern both for other political communities, and for individuals qua individuals in other communities.

IV. Anti-Universalism and Insiders

For obvious reasons, a moral theory that justifies the invasive acts of a society so long as these reflect its shared understandings about the common good, must also justify that society's acts of internal oppression and violence so long as these reflect shared understandings. In such a theory, the deviant individual's (or individuals') deviant understanding can have no moral force.

This is starkly illustrated in Walzer's discussion of the Indian caste system, a system that greatly restricts the liberty of the lowest castes—the Sudras or "untouchables"—to choose their occupations, or live or marry where or whom they will—a system that even, not infrequently, justifies killing those "overreaching" individuals who violate the general understanding. Notwithstanding all this, Walzer claims (as he and other communitarians must), that the caste system is just if it rests on the shared understandings of Indian society.[34] Moreover, the logic of the communi-

---

principled way to draw a line between rights-based and distributive justice, then a priority of universal rights over relativistic justice will end up invalidating the latter altogether. For other problems with Walzer's theory, see Ronald Dworkin, "What Justice Isn't," in Dworkin, *A Matter of Principle* (Cambridge: Harvard University Press, 1985), pp. 214–20; and Galston, "Community, Democracy, Philosophy," pp. 122–27. Both point out that, among other things, Walzer's theory is unfaithful to *our* self-understandings, *our* conception of justice, which *we* see, in Dworkin's words, as "our critic not our mirror" (p. 219).

This points to a problem with communitarian morality in general. Since communitarians regard their view of morality as a social product as applicable to all societies, they all face a difficulty with respect to societies that understand their own morality as embodying universal principles. And these probably include all societies, both liberal and illiberal. For a discussion of this and related issues, see Jeremy Waldron, "Particular Values and Critical Morality," *California Law Review*, vol. 77, no. 3 (May 1989), pp. 561–89.

[34] Walzer, *Spheres of Justice*, pp. 313–15. If "shared understandings" simply means "shared by most people" rather than "shared by all," then Walzer is, of course, right to suggest that the caste system, unlike slavery (p. 250n), rests on shared understandings. However, aside from the fact that this is irrelevant to the issue of justice for each individual, Walzer underestimates the problem of the oppressed internalizing the understandings of the oppressors and, thus, the possibility that the Sudras have internalized the understandings of the upper castes. Indeed, it appears that even some slaves internalized their masters' understanding of slavery; see *The Slave's Narrative*, ed. Charles T. Davis and Henry L. Gates, Jr. (Oxford: Oxford University Press, 1985). In any case, it is not clear what Walzer means by shared understandings; see Will Kymlicka's discussion of this point in Bell, *Communitarianism and Its Critics* (*supra* note 2), Appendix 1, pp. 211–15. Bell suggests that "deepest understandings" be understood as "those beliefs that we can consciously articulate and rationally endorse as our guiding principles" (Appendix 2, p. 224). But the reference to rational endorsement just gives the game away to the liberal, unless the notion of rationality itself is relativized to a community; and this leaves the communitarian conception of justice also relativized, and therefore still open to the objections already made.

tarian argument implies that the Indian government is wrong to prohibit acts of violence against "errant" Sudras, and wrong to recognize them as equal citizens. For a government ought to *express* the shared understandings of its citizens, not *override* them: the latter is always unjust.[35] Walzer does claim that once a government has done this and changed people's shared understandings, so that the lowest castes start talking about the injustice of the caste system (as they have begun to do), then, indeed, the caste system will become unjust. Nevertheless, it follows from his view that the initial act of the government in recognizing the rights of Sudras remains unjust, and that if members of the higher castes complain about the loss of their status (as many do), then at least with respect to this initial act, their complaint remains justified.

Walzer's view also seems to imply that deviant nonpolitical communities cannot be tolerated, despite his claim that when there is disagreement over social matters, society ought to reflect them in its scheme of justice.[36] For it is hard to see — nor does Walzer ever explain — how this can be done when the disagreement is radical, e.g., when the lowest caste disagrees with the other castes over its subordination. Nor is it clear *why*, on his conception of justice as reflecting shared understandings, the lowest caste should be heard rather than dismissed as deviant. As he himself proceeds to point out, understandings can count as shared even if they are not harmonious; and so, a partial community's disagreement with all the others may reasonably be seen as a rejection or violation of the society's shared understandings. If this were not the case, then the concept of justice as living by society-wide shared understandings would be hostage to every disagreement and, thus, largely otiose.

To summarize the discussion so far: The communitarian conception of morality grants to the norms of the political community the authority to override even the most basic norms of respect and concern for individuals qua individuals, both outside and inside the political community. In doing so, it also justifies total nonconcern for other political communities and for deviant nonpolitical communities within its own borders.

V. SELF-UNDERSTANDING, AGENCY, AND COMMUNAL NORMS

We have seen that one common justification given by communitarians for granting communal norms such preeminence is that it is only by

---

[35] Walzer, *Spheres of Justice*, pp. 313–15; MacIntyre, *After Virtue*, p. 236. This view also justifies communities of hard-line Muslim clerics and their followers around the world vis-à-vis governments with reformist (or relatively reformist) tendencies. A case in point is the example of the Bangladeshi feminist Taslima Nasrin, who was targeted for death by Muslim hard-liners, but supported by the Bangladeshi government in her attempt, with Western help, to escape to Sweden (*San Francisco Sunday Examiner and Chronicle*, October 23, 1994, p. C-13).

[36] Walzer, *Spheres of Justice*, pp. 313–14.

doing so that we can understand ourselves as (and continue living as) the particular persons we are. Trying to live by universal principles of respect and concern will lead to a disruption of our identities and render us incapable of moral depth and of leading a meaningful life.

However, even if this is true, it has moral force for the universalist only if the *kind* of moral depth and the *kind* of meaningful life in question are justifiable by independent criteria. To take the example of the caste system again, even if it is true that this system with its oppressions is part of a meaningful way of life and the deep identity of (nearly all) of those who live (or die) by it, it does not follow (without prior acceptance of the communitarian position) that the system is morally good and its disruption or loss, therefore, a moral loss. MacIntyre, however, provides an additional reason for regarding our identity-constituting communal loyalties and obligations as having overriding moral force, namely, that doing so is necessary for moral agency itself.

MacIntyre argues that the ability to understand one's life as a narrative "embedded in the history of . . . [one's] country" is necessary not simply for ensuring depth and meaning in one's life, but even for understanding our mutual obligations, for understanding what is good or bad about one's community, and for being motivated to act according to these understandings.[37] Moreover, he claims that moral understanding and motivation can only be sustained in the context of one's community; without this context, the individual is likely to lose grasp of "all genuine standards of judgment."[38] Hence, preserving one's way of life and one's identity through loyalty to one's community and its norms — unconditional, unquestioning patriotism — is a condition of moral understanding and motivation.[39] Correlatively, disloyalty to one's community is a threat to one's very moral agency, and the rational criticism of one's social ties called for by liberal morality is a form of disloyalty.[40]

MacIntyre concedes that communitarian morality is dangerous insofar as its survival or flourishing may require allegiance to a communal enterprise that is (on the liberal understanding) unjust to other human beings.[41] But he asserts that liberal morality is equally dangerous because, in calling for rational criticism, it undermines our ability to understand ourselves as part of a communal narrative and, thereby, our ability for effective moral agency.[42]

If MacIntyre is right about the nature of moral agency and liberal moral-

---

[37] MacIntyre, "Is Patriotism a Virtue?" p. 16.
[38] *Ibid.*, p. 11.
[39] *Ibid.*, p. 18.
[40] *Ibid.*, pp. 13, 18.
[41] *Ibid.*, pp. 14–15.
[42] *Ibid.*, p. 16.

ity's threat to it, then what we have is not a standoff between liberal and communitarian morality, as he goes on to suggest, but rather, a rout of liberal morality by communitarian morality. For whereas communitarian morality only leads to injustice (as understood from the impartial standpoint) under certain circumstances, liberal morality opens the very floodgates of injustice by threatening our moral agency and, hence, our sense of justice itself (however understood).

But it would be hasty to conclude that MacIntyre is right about the nature of moral agency and the dangers of rational criticism. Even if we accept the idea that self-understanding must have a narrative form, in that we must understand our lives in terms of a past, present, and future united by a *telos*, and the idea that moral agency — the capacity for "genuine" moral understanding and action — requires this sort of self-understanding, we have no reason to accept the further idea that this *telos* must be *political-historical*. This assertion is no more plausible than the assertion that a good work of literature must not only be a narrative but a political epic. It is even less plausible when we remind ourselves that all it means is that we can understand ourselves as moral agents only insofar as we can understand ourselves as citizens.[43] And in the absence of any philosophical, psychological, historical, or sociological support for this claim, it only begs the question against a universalist morality. For according to a universalist morality, it is precisely because our personhood, our moral agency, is distinct from our citizenship, that we can be good persons and bad citizens (as Aristotle, famously, pointed out).[44]

Moreover, MacIntyre's argument has breathtakingly implausible implications. It implies, for one thing, that those who do not identify with their country's political-historical commitments lack self-understanding and genuine moral understanding, a description that applies to any critic who questions his nation's injustices by invoking impartial ideals alien to its way of life. Such critics include men whom many would regard as moral exemplars, such as Andrei Sakharov, who had to invoke liberal (rather than traditional Russian) ideals to criticize Soviet authoritarianism, and Mohandas Gandhi, who had to invoke liberal (rather than Hindu) ideals to criticize the ancient caste system of India. Again, the assertion that a loosening or loss of one's communal ties results in a loss of moral agency applies to anyone anywhere who feels alienated from her country, to every immigrant — and, of course, to every individual anywhere who has internalized impartial, universal principles, whether or not she lives in a

---

[43] See also MacIntyre, *After Virtue*, pp. 236–37, where "moral community" is characterized as "the moral community of citizens" or one's "country," and patriotism is characterized as loyalty to this community and obedience to a government that represents it. Recall, also, Sandel's assertion (in *Liberalism and Its Critics*, p. 5) that our personhood is inconceivable apart from our role as citizens (see Section II above).

[44] Aristotle, *Politics*, 1276b30–35, 1278b1–5, 1293b5–8.

liberal society.[45] If these implications are too outlandish to be credible, then even if we accept that rational criticism necessarily threatens our communal ties (and I will discuss this claim later), we cannot accept that it threatens moral agency.

Suppose, however, that we accept the central communitarian contention about the nature of moral agency, namely, that it is particularist and situated, not universalist and impartial. Does this contention justify the communitarian assumption that it is in the *political* community that we are primarily situated? Not quite: it would be justified only if the political community were the dominant influence in shaping us, only if the shared understandings of *this* community were the understandings that most thickly defined us. In fact, however, in almost every society, both liberal and illiberal, the communities in which people are most deeply situated are nonpolitical (partial) communities, such as the community of two friends or lovers, the family, the national community of Planned Parenthood, or the international community of Baha'is. For it is in such partial communities, where a common conception of the good is the very basis of the community, that shared understandings are the most intense, the most thickly definitive of our identity. In comparison to these, for most of us, most of the time, our identities as citizens are secondary (which helps explain why partial communities are so often made up of citizens of different lands).

Walzer recognizes that there may be a greater sharing of sensibilities and intuitions in partial communities than in a political community (which, he also acknowledges, is often not a historical community). He still believes, however, that "distributive decisions" to accommodate the requirements of those partial communities have to be made by the political authority, according to citizens' shared understandings about how much and what type of cultural diversity and local autonomy to permit or require.[46] But neither he nor other communitarians can have it both ways. If the moral authority of a community is to be derived from shared understandings, then, for any individual, the community she most strongly identifies with, the community with which she shares the deepest understandings, must be the preeminent moral authority. This preeminent moral community would, then, provide the individual with the context and standard for evaluating her other particular goods, giving content to the virtues she is expected to have, and defining the norms that are authoritative for her. If, however, the political community is to

---

[45] It is part of the communitarian contention that liberal society is not a genuine community precisely because it refuses to inculcate a single, politically defined conception of the good in its citizens. I am not sure how communitarians, living in a liberal society, explain their own grasp of genuine moral standards. (MacIntyre seems to see himself as belonging to the community of ancient and medieval philosophers, but this, of course, is an intellectual, and not a political, community.)

[46] Walzer, *Spheres of Justice*, p. 29.

have preeminent moral authority, then the basis for this cannot be simply (or even primarily) shared understandings and the need for a communal normative context.

It might be objected that this line of criticism is uncharitable. For it should be obvious that the reason the preeminent moral authority must be the political community, rather than different partial communities for different individuals, is that one single normative standard is needed for people living in the same territory. Since, according to the argument about the particularist nature of moral agency which I have provisionally accepted, this single standard cannot be a universal, impartial standard, it must be a single communal standard, and the norms of the political community are the closest we can come to such a standard.

This response, however, will not do. For if the aim is a single moral standard compatible with our most intensely shared understandings, then the communitarian should propose not a politicized morality but, rather, a morality guided by the principle of equal respect for all compossible partial communities, i.e., all partial communities willing and able to coexist peacefully. This would still be a communitarian morality, because it would appeal not to any impartial, universal principle enjoining respect for all individuals qua individuals, but to a communally shared principle enjoining respect for all compossible partial communities within the boundaries of the political community. On this modified communitarian morality, each community would have its own conception of the right and the good, but each communal conception would include a principle of noninterference with other communities. Each community would be free to decide on policies of exit for its members and criteria of new membership, and (since the basic normative principle would be shared understandings rather than history when the two diverged) new communities of like-minded people could form and existing ones dissolve. Such a communitarian polity would thus resemble a liberal polity in making room for a capacious realm of diverse, private (nonpolitical) communal goods and pursuits.

But perhaps the resemblance is too great to be theoretically comfortable for the communitarian. For if partial communities are allowed this kind of moral standing, then partial communities committed to impartial, universal principles of respect for individuals qua individuals, such as Amnesty International and Asia Watch, must also be recognized. Moreover, since commitment to such principles and the goods they protect are the very raison d'être of these communities and the primary bond of their members, they would have to be recognized as genuine "constitutive" communities, i.e., communities whose norms and goals are partly constitutive of the identities of their members.[47] On the other hand, a com-

---

[47] Sandel, *Liberalism and the Limits of Justice*, pp. 62, 150, 172, 173. There are also, of course, organizations of people united by universal principles of charity or compassion, such as the Sisters of Charity, or *Children*, Incorporated.

munitarian polity based on the modified communitarian morality I have
proposed would *not* be a constitutive community, because the conception
of the common good holding it together would simply be a shared concern and respect for partial communities. This conception is no thicker
than the conception of the good holding together pluralistic liberal polities; the sole difference is that the former conception is nonindividualis-
tic, the latter individualistic. Hence, if such modified communitarian
polities have moral and political standing on account of their basis in
shared understandings, so do liberal polities.

The upshot, then, is that if communitarian morality emphasizes shared
understandings about the good as the ultimate moral court of appeal, it
must accept the modified polity described above as the only legitimate
communitarian regime. If, on the other hand, it emphasizes the political
community as the preeminent moral authority, it must abandon the
appeal to shared understandings and present a new justification. As we
have seen, such a justification is not forthcoming. A closer look at some
of the communitarian literature does, however, suggest an *explanation* for
the preeminence of the political community.

The explanation lies, I believe, in the unargued-for assumption that a
good society is a morally unified society, a society that lives by the same
thick communal norms. Since the only way to guarantee such unity is
through the law, the political community must be the morally authoritative community. The law may, indeed, enforce different norms about certain moral matters in different jurisdictions, but in each jurisdiction moral
unity is guaranteed through the law. In other words, in each jurisdiction
it is the political community that is morally supreme, rather than partial
(and mostly voluntary) communities, whose moral authority is informal
and limited to their own members.

The moral-unity assumption is clearly evident in MacIntyre's and Sandel's criticisms of liberal individualism and freedom of choice, and in their
celebrations of real or imaginary societies where individuals are less individualistic and choices less free. They criticize the voluntariness of social
relations protected by individual rights in favor of tradition and inherited
obligations — the individual's moral authority over her own decisions in
favor of the authority of the community — the ideal of a community of
flourishing individuals in favor of the ideal of a community with a flourishing intersubjective self — and the idea of a good community as a pluralistic community united in allegiance to justice in favor of the idea of a
good community as one that is united in "allegiance to some highly specific conception of the human good" pursued under the tutelage of the
law.[48]

---

[48] MacIntyre; "Moral Rationality" (*supra* note 24), p. 465. See also MacIntyre, *After Virtue*, pp. 160, 209, 236–37.

Walzer does not seem to rely on the idea of moral unity through an intersubjective good or intersubjective self in calling for the legal enforcement of communal norms. Indeed, as already noted, in his discussion of the caste system he expresses the view that if the lowest castes have different norms, the law can and should reflect them. We have also seen, however, that he neither shows how the disparate norms of all the castes *can* be legally recognized, nor, more importantly, *why* they should be recognized if they are not widely shared in a given jurisdiction. Nor can such a reason be given without recourse to the kind of principle of respect for all partial communities I suggested above. But the only kind of legal recognition *this* principle allows is the kind that leaves partial communities free to transact voluntarily with each other, and leaves subgroups who disagree with the larger partial community free to break off and form their own community. This kind of legal recognition could not lead to the imposition of a single set of norms on deviant communities, as Walzer's proposal would. So, even though Walzer does not explicitly endorse the principle of moral unity, this principle is implicit in his assumption that the law must enforce a single set of moral norms on society.

The requirement of moral unity explains why the political community has the authority to erase or control conflicts between contending partial communities, regardless of how this authority affects the actual situated agency of people—i.e., their actual shared understandings and moral identities. Thus, moral unity turns out to be more important in communitarian morality than its view of the nature of moral agency and the moral standpoint.

The politically defined good and the moral self as citizen are the communitarian antidote to the "divisive" individualism and pluralism of liberalism. The communitarian criticism of liberalism's neglect of the situated nature of moral agency is, thus, highly selective: the only "situated" viewpoint communitarianism is concerned to defend against the impartial, universal viewpoint is the viewpoint of the political community—more precisely, of the *communitarian* political community.

These observations also shed light on what communitarians mean when, despite their rejection of the impartial viewpoint and impartial reflection, they claim to be in favor of "critical reflection" on one's political community. To this claim I now turn.

VI. Impartial Reflection and Constitutive Particular Commitments

MacIntyre and Sandel allow that, as "self-interpreting" beings, we may reflectively distance ourselves from the historical communities that determine our moral identities, and question their moral limitations.[49] Likewise, Walzer sees the capacity for critical reflection as essential to the moral life, and sees exposure of "the false appearances of his own society" as one of the most important tasks of the critic.[50] Are communitarians simply being inconsistent in endorsing critical reflection while rejecting impartial reflection?

I believe not. For, in contrast to liberals, the reflection that communitarians endorse must always be undertaken on the basis of the political community's defining norms. Even when the aim is to find the universal human good, as in MacIntyre, we are reminded that because "particularity can never be simply left behind," the question must always be how *we* as members of a particular community, as sharing certain beliefs, ought to resolve this issue — and never how *I* as a rational human being, subscribing to universal normative principles, ought to resolve this issue.[51] There is no such thing as a universal morality or rationality; there are only particular moralities and rationalities.[52] And so the search for the universal must be for the universal *as understood in our society*, and a critique of our society's conception of the good must appeal to its own traditions and self-understandings.

Similarly, the distancing from one's history that Sandel talks about as a possibility can never amount to a departure from one's history. Rather, it must be "always precarious and provisional, the point of reflection never finally secured outside the history itself."[53] In other words, we cannot take a perspective on our inherited moral norms or identities that is not already a part of our moral heritage, much less reject these norms (or not, at least, without self-damage). As already noted, Walzer also holds that any attempt to reject communal norms from an impartial viewpoint in favor of a new theory will be either utterly unconvincing, or merely a disguised interpretation of social norms. The critical reflection he finds essential to the moral life is provided, like everything else that is essential to it, by our communal morality; this is what makes this morality "authoritative" for us.[54] Valid criticism is, necessarily, (politically) situated criticism: the critic must criticize his society by giving "expression to his people's deepest sense of how they ought to live."[55]

The communitarian opposition to the liberal idea of critical reflection is, thus, opposition only to criticism from the impartial, universal viewpoint,

---

[49] MacIntyre, *After Virtue*, p. 205; Sandel, *Liberalism and the Limits of Justice*, p. 179.

[50] Walzer, *Interpretation and Social Criticism*, pp. 20–21; Walzer, *The Company of Critics*, p. 232.

[51] MacIntyre, *After Virtue*, pp. 205–6; MacIntyre, "Moral Rationality," p. 451.

[52] MacIntyre, "Moral Rationality," p. 459; MacIntyre, *Whose Justice? Which Rationality?* (Notre Dame: University of Notre Dame Press, 1988), pp. 3–10.

[53] Sandel, *Liberalism and the Limits of Justice*, p. 179.

[54] Walzer, *Interpretation and Social Criticism*, p. 21.

[55] Walzer, *The Company of Critics*, p. 232.

the criticism that purports to enable us to engage in a critique of the political community's norms themselves. There is no opposition to subjecting the norms of the nonpolitical communities to such a critique, a critique that may require their rejection or sacrifice, so long as this is done from the politically situated viewpoint.

Leaving aside the point that the adoption of the situated viewpoint does not entail adoption of the politically situated viewpoint, communitarian or noncommunitarian, let us now ask exactly what kind of situated viewpoint is opposed to the impartial viewpoint.

If a situated agent is merely someone who is, and who sees himself as, centrally constituted by a shared conception of the good, a conception that defines a community, then there is no necessary opposition between the situated and the impartial viewpoints. For we have already seen (in Section V) that impartial principles can define a community and centrally constitute an agent. The "particular" goods and norms of such communities and such agents are themselves grounded in impartial, universal norms. Even communities not formed for the sake of doing justice by protecting individual rights may be committed, implicitly or explicitly, to impartial norms. This seems to have been the case with many groups which took part in rescuing Jews in Nazi Europe, such as the residents of Le Chambon, who acted as a community to rescue fifteen hundred Jews. The important fact and motivating thought for the Chambonnais was that fellow human beings were being unjustly persecuted and needed their help, rather than the thought that by helping them they would endanger their community, their families, and themselves.[56] Their identity, too, as members of their community was partly constituted by their historical commitment to justice for all human beings qua human beings.[57]

The only kind of situated viewpoint that is incompatible with the impartial viewpoint is the viewpoint of an agent or community that rejects impartial norms and goods, or regards them as secondary to com-

---

[56] Richard Rorty claims that our "sense of solidarity is strongest when those with whom solidarity is expressed are thought of as 'one of us', where 'us' means something smaller and more local than the human race. That is why 'because she is a human being' is a weak, unconvincing explanation of a generous action" (Rorty, *Contingency, Irony, and Solidarity* [Cambridge: Cambridge University Press, 1989], p. 191; cited in Bell, *Communitarianism and Its Critics*, p. 150 n. 33). Ironically, research on the rescuers of Jews in Europe during World War II reveals that the thought "because she (or he) is a human being, one of us" is the very thought most rescuers report as the (rather obvious) explanation for their actions. See Philip Hallie, *Lest Innocent Blood Be Shed: The Story of the Village of Le Chambon, and How Goodness Happened There* (New York: Harper and Row, 1979); Samuel P. Oliner and Pearl M. Oliner, *The Altruistic Personality: Rescuers of Jews in Nazi Europe* (New York: The Free Press, 1988); and Kristen R. Monroe et al., "Altruism and the Theory of Rational Action: Rescuers of Jews in Nazi Europe," *Ethics*, vol. 101, no. 1 (October 1990), pp. 103–22.

[57] I defend this and related points, including the contextual nature of identity, in "Altruism Versus Self-Interest: Sometimes a False Dichotomy," *Social Philosophy and Policy*, vol. 10, no. 1 (Winter 1993), pp. 90–117. For an account of the rescue effort launched by the village of Le Chambon, see Hallie, *Lest Innocent Blood Be Shed*.

munal norms on the grounds that our universally shared features are relatively unimportant. We have seen ample reason to dismiss such a conception of moral agency. Nevertheless, there is one communitarian criticism of the impartial viewpoint which is independent of this conception and which, therefore, merits consideration. This is the criticism that reflection from a point of view that takes into account everyone's basic interests, those interests that are protected by justice, is incompatible with deep commitment to particular persons and projects.[58] So individuals or communities that internalize impartial, unconditional norms, are incapable of such commitments. But what is supposed to justify this criticism?

One suggestion often made by MacIntyre and Sandel is that a genuine commitment requires unconditional loyalty, a loyalty that is incompatible with a commitment to liberal impartiality. On the second point they are, of course, right: liberal impartiality requires that we not value our commitments unconditionally, i.e., regardless of their compatibility with justice. But the claim that unconditional loyalty or valuing is necessary for a genuine commitment to a person or project is neither defended nor, I believe, defensible.

What *is* undoubtedly necessary is that we value the project (or person) to which we are committed *intrinsically*, i.e., for its own sake and for what it is. What this amounts to I will consider below, but the point to note here is that valuing something (or someone) intrinsically is not the same as valuing it *unconditionally*: for most, if not all, of our intrinsic values, from the trivial to the profound, are conditional. For example, someone may value the exhilarating experience of skiing down a slope for its own sake, but only on the tacit assumption that it will not jeopardize his life or limbs. Or he may value contributing his hard-earned millions to the recovery of Hungary's economy out of a deep and abiding concern for Hungary, but only on the assumption that this recovery will not be used for an expansion of governmental power. Most of our intrinsic commitments are shaped and sustained by tacit conditional assumptions of this

---

[58] This criticism is made by MacIntyre and Sandel in their discussions of family, friends, and country. Walzer makes a similar point with respect to the critic who takes the impartial point of view. Even some liberals seem to have accepted that liberal norms are, at least, not quite in harmony with deep commitment. For example, Stephen Macedo agrees that the requirement of liberal justice that we subordinate our particular commitments to liberal norms will lead to affections that are "broader but less intense or deep than pre-liberal ones . . ." (Macedo, *Liberal Virtues* [Oxford: Clarendon Press, 1990], pp. 244, 267–68). And Buchanan, "Assessing the Communitarian Critique of Liberalism" (*supra* note 3); Charles Larmore, *Patterns of Moral Complexity* (Cambridge: Cambridge University Press, 1987); and Jeremy Waldron, "When Justice Replaces Affection: The Need for Rights," *Harvard Journal of Law and Public Policy*, vol. 2 (Summer 1988), pp. 635–47, all seem to think that the communitarian thesis that liberal justice and community are inversely related is, at least, highly plausible. I discuss these issues in "The Circumstances of Justice: Pluralism, Community, and Friendship," *Journal of Political Philosophy*, vol. 1, no. 3 (1993), pp. 250–76; reprinted in *Philosophical Perspectives on Sex and Love*, ed. Robert Stewart (New York: Oxford University Press, 1994), where I argue that rights and justice play a constitutive role in friendships and other communities.

sort, assumptions that they satisfy certain conditions. All that an acceptance of liberal impartiality adds to them is the condition of concern for
others' rights.

But perhaps the thought is that this condition is incompatible with
intrinsic valuing of persons or projects because it is entirely alien or irrelevant to such valuing, and imposing an alien condition on our commitments to persons or projects somehow misses their value and devalues
them. Let us therefore ask whether the impartiality condition really is
alien to intrinsic valuing. Valuing something intrinsically requires, minimally, recognizing its full value. And this involves valuing it for its own
sake rather than as a mere means to an entirely independent goal, and
valuing it for what it is rather than for incidental or extraneous reasons.[59]

The first requirement is the requirement of noninstrumentality. If
something is valued primarily as a means to an entirely independent goal,
then it is replaceable by anything better suited to serve this goal. Some
Kantian defenses of liberal impartiality do, arguably, treat particular values as only means to the goal of greater justice, and are thus incompatible with valuing them intrinsically.[60] The second requirement has to do
with valuing something for its inherent features, the features that make
it what it is. If a thing is valued for incidental or extraneous reasons, reasons that have no essential connection to its inherent features, then *it* is
not really the object of value. For example, to value Picasso's *Guernica* just
because doing so is artistically or politically chic, rather than because of
its artistic features, is to fail to value the painting itself. But accepting an
alien or irrelevant condition for valuing something—for example, accepting that *Guernica* be valued for its artistic features only if it helps raise
funds to alleviate hunger—is also an example of failing to value it for
what it is. For to accept such a condition is to miss out on the function of
art in our lives as an aesthetic embodiment of value, rather than as a practical aid to our moral causes. Similarly, if the impartial viewpoint is alien
to our particular commitments, as communitarians contend, then to

---

[59] I give a fuller argument for these conditions in "Friends as Ends in Themselves," *Philosophy and Phenomenological Research*, vol. 48, no. 1 (September 1987), pp. 1–23; reprinted
in Alan Soble, ed., *Eros, Agape, and Philia* (New York: Paragon House, 1990) pp. 165-86; the
essay is also reprinted in Richard T. Hull, ed., *Histories and Addresses of Philosophical Societies*,
Value Inquiry Book Series (Amsterdam: Rodopi Publishers, 1995); and in Clifford Williams,
ed., *On Love and Friendship: Philosophical Readings* (Boston: Jones and Bartlett Publishers,
1995).

[60] See Bernard Williams, "Persons, Character, and Morality," in Williams, *Moral Luck:
Philosophical Papers, 1973–1980* (Cambridge: Cambridge University Press, 1981); and Michael
Stocker, "The Schizophrenia of Modern Ethical Theories," *Journal of Philosophy*, vol. 63,
no. 14 (August 1976), pp. 453–66. Interestingly, Alan Gewirth sees John Rawls's difference
principle and Ronald Dworkin's principle of equal concern and respect as forms of distributive consequentialism, because they justify unequal distributions as a means to some form
of overall equality; see Gewirth, "Ethical Universalism and Particularism," *Journal of Philosophy*, vol. 85, no. 6 (June 1988), p. 289. Gewirth's own universalist rights-based justification
of certain particularist attachments escapes this problem.

require that our commitments meet its demands is to fail to value them for what they are.

The question, then, is: Is impartiality thus alien? That it is often *treated* as alien by liberals is undeniable. For liberal theories often justify the principle of impartiality completely independently of particular values, as though there were no connection between impartial and particular values.[61] This not only devalues particular values, for reasons we have just seen, it also devalues impartiality. For it turns impartiality into a sort of forbidding monitor of the particular values that give our lives their color and texture, rather than a part of that color and texture. The truth in the communitarian contention that our moral norms must be derived from our particular values, that particularity can never be left behind, is that our moral norms are implicit in, and therefore to be derived from, those of our values that have an intrinsic importance in human life. Contrary to the communitarian view, however, it is not *communitarian* norms that can be so derived, for there is no necessary connection between commitment to one's political community and commitment to other sorts of particular values that have an intrinsic human importance.

By contrast, I will now argue, there *is* a necessary connection between liberal impartiality and particular intrinsic values. For the *understanding* that grounds the liberal agent's commitment to treat all persons as equally real, as equally bearers of rights to their own (compossible) values and pursuits by virtue of their common humanity, is implicit in valuing particular persons intrinsically. And valuing someone intrinsically involves valuing her for what she is, and as a human being; she is both one person among others equally real, and that particular individual.

Consider, for example, what is involved in a friendship in which each friend values the other intrinsically. In such a friendship, there is mutual well-wishing and concern for the other's good for her or his own sake. This good includes both the relational or social goods central to this friendship, and the goods central to the life of each friend as a separate and distinct individual, with her or his own perspective on things. Yet neither the relational goods central to the friendship, nor the good of a friend as a separate and distinct individual, is entirely unique. Both are grounded, in part, in universally shared features of their natures as essentially social, but equally essentially distinct, individuals.

As distinct individuals, their good requires the satisfaction of certain aspirations and needs—in particular, the aspiration to guide their lives from their own perspectives, as well as the need to see things from oth-

---

[61] Even Gewirth's justification of rights-respecting commitments seems to treat rights as justified entirely independently of considerations inherent in these commitments (*ibid*). Williams's and Stocker's criticisms of certain sorts of impartial theories suggest the worry that impartiality may be incompatible with intrinsic valuing of persons and projects.

ers' perspectives; the desire to be the originators of their actions, as well as to entrust their well-being to others; the need to give material form to their ideas, as well as to admire others' achievements; the desire to be a source of benefit for others, as well as to be a beneficiary of their actions. These aspirations and needs are universally shared, and their satisfaction is part of the good of any individual as a separate and distinct individual. Further, the satisfaction of these aspirations and needs requires both friends to have certain virtues, not only the virtues usually seen as central to friendship, such as kindness, generosity, or sympathy, but also virtues like mutual respect for each other's autonomy and freedom of action, fair-mindedness in such matters as praise and blame or division of labor, and reliability and responsibility. In other words, the mutual satisfaction of friends' universally shared aspirations and needs as part of their good requires the virtues both of justice and of benevolence.

The mutual well-wishing of friends, then, implies an understanding of each other's good as separate and distinct individuals, and a commitment to act accordingly. Without this understanding and the virtues in which it is manifested, such well-wishing would not amount to valuing each other intrinsically, because it would neglect the good of each as a separate and distinct individual. But an understanding of the individualistic dimension of a friend's good implies a general understanding of the individualistic dimension of a good human life, an understanding that extends to other human beings. Someone who lacked this general understanding would fail to understand even his own friendships adequately, just as someone who lacked a general understanding of the word "flower" would fail to truly understand what it meant to call the geraniums on his window-sill "flowers." And someone who failed to act on this understanding toward other human beings would fail to act rationally.

The other component of a friend's good mentioned above is the relational or social component. The good of each friend includes the attainment of relational goods central to the friendship, and the mutual well-wishing of friends implies wishing and acting for the relational goods central to the friendship. As in the case of the individualistic goods discussed above, however, the relational goods central to the friendship include, among other things, the satisfaction of aspirations and needs that are central to any friendship—the aspiration for a fuller knowledge of another person and of oneself than otherwise possible, the need for self-disclosure in a context of mutual trust and concord, the desire for a differential and exclusive mutual love and concern, and so on. So anyone capable of understanding the value of relational goods and pursuits in his own friendship is capable of understanding their value in others' friendships, and anyone who sees himself as entitled to such differential sharing and mutuality must also see others as similarly entitled. Moreover, since mutual entitlements entail mutual obligations of noninterference, he must see others and himself as mutually obligated to respect each other's right to such partiality.

Thus, a general understanding of the universally shared individualistic and relational dimensions of a committed friendship is implicit in an adequate understanding of one's own friendships. This point can be generalized to apply to larger communities as well as to the individual qua individual. Any good community must enable its members to achieve their individual as well as social good, and so it must understand both the individualistic and the social dimensions of a good life for its members, an understanding that, necessarily, extends to the members of other communities. Again, insofar as an individual understands her own good as an individual adequately, she must understand herself both as someone whose life is irreducibly separate and distinct, and as someone whose life is inextricably social. Under both aspects, she must see herself as one among others whose good, too, involves both the individualistic and the social dimensions. Since this kind of understanding of others and oneself is necessary for valuing persons (including ourselves) intrinsically, it follows that the point of view from which we value particular persons intrinsically is necessarily both particularist and universalist, both partial and impartial. This is just to say that there is a necessary connection between the ability to value particular people intrinsically and the ability to value persons as such, between the ability to see the value of one's particular goods as essential to one's own life and the ability to see the value of such goods as essential to a good human life.

Hence, the requirements of an impartial, universalist morality can and should be justified not simply by the fact that each one of us is equally real and that rationality requires consistency of response, but also by the fact that a recognition of this fact is a necessary element of valuing particular persons intrinsically and that such valuing is part of our own individual good. So, whereas it is true (as communitarians insist) that we ought not to simply leave particularity behind in matters of morality, it is equally true that we ought not to simply leave universality behind in matters of commitment—at least not if we want our commitments to have intrinsic value.

A commitment that is faithful to the communitarian account of the good fails to have such value because it fails to understand or respect the universally shared features of human life. In doing so, it fails to understand or repect both the individualistic and the social dimensions of human good.

To say that there is a necessary connection between impartial, universal values and intrinsic particular values, and that rationality requires consistency of response, is not to say that what we owe to those with whom we have special bonds of care and concern is no greater than what we owe to all others. Differential care can (as I have argued elsewhere) justify differential obligations.[62] What rationality requires on this point is that we recognize the differential obligations of others. Again, to say that the impartial point of view is implicit in an adequate understanding of our particular commitments is not to say that there cannot be a conflict between what we owe to all persons and what we owe to some. It is, rather, to locate the source of the conflict in the existence of plural concerns or values rather than in a clash between particularity and universality or between partiality and impartiality. The Soviet dissident who is willing to be tortured rather than to betray her comrades and her cause (and, thus, betray herself), but not willing to let her torturers torture her daughter (and thus, again, betray herself), is torn between two loves and commitments, two betrayals of her own identity, even as she is torn between two demands of justice.[63]

This kind of conflict is a necessary feature of human life, but a totalitarian regime committed to eradicating plurality can only make it more acute. For in such a regime political intrusion in the private lives of citizens is frequent and extreme, in an attempt to detach them from their private pursuits and attach them to the common good. The same, too, must hold for a regime that aspires to realize a constitutive political community in a liberal society: it must exacerbate conflict through frequent intrusions in individuals' lives. On the other hand, if such a regime *is* successful in subordinating private interests to political ones, and thus eradicating conflict between private and political interests, it is successful only at the price of eradicating differential and exclusive attachments. Thus, a society with a communitarian regime must either suffer a constant conflict between political and personal attachments, or it must purchase harmony by submerging individual identity and individual interests in the political community, at the cost of truly personal attachments.[64] In either case, a society with a communitarian regime fares far worse than a society with a liberal regime.

VII. CONCLUSION

I have argued that the preeminence of the political community in communitarian morality is unjustified by the communitarian conception of the

---

[62] Neera K. Badhwar, "Friendship, Justice, and Supererogation," *American Philosophical Quarterly*, vol. 22, no. 2 (April 1985), pp. 123–31.

[63] See Aleksandr Solzhenitsyn's description of interrogative methods in Soviet camps that create such conflicts in Solzhenitsyn, *The Gulag Archipelago 1918–1956: An Experiment in Literary Investigation, I–II* (New York: Harper and Row, 1973), pp. 106–8.

[64] In "Assessing the Communitarian Critique of Liberalism," pp. 871–72, Buchanan argues that communitarian society may leave so little room for autonomy, that it may be unable to accommodate any genuine commitment (as distinct from blind obsession).

moral agent and the moral standpoint, and incompatible with our particular, nonpolitical commitments. By contrast, commitment to the liberal
conception of the moral standpoint is compatible with particular commitments insofar as they have an intrinsic human importance, because the
understanding on which the commitment to impartiality is based is inherent in our capacity for such particular commitments.

Philosophy, University of Oklahoma

COMPASSION: THE BASIC SOCIAL EMOTION*

By Martha Nussbaum

I. Misfortune and Response

Philoctetes was a good man and a good soldier. When he was on his way to Troy to fight alongside the Greeks, he had a terrible misfortune. By sheer accident he trespassed in a sacred precinct on the island of Lemnos. As punishment he was bitten on the foot by the serpent who guarded the shrine. His foot began to ooze with foul-smelling pus, and the pain made him cry out curses that spoiled the other soldiers' religious observances. They therefore left him alone on the island, a lame man with no resources but his bow and arrows, no friends but the animals who were also his food.

Ten years later, according to Sophocles' version of the story, they come to bring him back: for they have learned that they cannot win the war without him. The leaders of the expedition think of Philoctetes as a tool of their purposes; they plan to trick him into returning, with no empathy for his plight. The Chorus of soldiers, however, has a different response. Even before they see the man, they imagine vividly what it is like to be him—and they enter a protest against the callousness of the commanders:

> For my part, I pity him—thinking of how, with no living soul to care for him, seeing no friendly face, wretched, always alone, he suffers with a fierce affliction, and has no resources to meet his daily needs. How in the world does the poor man survive? [1]

As the members of the Chorus imagine a man they do not know, they stand in for the imaginative activity of the audience, for whom the entire tragic drama is a similar exercise of sympathy.

Philoctetes' story displays the structure of the emotion that I shall call "pity" or "compassion," the emotion that lay at the heart of ancient Athe-

* This essay contains material from the fifth and sixth of my Gifford Lectures given at the University of Edinburgh in 1993, and forthcoming from Cambridge University Press in 1997, under the title *Upheavals of Thought: A Theory of the Emotions.* For comments on those lectures I am indebted to Richard Posner, Jerome Schneewind, and Cass Sunstein. I am also indebted to George Fletcher, John Haldane, Fred Miller, and John Tomasi for comments on an earlier draft of this essay.

[1] Sophocles, *Philoctetes*, lines 169–76.

© 1996 Social Philosophy and Policy Foundation. Printed in the USA.

nian tragedy. My plan is to investigate this emotion and its social role. First I shall examine the emotion itself, following the fine analysis given by Aristotle in the *Rhetoric*. (This analysis is continuous with less systematic earlier treatments in the tragic poets and in Plato; it is taken over, in most respects, by a long tradition in Western philosophy—major later exponents include both defenders of pity such as Rousseau, Schopenhauer, and Adam Smith, and opponents of the emotion such as the ancient Stoics, Spinoza, Kant, and Nietzsche.) With this analysis before us, we can then proceed to adjudicate a long debate about the suitability of pity as a basic social emotion.

Why should this be important for people who are thinking about the relationship between the individual and the community? I can give three reasons. First, compassion, in the philosophical tradition, is a central bridge between the individual and the community; it is conceived of as our species' way of hooking the interests of others to our own personal goods. It would therefore be a good thing to think hard about the structure of this moral sentiment, so that we might understand better how to produce it and how to remove obstacles to it.

Second, some modern moral theories—liberal and individualist moral theories in particular—have treated compassion as an irrational force in human affairs, one that is likely to mislead or distract us when we are trying to think well about social policy. (I shall give some examples of this below.) Once again, it would behoove us to scrutinize this claim by investigating the structure of compassion. I shall argue that such an investigation will undermine the simple dismissal of the emotion and will show it to be based on thought and evaluation.

Third, this simple opposition between emotion and reason has also been invoked by communitarian critics of liberalism, who have suggested that if we are to make room for sentiments such as compassion, which do not seem to be much honored in liberal theory, this will mean basing political judgment upon a force that is affective rather than cognitive, instinctual rather than concerned with judgment and thought.[2] The analysis of compassion for which I shall argue will undermine that claim as well, by showing that compassion is, above all, a certain sort of thought about the well-being of others. The upshot of this will be to show that a certain type of objection to the project of the Enlightenment fails, and that Enlightenment thinkers (such as Kant and John Rawls) who do not give this emotion a central place could do so without altering very much in the substance of their moral theories. If we want a compassionate community, we can have one without sacrificing the Enlightenment's commitment to reason and reflection—because compassion is a certain sort of reasoning.

---

[2] See, for example, the treatment of compassion in the legal theorists cited in note 6 below.

A brief note on terms: When I use the words "pity" and "compassion," I am really speaking about a single emotion. The analysis I shall offer focuses on an experience that remains remarkably constant from Sophocles to the present day, even though many terms in many languages have been used to name it. Such variation reveals some real, subtle difference in the understanding and the experience of the emotion itself;[3] but on the whole the philosophical tradition is in such vigorous conversation that the terms are frequently heard as translations of one another, and are thus pulled toward one another in meaning.[4] I shall use the term "pity" when I am talking about the historical debate, since that is the term generally used in English to translate both Greek *eleos* and French *pitié*; but since, from the Victorian era onward, the term has acquired nuances of condescension and superiority to the sufferer that it did not have formerly, I shall switch over to the currently more appropriate term "compassion" when I am talking about contemporary issues.

The Greek debate about pity and its philosophical legacy are, as I have already suggested, of more than historical interest. They have important implications for contemporary thought about public reasoning. In contemporary discussions of public rationality, we find, in fact, traces of the debate, but in an unclear and degenerate form. In economics, in politics, and especially, perhaps, in the law, we find a recurrent contrast between "emotion" and "reason," especially where appeals to compassion are at issue. (Later on, I shall give examples of this.) Both compassion's defenders and its opponents in legal theory seem to grant that this emotion is "irrational." Some would exclude it from legal reasoning on that account; some, by contrast, wish to let it in as irrational and yet valuable in addition to reason — a weak position, and one that opponents eagerly assail. Thinkers in the law-and-economics movement — for example, Richard Posner — are in the vanguard of the theoretical attack, claiming that emotions, being irrational, have nothing valuable to contribute to public reasoning.[5] Feminist legal scholars such as Lynne Henderson, Toni

---

[3] Nietzsche emphasizes, for example, the fact that the word *Mitleid* stresses the concurrent suffering of the onlooker; he typically uses it when he wants to argue that pity simply doubles the amount of suffering. On the other hand, the onlooker's pain is part of the definition of *eleos* in Aristotle and *misericordia* in the Roman Stoics, and still figures today in definitions of pity or compassion: see, for example, the excellent analysis in Andrew Ortony, Gerald L. Clore, and Allan Collins, *The Cognitive Structure of Emotions* (Cambridge: Cambridge University Press, 1988).

[4] Thus, Cicero uses *misericordia* to translate the Greek *eleos*; Nietzsche employs the German *Mitleid* to render Rousseau's *pitié* and also *eleos* and *misericordia*; Kant, alluding explicitly to the ancient Stoics (whether Greek or Roman) uses *Mitleid*; modern translators of both Aristotle and the Greek tragedians use "pity" for *eleos*, as they also do for Rousseau's *pitié*.

[5] Richard A. Posner, *The Economics of Justice* (Cambridge: Harvard University Press, 1988), pp. 1–2. Having assumed "that people are rational maximizers of satisfactions," Posner now asks:

> Is it plausible to suppose that people are rational only or mainly when they are transacting in markets, and not when they are engaged in other activities of life, such as

Massaro, and Martha Minow have tended to lead the defense, holding that "irrational" factors make a valuable public contribution.[6] Much the same opposition can be found in practice, in recent judicial opinions. For example, in a recent jury-instruction case, Justice Sandra Day O'Connor condemns appeals to compassion as irrational, contrasting them with a "reasoned moral response," while Justice Harry Blackmun, employing the very same contrast between reason and emotion, argues that such "irrational" motives should play a part in the deliberations of the juror.[7] Again, Blackmun puts himself in a weak position, one that seems unlikely to persuade.

Both sides in this debate go wrong because they fail to examine this strong opposition between compassion and reason. The claim that compassion is "irrational" might mean one of two things. First, it might mean that compassion is a noncognitive force that has little to do with thought or reasoning of any kind. This position, I shall argue, cannot bear serious scrutiny. Second, the claim might mean that the thought on which compassion is based is in some normative sense bad or false thought; this is in fact what the serious anti-pity tradition holds. To hold this, however, as we shall see, one must defend a substantive and highly controversial ethical position, one that very few of the contemporary opponents of the emotion would actually be prepared to endorse. In this way, a more precise analysis of the emotion and the historical debate about its normative role can clear the ground for a more adequate contemporary approach. I believe that I will be able to show that a good deal of the public reasoning that would be endorsed even by theoretical opponents of compassion actually makes essential use of compassion, properly understood.

I shall also try to show, however, that those who look to compassion for an intuitive or nonreasoned alternative to judgments based on principle — and, in general, for an alternative to Enlightenment conceptions of the basis of morality — are looking in the wrong place. I shall argue that all compassion is "rational" in the descriptive sense in which

---

marriage and litigation and crime and discrimination and concealment of personal information? . . . But many readers will, I am sure, intuitively regard these choices . . . as lying within the area where decisions are emotional rather than rational.

In other words, we can respect people's choices as rational in the normative sense only if we can show that they do not reflect the influence of emotional factors.

[6]For two examples, see Lynne N. Henderson, "Legality and Empathy," *Michigan Law Review*, vol. 85 (1987), pp. 1574-1653; and Toni M. Massaro, "Empathy, Legal Storytelling, and the Rule of Law: New Words, Old Wounds," *Michigan Law Review*, vol. 87 (1989), pp. 2099-2127; see also Martha Minow and Elizabeth V. Spelman, "Passion for Justice," *Cardozo Law Review*, vol. 10 (1988), pp. 37-76; and Paul Gewirtz, "Aeschylus' Law," *Harvard Law Review*, vol. 101 (1988), pp. 1043-55. Among these authors, only Minow and Spelman criticize the emotion-reason dichotomy. None presents any analysis of emotion that would clarify the role of cognition in emotion.

[7] *California v. Brown*, 479 U.S. 538ff. (1986); for further discussion, see Section VI.D below.

that term is frequently used — that is, not merely impulsive, but involving thought or belief. Nevertheless, not all compassion is rational in the normative sense, that is, based upon beliefs that are true and well-grounded. Properly filtered, however, compassion proves to be an essential ingredient in an Enlightenment moral conception — as Rousseau and Adam Smith saw clearly. Because compassion frequently has deep roots in early moral development, it can be legitimate to contrast it with more fully theorized forms of reasoning; for this same reason, it can be appropriate at times to trust its guidance when it conflicts with theory. None of this, however, shows that it is not suffused with thought, and thought that should be held to high standards of truth and appropriateness.

II. An Analysis of Pity

Let us now ask what pity actually is, following the general lines of the analysis in Aristotle's *Rhetoric*.[8] Pity, Aristotle argues, is a painful emotion directed at another person's misfortune or suffering (*Rhet.* 1385b13ff.). It requires and rests on three beliefs: (1) the belief that the suffering is serious rather than trivial; (2) the belief that the suffering was not caused primarily by the person's own culpable actions; and (3) the belief that the pitier's own possibilities are similar to those of the sufferer. Each of these seems to be necessary for the emotion, and they seem to be jointly sufficient. Let us examine each of these beliefs in turn.

Seriousness first. Pity, like other major emotions,[9] is concerned with value: it involves the recognition that the situation matters deeply for the life in question. Intuitively we see this easily. We do not go around pitying someone who has lost a trivial item, such as a toothbrush or a paper clip, or even an important item that is readily replaceable. Internal to our emotional response itself is the judgment that what is at issue is indeed serious — has "size," as Aristotle puts it (1386a6–7). The occasions for pity enumerated by Aristotle are also the ones on which tragic plots most commonly focus: death, bodily assault or ill-treatment, old age, illness, lack of food, lack of friends, separation from friends, physical weakness, disfigurement, immobility, reversals to expectations, or absence of good prospects (86a6–13).

An important question now arises: From whose point of view does the pitier make the assessment of "size"? Consider the following two exam-

---

[8] I discuss this account in Nussbaum, *The Fragility of Goodness: Luck and Ethics in Greek Tragedy and Philosophy* (Cambridge: Cambridge University Press, 1986), Interlude 2; and also in Nussbaum, "Tragedy and Self-Sufficiency: Plato and Aristotle on Fear and Pity," in *Essays on Aristotle's Poetics*, ed. Amélie O. Rorty (Princeton: Princeton University Press, 1992), pp. 261–90; a longer version appears in *Oxford Studies in Ancient Philosophy*, vol. 10 (1992), pp. 107–60. See also the very perceptive analysis of both Aristotelian and tragic pity in Stephen Halliwell, *Aristotle's Poetics* (London: Duckworth, 1986).

[9] To analyze the connection between emotion and evaluative thinking is the central purpose of the Gifford Lectures: see note * above.

ples. Q, a Roman aristocrat, discovers that his shipment of peacocks' tongues from Africa has been interrupted. Feeling that his dinner party that evening will be a total disaster in consequence, he weeps bitter tears, and implores his friend the Stoic philosopher Seneca to pity him. Seneca laughs. R, a woman in a rural village in India, is severely undernourished, and unable to get more than a first-grade education. She does not think her lot a bad one, since she has no idea what it is to feel healthy, and no idea of the benefits and pleasures of education. So thoroughly has she internalized her culture's views of what is right for women that she believes that she is living a good and flourishing life, as a woman ought to live one. Hearing her story and others like hers, workers in the province's rural-development agency feel deeply moved, and think that something must be done.

What these examples bring out is that people's judgments about what is happening to them can go wrong in many ways. Suffering and deprivation are usually not ennobling or educative; they more often brutalize or corrupt perception. In particular, they often produce adaptive responses that deny the importance of the suffering; such adaptive responses are especially likely to arise when the deprivation is connected to oppression and hierarchy, and taught as proper through religious and cultural practices.[10] Adaptation works in both directions: people can become deeply attached to things that on reflection we may think are either trivial or bad for them; their suffering at the loss of these things may be real enough, even though the onlooker is not disposed to share in it. Pity takes up the onlooker's point of view, informed by the best judgment the onlooker can make about what is really happening to the person being observed — taking the person's own wishes into account, but not always taking as the last word the judgment that the person herself is able to form. Adam Smith, following the Greeks, makes this point powerfully, using as his example a person who has altogether lost the use of reason. This, he argues, is "of all the calamities to which the condition of mortality exposes mankind . . . by far the most dreadful." It will be an object of pity to anyone who has "the least spark of humanity." The person affected does

---

[10] Aristotle was aware of this to some extent, since he frequently stresses the fact that one's sense of pleasure and pain, and related emotional responses, are influenced by moral education. His examples of cultural deformation, however, tend not to focus on poverty (they involve, for example, the excessive valuation of money and honor). For modern work on adaptive preferences, see Jon Elster, *Sour Grapes* (Cambridge: Cambridge University Press, 1983), and Elster, "Sour Grapes — Utilitarianism and the Genesis of Wants," in Amartya Sen and Bernard Williams, eds., *Utilitarianism and Beyond* (Cambridge: Cambridge University Press, 1988), pp. 219–38. See the related criticism of deformed preferences in John Harsanyi, "Morality and the Theory of Rational Behaviour," in Sen and Williams, *Utilitarianism and Beyond*, pp. 39–62. The adaptation of preferences to circumstances in situations of poverty and hierarchy is a major theme in Amartya Sen's work on development: see, for example, the essays in his *Resources, Values, and Development* (Oxford: Basil Blackwell, 1984).

not judge that his condition is bad, however—that, indeed, is a large part of what is so terrible about it.[11]

In short: implicit in pity itself is a conception of human flourishing, the best one the pitier is able to form.

Now I turn to *fault*. Insofar as we believe that a person came to grief through his or her own fault, we will blame and reproach, rather than pitying. Insofar as we do pity, it is either because we believe the person to be without blame for the loss or impediment, or because, though there is some fault, we believe that the suffering is out of proportion to the fault. Pity, Aristotle insists, sees its object as "undeserving" (*anaxios*) of the suffering.[12]

This point about desert is strongly emphasized in Greek tragic appeals for pity. The horrible suffering of Philoctetes becomes a focus for the soldiers' pity without further debate, since his innocence is agreed. Where there is disagreement about culpability, however, the appeal for pity comes closely linked with the assertion of one's innocence. Throughout *Oedipus at Colonus*, for example, Oedipus, asking for pity, insists on the unwilling nature of his crimes. Where there is some fault, the sufferer attempts to establish a discrepancy between fault and punishment. Thus, Cadmus, at the end of Euripides' *Bacchae*, joins to his admission of wrongdoing a claim that the god, by inflicting "unmeasurable sorrow, unbearable to witness"[13] has exceeded the just penalty. Only this justifies his claim to pity from the other characters.

Putting seriousness and fault together, we see that pity requires the belief that there are serious bad things that may happen to people through no fault of their own, or beyond their fault. In pitying another, the pitier accepts a certain picture of the world, according to which the valuable things are not always safely under a person's own control, but can be damaged by fortune. This picture of the world is profoundly controversial. Nobody can deny that the usual occasions for pity occur: that children die, that cities are defeated, that political freedoms are lost, that age and disease disrupt functioning. But how important, really, *are* these things? This is the question that the anti-pity tradition will ask.

I now turn to the third requirement of pity, as Aristotle and writers in

---

[11] Adam Smith, *The Theory of Moral Sentiments* (New York: Liberty Press, 1976), p. 12. Smith uses his device of the "judicious spectator" to distinguish proper from improper emotions; but it is important that this spectator—a model for public rationality—is rich in emotion. I discuss Smith's conception of impartiality in chapters 3 and 4 of *Poetic Justice: The Literary Imagination in Public Life* (Boston: Beacon Press, 1996), with detailed discussion of texts from *The Theory of Moral Sentiments*. For a related discussion of Smith, see my essay "Steerforth's Arm: Literature and the Moral Point of View," in Nussbaum, *Love's Knowledge* (New York: Oxford University Press, 1990).

[12] Aristotle, *Rhetoric*, 1385b14, 1385b34–1386a1, 1386b7, b10, b12, b13; *Poetics*, 1453a4, 5.

[13] Euripides, *Bacchae*, line 1244; see, e.g., the excellent English version by C. K. Williams (New York: Farrar, Straus, and Giroux, 1990), with an introduction by M. Nussbaum.

the poetic tradition understand it. This is a judgment of *similar possibilities*: pity concerns those misfortunes "which the person himself might expect to suffer, either himself or one of his loved ones" (*Rhet.* 1385b14–15). This fact is repeatedly stressed in poetic appeals to pity: thus, Philoctetes reminds his visitors that they, too, may encounter uncontrollable pain. This element in pity is the focus of the marvelous discussion of that emotion in Rousseau's *Emile*. Drawing his account from the classical tradition, Rousseau argues, agreeing with Aristotle, that an awareness of one's own weakness and vulnerability is a necessary condition for pity; without this, we will have an arrogant harshness:

> Why are kings without pity for their subjects? Because they count on never being human beings. Why are the rich so hard toward the poor? It is because they have no fear of being poor. Why does a noble have such contempt for a peasant? It is because he never will be a peasant.... Each may be tomorrow what the one whom he helps is today.... Do not, therefore, accustom your pupil to regard the sufferings of the unfortunate and the labors of the poor from the height of his glory; and do not hope to teach him to pity them if he considers them alien to him. Make him understand well that the fate of these unhappy people can be his, that all their ills are there in the ground beneath his feet, that countless unforeseen and inevitable events can plunge him into them from one moment to the next. Teach him to count on neither birth nor health nor riches. Show him all the vicissitudes of fortune.[14]

There is much debate in the tradition about how this identification with the sufferer works. Does one actually think, for the time being, that one *is* the sufferer?[15] Does one imagine one's own responses as *fused* in some mysterious way with those of the sufferer?[16] These analyses seem

---

[14] Jean-Jacques Rousseau, *Emile*, trans. Allan Bloom (New York: Basic Books, 1976), p. 224; I have altered Bloom's translation in several places, in particular substituting "human being" for "man." Bloom, it is clear, intends "man" in a gender-neutral sense, as the French strongly suggests, and as the Greek discussions that Rousseau is following would require (Greek, unlike French, has two words commonly translated as "man": *anthrôpos* for the species, *anêr* for its male members). A gender-neutral translation is essential to make sense of Rousseau's overall argument. By now, however, it is probably wrong to assume that the word "man" would be understood gender-neutrally by readers.

[15] This appears to be the view of Adam Smith in some passages: "By the imagination we place ourselves in his situation, we conceive ourselves enduring all the same torments, we enter as it were into his body, and become in some measure the same person with him, and thence form some idea of his sensations ..." (Smith, *The Theory of Moral Sentiments*, p. 9). This is, however, corrected by his later observation that the relevant viewpoint is that of the judicious spectator—not that of the sufferer, which may be ill-informed.

[16] This seems to be the view of Arthur Schopenhauer, *Preisschrift über das Fundament der Moral* (Prize essay on the foundation of morality) (Berlin: de Gruyter, 1979), p. 107: Compassion requires "that in *his* pain as such I directly feel, with suffering, *his* pain as I otherwise feel only my own, and on that account want his good directly, as I otherwise want only

wrong, if we think back to what we have already said about the estimation of "size." Pity does indeed involve empathetic identification as one
component: for in estimating the seriousness of the suffering, it seems
important, if not sufficient, to attempt to take its measure as the person
herself measures it. But even then, in the temporary act of identification,
one is always aware of one's own *separateness* from the sufferer — it is for
another, and not oneself, that one feels; and one is aware both of the bad
lot of the sufferer and of the fact that it is, right now, not one's own. If
one really had the experience of feeling the pain in one's own body, then
one would precisely have failed to comprehend the pain of another *as
other*.[17] One must also be aware of one's own *qualitative difference* from
the sufferer: aware, for example, that Philoctetes has no children and no
friends, as one does oneself. For these recognitions are crucial in getting
the right estimation of the meaning of the suffering.

While retaining awareness of her separateness, however, the pitier at
the same time acknowledges that she has possibilities and vulnerabilities
similar to those of the sufferer. She makes sense of the suffering by recognizing that she might herself encounter such a reversal; she estimates
its meaning in part by thinking about what it would mean to encounter
that herself, and she sees herself, in the process, as one to whom such
things might in fact happen. That is why pity is so closely linked to fear,
both in the poetic tradition and in philosophical accounts such as those
of Aristotle and Rousseau.[18]

Why is this important? The point seems to be that the pain of another
will be an object of my concern only if I acknowledge some sort of community between myself and the other, understanding what it might be
for me to face such pain. Without that sense of commonness, both Aristotle and Rousseau claim, I will react with sublime indifference or mere
intellectual curiosity, like an obtuse alien from another world; and I will
not care what I do to augment or relieve the suffering.

This fact explains why so frequently those who wish to withhold pity
and to teach others to do so portray the sufferers as altogether dissimi-
lar in kind and in possibility. In *The Destruction of the European Jews*, Raul
Hilberg shows how pervasively Nazi talk of Jews, in connection with their
murder, portrayed them as nonhuman: either as beings of a remote animal kind, such as insects or vermin, or as inanimate objects, "cargo" to
be transported. When by surprise an individual sufferer was encountered

---

my own. This, however, requires that in a certain manner I should be *identified* with him,
that is to say, that the entire *distinction* between me and that other person, which is the basis
for my egoism, should be, at least to a certain extent, removed" (my translation).

[17] See Stanley Cavell, "Knowing and Acknowledging," in Cavell, *Must We Mean What We
Say?* (New York: Scribner's, 1969; reprint, Cambridge: Cambridge University Press, 1976),
pp. 238–66.

[18] See Aristotle, *Rhetoric*, 1386a22–28, 1382b26–27; *Poetics*, 1453a5–6. For discussion, see
Halliwell, *Aristotle's Poetics*; and Nussbaum, "Tragedy and Self-Sufficiency," pp. 274–75.

in a manner that made similarity unavoidably clear, one frequently saw what might be called a "breakthrough," in which the seriousness of the suffering was acknowledged and pity led to shame and confusion.[19]

In short, the judgment of similar possibilities is part of a construct that bridges the gap between prudential concern and altruism. Equipped with her general conception of human flourishing, the spectator looks at a world in which people suffer hunger, disability, disease, slavery, through no fault of their own or beyond their fault. In her pity she acknowledges that goods such as food, health, citizenship, freedom, do all matter. Yet she acknowledges, as well, that it is uncertain whether she herself will remain among the safe and privileged ones to whom such goods are stably guaranteed. She acknowledges that the lot of the poor might be (or become) hers. This leads her to turn her thoughts outward, from her own current comfortable situation to the structure of society's allocation of goods and resources. For, given the uncertainty of life, she will be inclined to want a society in which the lot of the worst off — of the poor, of people defeated in war, of women, of servants — is as good as it can be. Self-interest promotes the selection of principles that raise society's floor. The floor does not get very high up in most of Greek literature, where a beggar gets a handout rather than a living; but as time goes on, there is a tendency for the exercise of imagination to yield more and more egalitarian results. Rousseau seems right that, followed through rigorously enough, it supports something like democratic equality: democracy because pity sees the value to each person of having a choice in his or her way of life and in the political conception that governs it; equality because it concerns itself at least with the provision to all of a basic minimum welfare.[20]

We can now observe that pity constructs an emotional analogue of the original position in John Rawls's *A Theory of Justice*,[21] in which prudentially rational agents are asked to select the principles that will shape their society, knowing all the relevant general facts but not knowing where in the resulting society they will themselves end up. (This similarity is no accident, since Rawls is in many ways indebted to Smith, who follows the ancient pity tradition.) There is one great difference between Rawls's parties and my pitier. Rawls's parties are determined to be fair to all conceptions of the good that the citizens in the resulting society might have; they therefore refuse themselves knowledge of their own conceptions of the

[19] See Raul Hilberg, *The Destruction of the European Jews*, abridged edition (New York: Holmes and Meier, 1985), pp. 274–93; on "breakthroughs," I am grateful for Jonathan Glover's discussion in an unpublished paper.

[20] On the relationship between that basic minimum and equality, see my "Human Capabilities, Female Human Beings," in Martha Nussbaum and Jonathan Glover, eds., *Women, Culture, and Development* (Oxford: Clarendon Press, 1995).

[21] John Rawls, *A Theory of Justice* (Cambridge: Harvard University Press, 1971).

good. My pitier, by contrast, like the spectator at a tragic drama, operates with a general conception of human flourishing that is the best one she can find; and although she does not fail to notice that the concrete spec-ification of flourishing will be different in different times and places and forms of life, and does not fail to note the value of choice in selecting the conception by which one lives, she does stake herself to a single general conception, when asking whether and to what extent disease, hunger, losses of children, losses of freedom, and so forth, are really bad things. She does not neglect the sufferer's view of things, as I have said; but she is prepared to find his or her preferences and judgments distorted, and to pity in accordance with her own view of the good. A deep similarity to Rawls remains, however: for in both cases the structure of self-interested prudential reasoning is mined to yield altruistic principles. The extent to which this yields a determinate political program may be ques-tioned.[22] What we see clearly, however, as in the case of Rawls, is that it makes political thought attend to certain human facts, and in a certain way, with concern to make the lot of the worst off as good, other things equal, as it can be, since one might oneself be, or become, a member of that worst-off group.

Compassion is in this way intimately related to justice. It is not sufficient for justice, since it focuses on need and offers no account of liberty, rights, or respect for human dignity. And there is another difference as well. Although compassion does presuppose that the person does not deserve the (full measure of) the hardship he or she endures, it does not entail that the person has a *right* or a just claim to relief. Further argument would be required to get to that conclusion. On the other hand, compas-sion at least makes us see the importance of the person's lack, and con-sider with keen interest the claim that such a person might have. In that sense it provides an essential bridge to justice.

It is natural to ask at this point whether one could not have all the judg-ments involved in pity without having the painful emotion itself. I see a stranger in the street. Someone tells me that this woman has just learned of the death of her only child, who was run over by a drunken driver. I have no reason not to believe what I have been told. I therefore believe that this woman has suffered an extremely terrible loss, through no fault of her own. I know well that I myself might suffer a similar loss. Now I might at this point feel compassion for the woman; but then again, I may not. As Adam Smith says, using a similar example, the fact that she is a stranger might make it difficult for me to picture her suffering; or I might

---

[22] For some attempts to describe the political consequences of this difference from Rawls, see the essays by Nussbaum and Sen, and Nussbaum's commentary on O'Neill, in *The Qual-ity of Life*, ed. Martha Nussbaum and Amartya Sen (Oxford: Clarendon Press, 1993); and also Nussbaum, "Aristotelian Social Democracy," in *Liberalism and the Good*, ed. R. B. Douglass et al. (New York: Routledge, 1992), pp. 203–56.

simply be too busy and distracted to focus on what I have been told.[23] Doesn't this show that I can, after all, have all the judgments without the emotion?

The answer is, I think, that we have to distinguish between really accepting a proposition and simply mouthing the words.[24] If I really am too distracted to focus on the woman's predicament, then I may be able to parrot the sentences in question, but it seems wrong to say that I really *believe* them, am prepared to defend them in argument, etc. One way we could see this would be to see how and whether they affect the pattern of my other actions and beliefs. But if the propositions lodge deep enough in me to alter my cognitive life, my motives for action, and so forth, then I think they do prove sufficient for the emotion. We all learn in books that human beings are mortal and subject to various diseases. I think it is fair to say, however, that being able to parrot these sentences does not suffice for really having the judgment: to have the judgment, one must understand what those facts really mean. Rousseau describes an Emile who has suffered himself, and who has it on good authority that others suffer too. He sees gestures indicative of suffering, and his teacher assures him that they mean in the case of others what they would in his own. But, Rousseau claims, he does not really believe or judge that this is so, until he has become able to imagine their suffering vividly to himself, and to suffer the pain of pity: "To see it without feeling it is not to know it."[25] By this he means something very precise: that the suffering of others has not become a part of Emile's cognitive repertory in such a way that it will influence his conduct, provide him with motives and expectations, and so forth. He is merely paying it lip service, until he can imagine in a way that is sufficient for being disturbed.

On the other side, if Emile really does the cognitive work, if his imagination really contains the thoughts of pity, with all their evaluative material, in such a way that they become part of his cognitive makeup and his motivations for action, then he has pity whether he experiences this or that tug in his stomach or not. No such particular bodily feeling is necessary.[26] To determine whether Emile has pity, we look for the evidence of a certain sort of thought and imagination, in what he says, and in what he does.

---

[23] Smith, *The Theory of Moral Sentiments*, pp. 17–18.

[24] I develop this position in much more detail, with regard to emotions in general, in Gifford Lecture 1 (*supra* note *).

[25] Rousseau, *Emile*, p. 222. One might, following Ludwig Wittgenstein, try a different line of argument, saying that the connection between the emotion and action taken to relieve suffering is criterial, not causal. In the Gifford Lectures (Lecture 2), I give the reasons why I do not want to take this route. Although in many cases emotions will lead to related action, there are many reasons why that might not occur in a particular case, and I see no reason why we should withhold ascription of the emotion.

[26] Again, this is a position for which I argue in detail in Gifford Lecture l. In Lecture 2, I show that recent work in cognitive psychology supports this conclusion.

III. PITY AND TRAGIC DRAMA

How could such a complex sentiment be learned? There is a great deal to say here, but I shall focus simply on one point, of great importance both to the philosophical tradition and to our contemporary concern with moral development: the moral importance of tragic drama and related narrative literature.

Tragedy, as ancient Athenian culture saw it, is not for the very young; and it is not just for the young. Mature people always need to expand their experience and to reinforce their grasp on central ethical truths.[27] To the young adolescent who is preparing to take a place in the city, however, tragedy has a special significance. Such a spectator is learning pity in the process. Tragedies acquaint young people with the bad things that may happen in a human life, long before life itself does so: they thus enable concern for others who are suffering what the spectator has not suffered. Moreover, they do so in a way that makes the depth and significance of suffering, and the losses that inspire it, unmistakably plain— the poetic, visual, and musical resources of the drama thus have moral weight. By inviting the spectator to identify with the tragic hero,[28] and at the same time portraying the hero as a worthy person, whose distress does not stem from his own deliberate badness, the drama sets up pity; an attentive spectator will, in apprehending it, have that emotion.

In the process, tragedy leads the spectator to cross boundaries that are usually regarded as firm in social life. Through sympathetic identification, it moves him from Greece to Troy, from the male world of war to the female world of the household. It asks him to identify himself not only with those whom he in some sense might be—leading citizens, generals in battle, exiles and beggars and slaves—but also with many whom he never in fact can be, though one of his loved ones might—such as Trojans and Persians and Africans, such as wives and daughters and mothers. In the process of playing the spectatorial role, as the drama constructs it, then, a young Athenian male would suspend knowledge not only of his wealth and comfort, but also of his national and ethnic origins, even of his gender. He would be asked to see the distresses of human life from points of view that include those of young women who are raped in wartime, queens who are unable to enjoy the full exercise of power on account of their gender, a sister who must violate all the conventional norms of a woman's life to behave with courageous piety. Becoming a woman in thought, he would find that he can remain himself, that is to say, a reasoning being with moral and political commitments. He would,

---

[27] See Nussbaum, "Tragedy and Self-Sufficiency" (*supra* note 8).

[28] On identification, see Halliwell, *Aristotle's Poetics* (*supra* note 8), where Halliwell argues that this is promoted by keeping the tragic hero within the bounds of human frailty and imperfection. Though the hero does not fall through wickedness, his having flaws makes possible the audience's sympathetic response to the tragedy.

however, be confronted with the fact that this group of able people face
disaster in ways, and with a frequency, that males do not, on account of
their powerlessness.

What this means is that when tragic drama constructs the original position, it does so in an especially radical way. Rawls himself did not stip-
ulate that the parties in the original position are ignorant of their gender,
though Susan Moller Okin has forcefully argued that his account of the
moral point of view should be so extended.[29] By investigating both the
common humanity of foreigners and women, and, at the same time,
the special vulnerabilities that they have simply in virtue of being foreigners or women, the spectator is getting an education in social justice. Some
disasters are inevitable, some are not; there are ways of making the world
so that the lot of the worst off does not include rape and slavery. The reality of this suffering might not have dawned on the mind of the young
spectator, without the experience of tragic pity. This does not mean that
he will go out and make radical social changes; nor are my claims about
the radical content of the tragic genre falsified by the evident fact that this
genre existed in an extremely hierarchical and unjust society. Certain
ideas about humanity may be grasped for a time, and yet not enacted, so
powerful are the dulling forces of habit, the entrenched structures of
power. What I want to say is simply that tragic pity provides a powerful
vision of social justice.

The tragic form is radical, in a sense. It is, however, so abstract—it
omits so much of the structure of daily civic life, with its distinctions of
class and race and gender and their concrete institutional forms—it
focuses so much on the sufferings of ruling classes—that an advocate of
a more thoroughy democratic approach to pity might find it education-
ally insufficient. Just as Rousseau applied the essential insights of the
ancient pity tradition to the new problem of constructing democracy, so
the novel, a literary form in which Rousseau was one of the great pio-
neers, develops the educational insights of ancient tragedy, affording its
reader a more concrete thought experiment about class and daily life. In
reading a realist novel with eager participation, the reader does all that
the tragic spectator does—and something more. She embraces the ordinary. She cares not only about the children of kings, but about David
Copperfield, painfully toiling in a factory, or walking the twenty-six miles
from London to Canterbury without food. These small realities of the life
of poverty are brought home to her with a textured vividness unavailable
in tragic poetry; and she is made a participant in that form of life. The
contemporary realist novel takes advantage of this feature of the genre to
explore the experience of marginalized groups whose experience it would

---

[29] See Susan Moller Okin, *Justice, Gender, and the Family* (New York: Basic Books, 1991),
reviewed by Nussbaum in *New York Review of Books*, October 2, 1992.

be especially important for a citizen to understand. The reader of E. M. Forster's *Maurice* is asked to identify with a young man who may be in many ways similar to the reader in education and class—but who has one difference, and for whom this difference (of sexual orientation) shapes the whole of his experience. The reader of Richard Wright's *Native Son* comes upon rich liberal Mary Dalton's wish that she could know how "your people" really live—at a time well after the reader has herself crossed "the line" in participatory imagination, entering Bigger Thomas's enclosed, enraged world, "living" in a tenement in which morning begins with the killing of a large rat. Such a reader understands some crucial social differences more clearly than the spectator at a drama of Sophocles, and also the difference between the vulnerabilities common to all human beings and those constructed for the powerless by the empowered. Her attention has, therefore, a more determinedly egalitarian form than would that of the tragic spectator—again, whether or not this has any practical consequence. And all this she grasps in her pity itself.

IV. The Socratic/Stoic Assault on Pity

Defenders of pity, such as the tragic poets, Aristotle, and Rousseau, assume that many of life's misfortunes do serious harm to good people. But for Socrates, as for the Stoics who follow his lead, a good person cannot be harmed;[30] and Socratic/Stoic thinking about virtue and self-sufficiency inaugurated a tradition of thought that opposes pity, as a moral sentiment unworthy of the dignity of both pitier and recipient, and one based on false beliefs about the value of external goods. According to this tradition, the most important thing in life is one's own reason and will. One can achieve a virtuous reason and will by one's own effort, without the aid of external resources; and virtue, once achieved, is indestructible. The only way to be seriously damaged by life, then, is to make bad choices or become unjust; the appropriate response to that would be blame, not pity. As for the events of life that most people take to be occasions for pity—losses of loved ones, loss of freedom, ill health, and so on—these are of only minor importance.[31] Thus, pity has a *false* cognitive-evaluative structure, and is objectionable for that reason alone. It acknowledges as important what has no true importance. Furthermore, in the process, pity insults the dignity of the person who suffers, implying that this is a person who really needs the things of this world, whereas no vir-

---

[30] Plato, *Apology*, 41D, cf. 30D–C; on this, see Gregory Vlastos, *Socrates: Ironist and Moral Philosopher* (Cambridge: Cambridge University Press, 1991).

[31] It appears that for Socrates such events can affect the *degree* of one's flourishing, though not flourishing itself: see Vlastos, *Socrates*. The Stoics refuse to admit even this much.

tuous person has such needs.[32] (Kant calls this an "insulting kind of beneficence, expressing the sort of benevolence one has for an unworthy person.")[33] Given the judgment of similar possibilities, pity also insults the dignity of the person who gives pity.[34] As Kant puts it, adopting the Socratic/Stoic position: "Such benevolence is called softheartedness and should not occur at all among human beings."[35]

This position on pity becomes the basis for Plato's assault on tragedy in the *Republic*.[36] The good person, he argues, will be "most of all sufficient to himself for flourishing living, and exceptionally more than others he has least need of another. . . . Least of all, then, is it a terrible thing to him to be deprived of a son or brother or money or anything of that sort" (387d–e). Accordingly, speeches of lamentation and requests for pity, if retained at all, must be assigned to characters whom the audience will perceive as weak and error-ridden, so that these judgments will be repudiated by the spectator. The Stoics take this line of thought further, insisting that the true hero for the young should be Socrates, with his calm, self-sufficient demeanor in misfortune, his low evaluation of worldly goods. Tragic heroes, by contrast, should be regarded with scorn, as people whose errors in evaluative judgment have brought them low. (Epictetus defines tragedy as "what happens when chance events befall fools.")[37] This Stoic position on pity and value is taken over with little change by Spinoza and Kant, and seriously influences the account of Adam Smith, who approves of pity up to a point, but thinks that all emotions must be kept strictly in bounds by a rather Stoic sort of "self-command." The position is given an especially complex and vivid development in the thought of Nietzsche, whose connection to Stoicism has not, I think, been sufficiently understood.[38]

[32] See the extensive development of this line of argument in Nietzsche—especially *Dawn*, 135 ("To offer pity is as good as to offer contempt"); and *Zarathustra*, "On the Pitying." Nietzsche actually makes three related points here: (l) pity denigrates the person's own efforts by implying that they are insufficient for flourishing; (2) pity inappropriately inflates the importance of worldly goods; and (3) pity has bad consequences, undermining self-command and practical reason.

[33] Kant, *Doctrine of Virtue*, 35, Akad., p. 457, trans. James W. Ellington (Indianapolis: Hackett, 1982). Kant's entire argument in this passage is very close to, is indeed appropriated as a whole by, Nietzsche—a fact that ought to give pause to those who think Nietzsche's view cruel or proto-fascist. Both Kant and Nietzsche add a further argument: that pity adds to the suffering that there is in the world, by making two people suffer rather than only one (Kant, *ibid.*; Nietzsche, *Dawn*, 134).

[34] See Nietzsche, *Dawn*, 251 (called "Stoical"), 133; *Zarathustra*, IV, "The Sign."

[35] Kant, *Doctrine of Virtue*, 34, Akad., p. 457, Ellington trans., p. 122.

[36] See Nussbaum, "Tragedy and Self-Sufficiency," for a detailed analysis.

[37] See Nussbaum, "Poetry and the Passions: Two Stoic Views," in *Passions & Perceptions*, ed. Jacques Brunschwig and Martha Nussbaum (Cambridge: Cambridge University Press, 1993).

[38] I analyze the Stoic roots of Nietzsche's position on pity, and draw some new interpretive consequences, in Nussbaum, "Pity and Mercy: Nietzsche's Stoicism," in *Nietzsche: Genealogy, Morality*, ed. Richard Schacht (Berkeley and Los Angeles: University of California Press, 1994), pp. 139–67.

The classic attacks on pity make two further objections. The first concerns the partiality and narrowness of pity; the second concerns its connection to anger and revenge. Pity, the first argument goes, binds us to our own immediate sphere of life, to what has affected us, to what we see before us or can easily imagine. This means, however, that it distorts the world: for it effaces the equal value and dignity of all human lives, their equal need for resources and for aid in time of suffering. This argument, which is first introduced in the ancient Stoics, is given an especially vivid form by Adam Smith, who argues that to rely on pity as a social motive will, on this account, produce very unbalanced and inconsistent results.[39]

Finally, the classic attack examines the connection between pity and the roots of other, more objectionable emotions. The person who pities accepts certain controversial evaluative judgments concerning the place of "external goods" in human flourishing. But a person who accepts those judgments accepts that she has given hostages to fortune. And to give hostages to fortune is to be set up not only for pity, but also for fear and anxiety and grief — and not only for these, but for anger and the retributive disposition as well. What Stoic analyses bring out again and again is that the repudiation of pity is not in the least connected with callousness, brutality, or the behavior of the boot-in-the-face tyrant. In fact, in this picture it is pity itself that is closely connected with cruelty. The pitier acknowledges the importance of certain worldly goods and persons, which can in principle be damaged by another's agency. The response to such damages will be pity if the damaged person is someone else; but if the damaged person is oneself, and the damage is deliberate, the response will be anger — and anger that will be proportional to the intensity of the initial evaluative attachment. The soft soul of the pitier can be invaded by the serpents of envy, hatred, and cruelty. When Seneca writes to Nero reproving pity,[40] he hardly aims to encourage Nero in his tendencies to brutality. On the contrary, his project is to get Nero to care less about insults to his reputation, and about wealth and power generally. This, Seneca argues, will make him a more gentle and humane ruler. But this project is not hindered by the removal of pity; indeed, it demands it, because it demands the removal of attachments to external goods.

This line of argument is developed vividly by Nietzsche, who argues, with the Stoics, that a certain sort of "hardness" toward the vicissitudes of fortune is the only way to get rid of the desire for revenge. The "veiled glance of pity," which looks inward on one's own possibilities with "a profound

---

[39] Smith, *The Theory of Moral Sentiments*, p. 136; see the excellent account of these aspects of Smith's thought in Ronald Coase, "Adam Smith's View of Man," *Journal of Law and Economics*, vol. 19 (1976), pp. 529–46.

[40] Seneca, *On Mercy*, Book II.

sadness,"[41] acknowledging one's own weakness and inadequacy — this glance of the pitier is, Nietzsche argues, the basis of much hatred directed against a world that makes human beings suffer, and against all those, in that world, who are not brought low, who are self-respecting and self-commanding: "It is on such soil, on swampy ground, that every weed, every poisonous plant grows. . . . Here the worms of vengefulness and rancor swarm."[42]

If pity is in this way bound up with the inclination to revenge, however, and if the task of a strong society is to contain and control the inclination to revenge, then one might conclude that society has reasons to extirpate pity in its citizens, and in its legal system, rather than fostering it. And this seems to mean removing the tragic poets from the city.

The debate over pity constructs, in effect, two visions of political community, and of the good citizen and judge within it. One sees the human being as both aspiring and vulnerable, both worthy and insecure; the other focuses on dignity alone, seeing in reason a boundless and indestructible worth. One sees a central task of community as the provision of support for basic needs; it brings human beings together through the thought of their common weakness and risk. The other sees a community as a kingdom of free responsible beings, held together by the awe they feel for the worth of reason in one another. Each vision, in its own way, pursues both equality and freedom. The former aims at equal support for basic needs, and hopes through this to promote equal opportunities for free choice and self-realization; the other starts from the fact of internal freedom — a fact that no misfortunes can remove — and finds in this fact a source of political equality. One sees freedom of choice as something that needs to be built up for people through worldly arrangements that make them capable of functioning in a fully human way; the other takes freedom to be an inalienable given, independent of all material arrangements. One attempts to achieve benevolence through softheartedness; the other holds, with Kant, that this softheartedness "should not occur at all among human beings." The debate between the friends and enemies of pity is not a debate between partisans of reason and partisans of some mindless noncognitive force. It is a substantive debate about ethical value. Both sides agree that pity is judgment; they differ about whether the judgments are true. To the adjudication of that debate I now turn.

V. A Defense of Pity

Let me address first the charge that pity ascribes to misfortunes an importance they do not really possess — insulting, in the process, the dignity of both the receiver and the giver of pity.

---

[41] Friedrich Nietzsche, *Genealogy of Morals*, trans. W. Kaufmann (New York: Vintage, 1967), Book III, ch. 14.

[42] *Ibid*.

The first thing we must say in response to this charge is that it is, so far, much too blunt. For why are we forced to make an all-or-nothing choice between pitying a suffering person and having respect for that person's dignity? Why can't we both pity the person for the wrongs luck has ' brought her way and at the same time have respect and awe for the way in which she bears these ills? Indeed, it is difficult to know what we would be admiring in such a case if we did take the Stoic position that the loss was not a serious loss. For then, where would the fortitude be in bearing the event with dignity?

In another way as well, the attack is too blunt. For it takes an all-or-nothing position on the importance of external goods for flourishing: either pity all over the place, or no pity at all. The pro-pity tradition, however, is not prevented from judging that some occasions for pity are illegitimate, and based upon false evaluations. As I have said, pity takes up not the actual point of view of any and every sufferer, but rather the point of view of a reflective spectator who asks which reversals are of true importance and which are not. Thus, pity will not be given to my Roman aristocrat who misses an evening of peacocks' tongues (discussed in Section II), no matter how much he minds this. On the other hand, pity will be given to the person who is unaware of the extent of her illness or deprivation because of mental impairment or the social deformation of preferences. The pro-pity tradition is in fact preoccupied with the criticism of those who attach inappropriate importance to money, status, or pleasure.

One further distinction can now be drawn. When the defender of pity depicts the best human life as vulnerable to fortune, she is not bound to embrace as good any and every sort of human neediness and dependency. Even with respect to those "external goods" that are endorsed by the pitier's own reflection as of enormous importance for flourishing, the pitier is not required to wish on people the maximum vulnerability. For there are ways of arranging the world so as to bring these good things more securely within people's grasp; and acknowledging our deep need for them provides a strong incentive for so designing things. There are some important features of human life that nobody ever fully controls; one cannot make oneself immortal, one cannot will that one's children should be healthy and happy, one cannot will oneself happiness in love. Nevertheless, differences in class, race, gender, wealth, and power do affect the extent to which the sense of helplessness governs the daily course of one's life. Taking up the reflective view of the tragic audience, one will see inequalities in vulnerability: therefore I argued, with Rousseau, that one will have reasons to raise the floor of security for all.

Nor is the anti-pity tradition prepared to repudiate concern for material well-being, as its own position might seem to demand. No member of this tradition expresses indifference to benevolence. Indeed, the tradition prides itself on promoting benevolence by minimizing competitive grasping for goods. Kant follows the Stoics in insisting that when we get rid of pity, that "insulting kind of benevolence," we will still be able to think of the needs of others with "an active and rational benevolence." This benevolent disposition will include an active attempt to understand the situation of another—what Kant calls *humanitas practica*—but will repudiate the softhearted commiseration characteristic of pity, which "can be called communicable (like a susceptibility to heat or to contagious diseases)."[43]

The question is, however, what sense such Stoic thinkers can make of the need for benevolence, when they hold the dignity of reason to be complete in itself. If people can exercise their most important capacities without material support, this very much diminishes the significance and the urgency of that support. The original Stoics at this point invoke teleology: Zeus's design asks us to be concerned with material necessities even though, strictly speaking, such things have no true worth.[44] But Kant and other modern Stoics can help themselves to no such religious picture; thus, the status of benevolence in their theories becomes problematic. We are put on our guard when Kant writes as follows:

> It was a sublime way of representing the wise man, as the Stoic conceived him, when he let the wise one say: I wish I had a friend, not that he might give me help in poverty, sickness, captivity, and so on, but in order that I might stand by him and save a human being. But for all that, the very same wise man, when his friend is not to be saved, says to himself: What's it to me? i.e. he rejected commiseration.[45]

Kant here accepts the Stoic view that there is no good way to respond with distress to the present distress of another. He immediately tries to salvage the motivational foundations of benevolence by insisting that, since active benevolence is a duty, it is also a duty to seek out circumstances in which one will witness poverty and deprivation:

> Thus it is a duty not to avoid places where the poor, who lack the most necessary things, are to be found; instead, it is a duty to seek them out. It is a duty not to shun sickrooms or prisons and so on in order to avoid the pain of pity, which one may not be able to resist. For this feeling, though painful, nevertheless is one of the impulses placed in us by nature for effecting what the representation of duty might not accomplish by itself.[46]

---

[43] Kant, *Doctrine of Virtue*, 34, *Akad.*, pp. 456–57, Ellington trans., p. 121.

[44] On the difficulties of interpreting the Stoic position here, see my discussion of the scholarly literature in Nussbaum, *The Therapy of Desire: Theory and Practice in Hellenistic Ethics* (Princeton: Princeton University Press, 1994), ch. 10.

[45] Kant, *Doctrine of Virtue*, 34, *Akad.*, p. 457, Ellington trans., pp. 121–22.

[46] *Ibid.*, 35, *Akad.*, p. 457, Ellington trans., p. 122.

This fascinating passage shows us as clearly as any text the tensions of the anti-pity position, when it tries to defend benevolence. In what spirit, we may ask, does the Kantian visit places "where the poor are to be found"? Should he do this in a truly Stoic spirit, performing a moral duty with no thought of the universality and importance of human need, no thought of his own personal similarity to the sufferers? But then what will the sight of this misery mean to him, and how will it inspire benevolence? Won't he be likely to have some contempt for these people, insofar as they are depressed by their lot? Won't he want to remind them, using Kant's own words, that "a good will is good not because of what it effects or accomplishes, . . . it is good only through its willing, i.e. good in itself"?[47] He might then reflect, gazing at them, that

> [e]ven if, by some especially unfortunate fate or by the niggardly provision of stepmotherly nature, this will should be wholly lacking in the power to accomplish its purpose . . . yet would it, like a jewel, still shine by its own light as something which has its full value in itself. Its usefulness or fruitlessness can neither augment nor diminish this value. Its usefulness would be, as it were, only the setting to enable us to handle it in ordinary dealings or to attract to it the attention of those who are not yet experts, but not to recommend it to real experts or to determine its value.[48]

And won't the Kantian then say to himself: I am a real expert, and I see here, in this place where the poor are to be found, not the squalor itself, not the poverty, but the pure light of human dignity, which has full value in itself and cannot possibly be increased by my gifts? But if, as Kant here acknowledges, this way of thinking might not lead to benevolence, if the motives connected with pity are also required, isn't this more than an accident of the hard-wiring of human psychology? Doesn't it mean that the *evaluations* characteristic of that emotion are also required, in order to inform the onlooker about what is going on here, and why it matters? Without these evaluations — which seem in any case to be endorsed in other parts of Kant's moral theory — he will be like a Martian onlooker, and only some external commandment — with which the Stoics can supply him, but Kant cannot — would make him intervene. Kant cannot consistently accept the full Stoic anti-pity position, if he really wishes to allow for the thoughts entailed by our duty to promote the happiness of others. This inconsistency escapes his notice, I think, because, unlike most of his philosophical predecessors, he does not investigate the cognitive foundations of the emotions, and tends to treat them as unintelligent (unthinking, nonreasoning) parts of our animal nature. It seems impor-

---

[47] Kant, *Grounding for the Metaphysics of Morals*, section 1, *Akad.*, p. 394, Ellington trans., p. 7.

[48] *Ibid.*, section 1, *Akad.*, p. 394, Ellington trans., pp. 7–8.

tant to point out that an endorsement of compassion, far from being inconsistent with Kant's Enlightenment interest in impartiality and universality, seems actually to be entailed by some parts of Kant's own position, although for the reasons given he does not see this.

I turn now to the objection about partiality. It is not exactly an objection to compassion or pity itself; but it says that people so rarely exhibit perfect universal compassion that it would not be good to rely on it too much. Any conception of public rationality that appeals to emotion will have to grapple with this issue; later I shall suggest some practical strategies. Nevertheless, I can begin my reply with two more-general arguments, one concerning development and one concerning adult deliberation.

The friend of pity should argue, I think, that pity is our species' way of connecting the good of others to the fundamentally eudaimonistic (though not egoistic) structure of our imaginations and our most intense cares. The good of others means nothing to us in the abstract or antecedently. Only when it is brought into relation with that which we already understand—with our intense love of a parent, our passionate need for comfort and security—does such a thing start to matter deeply. The Stoics, of whom I have otherwise been very critical in this essay, have a vivid metaphor for this process. Imagine, they say, that each of us lives in a set of concentric circles—the nearest being one's own body, the furthest being the entire universe of human beings. The task of moral development is to move the circles progressively closer and closer to the center, so that one's parents become like oneself, one's other relatives like one's parents, strangers like relatives, and so forth.[49] One has to build on the meanings one understands, or one is left with an equality that is empty of urgency—what Aristotle, attacking Plato's removal of the family, called a "watery" concern all around.[50]

But could adult rationality do without compassionate emotion—for example, by adopting an economic-utilitarian account of rational choice in terms of self-interest? Economics is so skeptical of compassion that it has excluded it from rationality by stipulative definition, simply assuming that all but the most deluded and perverse human behavior can be explained without it; but such accounts of human motivation are now under heavy attack within economic thought itself, precisely because they leave compassion out. A leading example of such criticism is Amartya Sen's famous essay "Rational Fools,"[51] which argues that we cannot

---

[49] This image is from Hierocles, a Stoic of the first-second centuries A.D.; see the discussion in Nussbaum, *The Therapy of Desire*, ch. 9. The job of a reasonable person is to "draw the circles somehow towards the centre," and "the right point will be reached if, through our own initiative, we reduce the distance of the relationship with each person." (See my discussion in *ibid.*, pp. 34–44.)

[50] Aristotle, *Politics*, Book II, ch. 4.

[51] Amartya Sen, "Rational Fools," *Philosophy and Public Affairs*, vol. 6 (Summer 1977), pp. 317–44, reprinted in Sen, *Choice, Welfare, and Measurement* (Oxford: Blackwell, 1982).

give either a good predictive account of human action or a correct normative theory of rationality without mentioning the concern people have for
the good of others, as a factor independent of their concern for their own
satisfactions. For people very often sacrifice their own interests and well-
being, and in many cases even their lives, for the well-being of those they
love, or for good social consequences that they prize. They also stand by
commitments and promises they have made, even when to do so requires
major personal sacrifice. One cannot, Sen argues, explain the behavior of
loving members of families, or of soldiers who give their lives for their
country, or of many other decent yet unselfish acts, without pointing to
patterns of action that are motivated by sympathetic emotion.[52] In short,
people may not be perfect in their compassion, but that is no reason to
deny that a good deal of human behavior is explained in this way. Neither
predictive nor normative analyses can afford to ignore this.

My argument, like Sen's, does not say that we should dismiss economic and mathematical analysis and rely on the the heart alone.
(Indeed, compassion itself is not a matter of the heart alone, if that means
being devoid of thought.) Later (in Section VI) I shall say what I think an
economics that takes emotion seriously would look like. Here I am saying that judgment that does not employ the intelligence of compassion in
coming to grips with the significance of human suffering is blind and
incomplete. Let the analysis be as sophisticated and as formal as science
requires it to be. Still, if, like the economic analyses of Dickens's Mr.
Gradgrind, it is concocted in a room that is like an astronomical observa-
tory without windows, where the economist can arrange the world
"solely by pen, ink, and paper,"[53] we should not be surprised to find it
lacking in vision concerning our world.

We now face the argument about revenge, which seems difficult for the
friend of pity to answer. For it tells her that she cannot have a form of reasoning that she prizes without also taking on attitudes that she herself
views with alarm. The defender of pity can insist once again, however,
that the opponent's picture of her position is far too crude. For just as she
is not committed to saying that any and every calamity is an appropriate
occasion for pity, so too she is not committed to saying that any and
every damage, slight, or insult is an appropriate occasion for retributive
anger. By far the largest number of the social ills caused by revenge concern damages to fortune, status, power, and honor, to which the
defender of pity does not ascribe much worth.

Furthermore, when we move the outer circles closer to the self, as an
education in pity urges, our inclination to revenge will diminish, in that

---

[52] Notice that the family altruism to which Sen alludes is not the "altruism" assumed in
standard economic models, which is really a kind of instrumental dependency, contingent
on the familial bond serving the good of the agent in some way.

[53] Charles Dickens, *Hard Times*, ed. David Craig (New York: Penguin, 1963), p. 131.

we will become concerned for others as for members of our own family, and see any damage befalling them as a damage to ourselves as well. Pity shows the significance of vindictive acts for those who suffer from them: by moving these victims closer to us, it makes us think twice before undertaking such acts.

At the conclusion of Aeschylus's *Oresteia*, the Furies are not banished from the city: instead, they are civilized, and made a part of Athena's judicial system. Now called "Eumenides," for their kindly intentions toward the people of Athens, they cease to snarl, to crouch like dogs, to sniff for blood. But they do not cease to demand punishment for crime: and in that sense to place them at the heart of the judicial institutions of the city is to announce that these dark forces cannot be cut off from the rest of human life without impoverishing it. For these forces are forms of acknowledgment of the importance of the goods that crime may damage.[54] Placing retribution under the control of law, however, is a signal way of limiting the domain of revenge in the city's life. The link between pity and revenge supports that move.

VI. COMPASSION IN CONTEMPORARY PUBLIC LIFE

Now that I have defended the pro-pity tradition against its opponents' most powerful objections, I want, more briefly, to sketch some of the roles that this emotion can and should play in public life.

A. Moral and civic education

If we believe that the ability to imagine the ills of another with vivid sympathy is an important part of being a good person, then we will want to follow Rousseau in giving support to procedures by which this ability is taught. Much of this will and should be done privately, in families.[55] But every society employs and teaches ideals of the citizen, and of good civic judgment, in many ways; and there are some concrete practical strategies that will in fact support an education in compassion. First of all, public education at every level should cultivate the ability to imagine the experiences of others and to participate in their sufferings. This, I think, means giving the humanities and the arts a large place in education, from elementary school on up. It also means recognizing that the arts serve a vital political function, even when their content is not expressly political— for they cultivate imaginative abilities that are central to the political life. This would give us special reasons for supporting the arts, and for giv-

---

[54] See Gewirtz, "Aeschylus' Law" (*supra* note 6); and Richard Posner, *Law and Literature* (Cambridge: Harvard University Press, 1988), where Posner perceptively suggests that this is one of the most important contributions literature can make to the law.

[55] For some valuable assistance in that task, see the section on compassion in William J. Bennett, *The Book of Virtues* (New York: Simon and Schuster, 1993).

ing artistic expression a high degree of protection from the repression that
so often threatens it.

This education of the imagination should take a particular form. I have
said that a crucial part of the ethical value of pity is its ability to cross
boundaries of class, nationality, race, and gender, as the pitier assumes
these different positions in imagination, and comes to see the obstacles
to flourishing faced by human beings in these many concrete situations.
I have argued that although Greek tragic drama already promoted this
sort of understanding to some degree, the novel goes further, by connecting the reader to highly concrete circumstances other than her own, and
by making her imagine what it would be like to be a member of both privileged and oppressed groups in these circumstances.

What I now want to suggest is that an education aimed at promoting
compassionate citizenship should also be a multicultural education. Our
pupil must learn to appreciate the diversity of circumstances in which
human beings struggle for flourishing; this means not just learning some
facts about classes, races, nationalities, and sexual orientations other than
her own, but being drawn into those lives through the imagination,
becoming a participant in those struggles. One ingredient in this education will certainly be the study of political, social, and economic history;
but another equally important ingredient will be contact with works of literature and other artworks that involve the spectator in the human meaning of these events. This does not commit us to cultural relativism, or to
any sort of hands-off attitude toward cultural criticism. In fact, the compassionate spectator is always attempting to compare what she sees with
her own evolving conception of the good; and though she is likely to
modify that conception during the educational process, she is also likely
to be keenly aware of hidden impediments to flourishing in the lives she
encounters.

B. Political leaders

We should demand political leaders who display the abilities involved
in compassion, who show not just mastery of pertinent facts about their
society and its history, but also the ability to take on in imagination the
lives of the various diverse groups whom they propose to lead. One may
find an example of this ability at an especially high level in Lincoln,
whose empathy for the situation of the slave was one of the most important sources of moral force in his public rhetoric.[56] It is also reassuring to
encounter, in President Clinton's inaugural address, the claim that the
idea of America is "an idea tempered by the knowledge that, but for fate,
we—the fortunate and the unfortunate—might have been each other."

---

[56] In Gifford Lecture 6, I give examples of this.

C. Economic thought: Welfare and development

I would argue that the compassionate imagination provides information essential for economic planning, by showing the human meaning of
the sufferings and deprivations different groups of people encounter. I
have insisted that I am not proposing to substitute emotion for economic
modeling; rather, I am urging that formal economic models take account
of compassion's information. Let me describe what I mean by this more
concretely.

When the well-being of a nation is measured by development agencies,
following the lead of development economists, by far the most common
strategy still is simply to list GNP per capita. This crude approach does
not tell us much about how people are doing: it does not even describe
the distribution of wealth and income, much less investigate the quality
of lives in areas not always well correlated with wealth and income — such
as infant mortality, access to health care, life expectancy,[57] the quality of
public education, the presence or absence of political liberties, and the
state of racial and gender relations. What development planners need to
know about the overall "political economy" of a nation is far more than
such approaches tell us, even where economic planning in the narrow
sense is concerned. For they need to know how the economic resources
of the nation are or are not supporting human functioning in these various areas, and how they might do so more effectively.

For these reasons, a number of development economists[58] have
recently argued that the focus of welfare and development economics
should not be resources as such, as if they had some value in themselves,
but the role of resources in supporting the *capabilities* of human beings to
function in important ways. The "capability" approach has begun to have
a major influence on the ways in which international agencies measure
welfare.

There is an intimate link between this approach to quality-of-life measurement and the thought experiment of compassion. For the point that
Sen has continually made, against liberal views that focus on resources,
is that we do not have information enough to tell us how these resources
are working, unless we see them at work in the context of human func-

---

[57] These may appear to be well correlated with GNP per capita, if one considers only
gross contrasts, such as those between Europe and North America on the one hand, and
the poorer regions of Africa on the other. If one breaks things down more finely, however,
large and significant discrepancies begin to appear; for many examples of this, see Jean Drèze
and Amartya Sen, *Hunger and Public Action* (Oxford: Clarendon Press, 1989); and the *Human
Development Reports* for 1993 and 1994, prepared by the United Nations Development Program (New York: United Nations, 1993, 1994).

[58] In addition to Sen and Drèze, this group includes the contributors to the *Human Development Reports*, including Sudhir Anand and others. For a similar approach, see Partha Das-
gupta, *An Inquiry into Well-Being and Destitution* (Oxford: Clarendon Press, 1993). For an
application of this approach to the situation of women in developing countries, see Nussbaum and Glover, eds., *Women, Culture, and Development* (*supra* note 20).

tioning. When we do so, however, we see that individuals have widely varying needs for resources, if they are to attain a similar level of capability to function. A person in a wheelchair needs more support in order to become mobile than a person who lacks this disability. A large and active person needs more food in order to be healthy than a small and sedentary person, and a pregnant or lactating woman more than a non-pregnant woman. Groups that have been disadvantaged with respect to education may need special educational investments to attain the same level of capability. Whether a government wishes to promote equality of capability is, of course, another story — though I have argued that compassion leads in an egalitarian direction, or at least in the direction of support for a basic level of capability, where the most important functions of life are concerned. What is important to me here is to say that the imaginative exercise itself, and the emotion itself, provide information without which no informed decision about allocation can be made.[59] Incorporating emotion in this way does not mean abandoning the aim of modeling human action scientifically; it does mean that science must be responsive to the human facts.

D. Legal rationality

What I have already said has many implications for legal and judicial rationality: for lawyers and judges are concerned with issues of human welfare, and will want to use the sort of deliberative rationality that is best equipped to handle welfare issues. They are also, some of them, leaders, to whom my argument about the importance of a compassionate leadership clearly applies. This means, I think, that it is especially important for judges and future judges to acquire the kind of information my imaginary curriculum for citizenship will offer — not just collecting facts about the diverse ways of life with which they are likely to come in contact, but entering into these lives with empathy and seeing the human meaning of the issues at stake in them.[60] Through compassion, the judge will be especially likely to discern the disadvantages under which certain people or groups have labored. The compassionate judge is committed to neutrality in the appropriate sense, that is, to the fair treatment of all the groups concerned and to judgments that are based upon articulable reasons. She has no tendency to suppose, however, that this pursuit of fairness requires her to stand at a lofty distance from the social realities of the cases before her.

This distinction goes to the heart of a famous and controversial argument made by Herbert Wechsler in his 1959 article "Toward Neutral Prin-

---

[59] See the introduction to Nussbaum and Sen, eds., *The Quality of Life* (*supra* note 22).

[60] For examples in this area, both good and bad, and further discussion, see Nussbaum, *Poetic Justice* (*supra* note 11).

ciples of Constitutional Law."[61] The opening of Wechsler's argument would find strong support from the friend of compassion: for he argues that judges need criteria that are not arbitrary or willful, not simply tailored to the "immediate result." A good decision is one "that rests on reasons with respect to all the issues in the case, reasons that in their generality and their neutrality transcend any immediate result that is involved." As the argument continues, however, Wechsler seems to take the demand for neutrality to entail ignoring certain specific social and historical facts that seem highly relevant to the equal and principled application of the law. In particular, he suggests, criticizing the reasoning in *Brown v. Board of Education* (1954),[62] that judges deciding cases relating to "separate but equal" facilities should refuse themselves concrete empathetic knowledge of the special disadvantages faced by minorities, in order to ensure that their principles should be applied without political bias. From this point of view, as Wechsler sees it, Southern blacks and whites suffer similar burdens from segregation: the fact that he and a black colleague cannot eat lunch together is an equal deprivation to both.

This, however, is all too like Kant taking a tour of places "where the poor are to be found." There is such a lofty distance here that the human facts are not correct. In terms of the human meaning of segregation for the two groups involved, the burden is not equal. The evidence that was presented in the arguments in *Brown v. Board of Education* showed the impediments to self-esteem, and thence to learning, that were unequally faced by black children in separate schools; like a tragic narrative, the materials presented in the case appealed to reasoned compassion. By taking his stand above emotion and the judgments involved in it, Wechsler prevents himself from seeing, and is thus unable to be truly fair. In this sense, when properly filtered for personal bias and when appropriately based on the evidence presented in the case, compassionate emotion is not the enemy but the indispensable ally of legal rationality. For the facts considered by the law are human facts, invested with the significance with which people endow them in their lives. Martian neutrality—or even Kantian neutrality—cannot so much as get at the facts, far less render an adequate judgment about them.

If a good judge cannot do without compassion of the appropriate sort, then one would expect to find compassion even in the opinions of a judge who in theoretical writings leads the opposition to emotion's public role— if, that is, he is a good judge in the sense I have described. When one examines the judicial opinions of Richard Posner, now chief judge of the

[61] Herbert Wechsler, "Toward Neutral Principles of Constitutional Law," *Harvard Law Review*, 1959, pp. 1ff. Wechsler's argument is discussed in greater detail in Nussbaum, *Poetic Justice*, ch. 4.

[62] *Brown v. Board of Education*, 347 U.S. 483 (1954).

U.S. Court of Appeals for the Seventh Circuit, one does indeed, I believe, find thoughts that (according to the long philosophical tradition) entail compassion.

The document I wish to examine here is an opinion written by Posner in a case of child sexual abuse, *Nelson v. Farrey* (1989).[63] The case concerns a father's abuse of his four-year-old daughter. The abusive father asks the court not to admit the testimony of a psychiatrist about the latter's lengthy interviews with the little girl, during which she gave very convincing evidence of her abuse, without giving the father an opportunity to confront the girl herself in court. Posner, ruling against the father, writes eloquently about the suffering of the little girl, about the clear evidence of sexual abuse that emerged in the psychiatric setting. He rejects summarily the father's claim that she could have learned what to say from the "anatomically correct" dolls given to her by the doctor: for, as Posner notes, she repeatedly said that she got "white mud" all over her face from her father's penis, and the dolls "are not *that* anatomically correct."[64]

Now recall that I insisted that there was no twinge or pang, no feeling of any particular sort, that was necessary for the emotion of pity or compassion. What is necessary, and sufficient, are certain value-laden thoughts and perceptions. This is not everyone's view, but it is the view for which I have been arguing, along with a great part of the philosophical tradition. This means that in order to find out whether Posner has compassion for the little girl, we do not need to ask him whether he feels a pain; we need only look at the perceptions and thoughts expressed in what he writes (assuming that he is sincere). When we do this, we see in his opinion all the materials of compassion: the judgment that the little girl has suffered serious harm through no fault of her own; the judgment that this is a very bad thing and must not be renewed by a courtroom confrontation, which would be, he writes, "psychologically harmful to her," indeed, a "monstrous cruelty";[65] and clearly, as well, the thought that this is not just an isolated sui generis case, but a case that displays a vulnerability to damage that is the lot of all too many human beings — for Posner writes that if this sort of psychiatric evidence were not admissible, "molesters of small children, especially incestuous molesters, would rarely be punished."[66] All this is arrived at by a process of empathy that is precisely what the pro-pity tradition demands. In short, Posner here is the compassionate judge I have been describing; and I think it is clear that

[63] *Nelson v. Farrey*, 874 F.2d 165 (7th Cir. 1989).

[64] *Ibid.*, p. 1229.

[65] *Ibid.*, pp. 1228, 1229.

[66] *Ibid.*, p. 1229. We do not exactly see the belief that Posner himself could suffer a similar damage, since the damage in question requires the victim to be very young; but we do have, I think, the sense that such damage is not an alien thing, that it might happen to someone that Posner knows or cares about.

this capacity for compassion is a vital part of his judicial equipment, and of his judicial rationality.[67]

What does this example show? In fact, it is not at all isolated in the judicial opinions of Posner.[68] To some extent, we see an increasing interest in sympathy in his more recent theoretical writings.[69] It is difficult to tell which shift is prior; but one may at least conjecture that the repeated confrontation with human misery that is a consequence of being a judge has had some bearing on the evolution of Posner's theoretical position.

E. Public institutions

What do we do, however, when we cannot rely upon compassionate actors in public life? It seems obvious that in some areas, such as the judiciary, we cannot embody everything we want in systems of rules; and individual actors will continue to exercise broad discretion. But the final point I want to make here is that compassion can and should inform the structure of public institutions themselves, so that we do not need in every case to rely on the perfect compassion of individual actors. (This is an important part of my answer to Adam Smith's point about partiality, discussed in Section IV.) I have compared the perspective of the compassionate spectator to John Rawls's "original position" — though with the difference that compassion embodies a highly general conception of the good. The original position, however, is a device that shows us how to design political institutions, and especially systems of distribution. Compassion, and the imaginings it prompts, is another such device, similar in spirit though different in some of its implications. We do not need to rely upon perfectly compassionate philanthropy, for example, since we can design a just welfare system, and a system of taxation to support it. It will be a complicated matter to determine how far we should take this course, and how far we ought to leave individual agents free to act compassionately by their own lights. In part, this will be an efficiency question, and will be settled by empirical trial and error. In part, it will also be a matter of the intrinsic worth of liberty; and we will need to ask carefully what sorts and what amount of liberty we should take to have intrinsic value. Aristotle was not wrong to conclude that in Plato's fully

---

[67] Compare Posner's criticism of the opinions in *Bowers v. Hardwick* (478 U.S. 1186 [1986]) for their lack of "empathy" with the situation of the homosexual in contemporary American society: Richard A. Posner, *Sex and Reason* (Cambridge: Harvard University Press, 1992), p. 345ff.

[68] In *Poetic Justice*, I discuss a recent sexual harassment case that contains similar material: *Mary J. Carr v. Allison Gas Turbine Division, General Motors Corporation*, U.S. Court of Appeals for the Seventh Circuit, July 26, 1994.

[69] In Richard A. Posner, *The Problems of Jurisprudence* (Cambridge: Harvard University Press, 1990), he presents a sympathetic discussion of appeals to sympathy under the rubric "Literary and Feminist Approaches"; see also his discussion of *Bowers v. Hardwick* in *Sex and Reason* (*supra* note 67).

controlled society there could be no generosity, since the scope for individual choice in matters of distribution was removed. On the other hand, we want institutions to take account of Smith's problem, and to find some way of solving it—whether his own way, with its heavy reliance on the operation of the market, or some other way.[70]

This point has two sides. If it is true that compassion can be embodied in the structure of legal and political institutions, it also seems true that the construction of these institutions influences the development of compassion in individuals. Because compassion requires fellow-feeling, its birth is very much aided by institutions that place people in similar circumstances, weakening or removing hierarchies of wealth, gender, and class. Alexis de Tocqueville argued that there was an unusually great potential for compassion in the American democracy, because the Constitution had situated citizens as equal to a degree unknown in Europe: "[T]he more equal social conditions become, the more do men display this reciprocal disposition to oblige each other."[71] As William Bennett says of this passage, "we are forced to ask ourselves: How does modern America measure up to the portrait he painted more than a century and a half ago?"[72]

In short, compassionate imagining and compassionate institutions reinforce one another. Institutions may compel behavior in the absence of virtue; but they are also educators of virtue, without which it will be far more difficult to bring up children who can imagine vividly another citizen's pain.

VII. Conclusion

Compassion is not the entirety of justice; but it both contains a powerful, if partial, vision of just distribution and provides imperfect citizens with an essential bridge from self-interest to just conduct. The spectators who watched Sophocles' *Philoctetes*, like readers of Richard Wright's *Native Son* today, did not live in a just society, nor did they go directly out to create one as a result of their compassionate experience. But this does not, I think, undercut the insights either of the literary works or of the emotions they construct. It simply shows that people are often too weak and confused and isolated to carry out radical political changes in their

[70] In this connection Smith's allegiance to Stoicism should be fully recognized: the "invisible hand" is not some blind natural force, but Zeus's Providence, deliberately, wisely, and justly arranging things. It is because markets are thought to embody ideal justice, and not because they promote interests, that Smith relies on them to the extent that he does. For criticism of the idea that market's *do* in fact have this high moral standing, see Amartya Sen, "The Moral Standing of the Market," *Social Philosophy and Policy*, vol. 2, no. 2 (Spring 1985), pp. 1–19.

[71] Alexis de Tocqueville, *Democracy in America*.

[72] Bennett, *The Book of Virtues* (*supra* note 55), p. 180.

own world. It shows that the power of the imagination is human and finite, and does not all by itself alter political reality. Without a just city in words, however, we never will get a just city in reality; without a compassionate training of the imagination, we will not, I think, get a compassionate nation. Without being tragic spectators, we will not have the insight required if we are to make life somewhat less tragic for those who, like Philoctetes, are hungry, and oppressed, and in pain.

Law and Ethics, University of Chicago

THE INDIVIDUAL, THE STATE,
AND THE COMMON GOOD

By John Haldane

The fellowship of society being natural and necessary to man, it follows with equal necessity that there must be some principle of government within the society. For if a great number of people were to live, each intent only upon his own interests, such a community would surely disintegrate unless there were one of its number to have a care for the common good.

  —St. Thomas Aquinas, *De regimine principium*, I, (1266)[1]

If there be not [virtue among us] we are in a wretched situation. No theoretical checks, no form of government, can render us secure. To suppose any form of government will secure liberty or happiness without any virtue in the people, is a chimerical idea. If there be sufficient virtue and intelligence in the community, it will be exercised in the selection of these men [of virtue and wisdom].

  —James Madison, *Debate on the Federal Constitution* (1788)[2]

I. Introduction

Let me begin with what should be a reassuring thought, and one that may serve as a corrective to presumptions that sometimes characterize political philosophy. The possibility, which Aquinas and Madison are both concerned with, of wise and virtuous political deliberation resulting in beneficial and stable civil order, no more depends upon possession of a philosophical theory of the state and of the virtues proper to it, than does the possibility of making good paintings depend upon possession of an aesthetic theory of the nature and value of art.

This is not to claim that theory is, or must be, irrelevant or unhelpful, let alone that philosophical understanding is gratuitous or inert. A superficial reading of conservative philosophers such as Michael Oakeshott and Roger Scruton is frequently taken to support an antitheoretical interpretation of their outlook, but, in addition to neglecting these authors' own understanding of their work, this interpretation begs the question of the

---

[1] See *Aquinas: Selected Political Writings*, ed. A. P. D'Entreves, trans. J. G. Dawson (Oxford: Blackwell, 1959), p. 3.

[2] See *The Debates in the Several State Conventions on the Adoption of the Federal Constitution*, ed. Jonathan Elliot (Philadelphia, PA: Lippincott, 1907).

© 1996 Social Philosophy and Policy Foundation. Printed in the USA.   59

nature and role of political theory.[3] Regarding the value of philosophy in relation to practice more generally, I agree with G. K. Chesterton when he writes that "[p]hilosophy is merely thought that has been thought out. . . . [M]an has no alternative, except between being influenced by thought that has been thought out and being influenced by thought that has not been thought out."[4] But to say that reflective understanding is worth having, and even that unless one has it one's practice will be confused and misdirected, is not to say that the possibility of a reasonable political order awaits the articulation and reception of an adequate general theory.

This much may seem obvious, but the scale and style of contemporary political philosophy assumes an importance for the subject which, viewed from the side of political and social life, it simply may not have. More germane to what follows, it is important to bring forward the idea that the fate of political order need not, indeed should not, depend upon the development of a general and generally acceptable theory of the state, the source of its authority, and the scope of its operations. I place that positive thought at the outset, because shortly I shall be suggesting that what John Rawls and many others involved in philosophical debates about liberalism have been trying to do cannot be done. In the circumstances in which we find ourselves there cannot be a full legitimation of the liberal or communitarian state as the arbiter of social justice.

This sort of thing is sometimes said by cultural relativists and by anti-realist pragmatists such as Richard Rorty;[5] but the standpoint I favor — in essentials a neo-Aristotelian-cum-Thomistic one — is certainly opposed to both of these. Indeed, it is because I believe in an objective moral order (a "moral law" even), and in its relevance for the conduct of political life, that I find what many liberals have to say on such issues as abortion, blasphemy, education, the public celebration of "alternative sexualities," pornography, and the provision of social services, for example, to be troublesome. Yet just as the morally neutral state seems an illusion, so the extensively morally committed state seems an impossibility. Communitarians are correct, I shall argue, in some of the criticisms they make of philosophical liberalism. They are wrong, however, to the extent

[3] See Michael Oakeshott, "The Concept of a Philosophy of Politics," in Oakeshott, *Religion, Politics, and the Moral Life*, ed. Timothy Fuller (New Haven: Yale University Press, 1993); and Roger Scruton, *The Meaning of Conservatism* (Harmondsworth: Penguin, 1980). "Conservatism may rarely announce itself in maxims, formulae or aims. Its essence is inarticulate, and its expression, when compelled, sceptical. But it is capable of expression . . ." (Scruton, *The Meaning of Conservatism*, p. 11).

[4] G. K. Chesterton, "The Revival of Philosophy — Why?" in Chesterton, *The Common Man* (London: Sheed and Ward, 1950), p. 176. Regrettably, Chesterton's writings have hardly been appreciated by social philosophers. See, for example, Chesterton, *What's Wrong with the World* (London: Cassell, 1910; San Francisco: Ignatius Press, 1994).

[5] See, for example, Richard Rorty, "The Contingency of Community," in Rorty, *Contingency, Irony, and Solidarity* (Cambridge: Cambridge University Press, 1989); and Rorty, "The Priority of Democracy to Philosophy," in *Reading Rorty*, ed. Alan Malachowski (Oxford: Blackwell, 1990).

that they think that moral community—in the precise sense that Augustine, for example, has in mind when he speaks of "a gathering of rational beings united in fellowship by their agreement about the objects of their love"[6] (and, one might add, of their aversion)—can be a general model for the legitimation of the modern nation-state. Here, indeed, I find myself in *qualified* sympathy with Rawls when he writes that "the hope of political community must indeed be abandoned, if by such a community we mean a political society united in affirming the same comprehensive doctrine"[7] (the nature of the qualification will become apparent).

In the remaining sections, then, I shall be arguing for the following claims. First, the project of liberal political theory, of the neutralist and individualist sort pursued by Rawls, fails and does so for foundational and structural reasons. Second, an important but still neglected notion in social philosophy is that of the common good—Aquinas's *"bonum commune."* Third, while communitarian conceptions of social life may include a nonreducible common good, it is certainly questionable whether the conditions necessary for the establishment of communitarian states generally exist. In these circumstances we should be grateful for the possibilities for moral development offered by various other forms of community—for which, following Augustine, I propose the term "fellowship." The acknowledgment that acceptance of a transcendent justification of the political order and its essential operations is not likely to come about (not: that such a justification is altogether impossible) suggests that the appropriate attitude toward the state is a blend of long-term moral aspiration, and short- to middle-term practical participation in limited political goals. Contrary to the position of Rawls, this latter element involves a defense of a form of political arrangement that probably is a *modus vivendi*. However, the proportions of this blend, as indeed the need of it, are matters of sociohistorical contingency; it is not inconceivable, therefore, that they may change over time, or differ geopolitically, as between the U.S. and the U.K. for example. Indeed, I end with the thought that English-language political philosophy suffers from a condition related to that noted by Oscar Wilde when he wrote of "two nations separated by a common language."

II. Rawls and the Unavoidability of Comprehensive Doctrines

The year 1993 saw the publication of two long-awaited, and since much-discussed, works on issues of values and prescriptions, namely, John Rawls's *Political Liberalism* and Pope John Paul II's *Veritatis Splendor*.[8] Thus far I have not seen these examined in tandem, though there is cer-

---

[6] Augustine, *De civitate dei* (London: Loeb, 1960), Book XIX, ch. 26.

[7] John Rawls, *Political Liberalism* (New York: Columbia University Press, 1993), p. 146.

[8] John Paul II, *Veritatis Splendor* (London: Incorporated Catholic Truth Society, 1993)—to which may be added a second much-heralded—and disputed—statement of fundamental Catholic doctrine: the *Catechism of the Catholic Church* (London: Chapman, 1994).

tainly scope for comparing and contrasting them. That is not my aim on this occasion; but I shall discuss a difficulty for Rawls's position arising from the existence of a work such as this encyclical addressed to the Roman Catholic Bishops—an encyclical directing them, in their teaching of the nine hundred million faithful, to uphold the unconditional and unlimited character of fundamental moral requirements.

First, however, recall the basic enterprise pursued in Rawls's recent work. His concern has been to give an account of how political institutions governed by principles of justice can be warranted in circumstances in which they are required to regulate the lives of people who may, indeed do, pursue different conceptions of their own good. Early on, Rawls presents this issue as a question: "[H]ow is it possible for there to exist over time a just and stable society of free and equal citizens, who remain profoundly divided by reasonable religious, philosophical, and moral doctrines?"[9] Although this form suggests a Kantian enquiry into the a priori conditions of the possibility of justice, the content of the question looks to be socioempirical; and certainly Rawls repeatedly emphasizes the nonmetaphysical character of his investigation and of its conclusions.

Already, however, that suggests a problem. To the extent that principles of justice carry normative force, they must appeal to considerations that can serve as justifying reasons and not mere psychological motives for those to whom they are addressed; but in order to do that they must have, if not a priori universal validity, at least some element of necessity or rational inescapability. Otherwise it will be too easy for the claims of justice to be evaded by those who fail to acquire, or choose to divest themselves of, the relevant desires. One possibility here would be to follow Aquinas (at least as I read him) and Aristotle (as he is traditionally read)[10] and argue that while prescriptions generated by practical reason are not categorical in Kant's sense, nonetheless in appealing to an agent's strivings they need not be void on account of the contingency of desire.[11] For the strivings in question may be ones the agent cannot fail to have inasmuch as they are partly constitutive of a normal (i.e., normative) human nature.

Such "assertoric hypotheticals" (to stay with Kantian terminology)[12] rooted in an animate essence *may* be available to those who reject the pure practical reason of the categorical imperative, but they remain too

[9] Rawls, *Political Liberalism*, p. 4.

[10] For a recent and influential departure from this tradition, see John McDowell, "Are Moral Requirements Hypothetical Imperatives?" *Proceedings of the Aristotelian Society*, supplementary volume 52 (1978), pp. 13–29; and McDowell, "The Role of Eudaimonia in Aristotle's Ethics," in *Essays on Aristotle's Ethics*, ed. Amélie Oksenberg Rorty (Berkeley: University of California Press, 1980).

[11] For Aquinas, see, for example, his *Summa Theologiae* [1265–1273], trans. Thomas Gilby (London: Eyre and Spottiswoode, 1976), Ia, IIae, q. 1, a. 6.

[12] See *The Moral Law: Kant's Groundwork of the Metaphysics of Morals*, ed. and trans. H. J. Paton (London: Hutchinson, 1976), ch. 2, p. 78.

deeply stained in the hue of metaphysics for Rawls's purpose. His opposition is not to the possibility of a philosophical justification of practical
reason. Though this disclaimer sometimes seems unconvincing,[13] he
insists that his objection is not an expression of skepticism, but rather an
implication of the concern to provide principles which can be drawn upon
to regulate the lives of those who hold competing philosophical doctrines:
"the conception of justice should be, as far as possible, independent of
the opposing and conflicting philosophical and religious doctrines that citizens affirm."[14] The avoidance of metaphysical theory is a consequence
of the application of the principle of toleration to philosophy itself. However, and setting aside the doubt about an underlying moral skepticism
on Rawls's part, the question remains of how, having disavowed philosophical justifications, what results can be anything other than an appeal
to contingent preferences.

A Rawlsian response to such an objection is likely to draw upon discussions offered in *Political Liberalism* under the headings "The Idea of an
Overlapping Consensus" and "The Idea of Public Reason" (Lectures IV
and VI respectively). To begin with, however, we are required to grant
a distinction between two branches or spheres of practical reasoning, that
associated with *ethical* and that concerned with *political* deliberation. The
latter is the site of Rawls's contractualist construction "the political conception of justice," while the former is the arena within which are to be
found "general and comprehensive doctrines." In these terms "generality" is a matter of range of application—to few, many, most, or all subjects (i.e., agents)—and "comprehensiveness" concerns aspects or
departments of life. Thus, a "fully comprehensive and entirely general
moral conception" would identify values and prescribe directives for all
persons in all aspects of their lives. *Ex hypothesi*, and assuming an organized social context, such a conception will include an account of justice
and other political virtues—as do the general and comprehensive views
drawn upon in *Veritatis Splendor* and the *Catechism of the Catholic Church*.

In contrast to comprehensive doctrines which present political values
as instances of more general principles, Rawls offers the idea of a "freestanding" political conception:

> [One that] is neither presented as, nor [i]s derived from, such a doc-
> trine applied to the basic structure of society, as if this structure were
> simply another subject to which that doctrine applied. . . . I assume

---

[13] See, for example, Rawls, *Political Liberalism*: "[T]his reasonable plurality of conflicting
and incommensurable doctrines is seen as the *characteristic* work of practical reason over time
under enduring free institutions"; "we also view the diversity of reasonable religious, philosophical, and moral doctrines found in democratic societies as a *permanent* feature of their
public culture"; and "[a]s always, we assume that the diversity of reasonable religious, philosophical and moral doctrines found in democratic societies is a *permanent* feature of the public culture and not a mere historical condition soon to pass away" (pp. 135, 136, 216–17; my
emphases). Why "characteristic" and "permanent" unless for skeptical reasons?

[14] *Ibid.*, p. 9.

all citizens to affirm a comprehensive doctrine to which the political conception they accept is in some way related. But a distinguishing feature of a political conception is that it is presented as freestanding and expounded apart from, or without reference to, any such wider background. . . . [I]t tries to elaborate a reasonable conception for the basic structure [of political society] alone and involves, so far as possible, no wider commitment to any other doctrine.[15]

Additionally, we are to consider a threefold distinction among a comprehensive doctrine, a political conception of justice, and a *modus vivendi*. For these purposes, the last is to be thought of as an agreement or treaty adhered to because the participants regard it as being to their individual benefit. Such a convergence of interest is contingent, and therefore any appearance of political unity among the parties is illusory; all that exists is a precarious arrangement sustained by self-interest. It is against the background of this tripartite division that the claims of political liberalism are elaborated. In answer to the question of how, given a pluralism of comprehensive doctrines, there can nevertheless be a just and stable society and not merely a *modus vivendi*, Rawls offers the idea of an overlapping consensus on a political conception of justice—that is, a principled agreement on values and norms whose content and justification are independent of any distinctive comprehensive doctrine, but are compatible with many, most, or all such doctrines. Unlike a *modus vivendi*, such a condition does express and sustain genuine social unity, but compatible with Rawls's requirement that liberalism be neutral between competing conceptions of the good, it is not the expression of one, as against another, comprehensive doctrine.

Such is the claim, but the problems seem resistant to this form of solution. First, the initial separation of practical reasoning into ethical and political spheres is not innocuous—if it were, it would hardly serve Rawls's argument, which requires a degree of independence of the political from the moral. There are several traditions, including the Aristotelian-Thomistic and the Kantian ones, which would deny that a political conception can be "freestanding," precisely because they assert the unity and continuity of practical reasoning. Put in terms of Thomism, for example, the counterassertion would be that there can be no account of a political "right" that does not derive from a theory of the good, and that this latter is the general presupposition of all individual and social action. A related claim is expressed by John Paul II in a section of *Veritatis Splendor* where he is considering objections to traditional natural-law moral theology:

---

[15] See *ibid.*, pp. 12–13; see also *ibid.*, Lecture V, "The Priority of the Right over the Good."

The separation which some have posited between the freedom of individuals and the nature which all have in common, as it emerges from certain philosophical theories which are highly influential in present-day culture, obscures the perception of the universality of the moral law on the part of reason. But inasmuch as the natural law expresses the dignity of the human person and lays the foundation for his fundamental rights and duties, it is universal in its precepts and its authority extends to all mankind.[16]

It is important to see that concerning the issue of the duality of practical reason and the further critical points that follow, Rawls may be in some difficulty even if Thomist, Kantian, and other theories are themselves defective, since it is central to his approach that it not rely on contentious philosophical doctrines. Thus, if it is controversial whether the moral and the political stand in the required relation, this fact alone undermines the possibility of advancing the political conception as the object of an overlapping consensus. Certainly one might argue directly for it, but to do so would be to violate the requirement of political autonomy.

Perhaps, however, that requirement is not absolute but admits of degree. Certainly Rawls sometimes suggests this. Earlier I quoted him writing that "the conception of justice should be, *as far as possible*, independent of the opposing and conflicting philosophical and religious doctrines that citizens affirm" (my emphasis), and at one point he considers directly the possibility of opposition to his political conception from an advocate of a comprehensive religious doctrine. What he says is very revealing and it faces, I believe, a serious objection. In order to show both points I need to quote at some length:

> [B]y avoiding comprehensive doctrines we try to bypass religion and philosophy's profoundest controversies so as to have some hope of uncovering a basis of a stable overlapping consensus.
> . . . Nevertheless, in affirming a political conception of justice we may eventually have to assert at least certain aspects of our own comprehensive religious or philosophical doctrine (by no means necessarily fully comprehensive). This will happen whenever someone insists, for example, that certain questions are so fundamental that to insure their being rightly settled justifies civil strife. . . . At this point we may have no alternative but to deny this, or to imply its denial and hence to maintain the kind of thing we had hoped to avoid.
> To consider this, imagine rationalist believers who contend that these beliefs are open to and can be fully established by reason (uncommon though this view might be). In this case the believers sim-

---

[16] John Paul II, *Veritatis Splendor*, section 51, p. 80.

ply deny what we have called "the fact of reasonable pluralism." So we say of the rationalist believers that they are mistaken in denying that fact; but we need not say that their religious beliefs are not true, since to deny that religious beliefs can be publicly and fully established by reason is not to say that they are not true. . . . [W]e do not put forward more of our comprehensive view than we think needed or useful for the political aim of consensus.[17]

First, then, it is conceded that the method of avoidance may fail and that when it does so it may be necessary, and is permissible, to defend the political conception against challenges from a comprehensive conception by invoking a rival — one's own — religious or philosophical doctrine. Second, however, it is supposed that in the imagined example of believers who deny the (purported) fact of "reasonable pluralism," one's doctrinal counter only challenges their epistemological claim and not the content of their own comprehensive conception. The point of this second observation is to emphasize the limited character of the departure from universal toleration. Against this, however, one should observe that any lapse from strict neutrality undermines the claim that a political conception can be founded on an overlapping consensus only and need not rest upon a distinctive comprehensive doctrine. Further still, the departure may not be as limited as Rawls supposes, since it might be part of the rationalist believers' doctrinal commitment that pluralism with regard to fundamental claims is *not* reasonable. In short, epistemological claims may fall within essential doctrine. Consider, for example, another papal document — Pope Pius XII's encyclical *Humani Generis* (*False Trends in Modern Teaching*):

> Notoriously, the Church makes much of human reason, in the following connexions: when we establish beyond doubt the existence of one God, who is a personal Being; when we establish irrefutably, by proofs divinely granted to us, the basic facts on which the Christian faith itself rests; when we give just expression to the natural law which the Creator has implanted in men's hearts.[18]

Here Pius is reiterating long-standing Catholic doctrines, the first of which is the provability of the existence of God — it being contrary to faith (not merely theological tradition) to deny that there can be such a proof. Earlier, having made similar claims, Pius asks why there should be disagreement over such matters and in response cites "the impact of the

---

[17] See Rawls, *Political Liberalism*, pp. 152–53.

[18] *False Trends in Modern Teaching: Encyclical Letter (Humani Generis) of Pius XII Concerning Certain False Opinions*, trans. Ronald A. Knox (London: Catholic Truth Society, 1950), Part II, "The Field of Philosophy," para. 29, section 1, p. 16.

senses and the imagination, [and] disordered appetites which are the consequences of the fall."[19] The interpretation of papal encyclicals is a fine art that philosophers now rarely practice,[20] but it is difficult to escape the idea that so far as Pius is concerned, pluralism with regard to the primary precepts of natural law (for example), though explicable, is not reasonable. In asserting otherwise, therefore, Rawls would be saying that the rationalist believers' religious beliefs are false.

Here my point is not that there can be no argument on behalf of a political conception against the claims of those who would pursue their creed to the point of unsettling civil peace.[21] On the contrary, I believe that one can and should fashion robust defenses of law and social order against, for example, those anti-abortionists who would murder clinic staff — or those who would assassinate blasphemers. As Rawls reluctantly concedes, however, the possibility of doing so depends upon bringing into the political domain a distinctive comprehensive moral doctrine. The tone in which he writes of this need suggests a socially regrettable necessity akin to the use of force to expel a drunk and boorish guest from a party; but the problem reveals faults in the very structure of political liberalism. By Rawls's own account, even though the political conception may not be the object of an overlapping consensus, it should nonetheless be affirmed (and upheld) because it is implied by a favored philosophical perspective.

In connection with this objection, consider what Rawls has to say about public reason. He asks: "How can it be either reasonable or rational, when basic matters are at stake, for citizens to appeal only to a public conception of justice and not to the whole truth as they see it?"[22] The answer elaborates interpretations of ideas that are supposed to be available and acceptable to all, and concludes with the demand that we live together politically on the basis of claims and justifications that everyone can reasonably be expected to endorse. As before, however, these formulations fail to withstand the test of real examples. Clearly almost everything turns on the interpretation of "reasonableness." Rawls writes:

> The only comprehensive doctrines that run afoul of public reason are those that cannot support a reasonable balance of political values. [And he continues, in a footnote whose importance it would be hard to exaggerate:]

[19] *Ibid.*, p. 3.

[20] For a distinguished exception, however, see Alasdair MacIntyre, "How Can We Learn What *Veritatis Splendor* Has to Teach?" *The Thomist*, vol. 58 (1994), pp. 171–95. I discuss philosophical aspects of *Veritatis Splendor* in "From Law to Virtue and Back Again: On *Veritatis Splendor*," in *The Use of the Bible in Ethics*, ed. M. Davis (Sheffield: University of Sheffield Press, 1995).

[21] I offer such an argument in "Religious Toleration," *Synthesis Philosophica*, Special Issue on Toleration, vol. 9 (1994), pp. 21–26.

[22] Rawls, *Political Liberalism*, p. 216.

As an illustration consider the troubled question of abortion. Suppose first that the society in question is well-ordered and that we are dealing with the normal case of mature adult women. . . . Suppose further that we consider the question in terms of these three important political values: the due respect for human life, the ordered reproduction of political society over time, including the family in some form, and finally the equality of women as equal citizens. . . . Now I believe any reasonable balance of these three values will give a woman a duly qualified right to end her pregnancy during the first trimester. The reason for this is that at this early stage of pregnancy the political value of the equality of women is overriding and this right is required to give it substance and force. . . . [A]ny comprehensive doctrine that leads to a balance of political values excluding that duly qualified right in the first trimester is to that extent unreasonable.[23]

Without entering into the abortion debate, it should be clear that any notion of reasonableness that renders an opinion contrary to that presented by Rawls "unreasonable" is almost certain to be (reasonably) contentious and thus not fitted to occupy a central role in a conception of justice that purports to apply the principle of toleration to philosophy itself — thereby "to bypass religion and philosophy's profoundest problems." In this connection consider again a view presented by an authoritative Roman document, this time an "Instruction" on abortion (*Donum Vitae*) issued by the Congregation for the Doctrine of the Faith:

The inalienable rights of the person must be recognised and respected by civil society and the political authority. These human rights depend neither on single individuals nor on parents; nor do they represent a concession made by society and the state. . . . Among such fundamental rights one should mention in this regard every human being's right to life and physical integrity from the moment of conception. . . . As a consequence of the respect and protection which must be ensured for the unborn child from the moment of conception, the law must provide appropriate legal sanctions for every deliberate violation of the child's rights.[24]

In the face of a clear conflict of views of the sort which this example makes vivid, Rawls's true position reveals itself to be far from neutral: try for an overlapping consensus, but where it is not available and where important issues are at stake, affirm your own comprehensive doctrine. The whole raison d'être of *Political Liberalism*, however, was to offer a way

---

[23] *Ibid.*, pp. 243–44.
[24] *Donum Vitae* (1987), as quoted in the *Catechism of the Catholic Church* (*supra* note 8), Part 3, section 2, paragraph 2273, p. 490.

forward that possesses the principles lacked by a mere *modus vivendi*, yet does not rely upon appeal to distinctive doctrines. It is apparent from the foregoing, therefore, that whatever its other merits this defense of liberalism fails in its own declared aim.

III. THE COMMON GOOD

One way of presenting some of the problems that Rawls runs into is by saying, as above, that he tries, unsuccessfully, to secure a political *right* — that of justice — without deriving it from any distinctive account of the *good*. This is a criticism that is increasingly voiced, in one form or another, particularly by advocates of "perfectionist" liberalism.[25] It might also be noted, though it rarely is, that although the notion of the right Rawls seeks is a commonly shared one, he conspicuously eschews any theory of the common good. So far as I am aware, he only mentions the idea once and that is in a passage characterizing views that contrast with his own account of justice as fairness:

> [W]hatever these religious and philosophical doctrines may be, I assume they all contain a conception of the right and the good that includes a conception of justice that can be understood as in some way advancing the common good.[26]

This, then, brings me to the issue of the role within political and social philosophy of the idea of the common good. The body of anti-Rawlsian criticism generally dubbed "communitarian" has several targets, but these can be gathered together under the general charge of "erroneous individualism." Thus, it has often been alleged that Rawls's use of the notion of an *original position* implies a view of the identity of persons as constituted independently of their social attachments and inherited values. This claim is usually made in an effort to show that Rawls has an incoherent metaphysical anthropology; but as with the criticisms of the previous section, it is important to see how political liberalism may be undermined by the mere fact that it draws upon substantive philosophical assumptions. One need not engage the question of whether those assumptions are coherent, let alone true. So, for example, while I agree with Rawls in his defense of the original position — holding it to be an epistemological device and not a metaphysical description of the social world — I think he is mistaken in arguing that the idea of citizens as free and equal persons is without controversial assumptions.[27] Ask yourself why citizenship should have

---

[25] Here I am thinking especially of recent writings by Joseph Raz: *The Morality of Freedom* (Oxford: Clarendon, 1986), and *Ethics in the Public Domain* (Oxford: Clarendon, 1994).

[26] Rawls, *Political Liberalism*, p. 109.

[27] See John Haldane, "Political Theory and the Nature of Persons: An Ineliminable Metaphysical Presupposition," *Philosophical Papers*, vol. 20 (1991), pp. 77–95, and "Identity, Community, and the Limits of Multiculture," *Public Affairs Quarterly*, vol. 7 (1993), pp. 199–214.

special normative significance ahead of some other aspect of a person's identity, such as his or her religious affiliation, to the extent that it can be appealed to as a trumping factor. The answer has to be that for Rawls these other identities are in some important sense secondary to that of our nature as free and equal persons. The exact sense in which the latter identity is prior and deeper may be held to be normative and not metaphysical, but in either event its assertion is philosophically controversial.

Having noted this distinction between kinds of criticism, it is unsurprising that those who complain of individualist assumptions are concerned to provide a communitarian alternative to liberalism. It is an interesting question what features are essential to such an option. One dominant strand in recent thinking has been the thesis of social constitution: the claim that persons are made to be such—advanced from the status of mere human animals—by being worked into a network of social relations. An analogy here might be with the process of sculptural assembly, whereby various items, each possessed of a pre-sculptural nature, have a new compositional identity bestowed upon them; for example, what was (and in one respect remains) a piece of windshield wiper is then a grinning mouth. I believe that there is something in this idea and that it shows itself in the fact that most action descriptions presuppose socially constituted patterns of behavior. However, here I am more interested in the claim that liberalism fails inasmuch as it neglects, and cannot accommodate, the fact that some or all of the goods we pursue, and which a system of rights is concerned to protect, are goods possessed in common.

By contrast with *Political Liberalism*, the term "common good" occurs frequently in recent Roman Catholic documents, including *Veritatis Splendor*. The history of the term's present prominence in Catholic social teaching goes back to the writings of Jacques Maritain and Yves Simon,[28] which in turn look to the moral theology of Thomas Aquinas. In the *Prima Secundae* of the *Summa Theologiae*, eight questions (qq. 90–97) are devoted to aspects of law (indeed, this group is often referred to as "The Treatise on Law"). In question 90, article 2, Aquinas writes as follows:

> [S]ince every part is ordered to the whole as the imperfect to the perfect and one man is part of the perfect society, it is necessary that the law properly regard the order to the happiness of the society. . . . Hence, since law is most of all ordered to the Common Good, it is necessary that any other precept concerning a particular matter must needs lack the nature of law except insofar as it is ordered to the Common Good. And therefore every law is ordered to the Common Good.[29]

[28] See, for example, Jacques Maritain, *The Person and the Common Good*, trans. John Fitzgerald (New York: Scribner, 1941); and Yves Simon, *The Tradition of Natural Law* (New York: Fordham University Press, 1965).

[29] See Thomas Aquinas, *The Treatise on Law*, trans. R. J. Henle (Notre Dame: University of Notre Dame Press, 1993), q. 90, a. 2, pp. 132 and 134.

It is important to understand what Aquinas means by the common good, since present-day writers sometimes speak of general or collective goods in ways which superficially resemble the Thomist notion, but which are in fact quite different from it.[30] Notice two elements in the quoted passage: man stands in relation to society as a part to a whole; *and every law is directed toward the establishment, maintenance, and improvement of the common good. The first is a familiar thesis of communitarianism—the irreducibility of society as a unified substance that bestows a form of moral identity on its members. As a corrective to a radical corporatist reading, it is relevant to add that Aquinas also regards individual persons as complete substances. By implication, then, he rejects a dichotomy that bedevils current debates, that which regards *persons as either parts of a greater whole—society—or else as preexisting individuals out of which society is formed. A way through lies in the direction of saying that persons are both wholes and parts—wholes as selves, parts as social selves.

This may seem evasive and invite the question: Are selves made by society or is society made by selves? Again, however, a way through the dilemma is offered by saying "both"; that is to say, there is a process of mutual determination. Think again of an artistic analogy. Consider, for example, an artist working on a composition by moving around cut-out shapes of different colors within a rectangular background. The composition is made out of parts which (in some, substance-involving, respects) can be described independently of it, but they also change their identities as aspects of a greater substantial whole as they move in relation to one another and the background. A more abstract account of the matter might be fashioned in terms of potentiality and actuality. One might say that a person has a range of potentialities some of which are actualized in society, while at the same time the potentialities of a style of social arrangement are actualized through the exercise of natural intrinsic powers of individuals. To adapt a formula of Hilary Putnam's, "the person and the society jointly make up the person and the society."

So far as concerns the common good, what is most striking is the idea that *every* law should have as its proper goal the well-being of society as a whole. This apparently radical anti-individualism is sometimes moderated by commentators who urge an interpretation of society as an aggregate, and thereby treat "common good" as a distributive notion, equivalent

---

[30] For recent accounts of the common good as it features in Aquinas and in modern Thomistic writings, see Louis Dupré, "The Common Good and the Open Society," in *Catholicism and Liberalism*, ed. David Hollenbach and Bruce Douglass (Cambridge: Cambridge University Press, 1993); Gregory Froelich, "Ultimate End and Common Good," *The Thomist*, vol. 58 (1994), pp. 609–19; Kibujjo Kalumba, "Maritain on 'The Common Good': Reflections on the Concept," *Laval Théologique et Philosophique*, vol. 49 (1993), pp. 93–104; and Thomas R. Rourke and Clarke E. Cochran, "The Common Good and Economic Justice: Reflections on the Thought of Yves R. Simon," *Review of Politics*, vol. 54 (1992), pp. 231–52.

to "the good of each and every member." At other times it is suggested that while some goods are indeed commonly possessed, they are social means to individual ends — in Aquinas's supernatural teleology, the beatific vision. On this account, law should promote civil order and public health, for example, because these are conditions that each may benefit from (since they and other public goods are objects of convergent interests).

However, neither of these interpretations is plausible exegesis, for neither takes seriously enough the phrase "*bonum commune*" and Aquinas's claim that this is a "*bonum honestum*," a genuine constituent of perfection. Consider first a modern attempt to interpret Aquinas's notion. I quote from Maritain's *The Person and the Common Good*:

> [T]hat which constitutes the common good of political society is not only: the collection of public commodities . . . a sound fiscal condition of the state and its military power; the body of just laws, good customs and wise institutions, which provide the nation with its structure; the heritage of the great historical remembrances, its symbols and its glories, its living traditions and cultural treasures. The common good includes all these and something more besides . . . the whole sum itself of these; a sum which is quite different from a simple collection of juxtaposed units. . . .
>
> It includes the sum or sociological integration of all the civic conscience, political virtues, and sense of right and liberty, of all the activity, material prosperity and spiritual riches, of unconsciously operative hereditary wisdom, of moral rectitude, justice, friendship, happiness, virtue and heroism in the individual lives of its members. For these things are, in a certain measure, *communicable* and so revert to each member, helping him to perfect his life of liberty and person.[31]

The emphasis on the *communicability* of the integrated sum of social and personal elements contrasts with a notion of commonality as a mere function of convergent interests. The common good is essentially shared: it is a good-for-many, taken collectively, rather than a good to many, taken distributively. Aquinas's claim that this good is a *bonum honestum*, a perfecting end in itself, might be thought to be incompatible with a Christian view of human destiny, which is usually treated individualistically; however, his trinitarian theology grants him the idea that, even eschatologically, the good of individuals resides in their participation in the life of a community of persons.

Theological interests aside, Aquinas's idea of the common good as a participatory end, for the sake of which civil society exists and must be regulated, has been insufficiently explored even by liberalism's "commu-

---

[31] Maritain, *The Person and the Common Good*, pp. 52–53.

nitarian critics." Yet something of this sort seems to be presupposed in a wide range of moral-cum-social judgments. Concerns about the conduct of nations in going to war and in prosecuting wars are not easily represented in individualistic terms. To cite two examples from recent history, the agonies felt in the U.S. about Vietnam present themselves as collective shame or guilt — not: a's plus b's plus c's, etc., but "ours"; likewise, the British experience of the Falklands war and subsequent reflection upon it are most perspicuously represented in terms of shared participation in honor and tragedy. It is too easy to respond to claims of communal good and evil with charges of romanticism. There is unquestionably something that is recognized, particularly but not exclusively within older traditional societies, as "our" well-being, or "our" corruption, and it is a serious omission not to give an account of this.

Rawls's political liberalism cannot find a place for the common good because of its commitment to neutrality between life-shaping values. At most it can register and even celebrate convergence in evaluations, seeing in this happy coincidence possibilities for establishing and extending an overlapping consensus. However, the idea of citizens as free and equal persons remains individualistic: the good of citizens that results from participation in an order regulated by the political conception of justice is a private one. This is sometimes overlooked on account of the regulated order being a public good; but therein lies a lesson: *public good does not equal common good.*

The argument in favor of the common good is not the failure of Rawls's project. My objections to the latter principally concerned its inability to meet one of its own main criteria, namely, the need to establish a case for the form and content of the political conception without reliance upon controversial comprehensive doctrines. However, unless one is willing and able to argue the case for greater moral indifference in the political order, the recognition that Rawls's neutrality lapses is likely to prompt the question of how the good should bear upon the right and what the nature of the right in question is. Having got that far, and recalling that the problem for resolution is the normative conditions of social life, one may then be better placed to see the possibilities offered by the idea of the common good — including, for example, the notion that what justifies the expenditure of society's resources upon universities wherein people are supported in their thinking about these very issues is the fact that the goods attained thereby are "communicable," reverting to each member. Regrettably, it has become all too natural to ask how the intellectual endeavor of philosophers could possibly be of instrumental benefit to taxpayers, since it is assumed that this is the only value at issue. From the perspective of Aquinas the question betrays a kind of corruption — not merely because it overlooks the possibility of noninstrumental goods, but because it neglects the idea that within a community *we* are *all* better when some of us achieve understanding. Thus, discussing the communal division of virtue in connection with the contemplative life, Aquinas writes:

> There are things required of the community which one individual alone cannot meet; this community-duty is discharged when one does this and another that. . . . [T]he command to be fruitful falls on the people as whole. They are bound not only to multiply in body but to grow in spirit. The human family is sufficiently provided for if some undertake the responsibility of bodily generation, while others devote themselves to the study of divine things, for the beauty and health of the whole human race.[32]

IV. STATES, NATIONS, AND COMMUNITIES

Not every state is a nation, nor every nation a state — as is indicated by the examples of the former Soviet Union and of Scotland respectively. Both sorts of social entities can be communities, but there is an internal connection between the ideas of nationhood and community that is absent between those of community and state. Let us say, then, that a state involves the organization of a collection of people under a system of justice and within a given territory, and that a nation is a people united by common history, language, customs, traditions, and interests. Given these features it is unsurprising that nations aspire to be states, or indeed that they regard this condition as their final end.

In a weak sense, a community is any social group whose members cooperate in pursuit of common interests. So defined, it easy to see how many states will acquire the character of communities even if they do not originate as expressions of them. Thus, although a collection of previously unassociated individuals may be brought together within a jurisdiction, it will generally not be long before they begin to interact in ways and under descriptions that indicate membership in a self-identifying social group. Earlier, however, I quoted Augustine's definition of a people as "a gathering of rational beings united in fellowship by a common agreement about the objects of its love." This clearly specifies a narrower, moral notion of community, one which I termed "fellowship." Restricted as it is, Augustine arrives at this after having set aside an even more exclusive definition of a people and of a state as a gathering united under proclaimed obedience to divine law.

Rawls writes that the hope of political community must be abandoned "if by such a community we mean a political society united in affirming the same comprehensive doctrine."[33] Obviously this would be taken to exclude the possibility of fashioning the state along the lines specified in

---

[32] Aquinas, *Summa Theologiae* (*supra* note 11), II, II, q. 152, a. 2, ad. 1, p. 173.
[33] Rawls, *Political Liberalism*, p. 146.

Augustine's more restrictive account. It is not that the latter requires as much as a theocracy, but that even the assumption of theism is no longer tenable as a basis for civil society. In a widely viewed and subsequently discussed television documentary, the Prince of Wales recently reflected upon his constitutional position as head of the Church of England and "Defender of the Faith," remarking that, assuming his succession, he might prefer to be "defender of faith." From the position within which Rawls develops his political liberalism, however, even this concession to religious pluralism harbors an unacceptable attachment to the politics of commitment if it presumes that the institutions of the state should acknowledge and give priority to one attitude toward religion (belief) as against others (agnosticism and atheism).

Even Augustine's modified account fails to meet the stated conditions for an adequate political conception of justice, since it violates what Rawls calls the "general facts of the political culture of a democratic society," namely: *the fact of reasonable pluralism* (that a diversity of comprehensive doctrines is a permanent feature); *the fact of oppression* (that common adherence to one comprehensive doctrine can only be maintained by state oppression); and *the fact of majority support* (that a secure regime requires the support of "a substantial majority of its politically active citizens").[34] Earlier I suggested that Rawls's insistence on the permanence of reasonable pluralism is difficult to make sense of save as an expression of skepticism. Equally, "the fact of oppression" is presented not so much as a historical datum but as a claim to the effect that things could not be otherwise, the implied explanation for this being the inevitability of pluralism as a characteristic result of the exercise of reason. These are controversial claims and the rationalist believer may want to oppose them, but even so it is hard to make plausible the idea that modern Western societies might come to exhibit the unity of Augustinian fellowships, let alone that they already are so beneath their visible and visibly variegated surfaces.

My purpose in observing this is not to reject the coherence of a communitarian polity, nor to distance myself from the implications of the earlier discussion of the common good — namely, that we are in some respects social beings, a genuine aspect of whose *telos* is participation in shared ends. Yet some acknowledgment of the claims of pluralism is certainly necessary, and in consequence a moderation of communitarian aspirations is called for. However, given the earlier criticisms of Rawls's attempts at neutrality, and the briefer charge that his account of citizens gives (unwarranted) priority to liberal identities over those deriving from membership in other communities — including ones defined in relation to comprehensive doctrines — there remains a need to consider just where one should stand between the poles of Augustinian fellowship and Rawlsian citizenship.

[34] *Ibid.*, pp. 37–38.

One's political nature is not independent of that "second nature" which
results from being born and raised within particular social groups sharing aesthetic, moral, philosophical, and religious inclinations communi-
cated to successive generations in part through the cultivation of a
complex sensibility. Real-world political personae rest upon these cultural
identities (which they rarely obscure). Accordingly, if the mask is to fit,
it must be shaped to the contours of the face, which tells against the
attempt to fashion it out of a universal mold. In consequence, the order
of construction in practical political philosophy should be to define the
characteristic values of given communities and reflect upon how these
might be expressed in the political order of a state. Among other things
this approach limits the scope for a priori reasoning about the conditions
of justice and political stability and directs attention toward the historical facts of community. In a way, of course, this is what Rawls himself
claims to be doing, but in order to maximize the acceptability of the political conception, he then tries, unsuccessfully, to detach the account from
distinctive conceptions of the good.

Elsewhere I have developed these reflections in support of the ideal of
nationhood and tried to respond to the familiar concerns that this notion
is anachronistic, ontologically problematic, and politically coercive.[35] I shall
not return to these matters now save, first, to emphasize that, as I understand it, the idea of a nation is a cultural and not a racial one—conjoining
history, tradition, and language, not color and blood-group—and, second, to acknowledge that its deployment involves the sometimes uncomfortable notion that the state may legitimately concern itself with social
formation.[36] In the present circumstance, however, I want to suggest
that while national identity may be an appropriate reference point for
political reflection in some contexts, it may not be so in others; and where
it is weakened or absent, there may be no other unifying cultural form
that can serve as a naturally eligible, prepolitical foundation for civil society. Attempting to establish political divisions along ethnic lines is always
possible; but if this is the true condition of things then it may be better
to acknowledge that in these circumstances politics is a solution to a problem of disunity rather than the expression of prior community. For some,
this picture of the political order as no more than a procedural arrangement for regulating the interactions between "strangers" will be dispir-
iting, especially if they are attracted by the many-layered richness of a
cultural-cum-nation-state such as Great Britain; but it is often, if not
always, possible to combine political thinness with a rich community life;

[35] See Haldane, "Identity, Community, and the Limits of Multiculture," section IV.

[36] For an example of what this might validate, see John Haldane, "Religious Education
in a Pluralist Society: A Philosophical Perspective," *British Journal of Educational Studies*,
vol. 34 (1986), pp. 161–81.

and in circumstances of radical pluralism, wisdom may caution against granting a greater role to the state than the maintenance of civil peace.

V. A Modus Vivendi and Political Philosophy in Context

By now the thought is emerging that in certain circumstances, and some might argue that these are coming to be general within Western societies, the hope of political community having had to be abandoned and the prospect of political liberalism having proved illusory, the way forward may lie in the development of political order as a *modus vivendi*. For Rawls, this is an unsatisfactory condition that must be sharply distinguished from an overlapping consensus on a political conception of justice. The difference is marked by three features: (1) an overlapping consensus focuses on a moral conception of justice; (2) it is affirmed on moral grounds; and (3) because of these facts it enjoys a kind and degree of stability different from that of a mere *modus vivendi*, which can only depend on "happenstance and a balance of relative forces."[37]

At this stage in the discussion I shall not begin to consider whether Rawls is entitled to or justified in his claims on behalf of the moral superiority of an overlapping consensus. All I am concerned with is the suggestion that it possesses a greater stability than a *modus vivendi*. For this possibility may seem to force a less critical reassessment of political liberalism. In fact, Rawls allows that an overlapping consensus may not be necessary for social unity and stability and goes on to address the concern that it is utopian to believe that it is sufficient for it. However, the idea remains unquestioned that while stability may be achieved by other means it is then a very precarious condition.

Why should this be thought to be so? I suspect that part of the reason is that although he refers back to the religious wars of Europe, Rawls is thinking in terms of American society and political life, which may sometimes bear the appearance of an arrangement that could easily come apart as the balance of forces changes, and with it the distribution of power. This prospect seems far less likely in a political culture such as that of Great Britain. Yet it is doubtful that the stability of British society is due to an overlapping consensus on a political conception in Rawls's sense. If any perspective of noble principle is entitled to claim credit for this civil order, it is a communitarian one.

But that is too quick and too simple. From the point of view of articulated theory, British political society is an enigma shrouded in a mystery. On the one hand, the intellectual demeanor of its public institutions owes much to the civil and eudaimonistic liberalisms of John Locke and John Stuart Mill, both of which are respectful of individual conscience. On the

---

[37] Rawls, *Political Liberalism*, pp. 147–48.

other hand, and notwithstanding its lack of a formulated constitution, it is ruled by a "constitutional" monarch who is the head of an established church and whose government is conducted in part by an unelected nobility which is most effective when rallying to such causes as the preservation of rural bus services and the maintenance of Christian education in state schools. That education derives nominally from the Church of England (and from the Presbyterian Church in Scotland — of which the sovereign is also a protector), yet the largest worshipping denomination is Roman Catholic, whose members, by the act of succession, are debarred from ascending to the throne or marrying the sovereign.

It is difficult to discern a principled justification for this general pattern of arrangements, and I believe it is a mistake to seek one — both insofar as there is no coherent set of organizing principles and, more importantly, because the whole set-up has no obvious political purpose independent of its own continuation. Piece by piece, the elements may have been fashioned to serve particular purposes — some internal, some external — but over time they have become part of a system that remains stable because it is an embodiment of a social order that is found congenial to a civilized life.

I realize this may sound self-satisfied; however, the point I want to end on is not the supposed superiority of the British political order but the fact that for good or ill this order exists, and (to the extent that it offers any justification) justifies itself independently of a theory of the right. Even if it originates in and is maintained by a series of pragmatic resolutions, these quickly come to be the object of civic allegiance, particularly as they are given the protection of law. If this is a *modus vivendi* writ large, it certainly seems no less stable than an overlapping consensus, and it is a way of going on socially that is compatible with active participation in a range of subordinate moral communities, and with the periodic accomplishment of principled political goals.

It would be presumptuous of me to speculate at any length on the extent to which a similar account might be given of the United States (not to mention the interesting case of Canada). However, if there are real differences, as the emphasis on individual rights and the recurrent preoccupation with the meaning of the founding constitution suggest, then it would be as well for political philosophers on both sides of the Atlantic to consider the possibility that these cultural and political differences may have found their way into the reflective understanding of such concepts as community, individual, and state, and that most of the foundational work done during the renaissance of English-speaking political philosophy initiated by Rawls has really concerned the political foundation of North American society — an issue formulated not inappropriately, but not altogether accurately either, as "the problem of liberalism." Of course, it may be that even if this diagnosis were once true, the influence of U.S. culture in Europe and elsewhere has been such that we are all now in the same moral and political situation. I doubt that this is so, however, and I certainly hope that current uncertainties about the direction of political philosophy may lead to some cultural differentiation of issues, methods, and doctrines, and to a more extensive investigation of what is available from "old" and "new world" writers of the past, such as those with whom I began.

VI. Codicil

In challenging the project of liberal political theory, I have been concerned principally with Rawls's neutralist and individualist version of it. Directed criticism of this sort raises both a general question of the adequacy of other forms of liberalism, and, given the perspective developed in later sections, a more specific question concerning the compatibility of Catholic social teaching with *any* kind of liberalism. In an earlier essay, addressed to the question of whether a Catholic can be a liberal, I described the opposition between liberal theory and Catholicism in terms of fundamental disagreements about the place of morality in politics, and the status of the community and the common good.[38] There as here, the liberalism in question was principally that associated with authors such as Rawls and Ronald Dworkin, rather than Locke and Mill. While the implied distinction between "old" and "new" liberalisms may not be as great as some like to suppose, there is certainly a question as to whether ideas of political liberty other than those associated with contemporary contractualism, better accommodate the value of community and the claims of morality in the public sphere. In a (loose and popular) sense, we are all liberals now, or should be; and the acknowledgment of this presents a challenge to advocates of general and comprehensive doctrines to show how they can endorse commonly held liberal values. Secular perfectionists such as Joseph Raz do so by arguing that personal political freedom is an aspect of the good life (deriving from the value of autonomy and from value pluralism),[39] and something similar is being developed by American Catholic writers influenced by the likes of Maritain and John Courtenay Murray.[40] However, while I hope for success in these ventures, the arguments generally presented seem either to beg the important questions or to fall short of their conclusions. For now, and perhaps forever, the best hope of liberty lies in a liberal sensibility.

Moral Philosophy, University of St. Andrews

---

[38] See John Haldane, "Can a Catholic Be a Liberal?" *Melita Theologica*, vol. 43 (1992), pp. 44–57.

[39] See Raz, *The Morality of Freedom*, esp. chs. 14 and 15.

[40] See, for example, the essays in Hollenbach and Douglass, eds., *Catholicism and Liberalism*.

LIBERALISM, COMMUNITARIANISM, AND POLITICAL COMMUNITY*

By Chandran Kukathas

We need to cut off the King's head; in political theory that has still to be done.

— Michel Foucault, "Truth and Power"[1]

I. Introduction

The primary concern of this essay is with the question "What is a political community?" This question is important in its own right. Arguably, the main purpose of political philosophy is to provide an account of the nature of political association and, in so doing, to describe the relations that hold between the individual and the state. The question is also important, however, because of its centrality in contemporary debate about liberalism and community.

Liberal political theories generally argue that the good society is best understood as a framework of rights (or liberties) and duties within which people may pursue their separate ends. On this view, the good society is not governed by particular common ends or goals; it is simply governed by law, consistent with principles of justice—principles which do not themselves presuppose the rightness or betterness of any particular way of life. While there are different strands in the liberal tradition, which encompasses thinkers as different as John Rawls, Robert Nozick, and F. A. Hayek (among contemporary writers), they all share these fundamental premises.

The most common criticism put against liberal political theory by its communitarian critics is that it not only undervalues community, but also rests on premises which are unable to account for the place of the individual in the political order. The deepest problem with liberal theory, the argument goes, is that it "continues to pay homage to the enlightenment ideal of the autonomous subject who successfully extricates herself from the immediate entanglements of history and the characteristics and values that come with that entanglement."[2] Ultimately, liberal theory is

* I am grateful to Ellen Frankel Paul and Emilio Pacheco for their detailed comments on an earlier draft of this essay. My thanks also to the other contributors to this volume for some helpful discussion and criticism.

[1] Michel Foucault, "Truth and Power," in Foucault, *Truth and Power: Selected Interviews and Other Writings 1972-1977*, ed. Colin Gordon (New York: Pantheon Books, 1980), p. 121.

[2] Daniel Bell, *Communitarianism and Its Critics* (Oxford: Clarendon Press, 1993), p. 29.

 © 1996 Social Philosophy and Policy Foundation. Printed in the USA.

unable to explain why such disentangled individuals should accept the obligations that arise out of their membership in the political sphere.[3] Thus, liberalism mistakenly advocates a way of life which emphasizes reflection, self-examination, and choice, while assuming that individuals are not "deeply bound up in the social world" in which they find themselves.[4] The fact of the matter is that the existence of political community (and our attachment to it) should be the starting-point of our philosophical reflections, and the value of political community should be the conclusion. Once this point is recognized, we should begin to consider the question of how community, in the form of common social practices and shared understandings, can be protected. This would require rethinking the liberal emphasis on justice and rights.

Communitarianism is, thus, a philosophy which takes the common good of the political community as its first object of concern. As with liberalism, there are many strands in this tradition, which includes philosophers as diverse as Michael Sandel, Alasdair MacIntyre, Charles Taylor, and Michael Walzer—although the only substantial work by a *self-proclaimed* communitarian is Daniel Bell's *Communitarianism and Its Critics.*

Liberal political theory has generally responded to the communitarian critique in several ways. The first has been to argue that the fact of social pluralism makes it difficult to regard political community as a feasible ideal, and that political society cannot be a community. This view has been put forward by John Rawls. The second response has been to suggest that there is a sense in which liberal society does constitute a community insofar as there is a distinctive set of liberal virtues, settled around a shared commitment to the idea of public justification. Such a view has been defended, for example, by Stephen Macedo, who has argued that in liberal society there is a shared public morality, and a distinctive set of liberal virtues appropriate to such a community.[5] A third response, offered by Donald Moon, has been to defend a "political liberalism" which "takes political community itself as an aim, and not the realization of a particular vision of human flourishing or human excellence."[6]

My narrower purpose in this essay is to respond to the communitarian challenge by developing an account of political community. In so doing, however, I wish also to take issue with contemporary liberal thinking. My argument will seek to show that both communitarianism and contemporary liberalism exaggerate the value of political community, and mistak-

---

[3] See *ibid.*, p. 30.

[4] *Ibid.*, p. 31.

[5] See Stephen Macedo, *Liberal Virtues: Citizenship, Virtue, and Community in Liberal Constitutionalism* (Oxford: Clarendon Press, 1990).

[6] J. Donald Moon, *Constructing Community: Moral Pluralism and Tragic Conflicts* (Princeton: Princeton University Press, 1993), p. 8. Moon distances himself from those liberals who "take autonomy, the protection of rights, or the satisfaction of individual wants, as the objectives or values that the practices and institutions of society ought to realize."

enly assume its centrality as a starting-point for philosophical reflection.[7]
The communitarians have begun by asserting the importance of community as a social value; but in arguing the case for preserving political communities, they tend to undermine other forms of community. Liberals, on
the other hand, in responding to the communitarian critique, have themselves embraced a position which is insufficiently liberal insofar as it is
destructive of the kind of pluralism that liberalism is supposed to respect.

The argument will proceed as follows. In the next section, I will examine the question "What is a community?" and will offer a definition, taking issue with some alternative formulations. From here I will argue that
political society is a community, albeit one of a peculiar kind. I will then
offer a definition of political community. In Section III, I will examine the
arguments for political community put forward by communitarians who
are critical of the liberal outlook, and will seek to show that, in elevating
political community, this view undermines the value of community that
these writers claim to uphold. In Section IV, I will turn to contemporary
liberal arguments and attempt to show that these arguments, in assuming the primacy of the political community, also undermine other forms
of community in different ways. In Section V, I will suggest some reasons
why this should concern us, and why we should value political community less. I will conclude with some more-general observations about the
nature of political community.

II. DEFINING COMMUNITY

What, then, is a community? At the very least, a community is an association of individuals. While this much may be uncontroversial, however,
there is some dispute about the meaning of community because the character of that association is highly contested. The centrally important point
of contention is the relationship between the individual and the community and, more specifically, the question of whether the individual is
shaped or constituted by the community, or whether the community is
something to which individuals merely belong or are attached. The issue
here is one of identity.

The argument offered by communitarians in criticism of liberalism is
that liberal theory does not recognize how much individuals are in fact
constituted by their membership in particular communities. Thus, for
example, Michael Sandel complains that Rawls's theory of justice
assumes the existence of a self as an antecedently individuated subject
beyond the reach of experience—whose identity, having been fixed once

---

[7] The argument will be developed, in other words, both at the level of advocacy and of
ontology. See Charles Taylor, "Cross-Purposes: The Liberal-Communitarian Debate," in
Nancy Rosenblum, ed., *Liberalism and the Moral Life* (Cambridge: Harvard University Press,
1989), pp. 160-82.

and for all, is unaltered by communal attachments.[8] Yet our individual identities are not given independently of our membership in particular communities. Indeed, Sandel argues, our identities are partly *constituted* by our social contexts and the commitments we have as parts of a community. By this he means that the community shapes individual identity to such an extent that it cannot make sense to talk of a "self" that is abstracted from the community and is without attachments. The liberal response to this has been to question the claim that persons can be wholly constituted by their social contexts. To some extent, persons have the capacity to shape their own identities; and this point, liberals argue, is surely recognized by communitarians insofar as they recognize that persons are only *partly* constituted by their social contexts.[9] Yet at the same time, it has to be admitted that membership in a community can have a profound effect on individual identity—even to the extent that, "cut off from the relevant community, a person's life would lose an important part of its meaning."[10]

But recognizing that membership in a community has an important bearing on individual identity still does not tell us what a community is. The problem here is that there are so many kinds of human associations which are commonly described as communities. While neighborhoods and towns are often identified as communities, one also encounters references to, for example, the university community, the scholarly community, the Jewish community, the Aboriginal community, the medical community, the scientific community, the business community, and even the international community. This does little to give us a clearer idea about the meaning of community.

For further guidance we should turn to the literature on community, which, according to the English philosopher Raymond Plant, reveals three main models of community.[11] The first is a model associated with the work of the German sociologist Ferdinand Tönnies, for whom a community was distinguished from an association by the fact that its members shared not only a geographical locality but also some common origin. Associations could be contracted into, or built; but true community was organic, involving ties of blood and kinship, as well as shared habitats, attitudes, and experiences. Community, in this respect, was something one could only be born into; and because it was a matter of birth, status,

---

[8] Michael Sandel, *Liberalism and the Limits of Justice* (Cambridge: Cambridge University Press, 1983), p. 62.

[9] On this, see Amy Gutmann, "Communitarian Critics of Liberalism," *Philosophy and Public Affairs*, vol. 14 (1985), pp. 308–22; and Will Kymlicka, "Liberalism and Communitarianism," *Canadian Journal of Philosophy*, vol. 18 (1988), pp. 181–204.

[10] David Miller, *Market, State, and Community* (Oxford: Oxford University Press, 1989), p. 234.

[11] Raymond Plant, "Community," in *The Blackwell Encyclopaedia of Political Thought* (Oxford: Blackwell, 1990), pp. 88–90.

and attitude, rather than contract and interest, a shared locality was a necessary but not a sufficient condition for the existence of a community.[12]

A second model of community is associated with the writings of the political scientist Robert MacIver, who emphasizes the importance of commonality of interests. A community, for MacIver, can be the product of the will of its members; but it also has to be a will for the good or interests the members have in common. Like Tönnies, MacIver sees a shared locality as a necessary condition of community, but his model differs from the first insofar as historical ties or associations are not essential — as long as members share a common concern for the good of the community.

A third model of community departs from the first two by regarding community as encompassing "partial associations": groups related not by shared localities or a direct concern for some common good but simply by shared interests.[13] This understanding of community allows us to consider associations such as trade unions and professional organizations as, at least in some circumstances, embodying community. Moreover, since it does not insist on the importance of geographical proximity, it allows for the possibility of communities which cross geographical (including national) boundaries. Indeed, since it does not insist that the members have an explicit concern for the good of the group, it allows for the possibility that some communities will be united by relatively weak bonds of commitment.

In Raymond Plant's analysis, the first model of community has tended to find favor in some traditional conservative circles — particularly in view of its emphasis on natural identities and organic relations among individuals. The second model, with its emphasis on community as an order of "intentional" relations aimed at securing a genuine common interest, will more likely find favor among socialists (who would also tend to view traditional communities as embodying a certain amount of false consciousness about the real interests which constitute them). Liberals, however, will tend to favor the third model because of their pluralist commitments: since they regard the good society less as the embodiment of community than as an environment in which a variety of partial communities can coexist.

On this view, liberals do not generally view political society as a community so much as a framework within which communities might be found. Yet I think this view is inadequate, if not entirely mistaken; for there is no reason to doubt that political society is a kind of community. To see this, however, the analysis of community will have to be extended.

The argument I want to defend at this point about the nature of community is that *all* communities are in fact "partial associations," as is sug-

---

[12] See Ferdinand Tönnies, *Community and Association*, trans. C. P. Loomis (New York: Harper and Row, 1963).

[13] The term is Plant's; see his "Community," p. 89.

gested by the third model. A community is essentially *an association of individuals who share an understanding of what is public and what is private within that association*. This definition of community captures the idea, insisted upon by writers like Tönnies and MacIver, that it is something about the relationship among people (rather than merely their propinquity) that makes their association a community rather than just a social grouping. As many have recognized, it is the understandings people share that make them into a community.[14] But this definition also specifies what it is precisely that people must share if they are to constitute a community. They must recognize which matters are indeed matters of public concern within that association. This requirement indicates why many forms of association whose members are geographically dispersed are nonetheless communities.

A scholarly community, for example, exists insofar as the people who comprise it share an understanding about which matters are of legitimate concern to all of them as scholars and which are not. Generally, they would hold that a scholar's behavior in the conduct of research is a matter of public concern. Scholars who plagiarize, or falsify research findings, or try to use political connections or financial power to influence academic appointments would typically be seen as having acted in ways which the scholarly community can legitimately take an interest in – perhaps to the point of censuring such conduct. Even if there are disagreements within the community over the seriousness of the breach of standards of right conduct, there would be a measure of agreement that these are matters of public concern. Similarly, there would be agreement that other things are not of public concern: the religious beliefs or political allegiances or (after-class) drinking habits of scholars are, in this community, essentially private matters.

Within Islamic or Christian communities, however, religious belief and practice may not be a private matter. An adherent of either of these religious communities who departed from the community's teachings would have to expect others of his faith to have a legitimate interest in his conduct. Among Muslims, the consumption of alcohol is a public matter; among Catholics, the individual's contraceptive practices are not a personal matter.[15]

The members of a village or neighborhood may have enough of a sense of community to regard any of a whole range of matters to be of public concern, from the care of private gardens, to noise levels, to the behavior and control of pets. In modern societies, with mobile populations, such local communities are unlikely, however, to regard religious beliefs

---

[14] See, for example, Michael Walzer, *Spheres of Justice* (Oxford: Blackwell, 1983).

[15] This is not meant to deny that sometimes principles which are defended as vitally important are more honored in the breach than in the observance. Thus, while in principle, and officially, all Catholics may condemn (certain forms of) contraception, the practice is often to leave such matters to personal judgment.

or diets as public matters. What would define the village or neighborhood as a community, however, is the existence of some recognition by the members that certain things are of concern to the membership as a whole. More particularly, there would have to be some recognition of the (mutual) obligations generated by membership. Thus, the existence of shared interests does not make for a community: a group of people standing at a bus stop may share an interest in having the bus arrive on time, and in forming an orderly queue to board quickly – but this does not make it a community.

At the same time, it has to be stressed that in all of these cases, only some matters are of public concern. If a community is distinguished by its shared understanding of which matters are of public concern, it is because it also recognizes the existence of a private realm: a realm in which the public or the community has no business. In recognizing this, communities make clear that they are, ultimately, only partly involved in the identities of the individuals who make them up. How far they can constitute an individual's identity will thus be determined by a number of factors: by the number of other communities to which the individual belongs, by the extent to which the individual himself wishes to identify with the community in question, and by the opportunity the individual has to exit from the community (and perhaps also by the willingness of others to recognize the individual as a member of a particular community). Few, if any, communities can constitute an individual's identity because few, if any, individuals are locked in a single community which leaves no room for other attachments to which the group is indifferent. In this sense, all communities are partial communities.

It should also be noted that communities are stable entities only to a limited extent. They are usually marked by internal divisions – the more so if the community is a large one composed of a diversity of related traditions. They often break down, or experience secessions by sections of their membership. The boundaries of a community thus shift continually.

None of this is meant to deny that some community memberships bite more deeply into an individual's identity than others. This may sometimes be the result of personal commitment: a man of part Aboriginal descent may choose to identify himself as an Aboriginal and to embrace with gusto the way of life he might thus adopt. In other cases, membership might give one a sense of identity which is unwelcome in its intensity: many members of the Baha'i faith in postrevolutionary Iran, and many Jews in Nazi Germany, might have found religion much less important for their identities in other circumstances. Nonetheless, the point remains: community membership is only partly constitutive of identity; and communities are, generally, partial communities.

At this point we should turn, then, to consider the question of whether there can be such a thing as a *political community*. On the definition of community I have proposed, there can. A political community is essentially *an association of individuals who share an understanding of what is pub-*

lic and what is private within their polity. In this context, a matter is of public interest or concern if it is something which is generally regarded as an appropriate subject of attention by the political institutions of the society. It is private if it is regarded as lying beyond the bounds of legitimate political concern.

What are in fact regarded as matters of legitimate political concern will, of course, vary from polity to polity. In some societies, a wide range of questions are regarded as properly subject to political determination. In the Islamic tradition, for example, there is no distinction to be drawn between religious and secular authority: the distinction between church and state which is so much taken for granted in the modern West, has no equivalent in Islam or in the languages in which Islamic thought has developed.[16] For some, the idea of a secular jurisdiction and authority is an impiety, if not a betrayal of Islam. Thus, some political societies, whose members are more profoundly shaped by their Islamic faith, will be political communities in which the domain of the political is also the religious domain. Yet, in others, the scope of political authority will be considerably less. Some societies with predominantly Muslim traditions have made the distinction between religious and secular authority, and in such societies the political community is not coextensive with the religious community — modern Turkey and Indonesia are two examples.

In liberal societies, at the other extreme, historical traditions (and, sometimes, formal constitutional requirements) may impose very clear limits on the scope of political authority. Within such political communities, members may regard comparatively few matters as legitimate objects of public (i.e., political) concern. Religion, ethnicity, sexual orientation, and political belief might be viewed as matters in which the political public need (indeed, may) take no interest.

At both these extremes, however, there is political community. What makes for the existence of a community is some shared understanding of what is public and what is private. This is not to say that there can be no dispute or disagreement within a political community over what is appropriately public and what is private. Libertarians, conservatives, and social democrats, for example, all give different answers to this question. Communists within a political community may even be trying to subvert it. Yet this does not mean that they are not part of a political community. A political community continues to exist for as long as its members generally recognize the conventions which define it — conventions which identify the commonly accepted understanding of the public concerns of the polity.

These understandings may, of course, change: conventions are, characteristically, dependent upon the times. And communities, as has already been noted, are not homogeneous but are typically marked by

[16] See Bernard Lewis, *The Political Language of Islam* (Princeton: Princeton University Press, 1990), pp. 3–4.

divisions and disagreements. This is no less true of political communities, which are notoriously unstable entities. There is scarcely a state on the globe which has not seen its geographical boundaries shift at least once in this century; and there have been countless secessions, partitions, mergers, reunifications, and renamings of states. Yet stable or no, these have (to varying degrees) been political communities.

But if political communities are defined by shared understandings of the public concerns of political institutions, it will be asked, what exactly are *political* institutions? More particularly, is the political community the same thing as the state? The first point to be made in response to these questions is that the political community is geographically distinct from other political communities; a political community has a territorial base. This need not be the case with other forms of community, such as religious communities. The most significant institution of a political community is its government. However, this does not mean that a political community must be a state, since there can be territorially based communities, run by governments, but which are not states. Lawrence township, for example, is a political community with a government which raises (local) taxes and attends to the administration of a community within Indiana, which is in turn a political community within the nation-state.[17]

Now, all this said, it must be noted that at least one philosopher has denied that a political society is a community — or at least that "a well-ordered democratic society" is one. John Rawls, most recently in his book *Political Liberalism*, has argued such a society is neither an association nor a community. A community, he argues, is "a society governed by a shared comprehensive, religious, philosophical, or moral doctrine."[18] Once we recognize the fact of pluralism, he maintains, we must abandon hope of political community unless we are prepared to countenance the use of state power to secure it. "Liberalism rejects political society as community because, among other things, it leads to the systematic denial of basic liberties and may allow the oppressive use of the government's monopoly of (legal) force."[19]

It should be noted, however, that Rawls's argument is based on a very specific, and somewhat narrow, understanding of community. For him, a community is a society united in affirming the same comprehensive doctrine. On this understanding, a community identifies a form of association which exhibits a far greater degree of unity and stability than I have suggested is characteristic of community. Yet such an understanding of community (which I take to be *implicit* in Rawls's stance) is, I sug-

---

[17] There is insufficient space here to pursue a more detailed investigation into the relationships and differences between various types of political communities. See, however, the analysis offered by Susan Reynolds, *Kingdoms and Communities in Western Europe 900–1300* (Oxford: Clarendon Press, 1986).

[18] John Rawls, *Political Liberalism* (New York: Columbia University Press, 1993), p. 42.

[19] *Ibid.*, p. 146n.

gest, too restrictive, because it does not allow us to recognize a range of associations commonly regarded as communities: from neighborhoods and universities to townships. While collections of individuals must share something to be recognized as communities, they do not need to share as much as a "comprehensive doctrine." Rawls's understanding of community emphasizes the qualities of commonality and thus underestimates the extent to which communities are made up of individuals who are different from one another.[20]

If we recognize that Rawls's rejection of the possibility of liberal political community is based on a very particular understanding of community, it becomes clear that his concerns about the preservation of pluralism and the avoidance of reliance on state power do not tell against the possibility of political community. However, we should also then recognize that the understanding of political community implicit in my argument indicates that political community is a much less substantial thing than many might think. Political community, like other forms of community, is still only "partial community." Membership in such a community is thus not constitutive of an individual's identity, because political community is only one of the communities to which an individual may belong. Of course, it has to be recognized that, for some, national identity may be of singular importance — and a quick glance at the history of modern nationalism is all that is necessary to confirm how powerful this commitment can be. Yet for many, membership in a political community is only one dimension of a life — and often not the most important dimension. In the Islamic world, for example, *national* or *political* identity is a relatively modern and intrusive notion. Although the concepts of nation and country are not new in Islamic thought, "there is a recurring tendency in times of crisis, in times of emergency, when the deeper loyalties take over, for Muslims to find their basic identity in the religious community; that is to say, in an entity defined by Islam rather than by ethnic origin, language, or country of habitation."[21]

Recognizing the existence and the possibility of political community does not, then, require a commitment to valuing this form of community. Indeed, I would suggest that understanding community in the way I have described should make us wary of assuming that political community is in some way the most important or the fundamental form of community which somehow subsumes or subordinates all others. To be sure, the rise of the modern state and the power of national governments have to be recognized; but this in itself does not mean that the shaping of individual life or the domination of individual identity by political community

[20] On this point, see Bernard Yack's discussion of Aristotle's analysis of community in Yack, *The Problems of a Political Animal: Community, Justice, and Conflict in Aristotelian Political Thought* (Berkeley: University of California Press, 1993), ch. 1, esp. p. 29.

[21] Lewis, *The Political Language of Islam*, p. 4. See also Partha Chatterjee, *The Nation and Its Fragments: Colonial and Postcolonial Histories* (Princeton: Princeton University Press, 1993).

should be welcomed or promoted. This is the assumption made, however, by the communitarian critics of liberalism. And it is this viewpoint which should now be addressed.

III. Communitarianism and Political Community

According to Daniel Bell, "the whole point of communitarian politics is to structure society in accordance with people's deepest shared understandings."[22] While it would be a mistake to suggest that all communitarian thought is of a piece, I believe Bell's statement captures what is essential in the communitarian position.[23] Communitarians, such as Charles Taylor, Alasdair MacIntyre, and Michael Sandel, argue that political community is an important value which is neglected by liberal political theory. Liberalism, they contend, views political society as a supposedly neutral framework of rules within which a diversity of moral traditions coexist. The rules are justified by appeal to abstract and universal principles of justice. Attending to the common good, however, is no part of the concern of these rules, which try not to make any substantial commitments to any idea of the good life or morally desirable goals.

Such an ideal of a political society, argue the communitarians, even if plausible, is unattractive. Indeed, it is no kind of society at all. It neglects the fact that people have, or can have, a strong and "deep" attachment to their societies — to their nations. Liberalism tends, mistakenly, to reject the view that communal attachments are fundamentally important — because it views such attachments, not as constitutive of individual identity, but as voluntary commitments which might be chosen or discarded at will.

There are thus two aspects to the communitarian argument: one ontological and the other evaluative. The ontological aspect is an argument about the nature of the self and its relations with social reality. The communitarian view is that the self cannot be conceived of independently of society or the community: the self is *situated* or *embodied*. It is constituted by society. Social processes and institutions shape the person into a social being, whose desires and whose understandings and attitudes toward the world are thus a product of the community. This is, in part, an argument about human interdependence. In this context, it does not make sense to talk about individuals *choosing* their ways of life, as liberal theories tend to do.

On this view, liberalism makes a mistake by seeing allegiances as merely values one happens to have or espouse at a particular time. The most important allegiances we owe are not matters of choice but exist in

---

[22] Bell, *Communitarianism and Its Critics*, p. 141.

[23] For a brief typology of communitarian views, see Will Kymlicka, "Community," in Robert Goodin and Philip Pettit, eds., *Blackwell Companion to Contemporary Political Philosophy* (Oxford: Blackwell, 1993), p. 367f.

virtue of the enduring attachments and commitments which define a person. "To imagine a person incapable of constitutive attachments such as these is not to conceive an ideally free and rational agent, but to imagine a person wholly without character, without moral depth."[24]

The evaluative aspect of the communitarian argument is a claim about the importance of communal or public or collective goods. (This argument is independent of the ontological claims about the social construction of the self, although the fact of human interdependence is held by communitarians to have important political implications.) A view of humans as primarily social beings requires an emphasis on values which support mutuality. This means promoting cultural practices and institutions which strengthen norms of reciprocity, solidarity, and fraternity. In political deliberations, these values must take priority over the liberal emphasis on individual rights and individual freedom.

Ultimately, the communitarian position holds that, because individuals are shaped by community and can live well only as members of healthy communities, it is important that the focus of politics be not on individual rights or liberties but on the well-being of the political community itself. Liberalism, in emphasizing rights and liberties, which divide rather than unite us, overlooks the fact that in the end the human good is secured together with others rather than alone.

The liberal response to the communitarian critique has been substantial, and there is already a large literature dealing with the liberal-communitarian debate. I do not intend to go over the various points and counterpoints in this dispute.[25] However, I want to argue that the communitarian view only has persuasiveness or appeal to the extent that it ignores the "partial" nature of communities. It neglects the fact that, even if individuals are constituted by the communities to which they belong, they are invariably members of different communities which contribute to the shaping of their lives in different ways and to different degrees. To say this is not to suggest that individuals are completely free to choose their allegiances or their ends; but it is to recognize that the nature of those allegiances and the nature of individual identity is not fixed or stable but variable.

The point of recognizing individual rights and liberties is not to insist on the individual's choosing his or her allegiances. It is rather to acknowledge that individuals exist in different partial communities. To the extent that communitarians intend to make community an explicit concern of politics, they run the risk of undermining the communal attachments they purport to value. They do this in two ways. In the first instance, they

[24] Sandel, *Liberalism and the Limits of Justice*, p. 179.

[25] For a more thorough examination of the dispute, see Stephen Mulhall and Adam Swift, *Liberals and Communitarians* (Oxford: Blackwell, 1992); Elizabeth Frazer and Nicola Lacey, *The Politics of Community: A Feminist Critique of the Liberal-Communitarian Debate* (Toronto: University of Toronto Press, 1993).

do so by emphasizing the importance of the political community and national identity. The effect of this is to weaken communities within the political society insofar as efforts are made to strengthen the hold of the *political* community on the individual's identity. Political unity and solidarity can be better secured only by greater homogenization of the population. This is most strikingly the case when communitarians emphasize that we must have a "deep attachment to the nation," and that government policies such as compulsory national service are desirable as means of strengthening those attachments.[26] Yet social unity of this kind can only be increased by suppressing diversity — and more particularly by suppressing the diversity of parochial attachments. The more substantial the commitments and obligations that come with membership in a political community, the more likely there is to be conflict between the demands of the political community and those of other communities to which the individual belongs. Giving political community greater importance must mean weakening other communal ties.

The second way in which communal politics can undermine community is by explicit attempts to uphold particular communal practices. For this approach neglects the character of community as something changeable and fluid. Community is, to varying degrees, continually evolving, and the boundaries of community are not always stable. Community is, in a sense, continually recreated by the involvements of its members. Political efforts run the risk of undermining communities by attempting to fix their existence and character.[27] Communities which are no longer viable because of a dwindling membership might be kept alive by subsidies, or tax incentives, or by force (for example, through emigration restrictions). Yet such measures not only threaten the viability of other communities (which might bear the burden of taxation) but also risk creating communities marked by "dislocation" and "anomie" insofar as individuals are discouraged or prevented from reconstituting themselves into associations which serve their purposes.

For both these reasons we should be wary of communitarian politics.

IV. LIBERALISM AND POLITICAL COMMUNITY

At the same time, however, these considerations give us reason to be concerned about the arguments advanced by much of contemporary liberal theory. Having recognized the deficiencies of communitarianism, liberal philosophers like John Rawls have rightly stressed the importance of recognizing the rights and liberties which allow for and protect social plu-

---

[26] Bell, *Communitarianism and Its Critics*, p. 143.
[27] I have discussed this point at greater length in "Are There Any Cultural Rights?" *Political Theory*, vol. 20, no. 1 (1992), pp. 112–15.

ralism. In Rawls's case, liberalism goes to the other extreme, arguing that it will not even consider the possibility of political community since such community—by its very nature—requires the oppressive use of state power.

Yet even in refusing to consider political society as a community, this view nonetheless elevates political society by taking for granted that the fundamental questions of social order must be addressed only within political society. Political society is not just one community among many, but an order which subsumes all other communities. Thus, Rawls's theory, for example, begins by assuming that all issues of justice must be formulated and resolved (philosophically speaking) within the context of a closed society.[28]

Pluralism is recognized; but the quality of that pluralism is circumscribed by its subordination to the moral standards of a particular community: political society. Ultimately, in this conception, pluralism takes a back seat to the values which appear to be more solidly defended by Rawls's liberalism: the values of stability and social unity of the political order. This is evident throughout Rawls's recent writings, which view the task of political philosophy in a democratic society as one of securing stability and social unity.[29] It is made particularly clear in *Political Liberalism*, where Rawls stresses that the starting-point of his theory of liberalism is an affirmation of the autonomy of individuals as *citizens* of a political society.[30] Indeed, a major concern addressed by this view is the problem of social reproduction. It is assumed that political society has a legitimate interest in its own perpetuation. And in a good society political autonomy is properly realized by the individual's "participating in society's public affairs and sharing in its collective self-determination over time."[31]

[28] This is clear in *Political Liberalism*, where Rawls writes:

> [W]e have assumed that a democratic society, like any political society, is to be viewed as a complete and closed social system. It is complete in that it is self-sufficient and has a place for all the main purposes of human life. It is also closed . . . in that entry into it is only by birth and exit is only by death. (pp. 40–41)

[29] For example, in "The Idea of an Overlapping Consensus," *Oxford Journal of Legal Studies*, vol. 7, no. 1 (1987), p. 1, Rawls writes:

> In a constitutional democracy one of its most important aims is presenting a political conception of justice that can not only provide a shared public basis for the justification of political and social institutions but also helps ensure stability from one generation to the next.

[30] Thus, Rawls is not upholding the value of personal autonomy as such. The

> full autonomy of political life must be distinguished from the ethical values of autonomy and individuality, which may apply to the whole of life, both social and individual, as expressed by the comprehensive liberalisms of Kant and Mill. Justice as fairness emphasizes this contrast: it affirms political autonomy for all but leaves the weight of ethical autonomy to be decided by citizens severally in light of their comprehensive doctrines. (*Political Liberalism*, p. 78)

[31] *Ibid.*, p. 78.

This outlook is not peculiarly Rawlsian.[32] Many, if not most, contemporary liberal political theorists begin with the assumption that the political "community" occupies a position of moral authority. It is the preeminently important community, and its interests or values take priority whenever there is conflict over differing values. Thus, the institutions of political society are legitimately concerned with the education, health, and even the preferences of citizens.[33]

The implication of this standpoint is to weaken or reduce the independence and the authority of the other communities to which people belong. It maintains that the activities of such communities, and the manner in which they are pursued, are subject to the moral standards established by the political community; they are subject to political authority.

This emerges most strikingly in contemporary liberal discourse concerning the claims of cultural minorities. Here, despite the sympathy expressed for the plight of minority communities trying to sustain ways of life at odds with the modern world, liberals have been reluctant to allow more than a limited autonomy to such groups. Some argue that, although cultural diversity is a good thing, individuality can be stifled by cultural communities which deny members—and in particular, children—the opportunity to choose from the wider range of options available in the mainstream of society. This Millian argument is at the core of Justice William Douglas's dissenting opinion in the case of *Wisconsin v. Yoder*.[34] For Douglas, the Amish ought not to be allowed to school their own children if this form of socialization would effectively deny them the opportunity to leave the Amish community. John Rawls, while rejecting the comprehensive moral ideal of Millian individuality as an inappropriate basis for establishing principles of political justice, is equally unwilling to allow the Amish more than a limited autonomy—although he offers no principled reasons for denying that community independence from the values of the political society.[35]

Among contemporary liberal thinkers, Will Kymlicka is more wary of intervening in the practices of illiberal cultural minorities, arguing that a distinction should be drawn between *identifying* a liberal theory of minority rights and *imposing* that liberal theory.[36] Yet while he is reluctant to

---

[32] See, for example, Amy Gutmann, who defends the "ideal of citizens sharing in deliberatively determining the future shape of their society," and commends the democratic ideal as one of "conscious social reproduction" (Gutmann, *Democratic Education* [Princeton: Princeton University Press, 1987], p. 289).

[33] See, for example, Cass Sunstein, "Preferences and Politics," *Philosophy and Public Affairs*, vol. 20, no. 1 (1991), pp. 3–34.

[34] *Wisconsin v. Yoder*, 406 U.S. 205 (1972).

[35] For a powerful critique of Rawls on this issue, see Will Kymlicka, "Two Models of Pluralism and Tolerance," *Analyse & Kritik*, vol. 14 (1992), pp. 33–56.

[36] Will Kymlicka, "The Rights of Minority Cultures: Reply to Kukathas," *Political Theory*, vol. 20, no. 1 (1992), p. 145. See also my "Cultural Rights Again: A Rejoinder to Kymlicka," *Political Theory*, vol. 20, no. 4 (1992), pp. 674–80. Kymlicka's view is endorsed by Amy Gutmann, "The Politics of Multiculturalism," *Philosophy and Public Affairs*, vol. 22 (1993), pp. 171–206.

intervene in cultural communities to coerce illiberal minorities into liberal ways, this concession is made to a limited number of communities who have particular historical claims to noninterference: groups such as the Amish and the Mennonites, and aboriginal communities. Newly constituted communities such as those formed by immigrants, however, must accept the legitimacy of state enforcement of liberal principles within these communities (provided these voluntary immigrants knew in advance that this would be the case). On Kymlicka's view, the fundamental liberal commitment is to the value of autonomy; and thus, for him, a sound defense of liberalism should recognize the necessity of upholding autonomy in all communities within the polity.

These various liberal positions defended by Rawls, Douglas, and Kymlicka can be placed within a scheme of four categories, according to their adherence to or rejection of a comprehensive moral ideal as the basis of liberalism, and according to whether or not they are willing to see liberal values imposed on communities within political society. This can be expressed in the matrix depicted in Figure 1.

One who adheres to position A, position B, or position C holds that the political community is morally authoritative. The adherent of position B is reluctant to impose liberalism on some communities for pragmatic reasons, but still sees political society as the arena within which the issue of which ways of life are acceptable must be authoritatively settled. Adherents of all three positions take the stability and social unity of political society to be (to varying degrees) a fundamental concern. (Contemporary liberals have generally been reluctant to consider position D, which views

	Impose	Not Impose
Comprehensive Liberalism	A Douglas	B Kymlicka
Political Liberalism	C Rawls	D

FIGURE 1. Four categories of liberal positions.

the political community as possessing little or no authority over other partial communities.)

This concern about the stability and unity of political society, which is
shared by most contemporary liberals (including Rawls, Kymlicka, and
Douglas), is one which, in the end, tends to undermine other particular
communities. The reason for this is not that contemporary liberals, like
communitarians, explicitly seek to elevate the political community by
denying the separateness of persons or asserting that political attachments are ultimately what matter to us. Contemporary liberalism, as
evinced in the thought of Rawls and Kymlicka among others, has been
quite insistent about its individualist commitments. Thus, it has repeatedly stressed the importance of upholding vital individual rights and
liberties — notably rights of religious worship, and liberty of conscience.
Individuals may not be forced to take on unwanted religious commitments; nor may they be forced to be party to practices they could not, in
good conscience, condone. Yet while these rights and liberties provide
important protections for the individual against the oppressive exercise
of state power, contemporary liberals have come to regard these liberties
as claims which may be enforced by the political community against
most, if not all, of the other communities to which an individual might
belong.

What is asserted here, in effect, is that there has to be an ultimate
authority determining what practices or ways of life are permissible, and
that this authority resides in the institutions of the political community.
The possibility of there being contending authorities is rejected. Other
communities may not lock their doors or close their borders to deny to
political authority the right to scrutinize their workings — unless they are
themselves political communities.

This is a position which is very much the normal starting-point of contemporary liberal political philosophy. Yet this outlook, I think, departs
from liberalism — and shares a great deal with communitarianism. This is
because it ceases to view political society (or the state) as no more than
a partial community which, therefore, has only a limited claim on our
allegiance. It begins to view the political community as a form of association in which individuals are more deeply entangled.

Thus, a liberal critic of communitarianism such as Ronald Dworkin, for
example, regards it as a strength of his own account of political community that it confirms "the commitment necessary to make a large and
diverse society a genuine rather than a bare community." [37] Such a model
of political society as a "community of principle," he argues, "can claim
the authority of a genuine associative community and can therefore claim
moral legitimacy — that its collective decisions are matters of obligation
and not bare power — in the name of *fraternity*." [38] This outlook is strik-

---

[37] Ronald Dworkin, *Law's Empire* (London: Fontana Press, 1986), p. 214.
[38] *Ibid.*, p. 214 (emphasis added).

ingly communitarian inasmuch as it not only regards political community as specially valuable, but also "insists that people are members of a genuine political community only when they accept that their fates are linked in the following strong way: they accept that they are governed by common principles, not just by rules hammered out in political compromise."[39] In such an association, each individual "accepts political integrity as a distinct political ideal"; and general acceptance of this ideal is "constitutive of political community."[40]

This image of political society as something more than just another partial community can also be found in Rawls's understanding of a well-ordered society as a "social union of social unions."[41] In such a society, he argues,

> each person understands the first principles that govern the whole scheme as it is to be carried out over many generations; and all have a settled intention to adhere to these principles in their plan of life. Thus the plan of each person is given a more ample and rich structure than it would otherwise have; it is adjusted to the plans of others by mutually acceptable principles. Everyone's more private life is so to speak a plan within a plan, this superordinate plan being realized in the public institutions of society.[42]

Now such a plan does not, Rawls insists, establish any dominant end — such as religous unity or national power — to which the aims of all individuals and associations must be subordinated. The larger plan is simply a constitutional order which realizes the principles of justice. And yet there is more to it than this; for Rawls also adds that (in the well-ordered society) "this collective activity . . . must be experienced as a good."[43]

Much of contemporary liberalism tends, then, to view other forms of community as subordinate to political society. It also largely accepts the idea that this form of community is especially (even if not uniquely) valuable. In doing so, it shares with communitarianism the view that society should be structured "in accordance with people's deepest understandings." While it has rejected the communitarians' ontological claims about the identities of individuals being constituted by political membership, it has embraced their evaluative claims about the importance of the communal attachments to be found in political society; and it has given expression to this commitment to the value of political membership by viewing the political community as having the authority to set the moral standards to which other forms of community must (minimally) conform.

---

[39] *Ibid.*, p. 211.
[40] *Ibid.*
[41] John Rawls, *A Theory of Justice* (Oxford: Oxford University Press, 1971), p. 527.
[42] *Ibid.*, p. 528.
[43] *Ibid.*

This, I think, involves an undesirable departure of liberalism from its individualist commitments. It reveals a preoccupation more with social unity than with respecting the diversity of ways of life which struggle to coexist in the face of dominant powers — notably political powers. It values political society too much, and other forms of human association not enough.

There are, however, at least two responses which might be made to address these concerns. First, why should liberalism not value political community in this way? After all, liberal theory has commonly been criticized for failing properly to appreciate the value of political allegiance, or even the significance of political membership as the starting-point of reflection on questions of social philosophy. If, in the arguments of Rawls, Dworkin, and others, there is to be found some recognition of the importance of political community or fraternity, this is surely all to the good. And second, how else could political society be understood, if not as the dominant form of community which subsumes other forms of human association?

V. THE VALUE OF POLITICAL COMMUNITY

There are several considerations which should lead us to value political community less. The first is that endowing the political community with great significance means viewing it as more than just another partial community and, consequently, conceding to it the authority to subordinate (and disrupt) other forms of community. This is undesirable for two reasons. The first is that a powerful political community can be oppressive.

Oppression, as Iris Young has shown, can take many forms.[44] These include oppression that is manifest in exploitation, marginalization, powerlessness, cultural imperialism, and violence. The first three refer to "structural and institutional relations that delimit people's material lives, including but not restricted to the resources they have access to and the concrete opportunities they have or do not have to develop and exercise their capacities."[45] Yet while these forms of oppression are troubling to be sure, it is the fourth and fifth — cultural imperialism and violence — which are of interest here.

To experience cultural imperialism[46] means "to experience how the dominant meanings of a society render the particular perspective of one's

---

[44] Iris Marion Young, *Justice and the Politics of Difference* (Princeton: Princeton University Press, 1990), pp. 39-65.

[45] *Ibid.*, p. 58.

[46] I leave to one side my reservations about the terminology; Young herself, in adopting the term "cultural imperialism," is merely following a usage established by Maria Lugones and Elizabeth Spelman, "Have We Got a Theory for You! Feminist Theory, Cultural Imperialism, and the Demand for 'The Woman's Voice,' " *Women's Studies International Forum*, vol. 6 (1983), pp. 573-81.

own group invisible at the same time as they stereotype one's group and mark it out as the Other."[47] Cultural imperialism involves the "universalization of a dominant group's experience and culture, and its establishment as the norm."[48] Dominant groups tend to view their own experience as representative of humanity, and thus, when challenged by other groups with different ways of seeing the world, seek to reinforce their position "by bringing the other groups under the measure of [their] dominant norms."[49]

The greater the extent to which a political community is more than a partial community (that is, the greater the extent to which it subordinates all other forms of human association), the greater the extent to which it will serve to secure the dominant norms — presented as distillations of universal understandings and experience. This form of oppression has not been difficult to find in modern states, which have — to varying degrees — established national standards for all kinds of practices, ranging from education to medicine to law. Communities which might understand these practices differently are seldom able to maintain their independence.

Of course, it is also possible that many of the norms which become dominant in a society do not reflect the thinking or the attitudes of the majority — or even a plurality — of the population. They may, instead, reflect the dominant position of particular interests or the ideas of intellectual elites. But this is of no comfort to dissenters who find these dominant norms ubiquitous and oppressive.

The objection here, it should be noted, is not that political society is uniquely oppressive; local communities or religious communities can be no less so. The point is that there is no reason to think that political communities will not be oppressive. This gives us less reason to concede to political society the authority to entrench particular values. It also gives us less reason to see political community as an especially valuable form of community.

There is, of course, a further reason why conceding such authority to the political community is undesirable. The disruption or undermining of other partial communities threatens to leave individuals without other significant attachments or memberships. At the extreme, it threatens to atomize society by eliminating (through subsumption) the forms of association which exist in between the individual and the state.

This brings us to the second consideration which should lead us to value political community less: that, when the political community is the nation, commending it involves prescribing the concentration of power in a strong central state. The reason why this is so is that viewing the

---

[47] *Ibid.*, pp. 58–59.
[48] *Ibid.*, p. 59.
[49] *Ibid.*

political community as the dominant authority subsuming other communities must mean the centralization of legal power. Even the liberal political community, if defended as what Ronald Dworkin calls a "community of principle," will not tolerate a variety of competing legal authorities except insofar as they are subordinate to the principal authority. It will not readily countenance different legal jurisdictions which uphold different laws on fundamental issues. The integrity of the society under a single legal framework becomes of major importance. Thus, it "condemns checkerboard statutes and less dramatic violations of that ideal [of integrity] as violating the associative character of its deep organization."[50] The upshot of all this is that pursuing political community leads to a powerful central (national) state with the capacity (and inclination) to override local law.

Two objections may be raised against this point. The first is that it is possible to devise institutional arrangements which constrain the state to ensure that it does not act tyrannically. James Madison, in *The Federalist Papers*, argued that power under the Constitution of the United States had been effectively divided "by so contriving the interior structure of the government, as that its several constituent parts may, by their mutual relations, be the means of keeping each other in their proper places."[51] The answer to this objection is that this problem is not as readily solved as Madison suggested. In the United States, the constitution he recommended did not prevent the growth of a large, powerful central government and the weakening of the states that comprised the union.[52] (That the union became all-important is evident not least in the fact that the national government was prepared, in 1861, both to maintain slavery and to wage war to preserve the union.)[53] The weakening of the states com-

---

[50] Dworkin, *Law's Empire*, p. 214.

[51] James Madison, "The Federalist No. 51," in James Madison, Alexander Hamilton, and John Jay, *The Federalist Papers*, ed. George Carey and James McClellan (Iowa: Kendall Hunt, 1990), p. 266.

[52] In this regard, my sympathies are with the anti-federalists, who resisted the creation of a republic which reduced the thirteen states to one government:

> In so extensive a republic, the great officers of government would soon become above the controul of the people, and abuse their power to the purpose of aggrandizing themselves, and oppressing them. . . . They will use the power, when they have acquired it, to the purposes of gratifying their own interest and ambition, and it is scarcely possible, in a very large republic, to call them to account for their misconduct, or to prevent the abuse of power.

See Letter I by "Brutus" to "The Citizens of the State of New York," October 18, 1787, in *The Anti-Federalist: Writings by the Opponents of the Constitution*, ed. Herbert J. Storing, selected by Murray Dry from *The Complete Anti-Federalist* (Chicago: University of Chicago Press, 1985), p. 116.

[53] See President Lincoln's first inaugural address (delivered March 4, 1861, two weeks after the inauguration of Jefferson Davis as the first president of the Confederacy), in which he maintained that he had "no purpose, directly or indirectly, to interfere with the institution of slavery in States where it exists"; that "Perpetuity is implied, if not expressed, in the fundamental law of all national governments"; and that "no State upon its own mere motion

prising the union also weakened the second Madisonian safeguard against majority tyranny: the federal structure which separated power not only functionally but geographically.

The second objection, however, is to say that a powerful central government is not a bad thing: a strong, dominant political community may be necessary to resolve conflicts among other communities and to prevent one of them from dominating and oppressing the others. Any answer to this objection must concede the possibility (indeed, likelihood) of such conflicts and of the domination of the weak by the powerful. There is, however, no reason whatsoever to think that a dominant political community with a powerful central government will suppress petty tyrannies rather than perpetrate gross ones.[54] And this still leaves the question: "Who will guard the guardians?"

Generally, it has to be said that modern liberal polities have accepted the fact of concentration of power in the government of the dominant political community. The third consideration which should make us value political society less is that the state has always posed a threat to individual liberty. The danger here is in part that a dominant majority will use the power of the state to oppress weaker minorities. Equally worrying, however, is the tendency for the political apparatus of the state to be captured by particular movements or organizations bent on the forcible transformation of society. Soviet communism, German Nazism, and the communism of Pol Pot are only three of the more dramatic examples of this. In all of these cases, and in countless others, great appeal is made to the virtue of the political community, for whose glory (now and in perpetuity) great sacrifices of individual life and liberty must be made. Individual liberty is sacrificed in order to build a state and a nation.

It may, of course, be objected that these cases identify extremes and thus exaggerate the dangers to liberty posed by the pursuit of political community. Yet one does not have to look to Pol Pot's Cambodia to find troubling examples. In many developing countries, from Malaysia to the Philippines to Brazil, great modernizing efforts have been undertaken in the name of "state-building," despite the protestations of minorities and of the poor, whose identities and lives have been most vulnerable to the processes of change. Indeed, the struggle for power in much of the Third

---

can lawfully get out of the Union; that *resolves* and *ordinances* to that effect are legally void, and that acts of violence within any State or States against the authority of the United States are insurrectionary or revolutionary, according to circumstances." See *Inaugural Addresses of the Presidents of the United States from George Washington 1789 to George Bush 1989*, 101st Congress, 1st Session, Senate Document 101-10 (Washington, DC: U.S. Government Printing Service, 1989), pp. 134–36. Note also Lincoln's acknowledgment in his second inaugural address (March 4, 1865) that, in fighting the Civil War, while both parties deprecated war, "one of them would *make* war rather than let the nation survive, and the other would *accept* war rather than let it perish" (*Inaugural Addresses*, p. 142).

[54] Current examples abound: consider the Russian suppression of the Chechen insurrection; the Iraqi treatment of its Kurdish minority; and the Serbian war against Bosnia.

World, as Joel Migdal argues, has often been a struggle for control of these peoples:

> For vulnerable individuals, that struggle for control of their lives has frequently been little more than a conflict between the evils of exploitative local powers and the "justice" of an aggrandizing state intent on transforming and ridding them of some of their most cherished values.[55]

In part, the problem for the aggrandizing state has been that many peoples within its borders have been able to imagine a completely different set of alternatives for the organization of social life from that laid down by the dominant regime.[56]

It has, of course, been argued that it is important for such peoples to come under the authority of a strong state: "inhabitants of weak states have few or poorly enforced rights," according to Stephen Holmes. Without significant state capacities, he argues, "there is no possibility of imposing a single and impartial legal system—the rule of law—on the population of a large nation." And "without a well-organized political and legal system, exclusive loyalties and passions of revenge will run out of control."[57] But this exaggerates not only the extent of intergroup conflict but also the capacity of state institutions to bring such conflicts under control.[58] For one thing, the state is often less an impartial umpire than an interested player in such conflicts; and in such cases, the state apparatus becomes the object of capture by the contending parties vying for power. More importantly, it is not clear why there has to be a single legal system imposed over a large population for the rule of law to prevail.[59]

In the end, we should be reticent about attaching great value to political community, because this attachment is founded on an illusion that there is something so special about this form of association that we may be justified in committing great violence against other people to preserve

---

[55] Joel Migdal, *Strong Societies and Weak States: State-Society Relations and State Capabilities in the Third World* (Princeton: Princeton University Press, 1988), pp. xx–xxi.

[56] On this, see James Scott, *Domination and the Arts of Resistance* (New Haven: Yale University Press, 1990). For a discussion of the resistance of nomadic and semi-nomadic peoples who resist easy categorization and control by the state, see James Scott, "State Simplification," *Journal of Political Philosophy* (forthcoming).

[57] Stephen Holmes, "Liberalism for a World of Ethnic Passions and Decaying States," *Social Research*, vol. 61, no. 3 (1994), p. 605.

[58] Indeed, much of the nationalist conflict around the world, as Will Kymlicka plausibly argues, is the result of attempts by majority nations coercively to assimilate national minorities. See Kymlicka, "Misunderstanding Nationalism," *Dissent*, Winter 1995, p. 133.

[59] For historical accounts and analyses of the decentralized provision of law and other mechanisms of conflict resolution, see Bruce L. Benson, *The Enterprise of Law: Justice without the State* (San Francisco: Pacific Research Institute for Public Policy, 1990), esp. chs. 2 and 3; and Robert C. Ellickson, *Order without Law: How Neighbors Settle Disputes* (Cambridge: Harvard University Press, 1991).

it. At its worst, the praise of political community takes the shape of nationalism. To be sure, not all defenses of political community have been assertions of bellicose nationalisms: a more modest defense of the nation-state is quite possible.[60] Moreover, to defend political community is not to make the claim of the nationalist, whose defining characteristic is the desire to see a coincidence of "nation" and political community. Nonetheless, if we acknowledge that the "nation" is itself little more than an "imagined community" (in Benedict Anderson's celebrated phrase),[61] we should recognize that to give preeminence to political community is to take a step down the nationalist path. Some nationalists want the imagined nation to become a political community; other nationalists want the political community to become a nation. Both see the members of political society as members of a deeper community; and both should be resisted.

VI. Conclusion

Yet if we accept these considerations, it will be asked, what can a political community be? If a political community is not to be viewed as the dominant community to which other forms of human association are subordinated, how is it to be understood?

The view of political community implicit in the position I have presented is not one which sees it as a "community of principle," made up of people bound by deep ties of fraternal obligation. Rather, it regards political community as another form of "partial" association. It is undoubtedly a particularly significant form of association, since it has the capacity, through the institutions of the state (which, typically, assume powers of policing, lawmaking, and warmaking, among others), to affect other communities very profoundly. But it remains a partial association nonetheless.

This outlook is most consistent with a view of political community as a product of convention. Such community is the result of accidents of history and geography which have seen the emergence of a settlement or set of compromises among people who belong to other communities or associations with varying—and often conflicting—interests. Thus, the association we call political community is essentially an association among people who do not share any significant intentional relationship. The obligations they owe the political community are, therefore, relatively weak, since they do not spring from any deep commitment to the other members which is thought (mistakenly) to be a necessary feature of this form of association. The obligations individuals owe may, in some circum-

---

[60] See David Miller, "In Defense of Nationality," *Journal of Applied Philosophy*, vol. 10, no. 1 (1993).

[61] Benedict Anderson, *Imagined Communities: Reflections on the Origin and Spread of Nationalism* (London: Verso, 1991).

stances, be *indirect* inasmuch as they emerge not out of an immediate claim the political community has upon the individual, but out of the fact that other communities to which the individual belongs are party to the convention or settlement which creates or sustains the political society.

None of this is meant to deny that people can develop strong attachments to their political communities. Indeed, it would be surprising if they did not, since governments and political elites have always found it useful to foster, encourage, and play upon such sentiments. It is, however, meant to deny that there is any firmer—or loftier—foundation for political allegiance, or for political community, than this.

Will Kymlicka has argued (in his essay in this volume) that it is important that some basis be found for the "solidarity" or the "social unity" of what he calls "multination states." It is important to identify a model of social unity that can accommodate diversity—particularly ethnic diversity. The fundamental challenge facing liberal theorists, he avers, is to identify the sources of unity in a democratic multination state. These sources, he suggests, will only be identified if we can clarify the peculiar sentiment that people must share if social unity is to be secured. One possible basis of social unity is a shared appreciation or valuing (by citizens) of "deep diversity."

According to the view defended in the present essay, however, the task of finding the basis of social unity in a political order is not so urgent, because there is no deep basis for the bonds of association to be found. And no deep basis is necessary. If we are concerned about the problem of different peoples coexisting peacefully, there is no need for them to value "deep diversity," or the particular groups and cultures with whom they share the country. It is enough simply for them not to object to coexistence. A political community need be no more than an association of people who recognize the terms of coexistence.

If this account of political community had to be labeled, it would probably be best described as a skeptical, Humean view. It recognizes that political communities exist, and that they exercise authority—indeed, assert their sovereignty—over other forms of human association; and it accepts that this form of association may be useful, if unavoidable. But it still sees political association, and thus political authority, as something which is the product of accident and which amounts to a conventional settlement which we should respect only to the extent that "innovation" threatens to produce something worse.

Politics, University of New South Wales

SOCIAL UNITY IN A LIBERAL STATE

By Will Kymlicka

Around the world, multiethnic states are in trouble. Many have proven unable to create or sustain any sense of solidarity across ethnic lines. The members of one ethnic group are unwilling to respect the rights of the members of other groups, or to make sacrifices for them, and have no trust that any sacrifice they might make will be reciprocated.

Recent events show that where this sort of solidarity and trust is lacking, the consequences can be disastrous. In some countries, the result is violent civil war, as in Rwanda, Yugoslavia, and various parts of the former Soviet Union. In other countries, the state has dissolved in a more peaceful way, as in Czechoslovakia, albeit with significant economic and psychological costs. In yet other countries, particularly in Africa, the state has stayed together, but is little more than a shell, a loose confederation of more or less hostile groups who barely tolerate, let alone cooperate with, each other.[1]

Nor is this just a problem for the Second and Third Worlds. Various multiethnic democracies in the West whose long-term stability used to be taken for granted, now seem rather more precarious. Consider recent events in Belgium and Canada. Even though they live in prosperous liberal states, with firm guarantees of their basic civil and political rights, the Flemish and Québécois may be moving down the path to independence. The problem of ethnic conflict has arisen in both capitalist and communist countries, in both democracies and military dictatorships, in both prosperous and impoverished countries.

In this essay, I will try to determine the possible basis of social unity and political stability in a liberal state that contains significant ethnic cleavages. It is vitally important to identify a model of social unity that can accommodate ethnic diversity. Indeed, I think this should be one of the first tasks of any political theory. Yet most liberal political theorists have not explicitly addressed this question; and what little they have said is manifestly inadequate. They have misconstrued both the nature of social unity, and the sorts of challenges which ethnic diversity raises— or so I will argue in this essay.

I will begin (in Section I) by exploring two patterns of ethnic diversity, patterns which have very different implications for social unity: namely, voluntary immigration by individuals and families (what I call "polyeth-

---

[1] Peter C. Ordeshook, "Some Rules of Constitutional Design," *Social Philosophy and Policy*, vol. 10, no. 2 (1993), p. 223.

© 1996 Social Philosophy and Policy Foundation. Printed in the USA.

nic" diversity), and the involuntary incorporation of previously self-governing societies (what I call "multinational" diversity). I will argue that voluntary immigration has posed few challenges to social unity (Section II), but that the existence of incorporated groups has often given rise to destabilizing conflict (Section III). The most urgent task, therefore, is to identify a secure basis for solidarity in "multination" states. I will look at some recent discussions of social unity by liberals, communitarians, and postmodernists, and argue that none provides an adequate account of the "ties that bind" in multination states (Section IV). My focus will be on social unity in liberal-democratic states, and the conclusions may or may not be applicable to other sorts of regimes.

I. Two Patterns of Ethnic Diversity

The resurgence of nationalist movements in Eastern Europe, and the stresses created by an increasingly multicultural and multiracial population in Western Europe, have made it clear that the health and stability of a multiethnic democracy depends, not only on the justice of its "basic structure," but also on the qualities and attitudes of its citizens:[2] e.g., their sense of identity, and how they view potentially competing forms of national, regional, ethnic, or religious identity; their ability to tolerate and work together with others who are different from themselves; their willingness to show self-restraint and to act from a sense of justice. Without citizens who possess these qualities, "the ability of liberal societies to function successfully progressively diminishes."[3]

Yet there is growing fear that the public-spiritedness of citizens of liberal democracies may be in serious decline. Maintaining the required level of mutual concern is a serious enough challenge in ethnically homogenous democracies (like Iceland), but is much more difficult in multiethnic countries, for differences in ethnic and national identity often form a barrier to a wider solidarity. Even where the country is not faced with secessionist movements, the lack of solidarity can lead to political paralysis which inhibits the cooperation needed to promote social justice and to secure public goods.

What then can and should be done to develop or sustain a sense of shared civic purpose and solidarity across ethnic lines? Before we can

---

[2] John Rawls says that the "basic structure" of society is the primary subject of a theory of justice. See Rawls, *A Theory of Justice* (London: Oxford University Press, 1971), p. 7; and Rawls, *Political Liberalism* (New York: Columbia University Press, 1993), pp. 257–89. There is increasing recognition, however, that the focus on institutions needs to be supplemented with a theory of citizenship, including civic virtues such as tolerance and public-spiritedness. For further references and discussion, see Will Kymlicka and W. J. Norman, "Return of the Citizen: A Survey of Recent Work on Citizenship Theory," *Ethics*, vol. 104, no. 2 (January 1994), pp. 352–81.

[3] William Galston, *Liberal Purposes: Goods, Virtues, and Duties in the Liberal State* (Cambridge: Cambridge University Press, 1991), p. 220.

answer this question, we need to clarify the idea of ethnic diversity. It is a commonplace to say that modern societies are increasingly "multicultural"; but the term "multicultural" covers many different forms of cultural pluralism, each of which raises its own challenges. I will distinguish two broad patterns of ethnic diversity — which I will call "multinational" and "polyethnic" — and will argue that the former is much more destabilizing than the latter.

One source of cultural diversity is the coexistence within a given state of more than one nation, where "nation" means a historical community, more or less institutionally complete, occupying a given territory or homeland, sharing a distinct language and culture.[4] A "nation" in this sociological sense is closely related to the idea of a "people" or a "culture" — indeed, these concepts are often defined in terms of each other. A country which contains more than one nation is, therefore, not a nation-state but a multination state, and the smaller cultures form "national minorities." The incorporation of different nations into a single state may be involuntary, as occurs when one cultural community is invaded and conquered by another, or is ceded from one imperial power to another, or when its homeland is overrun by colonizing settlers. But the formation of a multination state may also arise voluntarily, when different cultures agree to form a federation for their mutual benefit.

Many Western democracies are multinational. For example, there are a number of national minorities in the United States, including the American Indians; Alaskan Eskimos; Puerto Ricans; the descendants of Mexicans (Chicanos) living in the Southwest when the United States annexed Texas, New Mexico, and California after the Mexican War of 1846–1848; native Hawaiians; the Chamoros of Guam; and various other Pacific Islanders. These groups were all involuntarily incorporated into the United States, through conquest, colonization, or imperial cession.[5] Had a different balance of power existed, these groups might have retained or established their own sovereign governments. And talk of independence occasionally surfaces in Puerto Rico or the larger Indian tribes. However, the historical preference of these groups has not been to leave the United States, but to seek autonomy within it.

[4] By "institutionally complete," I mean containing a set of societal institutions, encompassing both public and private spheres, which provide members with meaningful ways of life across the full spectrum of human activities, including social, educational, religious, economic, and recreational life. For a fuller discussion, see my *Multicultural Citizenship: A Liberal Theory of Minority Rights* (Oxford: Oxford University Press, 1995), ch. 5.

[5] The American Indians, native Hawaiians, and Chicanos were forcibly incorporated through military conquest; the Alaskan Eskimos were incorporated when Russia sold Alaska to the United States in the Treaty of Cession of 1867; Puerto Ricans were incorporated when Puerto Rico was transferred in 1898 from Spain to the United States during the Spanish-American War; various Pacific Islanders were incorporated through colonization at the turn of the century (Guam; American Samoa), or were ceded from Japan after World War II (Micronesia Trust Territory). In none of these cases did the national minority consent to the incorporation.

As they were incorporated, most of these groups acquired a special political status. For example, Indian tribes are recognized as "domestic dependent nations" with their own governments, courts, and treaty rights; Puerto Rico is a "commonwealth"; and Guam is a "protectorate." Each of these peoples is federated to the American polity with special powers of self-government.

These groups also have rights regarding language and land use. In Guam and Hawaii, the indigenous language (Chamoro and Hawaiian) has official status (along with English) in schools, in courts, and in other dealings with government, while Spanish is the sole official language of Puerto Rico. Language rights were also guaranteed to Chicanos in the Southwest under the 1848 Treaty of Guadalupe Hidalgo, although these were abrogated as soon as anglophone settlers formed a majority of the population. Native Hawaiians, Alaskan Eskimos, and Indian tribes also have legally recognized land claims, which reserve certain lands for their exclusive use, and which provide guaranteed representation on certain regulatory bodies. In short, national minorities in the United States have a range of rights intended to reflect and protect their status as distinct cultural communities, and they have fought to retain and expand these rights.[6]

Most of these groups are relatively small and geographically isolated. Together they constitute only a fraction of the overall American population. As a result, these groups have been marginal to the self-identity of Americans; and, indeed, the very existence of national minorities, and their self-government rights, is often ignored or downplayed by American politicians and theorists.

In other countries, the existence of national minorities is more obvious. Canada's historical development has involved the federation of three distinct national groups (English, French, and Aboriginals).[7] The original

---

[6] For a survey of the rights of national minorities in the United States (and their invisibility in mainstream American constitutional and political theory), see Sharon O'Brien, "Cultural Rights in the United States: A Conflict of Values," *Law and Inequality Journal*, vol. 5 (1987), pp. 267–358; Judith Resnik, "Dependent Sovereigns: Indian Tribes, States, and the Federal Courts," *University of Chicago Law Review*, vol. 56 (1989), pp. 671–759; T. Alexander Aleinikoff, "Puerto Rico and the Constitution: Conundrums and Prospects," *Constitutional Commentary*, vol. 11, no. 1 (1994), pp. 15–43. For the issue of secession by American Indian tribes, see Erik Jensen, "American Indian Tribes and Secession," *Tulsa Law Review*, vol. 29 (1993), pp. 385–96.

[7] That these groups see themselves as nations is evident from the names they have chosen for their associations and institutions. For example, the provincial legislature in Quebec is called the "National Assembly"; the major organization of Indians is known as the "Assembly of First Nations." It is important to note that Aboriginal peoples are not a single nation. The term "Aboriginal" covers three categories of Aboriginals (Indian, Inuit, and Métis), and the term "Indian" itself is a legal fiction, behind which there are numerous distinct Aboriginal nations with their own histories and separate community identities. (The term "Métis" refers to the descendants of mixed-race marriages between white [mainly French-Canadian] fur traders and Plains Indians. They formed a powerful and cohesive community in the Prairie provinces in the nineteenth century, and have remained a distinct

incorporation of the Québécois and Aboriginal communities into the Canadian political community was involuntary. Indian homelands were overrun by French settlers, who were then conquered by the English. While the possibility of secession is very real for the Québécois, the historical preference of these groups—as with the national minorities in the United States—has not been to leave the federation, but to renegotiate the terms of federation, so as to increase their autonomy within it.

Many other Western democracies are also multinational, either because they have forcibly incorporated indigenous populations (e.g., Finland; New Zealand), or because they were formed by the more or less voluntary federation of two or more European cultures (e.g., Belgium and Switzerland). In fact, many countries throughout the world are multinational, in the sense that their boundaries were drawn to include the territory occupied by preexisting, and often previously self-governing, cultures. This is true of most countries throughout the former Communist bloc and the Third World.[8]

The second source of cultural pluralism is immigration. A country will exhibit cultural pluralism if it accepts large numbers of individuals and families from other cultures as immigrants, and allows them to maintain some of their ethnic particularity. This has always been a vital part of life in Australia, Canada, and the United States, which have the three highest per-capita rates of immigration in the world. Indeed, well over half of all legal immigration in the world goes into one of these three countries.

Aboriginal group to this day.) Aboriginals in Canada can be divided into eleven linguistic groups, descended from a number of historically and culturally distinct societies. It has been estimated that there are thirty-five to fifty distinct "peoples" in the Aboriginal population. It is also potentially misleading to describe the French Canadians as a single nation. The French-speaking majority in the province of Quebec views itself as a nation—the "Québécois." There are Francophones outside Quebec, however, and the French nation in Canada was not always identified so closely with the province of Quebec. For the change in self-identity from *canadien* to *la nation canadienne-française* to *franco-québécois* to *québécois*, see Jean Crête and Jacques Zylberberg, "Une problématique floue: L'autoreprésentation du citoyen au Québec" (A difficult transition: Citizenship identity in Quebec), in *Citoyenneté et Nationalité: Perspectives en France et au Québec* (Citizenship and nationality: Perspectives in France and Quebec), ed. Dominique Colas, Claude Emeri, and Jacques Zylberberg (Paris: Presses Universitaires de France, 1991), p. 424. The tendency of Aboriginals and the Québécois to describe themselves as "nations" is discussed in Alan Cairns, "The Fragmentation of Canadian Citizenship," in *Belonging: The Meaning and Future of Canadian Citizenship*, ed. William Kaplan (Montreal: McGill-Queen's University Press, 1993), p. 188; Paul Chartrand, "The Aboriginal Peoples in Canada and Renewal of the Federation," in *Rethinking Federalism*, ed. Karen Knop et al. (Vancouver: University of British Columbia Press, 1995); Jane Jenson, "Naming Nations: Making Nationalist Claims in Canadian Public Discourse," *Canadian Review of Sociology and Anthropology*, vol. 30, no. 3 (1993), pp. 337–58.

[8] On the Communist world, see June Dreyer, *China's Forty Millions: Minority Nationalities and National Integration in the People's Republic of China* (Cambridge: Harvard University Press, 1979); Walker Connor, *The National Question in Marxist-Leninist Theory and Strategy* (Princeton: Princeton University Press, 1984). On the Third World, see Alemante Selassie, "Ethnic Identity and Constitutional Design for Africa," *Stanford Journal of International Law*, vol. 29, no. 1 (1993), pp. 1–56; Basil Davidson, *The Black Man's Burden: Africa and the Curse of the Nation-State* (New York: Times Books, 1992).

Prior to the 1960s, immigrants to these countries were expected to shed their distinctive heritage and assimilate to existing cultural norms. This is known as the "Anglo-conformity" model of immigration. Indeed, some groups were denied entry if they were seen as unassimilable (e.g., restrictions on Chinese immigration in Canada and the United States; the "white-only" immigration policy in Australia). Assimilation was seen as essential for political stability, and was further rationalized through ethnocentric denigration of other cultures.

This shared commitment to Anglo-conformity is obscured by the popular but misleading contrast between the American "melting-pot" and the Canadian "ethnic mosaic." While "ethnic mosaic" carries the connotation of respect for the integrity of immigrant cultures, in practice it simply meant that immigrants to Canada had a choice of two dominant cultures to assimilate to. While Canada is bi-national, the "uneasy tolerance which French and English were to show towards each other was not extended to foreigners who resisted assimilation or were believed to be unassimilable."[9]

However, beginning in the 1970s, under pressure from immigrant groups, all three countries (Australia, Canada, and the U.S.) rejected the assimilationist model, and adopted a more tolerant and pluralistic policy which allows and indeed encourages immigrants to maintain various aspects of their ethnic heritage. It is now widely (though far from unanimously) accepted that immigrants should be free to maintain some of their old customs regarding food, dress, religion, and recreation, and to associate with each other to maintain these practices. This is no longer seen as unpatriotic or "un-American."[10]

---

[9] John Porter, *The Measure of Canadian Society* (Ottawa: Carleton University Press, 1987), p. 154; cf. Jeffrey Reitz and Raymond Breton, *The Illusion of Difference: Realities of Ethnicity in Canada and the United States* (Ottawa: C. D. Howe Institute, 1994). Insofar as immigrant groups seem more cohesive in Canada, this is likely due to the fact that they contain a higher proportion of recent migrants than U.S. ethnic groups, which in turn is due to Canada's higher immigration rate. In 1991, 16.1 percent of Canadian residents were foreign-born, compared to 7.9 percent of Americans; see *Statistical Abstracts of the United States: 1993* (Washington: U.S. Bureau of the Census, 1993), p. 50; Jane Badets, "Canada's Immigrants: Recent Trends," *Canadian Social Trends*, vol. 29 (Summer 1993), p. 8; cf. Leslie Laczko, "Canada's Pluralism in Comparative Perspective," *Ethnic and Racial Studies*, vol. 17, no. 1 (1994), pp. 28–29.

[10] The adoption of a more "multicultural" immigration policy was official and explicit in Canada and Australia, reflected in several pieces of legislation and government reports. In the United States, the shift in policy was more implicit, although the federal Ethnic Heritage Studies Act of 1972 is an important manifestation of this shift, as are similar programs at the state level. On the move away from Anglo-conformity and assimilation to the acceptance and affirmation of pluralism in the United States, see Nathan Glazer, *Ethnic Dilemmas 1964–1982* (Cambridge: Harvard University Press, 1983), ch. 7. On Australia, see Stephen Castles et al., *Mistaken Identity: Multiculturalism and the Demise of Nationalism in Australia* (Sydney: Pluto Press, 1988), ch. 4. On Canada, see below. Of course, the Anglo-conformity model was never fully realized in practice. Immigrant groups in all three countries often showed considerable tenacity in retaining various aspects of their ethnic heritage, and ethnic associations often flourished. Indeed, the eventual abandonment of the Anglo-conformity model stemmed as much from the growing recognition of its futility as from recognition of its unfairness.

It is important, however, to distinguish this sort of cultural diversity from that of national minorities. Immigrant groups are not "nations," and do not occupy homelands. Their distinctiveness is manifested primarily in their family lives and in voluntary associations, and is not inconsistent with their institutional integration. They still participate within the public institutions of the dominant culture(s) and speak the dominant language(s). For example, immigrants (except for the elderly) must learn English to acquire citizenship in Australia and the United States, and learning English is a mandatory part of children's education. In Canada, they must learn either of the two official languages (French or English).[11]

The commitment to ensuring a common language has been a constant feature of the history of immigration policy. Indeed, as Gerald Johnson said of the United States: "It is one of history's little ironies that no polyglot empire of the old world has dared to be so ruthless in imposing a single language upon its whole population as was the liberal republic 'dedicated to the proposition that all men are created equal.' "[12] The rejection of Anglo-conformity has not meant a slackening in this commitment to ensuring that immigrants become Anglophones, which is seen

---

[11] The recent growth in bilingual education programs for Hispanics in the United States is not an exception to this trend. These programs were primarily developed as part of a broader effort to rectify the historical injustices suffered by (nonimmigrant) Chicanos and Puerto Ricans. Some recent Hispanic immigrants from Central or South America may benefit from the existence of these programs, if they happen to reside in the same areas as Chicanos or Puerto Ricans; but this is incidental to the main aim of the programs. As a general rule, immigrants to the United States who speak Spanish are expected to integrate into the mainstream anglophone society just as much as immigrants who speak Portuguese, or Urdu, or any other language. For a careful exploration of this, see Rodolfo de la Garza and Armando Trujillo, "Latinos and the Official English Debate in the United States," in *Language and the State: The Law and Politics of Identity*, ed. David Schneiderman (Cowansville: Les Editions Yvon Blais, 1991). In any event, bilingual education, even for nonimmigrant Hispanics, is seen as supplementing, not displacing, the learning of English.

[12] Gerald Johnson, *Our English Heritage* (Westport: Greenwood Press, 1973), p. 119. As I go on to discuss, most immigrant groups did not object to the requirement that they learn English, or to the absence of government services in their mother tongue. Hence their adoption of English was not primarily the result of "ruthless imposition." There was a period between 1890 and 1920 when extreme restrictions were placed on the use of immigrant languages — e.g., legal prohibitions on the teaching of immigrant languages alongside English even in private schools; or prohibitions on speaking immigrant languages over the telephone, or in public places. However, these prohibitions were rare, and were ultimately declared unconstitutional. (See Heinz Kloss, *The American Bilingual Tradition* [Rowley: Newbury House, 1977], pp. 52, 68–74.) By contrast, attempts to impose English on national minorities were often quite ruthless, since they required the coercive disbanding of longstanding educational, political, and judicial institutions which used the minority's mother tongue. For a comprehensive review of the history of language rights in the United States, and the differential treatment of immigrants and national minorities, see Kloss, *The American Bilingual Tradition*, passim; and Edward Sagarin and Robert Kelly, "Polylingualism in the United States of America: A Multitude of Tongues amid a Monolingual Majority," in *Language Policy and National Unity*, ed. William Beer and James Jacob (Totowa, NJ: Rowman and Allanheld, 1985), pp. 21–44. For the continuing centrality of English to immigration policy, see James Tollefson, *Alien Winds: The Reeducation of America's Indochinese Refugees* (New York: Praeger, 1989), chs. 3–4.

as essential if they are to be included in the mainstream of the economic, academic, and political life of the country.

Thus, while immigrant groups have increasingly asserted their right to express their ethnic particularity, they typically wish to do so within the public institutions of the English-speaking society (or French-speaking in Canada). In rejecting assimilation, they are not asking to set up a parallel society, as is typically demanded by national minorities. The United States and Australia, therefore, have a number of "ethnic groups" as loosely aggregated subcultures within the larger English-speaking society, and so exhibit what I will call "polyethnicity." Similarly, in Canada there are ethnic subcultures within both the English- and the French-speaking societies.

It is possible, in theory, for immigrants to become national minorities, if they settle together and acquire self-governing powers. After all, this is what happened with English colonists throughout the British Empire, Spanish colonists in Puerto Rico, and French colonists in Quebec. These colonists did not see themselves as "immigrants," since they had no expectation of integrating into another culture, but rather aimed to reproduce their original society in a new land. It is an essential feature of colonization, as distinct from individual immigration, that it aims to create an institutionally complete society, rather than integrating into an existing one. It would, in principle, be possible to allow or encourage immigrants today to view themselves as colonists, if they had extensive government support in terms of settlement, language rights, and the creation of new political units. But immigrants have not asked for or received such support. (Whether this is fair or not is a separate question, which I have discussed elsewhere.)[13]

There is a widespread perception that this polyethnic model no longer applies to Hispanic immigrants to the United States. These immigrants are said to be uninterested in learning English, or in integrating into the anglophone society. This is a mistaken perception, which arises because people treat Hispanics as a single category, and thus confuse the demands of Spanish-speaking national minorities (Puerto Ricans and Chicanos) with those of Spanish-speaking immigrants recently arrived from Latin America. If we look at Hispanic immigrants who come to the U.S. with the intention to stay and become citizens, the evidence suggests that they, as much as any other immigrants, are committed to learning English and participating in the mainstream society. Indeed, among Latino immigrants, "assimilation to the English group occurs more rapidly now than it did one hundred years ago."[14] (Obviously, this does

---

[13] See my *Multicultural Citizenship*, ch. 6.

[14] M. Combs and L. Lynch, quoted in de la Garza and Trujillo, "Latinos and the Official English Debate," p. 215. Cf. Linda Chavez, *Out of the Barrio: Toward a New Politics of Hispanic Assimilation* (New York: Basic Books, 1991), p. 42. Hispanic immigrant groups have expressed an interest in bilingual education, but they view Spanish-language education as supplementing, not displacing, the learning of English. This is unlike Spanish-language education in

not apply to those who have no expectation of staying—e.g., Cuban refugees in the 1960s, and illegal Mexican migrant workers today.)

Immigration is not only a "New World" phenomenon. Many other countries also accept immigrants, although not in the same magnitude as the United States, Canada, and Australia. Since World War II, Britain and France have accepted immigrants from their former colonies. Other countries which accept few immigrants nonetheless accept refugees from throughout the world (e.g., Sweden). In yet other countries, "guest workers" who were originally seen as only temporary residents have become de facto immigrants. For example, Turkish guest workers in Germany have become permanent residents, with their families, and Germany is often the only home known to their children (and now grandchildren). All these countries are exhibiting increasing polyethnicity.[15]

Obviously, a single country may be both multinational (as a result of the colonizing, conquest, or confederation of national communities) and polyethnic (as a result of individual and familial immigration). Indeed, all of these patterns are present in Canada—the Indians were overrun by French settlers; the French were conquered by the English, although the current relationship between the two can be seen as a voluntary federation; and both the English and the French have accepted immigrants who are allowed to maintain their ethnic identity. Thus, Canada is both multinational and polyethnic, as is the United States.

Those labels are less popular than the term "multicultural"; but that term can be confusing, precisely because it is ambiguous between multinational and polyethnic. This ambiguity has led to unwarranted criticisms of the Canadian government's "multiculturalism" policy, which is the term the government uses for its post-1970 policy of promoting polyethnicity rather than assimilation for immigrants. Some French Canadians have opposed the "multiculturalism" policy because they think it reduces their claims of nationhood to the level of immigrant ethnicity.[16] Other

---

Puerto Rico, in which Spanish is the dominant language; and indeed 60 percent of Puerto Ricans do not speak English.

[15] This has led to a growing debate in Europe about the nature of citizenship and its relationship with nationality (understood as membership in the national culture). On England, see Bhikhu Parekh, "British Citizenship and Cultural Difference," in *Citizenship*, ed. Geoff Andrews (London: Lawrence and Wishart, 1991), pp. 183–204; on France, see Colas et al., *Citoyenneté et Nationalité (supra* note 7); on Europe generally, see W. R. Brubaker, *Immigration and the Politics of Citizenship in Europe and North America* (Lanham: University Press of America, 1989).

[16] As René Lévesque, former premier of Quebec, put it, multiculturalism "is a 'Red Herring'. The notion was devised to obscure 'the Quebec business', to give an impression that we are all ethnics and do not have to worry about special status for Quebec" (quoted in Seymour Wilson, "The Tapestry Vision of Canadian Multiculturalism," *Canadian Journal of Political Science*, vol. 26, no. 4 [1993], p. 656 n. 33). Similar concerns have been raised by the Maori in New Zealand—i.e., that the rhetoric of "multiculturalism" is a way of denying their national claims, by lumping them in with the polyethnic claims of non-British immigrants; see Andrew Sharp, *Justice and the Maori: Maori Claims in New Zealand Political Argument in the 1980s* (Auckland: Oxford University Press, 1990), p. 228.

people have had the opposite fear: that the policy was intended to treat immigrant groups as nations, and hence support the development of institutionally complete cultures alongside the French and the English. In fact, neither fear is justified, since "multiculturalism" is a policy of supporting polyethnicity within the national institutions of the English and French cultures.[17] Since the term "multicultural" invites this sort of confusion, I will use the terms "multinational" and "polyethnic" to refer to the two main forms of cultural pluralism.

It is important to note that "nations," whether they be the majority national group or a national minority, are not defined by race or descent. This is obvious in the case of the majority anglophone society in both the United States and Canada. In both countries, there have been high rates of immigration for over 150 years, first from Northern Europe, then from Southern and Eastern Europe, and now mostly from Asia and Africa. As a result, anglophone Americans or Canadians who are of solely Anglo-Saxon descent are a (constantly shrinking) minority.[18]

Similarly, national minorities are increasingly multiethnic and multiracial. For example, while the level of immigration into French Canada was low for many years, it is now almost as high as the level in English Canada or the United States, and Quebec actively seeks francophone immigrants from West Africa and the Caribbean. There have also been high rates of intermarriage between the indigenous peoples of North America and the English, French, and Spanish populations. As a result, all of these national minorities are racially and ethnically mixed. The number of French Canadians who are of solely Gallic descent, or American Indians who are of solely Indian descent, is also constantly shrinking, and will ultimately become a minority in each case. In talking about national minorities, therefore, I am not talking about racial or descent groups, but about cultural groups.[19]

Immigration and the incorporation of national minorities are the two most common sources of cultural diversity in modern states. These two broad categories are applicable to most countries, and most ethnocultural

---

[17] Jean Burnet, "Multiculturalism, Immigration, and Racism," *Canadian Ethnic Studies*, vol. 7, no. 1 (1975), p. 36.

[18] Indeed, the terms "anglophone" and "francophone" were adopted in the 1960s precisely because language-group membership was no longer synonymous with ethnic origin. "English Canadian" and "French Canadian" were traditionally used to refer to those of Anglo-Saxon or Gallic ethnic origin, and hence another term was needed to describe the (multiethnic) members of the English-speaking and French-speaking societies in Canada. On the increasing disjunction between ethnic origin and language group membership, see Laczko, "Canada's Pluralism in Comparative Perspective" (*supra* note 9), p. 29.

[19] Some national groups employ a descent-based definition of membership – e.g., Germany, or the Afrikaners. This used to be true of French Canada as well, and 20 percent of Québécois still hold that immigrants cannot call themselves Québécois (Crête and Zylberberg, "Une problématique floue" [*supra* note 7], pp. 425–30). However, the majority of Quebecers, as with most other national groups in the West, define membership in terms of participation in a societal culture, not in terms of descent.

groups can be located within one or the other of these camps; but of course not all ethnocultural groups fit neatly into them. In particular, the situation of African Americans is quite distinct. They do not fit the voluntary-immigrant pattern, not only because most were brought to America involuntarily as slaves, but also because when they arrived they were prevented from integrating (rather than encouraged to integrate) into the institutions of the majority culture (e.g., through racial segregation, and laws against miscegenation and the teaching of literacy).[20] Nor do they fit the national-minority pattern, since they do not have a homeland in America or a common historical language. They came from a variety of African cultures, with different languages, and no attempt was made to keep together those with a common ethnic background. On the contrary, people from the same culture (even from the same family) were often split up once they arrived in America. And even if they shared the same African language, slaves were forbidden to speak it, since slave-owners feared that such speech could be used to foment rebellion.[21] Moreover, before emancipation, they were legally prohibited from trying to recreate their own culture (e.g., all forms of black association, except churches, were illegal).

The historical situation of African Americans, therefore, is very unusual. They were not allowed to integrate into the mainstream culture; nor were they allowed to maintain their earlier languages and cultures, or to create new cultural associations and institutions. They did not have their own homeland or territory, yet they were physically segregated. Thus, we should not expect policies which are appropriate for either voluntary immigrants or national minorities to be appropriate for African Americans, or vice versa. On the contrary, it would be quite surprising if the same measures were appropriate for all these contexts. Yet a surprising number of postwar American legal and political theorists have made this assumption.[22]

II. Social Unity in a Polyethnic State

Given the profound differences between immigrant groups and national minorities, it is unhelpful to talk in general terms about the impact of ethnic diversity on social unity. We need to specify what sort of group we have in mind. In this section, I will discuss the status of immigrant groups; in Section III, I will turn to national minorities.

---

[20] These restrictions on integration applied most clearly during the period before the Civil War, although legally mandated segregation continued in the South until the 1960s, and of course de facto segregation had a much wider scope.

[21] Sagarin and Kelly, "Polylingualism in the United States" (*supra* note 12), pp. 26–27.

[22] See, for example, Michael Walzer, "Pluralism in Political Perspective," in *The Politics of Ethnicity*, ed. Michael Walzer (Cambridge: Harvard University Press, 1982), p. 27. For other examples, see my *Multicultural Citizenship*, chs. 2 and 4.

Most countries throughout history have contained immigrants, but the United States was the first truly "immigrant country." The idea of building and populating a country through polyethnic immigration was quite unique in history, and many people thought it untenable. There were no historical precedents to show that an ethnically mixed country of immigrants would be stable. What would bind people together when they came from such different backgrounds—including every conceivable race, religion, and language group—sharing virtually nothing in common?

The answer, of course, was that immigrants would have to integrate into the existing anglophone society, rather than forming separate and distinct nations with their own homelands inside the United States. There was no hope for the long-term survival of the country if the Germans, Swedes, Dutch, Greeks, Italians, Poles, and so on each viewed themselves as separate and self-governing peoples, rather than as members of a single (polyethnic) American people. As John Higham puts it, the English settlers conceived of themselves as "the formative population" of the American colonies/states, and "theirs was the polity, the language, the pattern of work and settlements, and many of the mental habits to which the immigrants would have to adjust."[23]

Immigrants would not only have the right to integrate into the mainstream anglophone society (and thus would be protected against discrimination and prejudice); they also had the obligation to integrate (and thus they would be required to learn English in schools, and English would be the language of public life). The commitment to integrating immigrants was not just evidence of intolerance or ethnocentrism on the part of WASPs (although it was that in part), it was also an understandable response to the uncertainty about whether a country built through polyethnic immigration would be viable.

It was fundamental, then, that immigrants view themselves as ethnic subgroups within the larger nation, not as national minorities. And immigrants have generally accepted this arrangement. After all, immigrants come voluntarily (if they are not refugees), knowing that integration is expected of them. When they choose to leave their culture and come to America, they voluntarily relinquish their original cultural membership, and the rights which go with it. Uprooting oneself from one's family and place of birth is painful, and immigrants know that this decision will only be worthwhile if they make an effort to integrate into their new society. As Nathan Glazer puts it, immigrants

> had come to this country not to maintain a foreign language and culture but with the intention . . . to become Americanized as fast as

---

[23] John Higham, *Send These to Me* (New York: Atheneum, 1976), p. 6; cf. Stephen Steinberg, *The Ethnic Myth: Race, Ethnicity, and Class in America* (New York: Atheneum, 1981), p. 7.

possible, and this meant English language and American culture. They sought the induction to a new language and culture that the public schools provided—as do many present-day immigrants, too—and while they often found, as time went on, that they regretted what they and their children had lost, this was *their* choice, rather than an imposed choice.[24]

Similarly, Michael Walzer notes that because the immigrants "had come voluntarily" to America, the "call for self-determination" had no basis here. Nor was there any basis or reason for rejecting English as the public language.[25]

Both Glazer and Walzer emphasize that this process of integrating voluntary immigrants differs from the assimilation of conquered or colonized national minorities, where "intact and rooted communities" that "were established on lands they had occupied for many centuries" are deprived of mother-tongue education or local autonomy. Under these conditions, integration is an "imposed choice" which national minorities typically have resisted. The integration of immigrants, by contrast,

was aimed at peoples far more susceptible to cultural change, for they were not only uprooted; they had uprooted themselves. Whatever the pressures that had driven them to the New World, they had chosen to come, while others like themselves, in their own families, had chosen to remain.[26]

Some commentators think that the so-called "ethnic revival" in the 1970s began to challenge this traditional model. According to Glazer, some immigrant associations in the United States have adopted the language and attitudes of colonized "nations" or "peoples." They have labeled social pressures for integration as "oppression," and demanded their right to "self-determination," including state recognition of their mother tongue and state support for separate ethnic institutions.[27]

This idea that immigrant groups are looking to establish themselves as national minorities is, I believe, a complete misreading of the "ethnic revival" in the United States (or in Canada and Australia, which have exhibited similar "revivals"). The ethnic revival has not been a repudia-

---

[24] Glazer, *Ethnic Dilemmas* (*supra* note 10), p. 149.

[25] Walzer, "Pluralism in Political Perspective," pp. 6–7, 10.

[26] *Ibid.*, p. 9; cf. Glazer, *Ethnic Dilemmas*, pp. 227, 283.

[27] According to Glazer, the sense of being a colonized people with a right to self-government, which began with black and Puerto Rican nationalists, "spread rapidly to other groups," including various immigrant groups. He does not give any evidence or examples of this spread, other than the demand for publicly funded ethnic studies programs by "Italian, Jewish, Polish and other groups" (Glazer, *Ethnic Dilemmas*, pp. 110–11). As I go on to discuss, I do not think that the demand for such programs by immigrant groups can plausibly be seen as reflecting a desire to be treated as national minorities.

tion of integration into the mainstream society. Even the most politicized immigrant groups have not been interested in reconstituting themselves as distinct societies or self-governing nations alongside the mainstream society. On the contrary, the ethnic revival has essentially been a matter of self-identity and self-expression, disconnected from claims for the revival or creation of a separate institutional life. People want to identify themselves in public as members of an immigrant group, and to see others with the same identity in prominent positions of respect or authority (e.g., in politics and the media, or in textbooks and government documents). They are demanding increased recognition and visibility within the mainstream society.[28] The ethnic revival, in other words, involves a revision in the terms of integration, not a rejection of integration.

Immigrant groups are becoming more politicized, but their increasing demands provide evidence of how much they want to participate within the mainstream of society. Consider the case of Sikhs who wanted to join the Royal Canadian Mounted Police, but, because of their religious requirement to wear turbans, could not do so unless they were exempted from the usual requirements regarding ceremonial headgear. Or consider the case of Orthodox Jews who wanted to join the U.S. military, but who needed an exemption from the usual regulations so they could wear their yarmulkes. Such exemptions are opposed by many people, who view them as a sign of disrespect for one of our "national symbols." But the fact that these men wanted to be a part of the national police force or the national military is ample evidence of their desire to participate in and contribute to the larger community. The special right they were requesting should be seen as promoting, not discouraging, their integration.

The same is true about the other sorts of demands made by immigrant groups—e.g., affirmative-action programs, or changes to the curricula of public schools so as to recognize their distinctive contributions to society, or exemptions from Sunday-closing legislation.[29] Whatever one thinks of

[28] Herbert Gans calls this "symbolic ethnicity," to emphasize that it lacks any real institutionalized corporate existence. The ethnic revival aimed to make the possession of an ethnic identity an acceptable and normal part of life in mainstream society. In this respect, it was strikingly successful, which helps explain why the "revival" lost its political urgency. For helpful discussions of the ethnic revival, see Herbert Gans, "Symbolic Ethnicity: The Future of Ethnic Groups and Cultures in America," *Ethnic and Racial Studies*, vol. 2, no. 1 (1979), pp. 1–20; Joshua Fishman, "The Rise and Fall of the American Ethnic Revival," in Fishman, *Language and Ethnicity in Minority Sociolinguistic Perspective* (Clevedon: Multilingual Matters, 1989), pp. 666–68, 678–80; and Steinberg, *The Ethnic Myth*, pp. 58, 74.

[29] Affirmative-action programs for ethnocultural groups have typically been aimed at helping nonimmigrant groups which have been subject to widespread historical discrimination (e.g., American Indians, Chicanos, and African Americans in the United States; Aboriginal peoples in Canada). But they may also cover certain immigrant groups, if these groups are seen as facing particularly severe disadvantages in society (e.g., Jamaicans in Canada), or if their status is seen as inextricably intertwined with the primary (nonimmigrant) beneficiaries (e.g., non-Chicano Hispanics in the United States). Sunday-closing laws have not been an issue in the United States for many years, but they remain a source of controversy in Canada and Britain.

the justice of these demands, none of them reflects a desire to be treated as a separate and self-governing national minority. Rather, they aim to reform mainstream institutions so as to make immigrant groups feel more at home within them.

Some people fear that these measures impede the integration of immigrants by creating a confusing halfway house between their old nations and their citizenship in the new one, reminding immigrants "of their different origins rather than their shared symbols, society and future."[30] These worries seem empirically unfounded, however. The experience to date suggests that first- and second-generation immigrants who remain proud of their heritage are also among the most patriotic citizens of their new countries.[31] Moreover, their strong affiliation with their new country seems to be based in large part on its willingness not just to tolerate, but to welcome, cultural difference.

Indeed, there is strikingly little evidence that voluntary immigrants pose any sort of threat to the unity or stability of a country. This fear was understandable 150 years ago, when the United States, Canada, and Australia began accepting waves of non-English immigrants; but that was 150 years ago, and there is no longer any reason for such fears to persist. It has become clear that the overwhelming majority of immigrants want to integrate, and have in fact integrated, even during the periods of large-scale influxes. Moreover, they care deeply about the unity of their new country. To be sure, they want the mainstream institutions in their society to be reformed, so as to accommodate their cultural differences, and to recognize the value of their cultural heritage. But the desire for such measures is a desire for inclusion which is consistent with participation in, and commitment to, the mainstream institutions that underlie social unity.

Indeed, immigrant groups are often particularly concerned with clarifying the basis of national unity. As Tariq Modood notes,

> the greatest psychological and political need for clarity about a common framework and national symbols comes from the minorities. For clarity about what makes us willingly bound into a single country relieves the pressure on minorities, especially new minorities whose presence within the country is not fully accepted, to have to conform in all areas of social life, or in arbitrarily chosen areas, in order to rebut the charge of disloyalty.[32]

[30] Citizens' Forum on Canada's Future, *Report to the People and Government of Canada* (Ottawa: Supply and Services, 1991), p. 128.

[31] See John Harles, *Politics in the Lifeboat: Immigrants and the American Democratic Order* (Boulder: Westview Press, 1993); and Reginald Whitaker, *A Sovereign Idea: Essays on Canada as a Democratic Community* (Montreal: McGill-Queen's University Press, 1992), p. 255.

[32] Tariq Modood, "Establishment, Multiculturalism, and British Citizenship," *Political Quarterly*, vol. 65, no. 1 (1994), p. 64.

Why have so many commentators seen the increasing assertiveness of immigrant groups as destabilizing? In part, it is prejudice against new immigrants, most of whom are nonwhite and non-Christian. Moreover, it is likely that worries about the volatile relations between entrenched and long-standing national or racial groups get displaced onto newer immigrants. For example, in the Canadian case, it is easier to blame "the diversity associated with multiculturalism . . . for disunity" than to confront the self-government demands of the Québécois or Aboriginals.[33] Similarly, I think that fears about the relations between whites and blacks in the United States are often displaced onto the "ethnic revival." In each case, the modest demands of immigrants provide an easier target than the demands of larger and more settled minorities, even though the former, in fact, pose little threat to the unity or stability of the country.

III. Social Unity in a Multination State

While immigrants rarely pose a threat to political stability, national minorities are very different. When immigrants demand special political recognition, they generally take the authority of the larger political community for granted. They assume, as John Rawls puts it, that citizens are members of "one cooperative scheme in perpetuity."[34] Immigrants assume that they will work within the economic and political institutions of the larger society, demanding only that these institutions be adapted to reflect the increasing cultural diversity of the population they serve.

In the case of national minorities, however, the larger political community has a more conditional existence. In most multination states, the component nations demand some form of political autonomy or territorial jurisdiction, so as to ensure the full and free development of their cultures and the best interests of their people. At the extreme, nations may wish to secede, if they think their self-determination is impossible within the larger state. Indeed, all of the examples of violent ethnic conflict and secession that I gave at the beginning of the essay involve national minorities.

The right of national groups to self-determination is given limited recognition in international law. According to the United Nations Charter, "all peoples have the right to self-determination." However, the U.N. has not defined "peoples," and it has generally applied the principle of self-determination only to overseas colonies, not internal national minorities, even when the latter were subject to the same sort of colonization and

---

[33] Yasmeen Abu-Laban and Daiva Stasiulis, "Ethnic Pluralism under Siege: Popular and Partisan Opposition to Multiculturalism," *Canadian Public Policy*, vol. 18, no. 4 (1992), p. 378.

[34] John Rawls, "Justice as Fairness: A Briefer Restatement," unpublished manuscript, 1990, quoted in Allen Buchanan, *Secession: The Morality of Political Divorce from Fort Sumter to Lithuania and Quebec* (Boulder: Westview Press, 1991), p. 5.

conquest as the former. This limitation on self-determination to overseas colonies (known as the "salt-water thesis") is widely seen as arbitrary, and many national minorities insist that they too are "peoples" or "nations," and, as such, have the right of self-determination. They demand certain powers of self-government which they say were not relinquished by their often involuntary incorporation into a larger state.[35]

In short, national minorities claim that they are distinct "peoples," with inherent rights of self-government. While they are currently part of a larger country, this is not seen as a renunciation of their original right of self-government. Rather, it is seen as a matter of transferring some aspects of their powers of self-government to the larger polity, on the condition that other powers remain in their own hands. In cases where the process of incorporation was negotiated and consensual, this condition may in fact be explicitly spelled out in the constitutional agreements which specify the terms of federation.[36] Where the process of incorporation was coercively imposed, the implicit or explicit recognition of this condition may be needed if national minorities are to accept the legitimacy of their incorporation. In this sense, the authority of the larger political community is derivative. In countries that are formed from the federation of two or more nations, the authority of the central government is limited to the powers which each constituent nation agreed to transfer to it. And these national groups see themselves as having the right to take back these powers, and withdraw from the federation, if they feel threatened by the larger community.

In other words, the basic claim underlying self-government rights is not simply that some groups are disadvantaged within the political community, or that the political community is culturally diverse. Instead, the claim is that there is more than one political community, and that the authority of the larger state cannot be assumed to take precedence over the authority of the constituent national communities. If democracy is the rule of "the people," national minorities claim that there is more than one people, each with the right to self-rule.

---

[35] Some indigenous peoples have argued before the U.N. that they too have a right to self-determination under the U.N. Charter (see *Mikmaq Tribal Society v. Canada* [1984] U.N. Doc E/CN.4/Sub.2/204). For discussions of the "salt-water thesis," and the right of self-determination under international law, see Michla Pomerance, *Self-Determination in Law and Practice: The New Doctrine in the United Nations* (The Hague: Martinus Nijhoff Publishers, 1982); Patrick Thornberry, *International Law and the Rights of Minorities* (Oxford: Oxford University Press, 1991), pp. 13–21, 214–18; and James Crawford, ed., *The Rights of Peoples* (Oxford: Oxford University Press, 1988).

[36] This is evident, for example, in the 1867 Confederation agreement which specified the terms under which French Canadians agreed to form part of the new country of Canada, or in the 1870 Manitoba Act, which specified the terms under which the Métis agreed to join Canada. Other examples would include the 1840 Treaty of Waitangi, which specified the terms under which the Maori would accept British rule in New Zealand. For further discussion of these examples, and the theoretical issues such agreements raise, see my *Multicultural Citizenship*, ch. 6.

Self-government rights, therefore, divide the people into separate "peoples," each with its own historic rights, territories, and powers of self-government; and each, therefore, with its own political community.[37] The members of each "people" may view their own political community as primary, and the value and authority of the larger federation as derivative.[38]

The threat to social unity from self-government rights is obvious. If citizenship is membership in a political community, then in creating overlapping political communities, self-government rights necessarily give rise to a sort of dual citizenship, and to potential conflicts about which political community citizens identify with most deeply. Moreover, there seems to be no natural stopping-point to the demands for increasing self-government. If limited autonomy is granted to a national minority, this may simply fuel the ambitions of nationalist leaders, who may be satisfied with nothing short of their own nation-state.

Democratic multination states which recognize self-government rights are, it appears, inherently unstable for this reason. At best they seem to be a *modus vivendi* between separate communities, with no intrinsic bond that would lead the members of one national group to make sacrifices for the members of others. Yet, as I noted earlier, liberal democracy requires this sense of common purpose and solidarity within the country.

It might seem tempting, therefore, to ignore the demands of national minorities, avoid any reference to such groups in a country's constitution, and insist that citizenship is a common identity shared by all individuals, without regard to group membership. This is often described as the American strategy for dealing with cultural pluralism.

In fact, however, the Americans have only applied this strategy in the context of integrating voluntary immigrants, who arrived in America as individuals or families (and, more recently, in the context of integrating the descendants of slaves). Generally speaking, a different strategy has been applied in the context of incorporating historically self-governing groups whose homelands have become part of the larger community, such as the American Indians, Alaskan Eskimos, Puerto Ricans, and Native Hawaiians. Most of these national minorities are accorded some

---

[37] For example, Canada has formed a single sovereign country since it broke its colonial ties with Britain, but in important respects it has never formed a single sovereign people. As Peter Russell puts it, "not all Canadians have consented to form a single people in which a majority or some special majority have, to use John Locke's phrase 'a right to act and conclude the rest'. In this sense Canadians have not yet constituted themselves a sovereign people" (Peter Russell, "Can the Canadians Be a Sovereign People?" *Canadian Journal of Political Science*, vol. 24, no. 4 [1991], p. 692, quoting Locke's *Second Treatise of Government*).

[38] This political community may be directly or indirectly controlled by the national minority, depending on how its boundaries are drawn. The Puerto Ricans and Québécois indirectly form political communities, by forming the majority within one of the territorial units of the federal system. Most Indian bands/tribes, however, directly form a political community, tied to the system of Indian reserves/reservations.

level of self-government within the American federation. And where the common-citizenship strategy has been applied to national minorities, it has often been a spectacular failure. For example, the policy of pressuring American Indian tribes to relinquish their distinct political status, known as the "termination policy," had disastrous consequences, and was withdrawn in the 1950s.[39]

Indeed, there are very few democratic multination states that follow the strict common-citizenship strategy. This is not surprising, because refusing demands for self-government rights will simply aggravate alienation among national minorities, and increase the desire for secession. What is called "common citizenship" in a multination state usually involves supporting the culture of the majority nation—e.g., its language becomes the official language of the schools, courts, and legislatures; its holidays become public holidays. Moreover, a regime of common citizenship means that the minority has no way to limit its vulnerability to the economic and political decisions of the majority, since the boundaries and powers of internal political units are usually defined to suit the administrative convenience of the majority, not the self-government claims of the minority.[40]

It is not surprising, then, that national minorities have resisted attempts to impose common citizenship on them. Rawls suggests that common citizenship promotes the political virtues of "reasonableness and a sense of fairness, a spirit of compromise and a readiness to meet others halfway."[41] But attempts to impose common citizenship in multination states may in fact threaten these virtues.

In the Ottoman Empire, for example, compromise between groups was traditionally ensured by the system of self-government for each major religious group. The Ottomans allowed Christian and Jewish minorities not only the freedom to practice their religion, but a more general freedom to govern themselves in purely internal matters, with their own legal codes and courts. For about five centuries, between 1456 and the collapse of the empire in World War I, three non-Muslim minorities had official recognition as self-governing communities (or "millets")—the Greek Orthodox, the Armenian Orthodox, and the Jews—each of which was

---

[39] The termination policy rendered Indian tribes much more vulnerable to the greater economic and political power of the larger society, and quickly resulted in the loss of Indian lands, and the breakdown of Indian communities. For discussion, see Rachel Kronowitz et al., "Toward Consent and Cooperation: Reconsidering the Political Status of Indian Nations," *Harvard Civil Rights–Civil Liberties Law Review*, vol. 22 (1987), pp. 533–34.

[40] This is true of the United States, where a conscious decision was made to draw state boundaries, and/or to delay the granting of statehood, so as to ensure that national minorities would not form a majority in any state. See Kloss, *The American Bilingual Tradition* (*supra* note 12), pp. 128–29, 205–7, 291. I discuss this in more detail in *Multicultural Citizenship*, chs. 2 and 6.

[41] John Rawls, "The Idea of an Overlapping Consensus," *Oxford Journal of Legal Studies*, vol. 7, no. 1 (1987), p. 21.

further subdivided into various local administrative units, usually based on ethnicity and language. The legal traditions and practices of each religious group, particularly in matters of family status, were respected and enforced throughout the empire. In the mid-eighteenth century, however, the Ottomans stripped the millets of most of their self-governing power, and tried to promote a common-citizenship status that cut across religious and ethnic boundaries, so that everyone's political rights and identity were based on a common relationship to the Ottoman state, rather than membership in a particular millet. As Kemal Karpat notes, the result was disastrous; for once the self-governing status of the millets ended,

> the relative position of the religious and ethnic groups in the Ottoman Empire toward each other began to be decided on the basis of their numerical strength. Hence they were transformed into minorities and majorities. It was obvious that sooner or later the views of the majority would prevail and its cultural characteristics and aspirations would become the features of the government itself.[42]

A similar process occurred when indigenous peoples in North America were accorded citizenship (often against their will), and thus became a numerical minority within the larger body of citizens, rather than a separate, self-governing people. Rawls suggests that a strong sense of common citizenship is needed to deal with the danger that majorities will treat minorities unfairly. But common citizenship in a multination state helps create that danger in the first place, by transforming self-governing groups into numerical majorities and minorities.

The historical evidence suggests that rejecting self-government demands in the name of common citizenship simply promotes alienation and secessionist movements. Indeed, recent surveys of ethnonationalist conflict around the world show clearly that self-government arrangements diminish the likelihood of violent conflict, while refusing or rescinding self-government rights is likely to escalate the level of conflict.[43]

Yet, as we saw earlier, accepting self-government demands is likely to lead to a desire for ever-increasing autonomy, even independence. Providing local autonomy reduces the likelihood of violent conflict, yet the resulting arrangements are rarely examples of harmonious cooperation

---

[42] Kemal Karpat, "Millets and Nationality: The Roots of the Incongruity of Nation and State in the Post-Ottoman Era," in *Christians and Jews in the Ottoman Empire: The Functioning of a Plural Society*, ed. Benjamin Braude and Bernard Lewis (New York: Holmes and Meier, 1982), p. 163. I discuss the millet system in more depth in my essay "Two Models of Pluralism and Tolerance," *Analyse & Kritik*, vol. 14, no. 1 (1992), pp. 33–56; reprinted in *Toleration*, ed. David Heyd (Princeton: Princeton University Press, 1995).

[43] Ted Gurr, *Minorities at Risk: A Global View of Ethnopolitical Conflict* (Washington: Institute of Peace Press, 1993); Hurst Hannum, *Autonomy, Sovereignty, and Self-Determination: The Accommodation of Conflicting Rights* (Philadelphia: University of Pennsylvania Press, 1990).

between national groups. They often become "mere treaties of cooperation," in which quarrelsome groups "agree to cooperate only on a limited
set of issues, if they can cooperate at all."[44] The sense of solidarity
needed to promote the public good and to tackle urgent issues of justice
is lacking. This seems increasingly true, for example, in Belgium and
Canada.

We seem caught in a Gordian knot. Given this dynamic, some commentators conclude that the only solution to the problem of multination
states is secession. According to David Miller, where national identities
"already have become so strong that what we have is really two separate
nationalities living side by side . . . the best outcome is ultimately likely
to be the secession of one community."[45] Similarly, Walzer argues that
"[i]f the community is so radically divided that a single citizenship is
impossible, then its territory too must be divided."[46]

This recalls John Stuart Mill's famous claim that free institutions are
"next to impossible" in a multination state:

> Among a people without fellow-feelings, especially if they read and
> speak different languages, the united public opinion necessary to
> the workings of representative institutions cannot exist. . . . [It] is
> in general a necessary condition of free institutions that the bound-
> aries of governments should coincide in the main with those of
> nationalities.[47]

For Mill, democracy is government "by the people," but self-rule is only
possible if "the people" are "a people"—a nation. The members of a
democracy must share a sense of political allegiance, and common nationality is a precondition of that allegiance. Similarly, T. H. Green argued
that liberal democracy is only possible if people feel bound to the state by
"ties derived from a common dwelling place with its associations, from
common memories, traditions and customs, and from the common ways
of feeling and thinking which a common language and still more a common literature embodies."[48] According to this stream of liberal thought,
since a free state must be a nation-state, with a single national culture, it
follows that if national minorities are unwilling to assimilate, they must
secede and establish their own state.

[44] Ordeshook, "Some Rules of Constitutional Design," p. 223.

[45] David Miller, *Market, State, and Community: The Foundations of Market Socialism* (Oxford:
Oxford University Press, 1989), p. 288.

[46] Michael Walzer, *Spheres of Justice: A Defence of Pluralism and Equality* (Oxford: Blackwell,
1983), p. 62.

[47] John Stuart Mill, *Considerations on Representative Government*, in Mill, *Utilitarianism, Liberty, Representative Government* (London: J. M. Dent, 1972), pp. 230, 233.

[48] T. H. Green, *Lectures on the Principles of Political Obligation* (London: Longman's, 1941),
pp. 130–31. I explore how national minorities have been viewed throughout the liberal tradition in *Multicultural Citizenship*, ch. 3.

Perhaps we should be more willing to consider secession. We tend to assume that secession is a moral and political catastrophe, but I suspect that few people today condemn the secession of Norway from Sweden in 1905. In the Norwegian case, the process of secession was (relatively) peaceful, and the result was two healthy liberal democracies where there used to be one. There is good reason to think that any future secession of Quebec from the rest of Canada would be similar. It is difficult to see why liberals should automatically oppose such peaceful, liberal secessions. After all, liberalism is fundamentally concerned, not with the fate of states, but with the freedom and well-being of individuals; and secession need not harm those goals, particularly if the alternative is political paralysis, where national groups are unable to cooperate.

However, secession is not always possible or desirable. Some national minorities, particularly indigenous peoples, would have trouble forming viable independent states. In other cases, competing claims over land and resources would make peaceful secession virtually impossible (particularly if it creates irredentist minorities).[49] In general, there are more nations in the world than possible states, so we need to find some way to keep multination states together.

Some people might think that I have created a false problem. So far in this essay, I have simply taken as a given the existence of national minorities with a strong desire for cultural self-preservation and political self-government, and then asked how best to accommodate this desire. But national identity, one might say, is not a brute fact. Rather, it is a social construction, and what can be socially constructed can surely be deconstructed. If minorities view themselves as distinct nations or peoples, then perhaps the state should try to modify that national consciousness, so as to reduce or remove the minority's desire to form a distinct national society.

This option is endorsed by David Miller, who says that we should not "regard cultural identities as given, or at least as created externally to the political system," but rather should have "a stronger sense of the malleability of such identities, that is, the extent to which they can be created or modified consciously." Since "subcultures threaten to undermine the overarching sense of identity" needed for a generous welfare state, the state should promote "a common identity as citizens that is stronger than their separate identities as members of ethnic or other sectional groups."[50]

---

[49] For a comprehensive review of the moral issues raised by secession, see Buchanan, *Secession* (*supra* note 34). The breakup of Czechoslovakia is another example of peaceful secession, although it is too early to tell how healthy the resulting democracies will be. There is a significant threat of violence in the former Czechoslovakia, not between the Czechs and the Slovaks, but between the Slovaks and Hungary over the Hungarian minority in Slovakia. The potential for violence is always dramatically increased when there are irredentist minorities.

[50] Miller, *Market, State, and Community*, pp. 237, 279, 286–87.

This idea is echoed by many postmodernists, who look at the way that nationalist leaders are able to whip up a mythical conception of national identity, and conclude that it is relatively easy to "construct" cultural identities. If one set of political leaders can construct a mythical nationalist identity, postmodernists argue, surely a new set of leaders can construct a more inclusive and tolerant transnational identity?

Recent history suggests, however, that *to some extent* national identities must be treated as given, at least within the sort of time frame that matters for political decision-making. The character of a national identity can change dramatically, as the "Quiet Revolution" in Quebec shows (see below). Equally dramatic changes have occurred recently among indigenous communities. But the identity itself—the sense of being a distinct national culture—is much more stable. Governments in Canada and the United States have, at times, used all the tools at their disposal to destroy the sense of separate identity among their national minorities, from residential schools for Indian children and the prohibition of tribal customs, to the banning of French- or Spanish-language schools. Nevertheless, despite centuries of legal discrimination, social prejudice, or plain indifference, these national minorities have maintained their sense of having a national identity. Similarly, efforts by European governments to suppress the language and national identity of the Kurds, Basques, and other national minorities have had little or no success. And communist governments failed in their efforts to eradicate national loyalties. Despite a complete monopoly over education and the media, communist regimes were unable to create a genuine and enduring sense of "Yugoslav," "Czechoslovak," or "Soviet" identity in these multination states, or to get Croats, Slovaks, and Ukrainians to think of themselves in terms of these pannational identities.

It is no longer possible to eliminate the sense of distinct identity which underlies these groups' desire to form their own national societies. If anything, attempts to subordinate these separate identities to a common identity have backfired, since they are perceived by minorities as threats to their very existence, and thus have resulted in even greater indifference or resentment.

Much has been made in the recent literature of the social construction of national identity, and of the "invention of tradition";[51] and of course much of the mythology accompanying national identities is just that—a myth. But it is important not to confuse the heroes, history, or present-day characteristics of a national identity with the underlying national identity itself. The former are much more malleable than is the latter. Indeed, according to Walker Connor, few if any national groups in the last one hundred years have voluntarily assimilated, despite often signif-

---

[51] E. J. Hobsbawm, *Nations and Nationalism since 1780: Programme, Myth, Reality* (Cambridge: Cambridge University Press, 1990).

icant economic incentives and legal pressures to do so.[52] As Anthony Smith puts it, "whenever and however a national identity is forged, once established, it becomes immensely difficult, if not impossible (short of total genocide) to eradicate."[53] Any plausible theory of social unity in a multination state must come to terms with the durability of national identities.

IV. Two Views of Social Unity

What then are the possible sources of unity in a multination state which affirms, rather than denies, its national differences? I do not have a clear answer to this question. Indeed, I doubt that there are any obvious or easy answers available. We can begin to see what is required, however, if we examine what is wrong with some existing accounts of social unity.

I will begin with a popular liberal account of social unity, expressed clearly by Rawls, which emphasizes the role of a shared conception of justice in upholding social unity. According to Rawls, the source of social unity in modern societies is a shared conception of justice. As he puts it, "although a well-ordered society is divided and pluralistic . . . public agreement on questions of political and social justice supports ties of civic friendship and secures the bonds of association."[54]

It is true that there often *are* shared political principles within multination states, including a shared conception of liberal justice. However, it is not clear that these principles, by themselves, provide a reason for two or more national groups to stay together in one country. For example, there may be (and probably is) a remarkable convergence of political principles between the citizens of Norway and the citizens of Sweden; but is this any reason for them to regret their breakup in 1905? I don't think so. The fact that they share the same principles does not, by itself, explain why they should want to live together under one state.

Similarly, there has been a pronounced convergence in political principles between English- and French-speaking Canadians over the last thirty years, so that it would now be "difficult to identify consistent differences in attitudes on issues such as moral values, prestige ranking of professions, role of the government, workers' rights, aboriginal rights, equality between the sexes and races, and conception of authority."[55] If

---

[52] Walker Connor, "Nation-Building or Nation-Destroying?" *World Politics*, vol. 24 (1972), pp. 350–51.

[53] Anthony Smith, "A Europe of Nations — or the Nation of Europe?" *Journal of Peace Research*, vol. 30, no. 2 (1993), p. 131.

[54] John Rawls, "Kantian Constructivism in Moral Theory," *Journal of Philosophy*, vol. 77, no. 9 (1980), p. 540.

[55] Stéphane Dion, "Le nationalisme dans la convergence culturelle" (Nationalism in an era of cultural convergence), in *L'Engagement intellectuel: Melanges en l'honneur de Léon Dion* (Intellectual engagement: Essays in honor of Léon Dion), ed. Raymond Hudon and Réjean Pelletier (Sainte-Foy: Les Presses de l'Université Laval, 1991), p. 301; Stéphane Dion,

the "shared principles" approach were correct, we should have witnessed a decline in support for Quebec secession over this period, yet nationalist sentiment has in fact grown consistently. Here again, the fact that Anglophones and Francophones in Canada share the same principles of justice is not a strong reason for them to remain together, since the Québécois rightly assume that their own national state could respect the same principles. Deciding to secede would not require them to abandon their political principles, since they could implement the same principles in their own state. The same is true of the Flemish in Belgium.

Indeed, this reflects a very general trend. There has been a convergence of political values throughout the Western world, among both majority nations and national minorities. In terms of their political principles, the Danes, Germans, French, and English have probably never been as similar as they are now. This has not, however, had any appreciable impact on the desire of these majority nations to retain their national independence.[56] Why then should it diminish the desire of national minorities for self-government? This suggests that shared political principles are not sufficient for social unity. The fact that two national groups share the same principles of liberal justice does not necessarily give them any strong reason to join (or remain) together, rather than remaining (or splitting into) two separate countries.[57] If two national groups want to live together under a single state, then sharing political principles will obviously make it easier to do so. But sharing political principles is not, in and of itself, a reason why two national groups should want to live together.

"Explaining Quebec Nationalism," in *The Collapse of Canada?* ed. R. Kent Weaver (Washington: Brookings Institute, 1992), p. 99; cf. Charles Taylor, "Shared and Divergent Values," in *Options for a New Canada*, ed. Ronald L. Watts and Douglas M. Brown (Toronto: University of Toronto Press, 1991), p. 54.

[56] The evolution of the European Community is not a counterexample. The formation and extension of the EC involves sovereign countries voluntarily agreeing to relinquish some powers to a transnational organization, because it is in their national interest to do so, and on the condition that they can withdraw from the EC when they think it is no longer in their national interest to remain in it. Deciding to join the EC, in short, is one way of exercising a country's right of self-determination, not an abandonment of that inherent right. This is just the sort of relationship which national minorities seek vis-à-vis the sovereign states into which they have been incorporated. They too are willing to cede certain powers to a larger unit, on the condition that this transfer of powers is partial, consensual, and revocable. In both cases, the ceding of powers to a larger political unit is acceptable only if and insofar as it is seen as the voluntary and revocable choice of an inherently self-governing group. The fact that there are shared·political principles within Western Europe has undoubtedly made it easier to form entities such as the EC, but it has not diminished the insistence of states that they form separate and self-governing nations whose participation in the EC is consensual and revocable. The same applies to the demands of national minorities within European states.

[57] See Wayne Norman, "The Ideology of Shared Values," in *Is Quebec Nationalism Just?* ed. Joseph Carens (Montreal: McGill-Queen's University Press, 1995); cf. James Nickel, "Rawls on Political Community and Principles of Justice," *Law and Philosophy*, vol. 9 (1990), pp. 205–16.

Communitarians offer a different account of social unity. They rightly insist that any plausible account of social unity must be particularized; that is, it must show why people have an attachment to a particular, historical political community, rather than to abstract universal principles of justice. But what ties individuals to a particular historical community? Communitarians claim that this bond to a particular social group is based on shared ends or conceptions of the good life. They believe that members have a "constitutive" bond to the group's values—that is, a bond so deep that it is virtually impossible, even unintelligible, to question it. These ends define who we are, and therefore promoting these constitutive ends can sometimes justify limiting the ability of individuals to dissent from communal practices and traditional authorities. Hence, communitarians endorse a "politics of the common good," in which groups can promote a shared substantive conception of the good, rather than a "politics of rights," which emphasizes people's ability to form and pursue their own individual conceptions of the good.[58]

But this assumption of shared ends is clearly false at the national level.[59] The members of a nation, at least in a modern liberal society, do not share conceptions of the good or traditional ways of life. They share a language and history, but often disagree fundamentally about the ultimate ends in life. Here again the Québécois provide a nice illustration of the problem. Before the "Quiet Revolution" (1960–1966), the Québécois generally shared a rural, Catholic, conservative, and patriarchal conception of the good. Today, after a rapid period of liberalization, most people have abandoned this traditional way of life, and Québécois society now exhibits all the diversity that any modern society contains—e.g., atheists and Catholics, gays and heterosexuals, urban yuppies and rural farmers, socialists and conservatives, etc. Being a "Québécois" today, therefore, simply means being a participant in the francophone society of Quebec; and Francophones in Quebec no more agree about conceptions of the good than do Anglophones in the United States.

If the "shared conceptions of the good" approach were correct, we should have witnessed a decline in support for Quebec secession over this period of liberalization, yet nationalist sentiment has in fact grown consistently. And if there are no shared conceptions of the good within

[58] This, of course, is only a crude thumbnail sketch of communitarianism, focusing on one strand of that complex school of thought. For the idea of "constitutive" ends, and the contrast between a politics of the common good and a politics of rights, see Michael Sandel, "The Procedural Republic and the Unencumbered Self," *Political Theory*, vol. 12, no. 1 (1984), pp. 81–96. I provide a more systematic exposition and critique of communitarian views in my *Contemporary Political Philosophy* (Oxford: Oxford University Press, 1990), ch. 6.

[59] Some communitarians admit this. According to Sandel, for example, "the nation proved too vast a scale across which to cultivate the shared self-understandings necessary to community in the . . . constitutive sense" (Sandel, "The Procedural Republic," p. 93). Hence, most communitarians talk about our attachment to subnational groups—churches, neighborhoods, families, unions, etc.—rather than to the larger society which encompasses these subgroups. See David Miller, "In What Sense Must Socialism Be Communitarian?" *Social Philosophy and Policy*, vol. 6, no. 2 (1989), pp. 60–67.

each national group, then *a fortiori*, the communitarian approach cannot possibly explain what unifies two or more national groups in a multi-nation state.

There is a common problem in the liberal and communitarian approaches. Both give an overly cerebral account of social unity, in terms of shared normative beliefs regarding justice or the good life. It is clear, I think, that social unity cannot be based on shared beliefs. Conceptions of the good are not widely shared within national groups, and principles of justice are too widely shared across national groups.

What matters is not shared values, but a *shared identity*. A shared conception of justice throughout a multinational political community does not necessarily generate a shared identity, let alone a shared civic identity that will supersede rival national identities. Conversely, the lack of a shared conception of the good does not preclude a shared identity. People decide who they want to share a country with by asking who they identify with, who they feel solidarity with. What holds Americans together, despite their disagreements over the nature of the good life, is the fact that they share an identity as Americans. Conversely, what keeps Swedes and Norwegians apart, despite their shared principles of justice, is the lack of a shared identity.

Where does this shared identity come from? In nation-states, the answer is simple. Shared identity derives from commonality of history, language, and perhaps religion. But these are precisely the things which are not shared in a multination state. If we look to strongly patriotic but culturally diverse countries like the United States or Switzerland, the basis for a shared identity often seems to be pride in certain historical achievements (e.g., the founding of the American Republic). This shared pride is one of the bases of the strong sense of American political identity, constantly reinforced in America's citizenship literature and school curricula.

In many multination countries, however, history is a source of resentment and division between national groups, not a source of shared pride. The people and events which spark pride among the majority nation often generate a sense of betrayal among the national minority.[60] Moreover, the reliance on history often requires a very selective, even manipulative, retelling of that history. The nineteenth-century French theorist Ernst Renan once claimed that national identity involves forgetting the past as much as remembering it. To build a sense of common identity in a multination state probably requires an even more selective memory of the past.[61]

---

[60] On the divisive impact of history, see Lea Brilmayer, "Groups, Histories, and International Law," *Cornell International Law Journal*, vol. 25, no. 3 (1992), pp. 555–63.

[61] This raises some important questions about the nature of citizenship education, and the legitimacy of selective and manipulative use of history in schools, which I discuss in *Multicultural Citizenship*, ch. 9.

Shared values and an inspiring history no doubt help sustain solidarity in a multination state, but it is doubtful that either factor is sufficient by itself. How then can one construct a common identity in a country which contains two or more communities which view themselves as self-governing nations? The great variation in historical, cultural, and political situations in multination states suggests that any generalized answer to this question will likely be overstated.[62]

What is clear, I think, is that if there is a viable way to promote a sense of solidarity and common purpose in a multination state, it will involve accommodating, rather than subordinating, national identities. It may seem puzzling that people have a strong attachment to their national identity, particularly if their national culture is liberalized. After all, as a culture is liberalized—and thus allows members to question and reject traditional ways of life—the resulting cultural identity becomes both "thinner" and less distinctive. That is, as a culture becomes more liberal, the members are less and less likely to share the same substantive conception of the good life, and more and more likely to share basic political principles with people in other liberal cultures.

For example, as we have seen, liberalization in Quebec has meant both an increase in differences amongst the Québécois, in terms of their conceptions of the good, and a reduction in differences between the Québécois and the members of other liberal cultures. The same process is at work throughout Europe. The modernization and liberalization of Western Europe has resulted in both fewer commonalities within each of the national cultures, and greater commonalities across these cultures. As Spain has liberalized, the Spanish have become both more pluralistic internally, and more like the French or the Germans in terms of their modern, secular, industrialized, democratic, and consumerist civilization.

This perhaps explains why so many theorists have assumed that liberalization and modernization would displace any strong sense of national identity. As cultures liberalize, people share less and less with their fellow members of the national group, in terms of traditional customs or conceptions of the good life, and become more and more like the members of other nations, in terms of sharing a common civilization. Why then would anyone feel strongly attached to his or her own nation? Such an attachment seems, to many commentators, like the "narcissism of minor differences."[63]

Yet the evidence is overwhelming that the members of liberal cultures *do* value their cultural membership. Far from displacing national identity,

---

[62] Charles Taylor, "Quel principe d'identité collective?" (What is the basis of collective identity?), in *L'Europe au soir du siècle: Identité et démocratie* (Europe at the end of the century: Identity and democracy), ed. Jacques Lenoble and Nicole Dewandre (Paris: Editions Esprit, 1992), pp. 61–65.

[63] Michael Ignatieff, *Blood and Belonging: Journeys into the New Nationalism* (New York: Farrar, Straus, and Giroux, 1994), p. 21; cf. Dion, "Le nationalisme."

liberalization has in fact gone hand in hand with an increased sense of nationhood in many countries.[64] The fact that their culture has become tolerant and pluralistic has in no way diminished the pervasiveness or intensity of people's desire to live and work in their own culture.

Thus, people from different national groups will only share an allegiance to the larger polity if they see it as the context within which their national identity is nurtured, rather than subordinated. Accommodating these national identities is difficult enough in a country which simply contains two nations (e.g., Belgium). It gets even more complicated in countries which are not only multinational but also polyethnic, containing many national and indigenous groups, often of vastly unequal size, as well as immigrants from every part of the world. In this context, we need what Charles Taylor calls a theory of "deep diversity," since we must accommodate not only a diversity of cultural groups, but also a diversity of ways in which the members of these groups belong to the larger polity.[65] For example, a member of an immigrant group in the United States may see her citizenship status as centered on the universal individual rights guaranteed by the U.S. Constitution. Her ethnic identity, while important in various ways, may not affect her sense of citizenship, of what it is to be an American (or a Canadian, or an Australian). The United States, for her, may be a country of equal citizens who are tolerant of each other's cultural differences.

This model of belonging will not, however, accommodate national minorities like the Puerto Ricans or the Navajo. They belong to the United States through belonging to a national group that has federated itself to the larger country. According to a recent poll, 91 percent of the residents of Puerto Rico think of themselves as Puerto Ricans first, and Americans second.[66] They do see themselves as Americans, but only because this does not require abandoning their prior identity as a distinct Spanish-speaking people with their own separate political community. The United States, for them, is a federation of peoples — English, Spanish, Indian — each with the right to govern themselves.

Similarly, the immigrant model of belonging will not accommodate the Francophones and indigenous peoples in Canada, for whom "the way of being a Canadian (for those who still want to be) is via their belonging to a constituent element of Canada," such as the Québécois or the Cree.[67]

---

[64] William Peterson, "On the Subnations of Europe," in *Ethnicity: Theory and Experience*, ed. Nathan Glazer and Daniel P. Moynihan (Cambridge: Harvard University Press, 1975), p. 208.

[65] Taylor, "Shared and Divergent Values" (*supra* note 55), p. 75. For related speculations, see Philip Resnick, "The Crisis of Multi-National Federations," *Review of Constitutional Studies*, vol. 2, no. 1 (1994), pp. 189–202.

[66] Alvin Rubinstein, "Is Statehood for Puerto Rico in the National Interest?" *In Depth: A Journal for Values and Public Policy*, Spring 1993, p. 88.

[67] Taylor, "Shared and Divergent Values," p. 75.

For these groups, Canada is a federation of national groups which respect each other's right to be a distinct societal culture within Canada.

In countries that are both polyethnic and multinational, cultural groups not only are diverse, but have diverse images of the country as a whole. People not only belong to separate political communities, but also belong in different ways. This means that the members of a polyethnic and multination state must respect not only diversity, but also a diversity of approaches to diversity. As Taylor puts it, an immigrant might see herself "as a bearer of individual rights in a multicultural mosaic," but she must nevertheless accept that a Puerto Rican, Navajo, or Québécois "might belong in a very different way . . . through being members of their national communities." And reciprocally, the Puerto Ricans, Navajo, and Québécois "would accept the perfect legitimacy of the 'mosaic' identity." This sort of "deep diversity" is "the only formula" on which a united polyethnic, multination state can be built.[68]

What would hold such a multination state together? Taylor suggests that citizens might "find it exciting and an object of pride" to collectively build a society founded on deep diversity, and thus might be willing to make sacrifices to keep it together.[69] As Taylor admits, however, whether this is realistic is an open question. Why would citizens find this exciting rather than wearying, given the endless negotiations and complications it entails?

Nevertheless, Taylor is pointing in the right direction. A society founded on deep diversity is unlikely to stay together unless people value deep diversity itself, and want to live in a country with diverse forms of cultural and political membership. Even this is not always sufficient. For example, a sovereign Quebec would still be a very culturally diverse country, with immigrants from around the world, as well as a historically settled anglophone community and various indigenous peoples, including the Cree, the Mohawk, and the Inuit. Secession rarely if ever creates homogeneous nation-states, it simply rearranges the pattern and size of groups. For citizens to want to keep a multination state together, therefore, they must value, not just deep diversity in general, but also the particular immigrant groups and national cultures with whom they currently share the country.

The problem, of course, is that this sort of allegiance is the product of mutual solidarity, not a possible basis for it. If citizens already have a fairly strong sense of shared identity with the other ethnic and national groups in the country, they will find the prospect of sustaining their deep

---

[68] *Ibid.*, p. 76. While accommodating both polyethnic and multinational differences complicates the situation, I do not believe that the presence of immigrant groups substantially affects the likelihood that a multination state will successfully deal with its national differences. The fact that Canada contains many more immigrants than Belgium or Czechoslovakia does not, I think, have much bearing on the likelihood of Quebec's secession.

[69] Taylor, "Shared and Divergent Values," p. 76.

diversity inspiring and exciting. But a vague commitment to the value of cultural diversity, by itself, may not generate a strong sense of identification with the existing country, or with the particular groups that live within it.

Some multination states do have this strong sense of mutual identification. This is obviously true of the Swiss. Their sense of patriotism is so strong that the Swiss are, in some ways, a single "people," as well as a federation of peoples. This shows that there is no necessary reason why the members of a national minority cannot have both a strong national consciousness and a strong sense of patriotism and commitment to the larger polity.[70]

Canadians also have a reasonably strong sense of solidarity. For example, while over half of Quebecers attach priority, in their self-identity, to their status as Quebec citizens, compared with just under 30 percent who attach priority to Canadian citizenship, still 70 percent of Quebecers say they would be willing to make personal sacrifices that would benefit only Canadians outside Quebec.[71] This provides a level of goodwill that is not present in other multination states—and focusing on shared values, mythical history, or the excitement of deep diversity might help sustain that level of solidarity. Nevertheless, it is not clear how other multination states could try to create such a level of solidarity where it did not already exist. If two or more national groups simply do not want to live together, it may be impossible to create solidarity from scratch.[72]

V. CONCLUSION

In thinking about the impact of ethnic diversity on the stability of liberal democracies, we must avoid overgeneralizations about the goals or consequences of "multiculturalism." For example, opponents of multiculturalism often say that it ghettoizes minorities and impedes their integration into mainstream society; proponents respond that this concern for integration reflects cultural imperialism. Both of these charges are overgeneralizations which ignore differences among minority groups and misinterpret their actual motivations.

I believe that the demands of immigrants are primarily demands for inclusion, for full membership in the larger society. To view this as a threat to stability or solidarity is implausible, and often reflects an underlying ignorance or intolerance of these groups. The demands of national minorities, however, do pose a threat to social unity. The sense of being a distinct nation within a larger country is potentially destabilizing. Yet

---

[70] Jay Sigler, *Minority Rights: A Comparative Analysis* (Westport: Greenwood, 1983), pp. 188–92.

[71] *L'Actualité*, vol. 17, no. 11 (July 1992).

[72] David Miller, "In Defense of Nationality," *Journal of Applied Philosophy*, vol. 10, no. 1 (1993), p. 16 n. 14.

the denial of self-government rights is also destabilizing, since it encourages resentment and even secession. Concerns about social unity will arise no matter how we respond to self-government claims.

A fundamental challenge facing liberal theorists, therefore, is to identify the sources of unity in a democratic multination state. The nineteenth-century English theorist A. V. Dicey once said that a stable multination federation requires "a very peculiar state of sentiment" among its citizens, since "they must desire union, and must not desire unity."[73] Liberal theory has not yet succeeded in clarifying the nature of this "peculiar sentiment."

Philosophy, University of Ottawa

---

[73] A. V. Dicey, quoted in Reginald Whitaker, "Federalism and Democratic Theory," in Whitaker, *A Sovereign Idea* (*supra* note 31), p. 195.

CAPITALISM AND COMMUNITY

By David Conway

I. Introduction

Is capitalism inimical to community? Yes, say communitarians, a large
part of whose body of writing is given over to the elaboration and defense
of various forms of this thesis.[1] The aim of the present essay is to contest
this answer. Not only, I will argue, is there no good reason for supposing capitalism inimical to community, but there is reason to think it more
conducive to community than are the feasible alternatives to it.

Communitarians are undoubtedly correct to deplore the fragile state of
community in present-day Western societies. However, insofar as they
hold capitalism responsible, communitarians misidentify the real culprit.
What principally causes the lack of community in these societies today,
I will argue, is not their suffering from too much capitalism, but rather
their suffering from not enough of it.

In recent times, many public-policy measures designed to restrict the
market, or to correct its outcomes, have been supported through appeal
to community and to the need to defend it against the threat to it allegedly posed by unrestrained capitalism. These policy measures include
extensive provision of state welfare,[2] restrictions on capital mobility,[3]
state subsidies and support for religious and ethnic minorities,[4] and calls
for greater protection against Third World imports.[5] Many of these measures have already been adopted. Others lie in waiting. If my argument
is correct, none of them is likely to prove at all effective in stemming the
breakdown of community, and some will merely accelerate the process.

[1] Canonical communitarian texts include Alasdair MacIntyre, *After Virtue*, 2d ed. (London: Duckworth, 1985); Michael Sandel, "Democrats and Community," *New Republic*, February 22, 1988, pp. 20–23; Charles Taylor, "Legitimation Crisis?" in Taylor, *Philosophy and
the Human Sciences* (Cambridge: Cambridge University Press, 1985); and Michael Walzer,
Spheres of Justice (Oxford: Basil Blackwell, 1983). To this chorus of communitarian critics of
capitalism may now be added John Gray, *The Undoing of Conservatism* (London: The Social
Market Foundation, 1994).
[2] See, for example, David Harris, *Justifying State Welfare: The New Right versus the Old Left*
(Oxford: Blackwell, 1987), p. 27.
[3] See, for example, Michael Sandel, "Morality and the Liberal Ideal," *New Republic*, May
7, 1984, pp. 15–17; and Michael Walzer, "The Communitarian Critique of Liberalism," *Political Theory*, vol. 18, no. 1 (February 1990), pp. 6–23.
[4] Such measures have been argued for by, among others, Will Kymlicka, "Liberal Individualism and Liberal Neutrality," in *Communitarianism and Individualism*, ed. Shlomo Avineri
and Avner de-Shalit (Oxford: Oxford University Press, 1992), pp. 165–85; and Walzer, "The
Communitarian Critique of Liberalism."
[5] See Gray, *The Undoing of Conservatism*.

© 1996 Social Philosophy and Policy Foundation. Printed in the USA.

II. Terminological Prelude

In considering whether capitalism undermines community, we are liable to go seriously astray unless we are careful to make clear precisely what is to be understood by each term. Many discussions of this issue are seriously compromised, if not vitiated, by too ready a tendency for the participants to assume that what each term means on each occasion of its use is unproblematic. This is a most regrettable tendency. What is to be understood by each term is by no means unproblematic. This is, not least in part, because each has more than one perfectly standard sense. Assertions about the effects of capitalism on community can be true when the terms are understood in one way, but false when they are understood in another equally legitimate way. Unless one is fully aware of the different senses the terms have, it is all too easy to suppose that the truth of some assertion which results from understanding the terms in one way, suffices to establish the truth of the corresponding, but entirely different, assertion that results from understanding the terms in some other way.

The tendency to make this fallacious supposition is particularly prevalent in the case of the term "capitalism." This is because the term is multiply ambiguous. There are two potential sources of confusion here. The first is that the term can be, and often is, intended and understood to refer to either one of two intimately related, but nonetheless importantly different, sorts of entity. The first is *a particular kind or form of order* which an actual society or set of societies may exemplify to a greater or lesser degree. The second is *an actual society* exemplifying this particular form to some especially marked degree. The first understanding of the term refers to an ideal type in the Weberian sense. This type comprises a set of constitutive institutions and practices. The second understanding refers to those societies, such as present-day Britain, America, and Japan, which, in virtue of their instantiating the type to the degree that they do, are often also designated by the same term as designates the type of which they are tokens.

A second potential source of confusion connected with the term "capitalism" arises from the fact that, in the literature, there is no consensus regarding the type of order to which the term should always be understood as referring. It is possible to identify three different types of order to which it is sometimes used to refer. The first is that which is also sometimes designated by the expression *the market economy* or *the market* for short.[6] Its main constitutive institutions and practices include private ownership of the means of production, free labor (in the sense of freedom of contract and association), and production for profit. The second type

---

[6] Among notable of writers on capitalism to define the term in this way are Milton Friedman, *Capitalism and Freedom* (Chicago and London: University of Chicago Press, 1962); and Peter L. Berger, *The Capitalist Revolution* (Aldershot: Wildwood House, 1987).

of order combines the constitutive institutions of the market economy with *limited government*.[7] This form of government confines the role of the state to the provision of only such goods and services as citizens are deemed incapable of providing for themselves either through the market or through other non-state, and hence voluntary, institutions and agencies. Among the principal goods and services of this sort are the protection of the lives, liberty, and property of citizens, as well as the enforcement of legally recognized contracts between them. The third type of order also sometimes designated by the term "capitalism" results from combining the constitutive institutions of the second type with those of *representative democracy*.[8] This form of democracy confines the participation of citizens in affairs of state to the periodic election of its principal officers. Under this form of democracy, citizens also enjoy the legal right to stand for election to office and to participate in the electoral process through party membership, canvassing, campaigning, and so on, as well as some familiar rights of expression and assembly.

Clearly, these three different senses of "capitalism" are neither extensionally nor intensionally equivalent to one another. Which is correct? Since it is not a natural kind, capitalism cannot be said to have any real essence. Hence, none of the three senses can be said to be any more correct than any other. What can be correctly said, however, is that one is a more or a less common usage of the term than another. So far as that is concerned, the third of its three senses is the least common. In both common speech and academic writing, it is not customary to regard democracy as even an invariable accompaniment of capitalism, let alone a part of it. In spite of this, it is my intention in what follows to employ the term in the third of these three senses. My reasons for wishing to do so are two. First, as previously remarked, in debates over whether capitalism is inimical to community, what discussants are principally concerned about is the fate of community in the advanced industrial societies, such as the United States, the United Kingdom, and Japan. In addition to being capitalist in the first two senses of this term (relative, that is, to full-blown socialism), these societies are also capitalist in its third sense. Since this is so, the issue of greatest concern to discussants can be addressed most economically by including representative democracy among the constitutive institutions of capitalism. Such an inclusion enables them to take account of this variable, when considering the fate of community in these societies.

My second reason for proposing that representative democracy be included among the constitutive institutions of capitalism is that, ulti-

---

[7] One notable writer on capitalism who defines the term in this way is Arthur Seldon, *Capitalism* (Oxford: Basil Blackwell, 1990).

[8] One notable writer on capitalism who defines the term in this way is Michel Albert, *Capitalism against Capitalism* (London: Whurr Publishers, 1993).

mately, in both its other two senses, capitalism both requires and invariably leads to this form of government. As has been observed:

> While bastard forms of capitalism do seem able for a time to endure without democracy, the natural logic of capitalism leads to democracy. For economic liberties without political liberties are inherently unstable. Citizens economically free soon demand political freedoms. Thus dictatorships or monarchies which permit some freedoms to the market have a tendency to evolve into political democracies, as has happened in recent years in Greece, Portugal, Spain, and other nations.[9]

So long as it is clearly understood throughout that by the expression "capitalism" I intend that kind of societal order which incorporates the institutions of representative democracy as well as a market economy and limited government, all possible scope for misunderstanding as to which general type of societal order is being intended will have been eliminated.

Considerable scope for misunderstanding will still remain. For, as I have remarked, the term "capitalism" can be used to refer to actual societies as well as to a form of society. It is perfectly acceptable common practice for actual societies or sets of societies to be referred to by a term which, strictly, denotes the form they exemplify. However, there is a danger in so doing. No actual society has ever fully and perfectly exemplified a capitalist form. When the difference between the form and a partial and incomplete exemplar of the form is not clearly appreciated, it becomes all too easy to suppose endemic to the form itself some feature which, rightfully, belongs only to some actual society or set of societies which partially exemplify it, and which may possess this feature only because their exemplification of the form is only partial and not full. This error occurs over and over again in discussions of capitalism and community. I shall illustrate its prevalence in due course.

A similar, albeit far less troublesome, ambiguity attaches to the term "community." It can be used, first, to designate a specific kind of *character* or *quality* which some form(s) of association can have. Second, it can be used to refer to the various *concrete forms of association* that have this kind of character. It is rare for this ambiguity to give rise to any problems in the way the corresponding one does in the case of the term "capitalism."

When it is claimed that capitalism is inimical to community, in what sense is the latter term being used? Often, it goes undefined by those who level the charge, but I believe the following definition adequately captures its meaning in most present-day discussions:

---

[9] Michael Novak, *The Spirit of Democratic Capitalism* (New York: Touchstone Books, 1982), p. 15.

A community is any set of individuals who (1) share with one another, in whole or part, a common life or form of life; (2) attach — and are aware of themselves and each other as attaching — intrinsic value to that common life or form of life; (3) feel, or are disposed to feel, some degree of heightened regard for one another; and (4) cooperate, or are disposed to cooperate, with one another to preserve and foster that common life or form of life.

Two or more individuals share a *common life* if and to the extent that their individual lives bring them into direct contact with each other in ways which involve their cooperating with one another. Two or more individuals share a *common form of life* if and to the extent that they share the same native language, participate in the same customs and traditions, and have the same beliefs about the world as one another.

It is possible, although rare, for human beings to share a common life without sharing much by way of a common form of life. This happens when people of very different cultures begin to interact and cooperate with one another. It is far less rare for human beings to share a common form of life without sharing much, if anything, of a common life. For example, a devoutly orthodox Jew in Brooklyn may share much the same form of life as his or her counterpart in Minsk, yet the two individuals may never come into contact with one another or engage in any form of cooperation with one another.

A *group* is simply any set of individuals who each possess some feature or features in common. Not every human group forms a community. For example, the set of left-handed individuals is a human group in this sense, but hardly a community.

A human group does not always form a community in the relevant sense even when its members cooperate with one another for the sake of a common purpose. Consider, for example, the various members of a business corporation — its directors, managers, and employees. Suppose they all work for the corporation solely for the sake of their own individual self-interest. Suppose they have no interest in one another save *as* one another's employers or (fellow) employees, and suppose that they share no other common interests which they cooperate with each other to foster. They might all attach considerable instrumental value to the success of their firm, be pleased when its profits are good, and cooperate to achieve its success. However, they would still not form a genuine community in the relevant sense. For, as described, the goal of their common endeavor has, for them, only an *instrumental* value. In order for the members of some group who cooperate with one another for a common purpose to form a community in the relevant sense, the common purpose for the sake of which they cooperate has to be of some *intrinsic* or noninstrumental value to them. It is possible, over time, for the associates of a firm to develop some common intrinsic attachment to it, and some heightened regard for one another. When (but only when) this happens, they will have become a community in the relevant sense. In the case of a commercial firm, it is not obvious that this must—or even should—happen in order for it to be a commercial success.

It is worth noting that, according to the definition I have given, community is very much a matter of degree. The greater the degree of intrinsic value attached by the members of some group to some common object, and the greater the degree of cooperation in fostering that common value, the greater their degree of community will be—and the more of a community they will make.

I have now explained what I believe is generally understood by the term "community" when it is claimed that capitalism is inimical to it. In the next section, I shall identify which principal varieties of community are supposedly endangered by capitalism.

III. THE VARIETIES OF COMMUNAL EXPERIENCE

Four principal varieties of community have been deemed to be at risk from capitalism. These are, in ascending order of size: family, neighborhood, nation, and state.

At root, a *family* is a biological group. It comprises all and only those who are related to each other by way of kinship. The most direct and immediate of such kinship relations is the relation between biological parent and child. All other familial relations—such as those of grandparent, sibling, cousin, and so on—derive from this primary one. In considering the family, it is often useful to distinguish between the *immediate* or *nuclear family*, which comprises parents and their biological children, and the *extended family*, which includes all other biological relatives in addition to these.

According to the definition of community given above, in order for members of a family—nuclear or extended—to constitute a community, much must hold true of them. They must share and value a common life, feel a heightened regard for one another, and be disposed to cooperate with one another to foster that life in common. In practice, what the latter means is that, in order to be a community, family members must be disposed to celebrate or otherwise collectively mark significant events in the life-cycles of one another, such as births, weddings, and bereavements. In addition, in proportion as they form a genuine community, family members must be disposed to assist one another in time of need, as well as to seek and enjoy one another's company.

It is clear that, given what is involved in being a community, not every family is one. This is so, even when only nuclear families are considered. There are plenty of nuclear families whose members do not live together, or, if they do, do not intrinsically value doing so, or have any heightened mutual regard or disposition to foster the common life they all share. Immediate family members can be separated from one another and thus not share a common life. Or they can share a common life but be so estranged from one another as not to value doing so, remaining together not by choice but only from necessity. Even when they share and jointly value a common life and feel heightened mutual regard, the members of a family might, through force of circumstance, be unable to do much to foster their common life. For example, they might be afflicted by famine, war, or persecution.

Although families do not necessarily or always form communities, it has to be admitted that plenty of them do. Wherever they reside together and are linked by bonds of love and affection, family members will be disposed to value their common life. As a result, they will be disposed to cooperate with each other to foster that common life they share. Such happy families are bound to form very strong communities.

A *neighborhood* may be understood to be any relatively small, well-defined portion of territory inhabited by some set of human beings in independent dwellings or households. Among some social commentators, there is a regrettable tendency to describe each and every neighborhood as a community, irrespective of whether it satisfies the conditions set out in the definition of community that I have given. A neighborhood is a genuine local community, however, only when it satisfies these conditions. This is not something which by any means neighborhoods always do. Neighborhoods can be rent with strife and faction. They can also be inhabited by a mass of strangers indifferent to one another and with few intrinsic values in common.

Although neighborhoods do not always form genuine local communities, it must be noted that, as with families, there is a powerful tendency for them to do so. The members of any group of human beings, resident in some neighborhood for any length of time, tend, other things being equal, to acquire some attachment to it, some heightened mutual regard, and, also, begin to cooperate to preserve or enhance their local quality of life by, for example, conserving or improving local amenities.

The tendency for the residents of a neighborhood to become and remain a genuine community will be strong in proportion as they share and jointly value the same form of life. These common attachments can often be of far greater weight to the residents than any common attachment they might have to the neighborhood per se. For example, the residents of a neighborhood might all have a common ethnic background or religious affiliation. Or they might all have some other set of interests or predilections in common. For example, they might all be practicing homosexuals and might have settled in their chosen neighborhood precisely because of its reputation as a center for those of that orientation. In such cases, where the residents of a neighborhood are all aware of these special points of affinity among themselves (in addition to their simply all residing in the same neighborhood), they can and typically will cooperate to foster their shared common interests. In the process of so doing, they are likely to develop some degree of heightened regard for one another.

It is more difficult for the residents of a neighborhood to form and remain a genuine local community if they emanate from a wide variety of ethnic and cultural backgrounds, and hence share little by way of a common culture. In view of this, it is not surprising that there tends to develop in different neighborhoods, even within large cities, a substantial degree of ethnic and cultural homogeneity. People like to be with their own kind, however they individuate that.

The third principal variety of community deemed at risk from capitalism are communities whose members belong to the same nation as one another. A *nation* is simply any group of human beings who all share at least one — and, typically, more than one — of the following characteristics: some (actual or widely believed) common ancestry and history; a common native language; common traditions and customs; and, finally, common citizenship in the same state. A *state* is simply some piece of inhabited territory over which some individual or organized group exercises jurisdiction, that is, makes and enforces laws.

As the term "nation" has been defined, not every nation forms a community. This is especially so, when, as often happens, through being geographically dispersed over a wide area, the members of some nation are mixed up with members of other nations and are citizens of a number of different states. Quite independently of their geographical distribution relative to one another, the members of some nation may fail to attach any intrinsic value to their national form of life, or have any mutual regard, or any concern to preserve and foster their national culture. Although these things are neither universal nor necessary, there is among human beings a powerful tendency for them to identify themselves with and to value whichever distinct nation(s) they happen to belong to. Human beings tend to acquire some noninstrumental attachment toward their own national traditions and culture, some heightened regard for fellow nationals, and tend to cooperate with some of these to maintain their own distinct national traditions and customs. As with families and neighborhoods, therefore, nations tend to form communities.

In the case where some group forms a nation solely through being citizens of the same state, its members will constitute a genuine community only if they share a common patriotic attachment to the state to which they all belong. In virtue of their belonging to the same state, they share a common form of political life. In virtue of their sharing a common patriotic attachment to it, they will all attach intrinsic value to their common form of political life and be disposed to cooperate with one another to preserve and foster it. As is notorious, citizens of a state do not always feel any patriotic attachment to it. Some may wish to secede from their state, or may wish for it to be absorbed by some other state. Despite this, where a state is stable and well-ordered, there is a tendency for its citizens to acquire some patriotic attachment to it. When, and only when, they share such a sentiment will the citizens of a state constitute a genuine political community.

It is possible for the citizens of a state to share a common patriotic attachment to it, even though they share little else with one another by way of other common national affiliation, such as ethnicity or religion. Other things being equal, however, the members of any state are more likely to share a common patriotism toward it — and, hence, are more likely to form a genuine political community — in proportion as they share the same form of life, as well as simply a common form of political life.

Political community is the last of the four principal varieties of community which have been deemed to be imperiled by capitalism. Before considering the grounds on which this claim has been made, I wish very briefly to consider why each of these four varieties of community might be thought of value.

IV. The Value of Community

Every human being is a member of some biological family; each resides, however temporarily, in some neighborhood; each belongs to some nation or other; and, unless stateless or a slave, each is a citizen of some state. As previously noted, none of these four varieties of group invariably forms a community. Why, in general and other things being equal, might it be thought better, for every individual, that each of these four varieties of group be a genuine community rather than not? The reasons are not invariably the same in the case of each variety of group.

So far as the family is concerned, there would appear to be at least two central reasons for supposing that, other things being equal, it is better for families to be genuine communities than not. First, in general, people value both loving and receiving love, especially from those whom they love. In families which are communities, there is bound to be considerable reciprocal love between family members, almost certainly far more than is likely to exist in societies in which families are not communities. Thus, if love and affection are of value for their own sake, societies which contain strong family communities are likely to be more productive of this intrinsically valuable sentiment than are societies in which family community is weak.

Second, there is a considerable and growing body of increasingly incontrovertible evidence[10] to show that, according to virtually whatever

---

[10] For reviews of this evidence, see Barbara Dafoe Whitehead, "Dan Quayle Was Right," *Atlantic Monthly*, vol. 271, no. 4 (April 1993), pp. 47–84; Norman Dennis and George Erdos, *Families without Fatherhood*, 2d ed. (London: IEA Health and Welfare Unit, 1993); and James Q. Wilson, "The Family-Values Debate," *Commentary*, vol. 91, no. 2 (April 1993), pp. 24–31.

measure of success one chooses, children are far more likely to succeed, when raised lovingly and caringly by both natural parents, than they are when raised according to any other arrangement. Consider, for example, the findings of a nationwide survey of the family arrangements of sixty thousand children growing up in the United States carried out in 1988 by the Department of Health and Human Services. It found that

> [a]t every income level save the very highest (over $50,000 per year), for both sexes and for whites, blacks, and Hispanics alike, children living with a never-married or a divorced mother were substantially worse off than those living in two-parent families. Compared to children living with both biological parents, children in single-parent families were twice as likely to have been expelled or suspended from school, to display emotional or behavioral problems, and to have problems with their peers; they were also much more likely to engage in antisocial behavior. These differences were about as wide in households earning over $35,000 a year as they were in those making less than $10,000.[11]

From surveys such as this and many other studies, it may be inferred that, other things being equal, children whose (biological) families are genuine communities are likely to do better in life than they otherwise would. A society of strong and stable, loving families, therefore, is likely to be populated by better members than one which is not—and hence is likely to be a better society.

Consider next neighborhoods: Why, other things being equal and in general, might it be supposed better for neighborhoods to be communities than not? Fundamentally, the reason is that, when a neighborhood is a genuine local community, its residents are almost certain to be far more civil toward and supportive of one another than they otherwise would be. Other things being equal, goodwill and civility are better both in themselves and instrumentally than are animosity, indifference, or incivility. Accordingly, other things being equal, it is better for neighborhoods to be genuine communities than not.

Next, why might it be thought, in general, better for human beings that the various nations to which they each belong be national communities rather than not? Some deny that it is better on the grounds that strong nationalist sentiment invariably gives rise to xenophobia and chauvinism, with disastrous consequences. However, such pathological forms of nationalism no more establish that strong nationalist sentiment and affiliation are undesirable than the occurrence of rape renders the human sexual drive undesirable.

Several reasons may be offered for supposing that, in general, it is better for the members of each different nation to form distinct national com-

---

[11] Wilson, "The Family-Values Debate," pp. 26–27.

munities with other co-nationals than for them not to. First, every distinct nation can be regarded as a unique flowering of the human species, manifesting a different way in which it has attempted to make sense of and order human life. To the extent to which a distinct nation is neither predatory nor inherently oppressive, its continued existence can be considered a good thing. Given that the survival of any nation depends upon at least some members following its distinct traditions and customs, and given that they are more likely to do so if they attach some intrinsic value to them, it follows that, if distinct national cultures are desirable, then so are distinct national communities.

It is not only from an external point of view—that is, the point of view of a spectator—that distinct national communities can be thought of as being of value to human beings. There is, also, arguably, an unmistakable value, for each individual, in being able to identify with and participate as a member of whichever nation he or she belongs to. Without being able to do so, an individual is likely to lead a severely stunted and deracinated life. This is because so much of what gives meaning and value to any human life is bound up with and flows from the wider cultural matrices within which the individual is embedded. Assume that it is desirable for human beings to possess an understanding of and have an affinity for the cultural traditions of whichever nation they happen to belong to, and that such understanding and affinity is best acquired through participating in these cultural traditions with other members who already possess such an understanding and affinity. It follows that, in general and other things being equal, it is better, for every individual, that he or she be a member of some national community.

Finally, we come to consider why, in general, it might be supposed better for each state to be a genuine political community than not. In essence, the reason is that, unless the citizens of a state share a common patriotic attachment to it, that state will lack cohesion and stability, and hence will be unable to fulfill its essential function of protecting and supporting its citizens.[12] Assuming that a state is better able to protect and support its citizens in proportion as the latter feel patriotism toward it, then, other things being equal, it is better for the citizens of every state that they form a genuine political community than that they not.

Having briefly considered why all four varieties of community are worth preserving, we shall now consider why communitarians have claimed that capitalism poses a threat to each of them.

V. THE COMMUNITARIAN CASE AGAINST CAPITALISM

Two principal reasons have been offered by communitarians for supposing capitalism to be inimical to family community. First, capitalism has been said to engender in human beings an outlook of extreme individu-

---

[12] See Henry Sidgwick, *The Elements of Politics* (London: Macmillan, 1891), p. 213.

alism which makes them view even "marriage and the family as vehicles of self-realisation."[13] Such a mentality, it is said, is bound to result in a devaluation of "commitment and stability in personal relationships."[14] Second, capitalism has been said to require a degree of labor mobility so great as to break up and disperse extended families, and to expose even nuclear families to the stresses and strains of periodic uprooting and moving.[15]

Neighborhood communities have been said to be imperiled by capitalism for three principal reasons. First, in addition to its supposed deleterious effect on the family, the high degree of labor mobility required by capitalism is said to turn neighborhoods into congeries of transient strangers, thereby reducing their propensity to be communities.[16] Second, in permitting a degree of capital mobility that allows corporations to move their plants away from neighborhoods in which they were the principal source of employment, capitalism is said to be liable to create pockets of high local unemployment.[17] Such resulting structural unemployment has been claimed to have a profoundly debilitating effect upon the local communities that suffer it. Third, capitalism has been said to reduce the capacity of cities to serve as environments for genuine urban community through encouraging "their deformation as communities by the private motor car, and their hollowing out by such developments as warehouse shopping."[18]

National community has been deemed to be imperiled by the unrestricted immigration which capitalism is said to license. High levels of immigration are said to dilute and ultimately obliterate all national difference. If all restrictions on immigration were abolished, it has been claimed,

> [t]he result would be the world of the political economists . . . a world of radically deracinated men and women. Neighborhoods might maintain some cohesive culture for a generation or two on a voluntary basis, but people would move in, people would move out; soon the cohesion would be gone. The distinctiveness of cultures and groups depends upon closure, and, without it, cannot be conceived as a stable feature of human life. If this distinctiveness is a value . . . then closure must be permitted somewhere. At some level of political organization, something like the sovereign state must take

---

[13] Gray, *The Undoing of Conservatism*, p. 22. See also Taylor, "Legitimation Crisis?" pp. 283–84.

[14] Gray, *The Undoing of Conservatism*, p. 22.

[15] *Ibid.*, p. 19.

[16] Walzer, "The Communitarian Critique of Liberalism," p. 13.

[17] Sandel, "Democrats and Community," pp. 22–23.

[18] Gray, *The Undoing of Conservatism*, p. 44.

shape and claim the authority to make its own admissions policy, to control and sometimes restrain the flow of immigrants.[19]

Four principal reasons have been given for supposing capitalism to be inimical to political community. First, beyond its supposedly leading to the erosion and ultimately to the destruction of all distinct national communities, the large volume of immigration licensed by capitalism is said to be likely to create states of such great ethnic and cultural diversity as to make patriotism difficult, if next to impossible, for their citizens.[20] Second, through encouraging the breakup and dispersal of extended families, capitalism is said to create the need for extensive state provision of welfare for all those indigent members of society who can no longer rely on members of their own families to take care of them. Neither the recipients of state welfare, nor those required to meet its costs from their taxes, are much enamored of the giant welfare bureaucracies which dispense it. Indeed, taxpayers are said to find it difficult to see why they should meet its costs. The result is held to be high levels of political alienation and taxpayers' revolts. The latter heighten social dissension between society's have's and have-not's,[21] at the cost of genuine political community between them. Third, in favoring free trade between industrially developed countries and developing countries in which labor costs are much lower, capitalism has been deemed liable to create severe structural unemployment in the developed countries, which must further exacerbate the political antagonisms within them between rich and poor.[22] Finally, by opting for representative rather than direct democracy, capitalism has been said to preclude political community. To be a genuine political community, it is argued, the citizens of a state must possess a common will, which is said to require their direct participation in the political decision-making process.[23]

This completes my review of the main reasons offered by communitarians for supposing that capitalism is inimical to community. It remains now to consider how compelling they are.

VI. Appraising the Communitarian Case

I begin by considering the two reasons given by communitarians for supposing that capitalism is inimical to family community. These were, first, that it encourages an individualistic mentality in which the value of

---

[19] Walzer, *Spheres of Justice*, pp. 37–38.

[20] See *ibid.*, pp. 61–62. See also Roger Scruton, "In Defence of the Nation," in Scruton, *The Philosopher on Dover Beach* (New York: St. Martin's Press, 1990).

[21] Taylor, "Legitimation Crisis?" pp. 284–86.

[22] Gray, *The Undoing of Conservatism*, p. 28.

[23] See Benjamin Barber, "Strong Democracy," in *Communitarianism: A New Public Ethics*, ed. Markate Daly (Belmont: Wadsworth, 1994), pp. 213–24.

personal relationships is judged solely in terms of self-fulfillment, and, second, that it demands a degree of labor mobility which is disruptive of families.

So far as the first reason is concerned, an increased individualism in personal relations may readily be conceded to be among the principal immediate factors responsible for the recent dramatic decline of the family in Western societies. However, it is open to doubt whether capitalism can be deemed responsible for the increase in this mentality. Historically speaking, marriage and family community have flourished in both the United States and Great Britain during periods in which both societies were at least as capitalist as they have been during the period in which the much-heralded breakdown of the family took place in them. The start of this period of family breakdown dates approximately from the mid-1960s. Prior to this time, family stability in both societies had been high.[24] This is indicated by the rates of both illegitimacy and divorce. From the mid-1960s on, both illegitimacy and divorce started to increase rapidly in both societies. In England today, approximately one in three children are born out of wedlock, while, less than twenty years ago, fewer than one in ten were. Likewise, in the United States today, approximately one in four children are born out of wedlock, while only one in twenty were in the 1950s and early 1960s. In the United States, the rate of divorce is currently more than double what it was in the 1950s and 1960s, and, in England, it is currently six times what it then was. If, for the reasons given earlier, it is, in general, better for families to be communities than not, then these recent trends must be considered highly disturbing and undesirable.[25]

It is difficult to regard either the United States or Great Britain in the 1950s, or in the century before that, as having been significantly less capitalist than either was during the period in which their rates for both divorce and illegitimacy took off. Consequently, if, as communitarians claim, the prevalence of individualism in personal relations explains the recent breakdown of family in these societies, something other than their being capitalist in form must account for why, from the 1960s onward, both societies began to experience such an increase in individualism. What this might be we shall consider in the next section.

There remains the second putative reason for supposing that family breakdown is inevitable under capitalism. This, to recall, is the pressure

[24] See Friedrich A. Hayek, "Individualism: True and False," in Hayek, *Individualism and Economic Order* (Chicago: University of Chicago Press, 1948), pp. 1–32, esp. p. 23; Joseph A. Schumpeter, *Capitalism, Socialism, and Democracy* (London: George Allen and Unwin, 1976); and Robert Nisbet, *The Quest for Community* (New York: Oxford University Press, 1953).

[25] For a discussion of illegitimacy, see Gertrude Himmelfarb, *The De-moralization of Society* (London: IEA Health and Welfare Unit, 1995), pp. 223–24. For statistics on divorce in the U.K., see Paul Goodman, "The Future of the Family," *Salisbury Review*, vol. 10, no. 3 (March 1992), p. 15; for U.S. divorce figures, see Barbara Dafoe Whitehead, "Dan Quayle Was Right," *Atlantic Monthly*, vol. 271, no. 4 (April 1993), p. 50.

on extended-family community allegedly exerted by the high degree of mobility of labor required under capitalism. A high demand for labor mobility may certainly be considered endemic to capitalism. Likewise, it may readily be conceded that such a high degree of labor mobility is unlikely to be compatible with robust extended-family community. From these facts, however, it cannot safely be inferred that capitalism undermines family community, even extended-family community. To make this inference is to assume that, prior to (or in the absence of) capitalism, extended-family communities have been better able to thrive than they are able to under capitalism. This assumption, however, seems unwarranted.

For present purposes, the advent of capitalism may be regarded as having coincided with the Industrial Revolution of the eighteenth century. Before the Industrial Revolution, infant-mortality rates were high and life expectancy was low. The Industrial Revolution which capitalism brought about reversed the relative magnitudes of these two rates. It has been estimated[26] that, before the Industrial Revolution, between one fifth and one half of all children died within their first year, life expectancy at birth was between twenty and thirty-five years, and few who reached the age of five were likely to survive beyond the age of fifty. After the Industrial Revolution, infant mortality declined to less than 4 percent, and life expectancy at birth increased to over sixty years.

It is difficult to regard as paradigms of extended-family community those families of the precapitalist era, of which practically every one would have suffered the premature deaths of many members. Assuming that capitalist methods of agriculture are vastly more efficient than noncapitalist methods, an abandonment of capitalism would be unlikely to sustain the current world's population for long either. Accordingly, it seems questionable whether extended-family community did or could flourish any better without capitalism than it can and does with it.

In any case, it can only be correctly said that it is likely, not certain, that a high degree of labor mobility will lead to the undermining of strong family community. It is by no means necessary that it does. In the relatively highly mobile societies of today, such as the United States and the United Kingdom, strong extended-family communities can still be found, especially among ethnic minorities, such as Jews, Japanese, and Chinese. These minorities are noted for the strength of their family ties and have also been conspicuous in their ability to take full advantage of the opportunities afforded them by capitalism. In the United States, the average family income for each of these minorities is well above the national average.[27] If something has led to a significant breakdown of family commu-

---

[26] Carlo M. Cipolla, *The Economic History of World Population*, 7th ed. (Harmondsworth: Penguin, 1974), pp. 87–89.

[27] Thomas Sowell, *Ethnic America* (New York: Basic Books, 1981), p. 5.

nity in these societies today, therefore, it must be some factor not endemic to capitalism per se. What that is we shall have to postpone considering until the next section.

I turn next to consider the three reasons given for supposing that capitalism is inimical to neighborhood community. To recap, these were, first, that the high mobility of labor required by capitalism turns neighborhoods into dormitories of transient strangers; second, that unrestrained capital mobility creates high levels of structural unemployment destructive of community in the neighborhoods affected by it; and, third, that capitalist urban development is destructive of previously convivial urban environments.

With reference to the first of these reasons, it is undoubtedly harder for neighborhoods whose residents are strangers to one another to be communities. However, it may be doubted whether a high degree of labor mobility by itself has any necessary tendency to make strangers of neighbors. It is perfectly possible for a society to possess a high degree of labor mobility without neighborhoods becoming populated by transient strangers with neither the ability nor the will to form genuine local communities with one another. As I noted earlier, other things being equal, people tend to congregate with others who are similar to themselves. People like to be among their own kind. It is by no means obvious that a high degree of labor mobility prevents members of society from being able to do this, even if they are frequently called upon to move. This is especially so, where, besides ties of neighborhood, members of a society have other strong communal bonds and affiliations which unite them, such as a strong sense of national, ethnic, or religious identity and affiliation. Where these other forms of community attachment are strong, members of a society can be mobile and yet capable of moving to neighborhoods where they would not, at least for very long, remain strangers. For they would be linked to other residents by these other bonds. Thus, it does not seem necessary that high mobility per se must undermine neighborhood community. If, today, so many neighborhoods lack this character, this must be for other reasons.

Something similar applies in the case where, as a result of the relocation of a previous major source of employment, a neighborhood suffers prolonged high levels of structural unemployment. Some of its residents will move in search of work. Provided the new neighborhoods to which they move are genuine local communities into which the newcomers are capable of entering, they need suffer no loss of neighborhood community in moving. Nor need those who remain behind do so either, although life might in other ways be less happy than it formerly was. Neither material hardship per se nor declining numbers need be incompatible with neighborhood community. Many of our most potent images of neighborhood community are of small numbers of people similarly exposed to hardship who mutually support one another. If, today, a sense of community is so conspicuously absent from so many of our most depressed inner-cities and regions, it must be for reasons other than their high unemployment levels.

There remains to be considered the claim that capitalism undermines the environmental basis for neighborhood community in cities through permitting, if not positively encouraging, such forms of urban development as the creation of motorways and giant retail warehouses, which destroy local shops and other local amenities. Again, it must be conceded that many cities have suffered a significant deterioration, in both physical and social terms, as a result of such forms of urban development as these. However, it is not clear that capitalism itself can correctly be considered responsible for these forms of development. Throughout the entire period in which urban development has taken place, road building and maintenance have been responsibilities of government, although, as earlier centuries have shown, it is not necessary for the state to build and maintain roads in order for its citizens to be supplied with them. During the period in which the state has been responsible for road construction and maintenance in both the United States and Britain, the full economic costs of roads have not been anything like fully borne by those who make use of them. Rather, the costs of road construction and maintenance have been financed, in considerable part, from general tax revenues. For example, it has been estimated that, in the United States, "urban expressways have been built at a cost of from 6 cents to 27 cents per vehicle-mile, while users pay in gasoline and other auto taxes only about 1 cent per vehicle-mile."[28] Road users have thus received a substantial subsidy, which has inevitably increased the number of vehicles on the roads well above what there would have been had drivers been made to bear the full costs of road use. To deal with the traffic congestion created by its unnecessary involvement in road construction, the state in both countries has been obliged to embark on ever more extensive road-building programs, with all the attendant detrimental effects upon the urban environment already noted. If, as was perfectly possible, the state had never intervened in road construction and maintenance, it is likely that there would have been far fewer vehicles on the road, and hence less call or scope for the extensive urban motorway systems and shopping developments which have proved so destructive of established urban neighborhoods. Hence, it may be argued that those forms of urban development which have proved so environmentally damaging to cities in Britain and the U.S. have resulted less from the degree to which these countries have been capitalist in form than the degree to which they have not been.

The third variety of community on which capitalism has been said to have had a deleterious effect is that belonging to nations. It is through

---

[28] Murray Rothbard, *For a New Liberty*, 2d ed. (New York: Collier Books, 1978), p. 209.

permitting unrestricted immigration that capitalism is said to undermine distinct national cultures. There is certainly reason to think that, in a pure capitalist society, there would be no legal barriers to immigration. As a result, any such society could well attract substantial numbers of immigrants who belong to nations other than those to which the members of the indigenous population belong. It may be conceded, therefore, that a capitalist society is likely—or, at least, is able—to be highly cosmopolitan. Must any distinct national communities suffer as a result of such immigration? They must do so only if the members of any national community are incapable of residing in the same state as persons of other nationalities while simultaneously retaining an identification with and an affinity for their own distinct national traditions and culture. It is not obvious why this should not be possible. It is true that present-day Western societies harbor many rootless and deracinated members who lack any real sense of or interest in their own national traditions and cultures. Again, however, there are plenty of historical examples of distinct national communities being able to thrive within a cosmopolitan capitalist setting. The United States of America in the nineteenth century and the early part of the twentieth was a highly cosmopolitan society in which different ethnic and religious communities were able to thrive. Therefore, the destruction of distinct national communities need not be endemic to a pluralistic and ethnically heterogeneous and diverse capitalist society. If there is severe deracination in present-day Western societies, its source must be located somewhere other than in their capitalist form. Precisely where will be considered in the next section.

This leaves the fourth variety of community to which capitalism has been claimed inimical, namely, political community. As will be recalled, four principal reasons have been given for thinking capitalism to be so. First, through permitting unrestricted immigration, it is said to undermine the national cohesion and unity on which patriotism is said to rely. Second, by breaking up extended-family communities, it is said to create a poorly appreciated, and hence widely resented, need for extensive state welfare for indigents no longer able to rely for support on their families. Third, through permitting free trade between mature industrial countries with high labor costs and newly industrialized competitors with low labor costs, capitalism is claimed to induce, in the former, socially divisive high levels of structural unemployment. Fourth, through adopting representative democracy rather than direct democracy, capitalism is said to preclude the formation of a common will among citizens.

So far as the first of these reasons is concerned, just as there is no reason why the members of a highly cosmopolitan society must become deracinated, so there is no reason why they must be unable to share as much common patriotism as they need share to make them a genuine political community. Again, the United States during the first half of the twentieth century, particularly its early decades, may be cited as a graphic illustration of a political society whose citizens were drawn from a wide variety of nationalities and backgrounds and yet who shared a high degree of patriotism and national cohesion and unity.[29]

So far as the second reason is concerned, even if, as was previously brought into question, capitalism inevitably leads to the breakup of extended-family community, it may be contested whether such a breakup must generate a need for public welfare provision for the indigent. Public welfare provision, on the one hand, and support by family members, on the other, do not together exhaust the possible systems of aid for those unable to support themselves from current earnings. Alternatives to both include private charity and self-help in the form of membership in voluntary savings and insurance schemes. There is a considerable body of direct and indirect historical evidence to suggest that these alternatives to state welfare and assistance from extended families would and could perfectly well take care of all the problems connected with indigence in a capitalist society.[30] One notable example is the welfare role played by fraternal societies in the United States during the pre-Depression era. It has been estimated, for example, that, in 1920, one in three of all adults aged over twenty belonged to one or more fraternal societies which provided an extensive system of social welfare. The extent and effectiveness of self-help is illustrated by the fact that, in 1930, fewer than 4 percent of New York's aged depended upon either public or private charity.[31] One explanation of why the welfare state has come in for recent attack in contemporary Western societies such as America and Great Britain could well be that there is no real good reason for it, and many reasons against. What some of these might be we shall consider in the next section.

The third reason why capitalism has been said to undermine political community is that it supposedly creates unemployment in those developed countries which practice free trade with developing countries whose labor costs are lower. There is, however, not much reason to suppose that, when so practiced, free trade must invariably result in politically divisive high levels of structural unemployment. To make this supposition is to assume that the skills developed in a well-established industri-

[29] See Robert Nisbet, *The Twilight of Authority* (New York: Oxford University Press, 1975), pp. 64–70.

[30] For accounts of some of this evidence in relation to the United Kingdom, see David Green, *Reinventing Civil Society: The Rediscovery of Welfare without Politics* (London: IEA Health and Welfare Unit, 1993); and Seldon, *Capitalism*, ch. 11. For accounts of some of the evidence in relation to the United States, see Marvin Olasky, *The Tragedy of American Compassion* (Washington, DC: Regnery Gateway, 1992); Charles Murray, *In Pursuit of Happiness and Good Government* (New York: Simon and Schuster, 1988); and David T. Beito, "Mutual Aid for Social Welfare: The Case of American Fraternal Societies," *Critical Review*, vol. 4, no. 4 (Fall 1990), pp. 709–36.

[31] Beito, "Mutual Aid for Social Welfare," pp. 711–14 passim.

alized labor force are insufficiently transferable to enable alternative sources of employment to be found as a result of the collapse of traditional manufacturing industries in the face of foreign competition.

In any case, it is open to doubt whether domestic demand for the import of cheap manufactured goods could ever be so high as to create prolonged high levels of domestic unemployment. For how could there be such a high level of demand for imports unless there was enough domestic employment to generate the demand? *Ex hypothesi*, the cheap foreign imports are in lines formerly produced by and for the domestic market. Unless those who formerly produced these manufactured goods in the developed countries for domestic consumption were able to find alternative forms of employment, there would not be sufficient demand for these cheap foreign imports. Free trade may well alter the balance of wealth between trading partners under conditions of ideal capitalism, but, under these ideal conditions, it can never lead to prolonged structural unemployment.

There remains for consideration the fourth reason why capitalism has been claimed inimical to political community. To recall, the claim was that, through the adoption of representative rather than direct democracy, members of society are deprived of the political wherewithal to develop a common political will. The thesis that representative democracy is inimical to political community may be contested on two counts. First, it may be doubted whether, for a state to be a political community, anything more is needed than that its citizens share a common patriotic attachment to it. For such a sentiment to be possible, it is difficult to perceive why anything more should be necessary than that the citizens feel satisfied with the lives and opportunities open to them in their society. It is surely possible for citizens to feel such satisfaction without their state having to afford them the opportunity for direct democratic participation. Not everyone enjoys politics—other than as a spectator sport!

Second, even if it is conceded that genuine political community demands from citizens not only patriotism but a common will, it may be doubted whether representative democracy is any less able than direct democracy to engender such a will. Historically, direct democracy has not always issued in a high degree of common will. Ancient Athens, often cited as the paradigm case of a direct democracy, does not appear to have always enjoyed a high level of common will among its active citizenry. By the fourth century B.C. at least, it seems to have been a highly fractured political society held together more by compromise than by any genuine consensus.[32]

If direct democracy does not suffice to guarantee the presence of a common will among citizens, then representative democracy does not suffice

---

[32] Chester G. Starr, *The Aristocratic Temper of Greek Civilization* (New York: Oxford University Press, 1992), p. 27.

to guarantee its absence. As was once acutely observed of the British system of parliamentary democracy,

> [r]epresentative government is not merely an inferior substitute for government by general assembly; it is superior in many ways. . . . [F]irst, through the culmination of national deliberation among a selected group of representatives . . . in whose consciousness the nation . . . is most adequately reflected; secondly, by means of the party system, which ensures vigorous criticism and full discussion of all proposals . . . — in these two ways . . . the formal deliberations and decisions of the nation are raised to a higher plane than the collective deliberations of any assembly of men lacking such traditional organisation could possibly attain. . . . It is . . . acquiescence in accomplished legislation . . . which gives to the decisions of Parliament the status . . . of the expression of the will of practically the whole nation.[33]

The mere fact that a democracy is direct does not ensure that its citizens will enjoy a high degree of common will. Nor does the fact that a democracy is representative ensure that its citizens will not. If, as is arguably the case, neither Britain nor the United States today enjoys a notably high degree of common will among its citizens, it is not the fact that both countries are representative rather than direct democracies which explains why this is so.

But if it is not capitalism that undermines community in these four valuable forms, what has led these varieties of community to become so weak in present-day Western societies? With this question, we come near to the end of our enquiry. I shall attempt to address it in the next and last section, where I will try to show that these varieties of community would stand a far better chance of flourishing in these societies were they to become more rather than less fully capitalist.

VII. THE TRUE CULPRIT

As I have previously noted, recent years have witnessed a remarkable decline in family community in both the United States and the United Kingdom. Whether any anticapitalist inferences may be drawn from this decline, however, is moot. The societies in which it has occurred are by no means fully capitalist in form. Consequently, it is not possible to implicate capitalism in the decline simply in virtue of its having taken place in these currently most capitalist of societies. Since they are not fully capitalist in form, it is equally possible that the decline has occurred as a result

---

[33] William McDougall, *The Group Mind* (Cambridge: Cambridge University Press, 1920), pp. 190–91.

of recent changes which have made these societies become less rather than more capitalist than they previously had been.

So far as the increase in single-parent families is concerned, this would certainly appear to be the case. The sudden increase in the number of such families can be directly correlated with a correspondingly recent and no less massive increase in the levels of state support that have come to be provided for single mothers. Since the increase of single-parent families has been disproportionately great among the least well-off social classes, it would appear that the increased levels of support for single mothers have served to remove previously powerful economic disincentives for young women from such backgrounds to have children out of wedlock.[34]

Something similar can be said in connection with the recent increase in divorce. One recent change which has occurred in both the United States and Great Britain cannot but be regarded as intimately connected with this increase in divorce, and as a change which has made these societies less capitalist than they formerly were. This change has been the introduction of so-called *no-fault divorce*.[35] The term "no-fault" refers to two different issues. The first is that divorce may be secured without one marital partner's needing first to establish any fault in the conduct of the other, such as adultery or cruelty. The second is that, in the accompanying financial settlement, the conduct of the partners during the marriage is not taken into account in apportioning the assets between them. This form of divorce was introduced gradually into most American states in the course of the 1960s and early 1970s, and was introduced into Britain with the 1969 Divorce Reform Act and some subsequent case law, notably *Wachtel v. Wachtel* in 1973.

There is, no doubt, some close causal connection between, on the one hand, the recent increase in individualism in personal relations, as reflected in the increase in divorce, and, on the other, the introduction of no-fault divorce. But in which direction does the causal link flow? There is some reason for supposing that the introduction of no-fault divorce has given rise to the increase in individualism in personal relations rather than the other way around. By severing the terms of the financial settlement from the marital conduct of spouses, no-fault divorce removes a hitherto seemingly powerful disincentive against marital partners' engaging in marital infidelity or other forms of conduct which give grounds for

---

[34] See Charles Murray, *Losing Ground: American Social Policy, 1950–1980* (New York: Basic Books, 1984); Murray, *The Emerging British Underclass* (London: IEA Health and Welfare Unit, 1990); and Murray, *Underclass: The Crisis Deepens* (London: IEA Health and Welfare Unit, 1994).

[35] For a good discussion of the impact of no-fault divorce upon divorce rates, see Norman Barry, "Justice and Liberty in Marriage and Divorce," in *Liberating Women . . . From Modern Feminism*, ed. Caroline Quest (London: IEA Health and Welfare Unit, 1994), pp. 38–58; and John Campion, "Marriage, Morals, and the Law," *Salisbury Review*, vol. 13, no. 2 (December 1994), pp. 25–28.

divorce. The introduction of no-fault divorce may, therefore, be thought likely to have encouraged greater marital infidelity and marital misconduct than would otherwise have occurred.

No-fault divorce is not a form of divorce which any truly capitalist society could countenance. For it involves a deliberate abrogation on the part of the state of one of the essential functions of any genuinely capitalist state, namely, the enforcement of freely entered into, legally recognized contracts between private citizens. When two people get married, they make a vow or promise to one another of lifelong fidelity and support. These marital vows set up legitimate expectations in the marital partners of those who make them. In removing all legal sanction against those who unilaterally violate their marriage vows, and hence who frustrate the expectations that these vows have created in their marital partners, no-fault divorce, in effect, nullifies the legal force of the vows themselves, and in so doing subverts the institution of marriage. The enforcement of legally recognized contracts seems to be among the indispensable functions which any decent capitalist state must perform. If, as seems plausible, the introduction of no-fault divorce has been among the principal causes of the recent increase in divorce in both Britain and America, it would follow that this increase in divorce has been the result of these societies' having become less rather than more capitalist than they formerly were.

In a purely capitalist society, there would be far greater disincentive than there currently is for men and women to have children out of wedlock. Single mothers would not receive any of the state support they currently do. Likewise, in a purely capitalist society, there is likely to be far less infidelity and marital breakdown. For, in such a society, legally recognized contracts would be enforced, and, hence, unfaithful or cruel marital partners would, upon divorce, be liable for damages for breaking their marriage vows. For these reasons, therefore, it may be said that the recent breakdown of the family in such societies as the United States and Britain is due less to their being as capitalist as they are than it is to their not being as capitalist as they could be and once were.

Something similar can be said in connection with the significant and marked deterioration in neighborhood community that has taken place in both the United States and the United Kingdom since the mid-1960s. By far the biggest single way in which neighborhood community has declined in these societies has been through a massive increase in crime that has taken place during this period. Between 1963 and 1980, the rate of murder in the United States doubled, the rate of violent robbery almost tripled, and the rate of burglary almost doubled.[36] During this same period, comparable increases have been recorded for England. Until 1955, the crime rate in England had been low and comparatively static for a

---

[36] Murray, *Losing Ground*, p. 115.

hundred years. It then began to rise. Relative to its level in 1960, by 1965, the crime rate was more than double; by 1970, more than triple; and, by 1980, more than five times what it had been in 1960.[37]

What has been responsible for this massive increase in crime in both societies is a matter of much controversy. However, one major social change which has taken place during the period since 1960 has arguably had an important bearing on the increase; and this change, as was argued earlier, has been a direct consequence of these societies' having become less capitalist than they were formerly. The social change in question is the dramatic growth during this period in the numbers and proportion of single-parent families. The growth of such families has dramatically increased the number of young males growing up in neighborhoods lacking large numbers of responsible adult male role models. It seems likely that such males will be less able to internalize a work ethic and norms of social responsibility than those who grow up in neighborhoods densely populated by such role models. Since it is adolescent males who are the most frequent lawbreakers, there is some reason to suspect that the increase during this same period of single-parent households has been among the principal factors responsible for the recent increase in crime in both America and Britain. If this suspicion is sound, much of the recent decline of neighborhood community in the United States and Britain can be attributed to those social and legal changes connected with welfare benefits and divorce, changes which made these societies less rather than more capitalist in form. As levels of state welfare have increased above a critical threshold, previously powerful economic disincentives have been removed from women of low-income backgrounds to have children out of wedlock. With the introduction of no-fault divorce, incentives for marital fidelity and propriety have been weakened. If the rise in crime may be attributed to the increase in fatherless families, then the very same changes in social policy which (as I have argued) undermine family community may also be deemed responsible for much of the recent increase in crime which has proven so damaging to neighborhood community.

There is a still further way in which the same massive increase in state welfare of all sorts during this period may be thought to have contributed to the erosion of neighborhood community. This is by its having removed from private citizens both the need and, in some cases, the resources (be these time or money) to engage in philanthropic endeavors in their neighborhoods. As has been observed in this connection,

> [i]ndividuals are drawn to community affiliations and attach themselves to them in direct proportion to the functional value of these organizations. . . . Take away the functions, and you take away the

[37] Norman Dennis, *Rising Crime and the Dismembered Family* (London: IEA Health and Welfare Unit, 1993), p. 1.

community. The cause of the problem is . . . a centralization of functions that shouldn't be centralized, and this is very much a matter of political choice, not ineluctable forces.[38]

The cohesion of distinct national communities has remained remarkably and unexpectedly resilient in present-day American and British society. This is especially true among immigrants and ethnic minorities. Nevertheless, as I have noted, there has been a significant increase in deracination among all social strata. This remains so, despite the very recent emergence in both societies of what amounts almost to a cult of ethnicity.[39] A good part of the responsibility for this kind of loss can be attributed to the fact that the state in both societies has intervened unduly in the sphere of education. In both societies, the state has assumed effective responsibility for the provision of schooling for the vast majority, as well as for deciding the content of the school curriculum. However, there is no reason why it should assume such responsibility in order to ensure that all its citizens receive an adequate education. There is no need for the state to intervene in education, beyond, at most, requiring all parents to ensure that their children receive an education and supplying assistance to those unable to do so.

By assuming responsibility for schooling and for the content of the curriculum, the state in both societies has inexorably imposed upon members an unnecessary and unwarranted degree of cultural homogeneity. For it has crowded out the possibility of citizens of different nationality or religion making arrangements for the schooling of their own children. Where schooling is privately supplied, it is likely, for obvious reasons, to be provided through churches and other cultural organizations closely associated with different nationalities. By becoming the major provider of schooling for the majority of the population, the state, in both the United States and Britain, has reduced the scope for citizens to provide their children with a grounding in the cultural traditions of the nations to which they belong. Thus, by being less capitalist than it might be and once was, the state, in both the United States and Britain, has inadvertently subverted distinct national and cultural communities and contributed to the deracination of members of society.[40]

Educational curricula designed to do justice to the contemporary "multicultural" character of these societies do little to stem the undue homogenization and deracination produced by state intervention in the sphere of education. These curricula merely prevent any children taught under them from being able to receive a deep and thorough grounding

[38] Murray, *In Pursuit of Happiness and Good Government*, p. 279.

[39] See Arthur M. Schlesinger, Jr., *The Disuniting of America: Reflections on a Multicultural Society* (New York and London: W. W. Norton and Company, 1992).

[40] For the classic argument for this thesis, see E. G. West, *Education and the State* (London: Institute of Economic Affairs, 1965).

in any one single culture—rather than acquainting everyone with all cultures. By assuming responsibility for providing education, the state, in both the United States and Great Britain, has greatly reduced the variety of different types of school needed to enable societies as culturally diverse and ethnically pluralistic as these to maintain a rich diversity of national cultures and traditions within them.

Let us, finally, turn to consider what might truly have been responsible for the very real recent decline in patriotism, and hence in genuine political community, in countries such as Britain and the United States. I have argued that extension of government beyond the role to which it would be confined in a truly capitalist order has been responsible for the undermining of the family, neighborhood, and national communities. Since all these smaller varieties of community have been so profoundly undermined by the overextension of government, it is hardly surprising that political community itself has suffered a corresponding decline as well, both in terms of patriotism and in terms of the degree of common will. As has been well observed in this connection: "If they love not those whom they have seen, how shall they love those whom they have not seen?"[41]

In exonerating capitalism of the charge of undermining community in present-day Western societies, and levelling the charge instead against their overextended governments, I reach a conclusion similar to that reached half a century ago by Robert Nisbet in his remarkably prescient and still unsurpassed treatment of the subject.[42] "[W]ith all respect to the influence of capitalism," observed Nisbet, "I do not think it can be called the primary agent in the transmutation of social groups and communities. . . . [T]he single most decisive influence . . . has been the rise and development of the centralized territorial State."[43]

Nisbet's thesis was that the prime threat to community in modern societies comes not from capitalism but from the fact that the state in these societies has taken upon itself functions and tasks better left to local autonomous communities of family, church, and neighborhood. By removing from these associations their traditional educative and welfare functions, the modern welfare state has effectively destroyed the rationale of these varieties of group as communities, without itself having become, or being capable of becoming, an adequate substitute for the multifarious moralizing and socializing functions these forms of community previously fulfilled.

Only when we have correctly identified what is truly responsible for the sorry state of community in today's societies can we hope to know how best to begin to redress the problem. If my argument is sound, then

---

[41] This remark is attributed to Dean Inge in McDougall, *The Group Mind*, p. 181n.

[42] Nisbet, *The Quest for Community* (*supra* note 24).

[43] *Ibid.*, pp. 97–98.

none of the main prescriptions made by contemporary communitarians for strengthening community are likely to prove effective. All they do is further extend the role of the state, which has been the principal culprit in undermining community in the first place. Thus, they are, at best, likely to be ineffective, and, at worst, likely only to accelerate the demise of community. To arrest and reverse the decline of community, more capitalism is needed, not less. The crucial political choice that faces the modern world, therefore, is not the choice between capitalism and community. Rather, it is the choice between capitalism together with community, on the one hand, and super-Leviathan on the other. Communitarians should therefore either cease to inveigh against capitalism or cease to claim that concern for community is what moves them to do so.

Philosophy, Middlesex University

THE POSTMODERN SELF AND THE POLITICS
OF LIBERAL EDUCATION*

By Steven Kautz

I. Introduction

Richard Rorty is one of the principal architects of a new way of thinking about liberalism. He calls his way "liberal ironism": it is a postmodern liberalism, without Enlightenment rationalism, without the hopeless and finally enervating aspiration to discover an ahistorical philosophical foundation ("natural rights") for liberal principles and practices. The postmodern liberal ironist, unlike the classical liberal rationalist, "faces up to the contingency of his or her own most central beliefs and desires," says Rorty, including the characteristic liberal belief that "cruelty is the worst thing we do." Such postmodern liberals frankly admit the apparently unhappy consequence of that essential "contingency," that "there is no *neutral*, noncircular way to defend" liberal ways, no good argument to deploy against "Nazi and Marxist enemies of liberalism"; but no such argument is needed, says Rorty, since loyalty to one's own community is morality enough, even where that loyalty is without foundation. Here, I begin with a few words about Rorty's postmodern liberalism, as preface to a discussion of the effects of postmodern doctrines on liberal moral psychology.[1]

Postmodern liberalism is no strategic retreat, according to Rorty; his position is not that of an embattled liberal grudgingly conceding that Enlightenment rationalism is by now so thoroughly discredited that friends of liberalism must seek a more up-to-date, philosophically modest way of defending liberalism. Rather, says Rorty, we now see that "the vocabulary of Enlightenment rationalism, although it was essential to the beginnings of liberal democracy, has become an impediment to the preservation and progress of democratic societies." We have progressed beyond the need for Enlightenment rationalism, which was so useful when the enemies of freedom, priests and others, spoke a language of more-than-rational authority; now the enemies of freedom (above all, conservative partisans of prevailing authorities in Western liberal communities) have appropriated the formerly liberating language of reason and

* I would like to thank the Earhart Foundation and the Harry & Lynde Bradley Foundation, whose generous research support helped to make possible the preparation of this essay.
[1] Richard Rorty, *Contingency, Irony, and Solidarity* (Cambridge: Cambridge University Press, 1989), pp. xv, 53, 197. In *Liberalism and Community* (Ithaca: Cornell University Press, 1995) — from which this paragraph and the next are taken — I discuss Rorty's liberalism.

 © 1996 Social Philosophy and Policy Foundation. Printed in the USA.

nature, crushing the poetry in our souls—those self-creative impulses that enable human beings to liberate themselves from inherited, tired, used ways of life. Thus, a new vocabulary, the vocabulary of liberal ironism, which "revolves around notions of metaphor and self-creation rather than around notions of truth, rationality, and moral obligation," is more suited to a progressive liberalism today than is the inherited language of inalienable rights, self-evident truths, and the rest. And a new "conception of the self"—one that makes " 'community constitutive of the individual' " (so that each of us is essentially "constituted" by his or her membership in particular communities) and that, on the other hand, honors idiosyncratic self-creation more than knowledge of our common humanity—"in fact comport[s] better with liberal democracy than does the Enlightenment conception of the self" as having an intrinsic nature that justifies certain moral understandings. So postmodern liberal ironism is a strategic advance over classical liberal rationalism, says Rorty: the liberal ironist describes prevailing liberal principles and practices more faithfully than the liberal rationalist; and he is more assured in his defense of liberal ways, because he is less troubled by the skepticism that is the flip side of the rationalist coin.[2]

To be sure, Rorty's strategy does not permit a defense of the old, robust liberalism of natural rights. We now know that our attachment to liberal democracy is a historically contingent faith, one among many such fighting faiths, and that liberal political principles are in no sense "the common interest of humanity." We are, says Rorty, "postmodern bourgeois liberals," products of the "institutions and practices of the rich North Atlantic democracies," tolerably comfortable (both physically and morally) with our way of life, but lacking the cultural arrogance of our ancestors: we are ethnocentric, but we do not insist on the superiority of our ways. After all, what is wrong, asks Rorty, with "the attempt to fulfill the hopes of the North Atlantic bourgeoisie"? If we must indeed abandon the naive hope of those starry-eyed early liberals, to vindicate by our example the *rights of man*, of human beings qua human beings, so what? Will *we* not still live comfortably as liberals, and even be able to defend our liberal way of life with, as Rorty says, "unflinching courage"?[3]

My aim in this essay is quite modest. I propose to raise certain questions regarding the psychological consequences of conceiving of liberalism, and of the relation between the individual and the community, in this new way. What sorts of human beings will emerge as we learn, more and more, to "face up to our contingency" (as beings without essential natures, who are wholly constituted by idiosyncratic or historical acci-

---

[2] Rorty, *Contingency, Irony, and Solidarity*, p. 44; and Richard Rorty, *Objectivity, Relativism, and Truth* (Cambridge: Cambridge University Press, 1991), p. 178 (quoting Charles Taylor).

[3] Rorty, *Objectivity, Relativism, and Truth*, p. 198; and Rorty, *Contingency, Irony, and Solidarity*, p. 47 and context.

dents)? I do not here aim to refute Rorty's major claim: that there is no escape from contingency either for individuals or for communities.[4] Rather, I argue that Rorty is mistaken, or at least unreasonably hopeful, regarding the psychological consequences of embracing his postmodern doctrines. I should add that Rorty invites a debate on these terms, for he does not himself claim to *prove* that there is no escape from contingency.[5] Rorty's task, in *Contingency, Irony, and Solidarity*, is to paint a pleasing portrait of the liberal ironist: to show that there is no need to worry, ironists are nice folks too. Thus, the issue here is whether a (politically and morally) healthy liberal ironism is possible or likely, not whether the antiphilosophical claims of the ironist can be refuted. I argue that certain pathologies of the postmodern soul can be traced to the increasingly widespread conviction that something like Rorty's account of the "contingency of the self" and the "contingency of community" is true; and I aim thereby to give rise to doubts regarding the *celebration* of contingency that characterizes much contemporary theorizing. But that is evidently the beginning of the argument, not the end.

Rorty suggests that his new way of thinking about liberalism entails a new way of thinking about liberal education. Since that is a more manageable topic than the more general question regarding liberal democracy, I propose to ask whether Rorty's postmodernist strategy for defending liberalism works in the particular case of liberal education. I shall raise two objections to Rorty's strategy. First, a conservative objection: In a world of self-creative liberal ironists who embrace altogether new and idiosyncratic ways of life, what reason is there to suppose that attachment to liberal principles and practices will endure? Next, a radical objection: In abandoning enlightenment rationalism, do we not thereby also abandon our capacity for reasonable self-criticism, for doubting our own ways in light of an understanding of the "common interest of humanity"?

---

[4] That is, I do not directly challenge Rorty's metaphysical or epistemological irrealism here; the question of whether Rorty's deeper philosophical views are true or not is almost entirely distinct from the question of whether embracing those views will yield illiberal and otherwise destructive psychological and political consequences. This essay addresses only the latter issue. Thus, I do not address the question of whether the absence of foundations necessarily or for philosophical reasons places us in a moral free-fall; rather, I argue that the natural and ordinary psychological consequence of this new liberalism without foundations is such moral confusion.

[5] As Rorty admits, he does not quite "argue" that this is so:

"argument" is not the right word. For on my account of intellectual progress as the literalization of selected metaphors, rebutting objections to one's redescriptions of some things will be largely a matter of redescribing other things, trying to outflank the objections by enlarging the scope of one's favorite metaphors. So my strategy will be to try to make the vocabulary in which these objections are phrased look bad, thereby changing the subject, rather than granting the objector his choice of weapons and terrain by meeting his criticisms head-on. (Rorty, *Contingency, Irony, and Solidarity*, p. 44)

II. Liberal Education

Liberal education as it is commonly understood has two dimensions: a conservative dimension and a radical dimension. This story is as old as Plato's *Republic*: higher education, the education most suitable for free men, is at once an education toward good citizenship and an education toward philosophy. And these two educations, which are in some sense aspects of a single education, have different imperatives, as Plato memorably reveals in a little joke about philosophers and noble puppies, that they are akin because they both love what they know.[6]

Consider, first, the conservative dimension—liberal education as education toward good citizenship. Regimes differ, nations differ, epochs differ: and thus an education toward good citizenship will also differ from time to time and from place to place. Put another way, a liberal education is in part an education toward membership in a particular (moral, political, sometimes religious) community; it is an education in a particular way of life, a tradition, a set of understandings about what it means to be, say, an Athenian or an American. (So we might also call this the communitarian dimension of liberal education.) Human beings cannot live well, it seems, outside such communities; in any case, we are all born into them, and we must learn to make our peace with them. Toward this end, a liberal education first of all teaches us who we are, where we come from, what we say we believe. E. D. Hirsch's *Cultural Literacy*, for example, seeks to reinvigorate this aspect of liberal education today. The core of *our* liberal education, then, must be a study of Western civilization, of the traditions that inform our way of life. Without this, we are in some sense homeless.[7]

There is doubtless more to the conservative or communitarian aspect of liberal education than this. Thus, for example, Rorty writes:

> When people on the political right talk about education, they immediately start talking about truth. Typically, they enumerate what they take to be familiar and self-evident truths and regret that these are no longer being inculcated in the young. . . . The left typically views the old familiar truths cherished by the right as a crust of convention

---

[6] Plato, *Republic*, trans. Allan Bloom (New York: Basic Books, 1968), 375a–376c. In this respect, the *Republic* offers a model of a liberal education, an education toward both citizenship (virtue) and philosophy (reason).

[7] In "Education without Dogma: Truth, Freedom, and Our Universities," *Dissent*, vol. 36, no. 2 (Spring 1989), Rorty distinguishes, as I do here, between conservative and radical understandings of liberal education, but he is a critic of both understandings. (His somewhat bloodless name for the conservative aspect of liberal education is "socialization.") But his account of the two dimensions of liberal education differs from my account in significant ways, some of which are noted below.

that needs to be broken through, vestiges of old-fashioned modes of thought from which the new generation should be freed.[8]

A conservative might quibble with some of this (especially since, as I will argue, conservatism in the sense at issue here is altogether compatible with a philosophical radicalism), and in particular with the implication that our truths precede our arguments, which is of course backwards. A more sporting response, however, would be a confession: Fair enough. So far as a liberal education is an education toward good citizenship, toward participation in the way of life of a particular community, it will inevitably see truths where outsiders and radicals see only questions and prejudices; for the defenders of any particular civilization or way of life will commonly say not only that this way of life is "one's own" but also that it is a "good" or even the "best" way. We may, of course, be wrong when we say such things, for example, about Western civilization. Yet there is something honorable about this aspect of traditional conservatism: it implies that there is some authority or horizon beyond the community itself, in the light of which one must distinguish between the best ways and inferior ways; such conservatism affirms the possibility and even the necessity (as, I will argue, Rorty and other postmodern communitarians cannot) of a certain kind of philosophical radicalism.

Let me now turn to the radical dimension of a liberal education: liberal education as education toward philosophy. Again, Rorty's description of this species of radicalism (in education) is fair enough, so far as it goes:

> When people on the political left talk about education, they talk first about freedom. . . . The left dismisses Platonic asceticism and exalts Socratic social criticism. It identifies the obstacles to freedom that education must overcome not with the passions or with sin but with convention and prejudice. . . . What the right thinks of as the triumph of reason, the left describes as the triumph of acculturation — acculturation engineered by the powers that be. . . . In the tradition of Rousseau, Marx, Nietzsche, and Foucault, the left pictures society as depriving the young of their freedom and of their essential humanity.[9]

The language of left and right is not especially helpful here, I think; the philosophical radicalism that gives rise to "Socratic social criticism" is of course compatible, as in the case of Socrates himself, with a sort of political conservatism. So too, Allan Bloom's The Closing of the American Mind also (borrowing Rorty's words) "pictures society as depriving the young of their freedom and their essential humanity." (Although Bloom is often

---

[8] Rorty, "Education without Dogma," p. 198.
[9] Ibid.

described as a political conservative, he is in this respect a philosophical radical in a way that Rorty cannot be, since Rorty denies that there is an "essential humanity.") Perhaps it would be better, then, to speak of a quarrel between community and philosophy; since communitarians are often on the left, thinking about the issue in these terms yields a provocative confusion by revealing a surprising kinship between political radicalism and philosophical conservatism today. However that may be, liberal education is surely (in part) a quest for freedom, as Rorty here says: freedom from community, from law and orthodoxy. Philosophy is the search for a place to stand outside the community, beyond the reach of the particular prejudices and conventions of a time and place. But where is this solid piece of ground? As Glaucon says in Plato's *Republic*, the daring lover of freedom seeks "what any nature naturally pursues as good"; such a human being "pursues a thing dependent on truth and does not live in the light of opinion." Law or convention "by force perverts [nature]," says Glaucon.[10] And this is true everywhere, since every community is constituted by some orthodoxy, some fundamental faith. In the *Republic*, Socrates teaches Glaucon that philosophy is the road to nature; from the vantage of this old-fashioned Socratic or philosophical radicalism, our homes appear to be our chains, as in the parable of the cave. And liberal education at its most inspiring breaks these bonds, stealing children from their parents, the pious from their parishes, citizens from their communities. But this is possible only if "there is something in man that is not altogether in slavery to his society"; liberal education aims to bring that something—our "essential humanity"—to light.[11] Here's the rub: Rorty and other postmodernists now deny that there is such a place as "nature" or such a natural kind as "humanity"; and thus Rorty is obliged to think again about liberal education, and especially the radical or philosophical dimension of liberal education (just as he was obliged, for the same reasons, to think again about the character of liberalism itself). That is the business of the essay now under consideration, Rorty's "Education without Dogma."

I need to make one further ancillary point regarding the traditional view of liberal education, before proceeding to Rorty's view. Since liberal education is both an education toward good citizenship and an education toward philosophy, and since these are not easily harmonized, it is tempting to assign priority to one dimension at the expense of the other. For political reasons, some might be inclined to emphasize the conservative dimension of a liberal education, the importance of making the honorable case for Western civilization in the face of old and new enemies, and to neglect the Socratic aspiration to find a way out of the cave. The

[10] Plato, *Republic*, 359c, 362a.
[11] Leo Strauss, *Natural Right and History* (Chicago: University of Chicago Press, 1953), p. 3.

temptation to respond to the challenge of postmodernism or multiculturalism in this way, which has not always been resisted on the right in
recent years, seems to me misguided, not only for the reasons already
sufficiently indicated but also because it leaves the field of radical social
criticism to the enemies of Western civilization, a tactical error that makes
it remarkably easy to portray defenders of the traditional understanding
of liberal education as stodgy and complacent partisans of "the powers
that be." But the opposite error is perhaps more interesting. For certain
defenders of old-fashioned liberal education are inclined to assign priority to the Socratic dimension: good citizenship for the kids, philosophy
for the wise few. It seems to me, however, that in the absence of a serious education toward participation in the way of life of a particular community, Socratic education will often be frivolous, lacking the gravity that
comes from knowledge of what is at stake. Only if we first come to know
who we are, where we come from, what we (willy-nilly) believe, can we
begin to achieve that liberation from the disabling orthodoxies of our time
and place which liberal education promises; otherwise we will be blind
to these too-familiar habits of thought and ways of living, hardly notic-
ing the chains that most confine us. What is more, only in this way can
we properly weigh the full price of liberation, the loss of our "homes."

   The drama of a liberal education consists just in this: we must somehow harmonize these respectable conservative and radical impulses,
standing now inside and then outside our community. Liberal education
enables human beings to move between the kind of thick description of
a way of life that Michael Walzer calls "interpretation" and the Socratic
quest for a way out of the cave that Walzer eschews (see his *Interpretation
and Social Criticism*).[12] The most impressive achievements of social criticism are of this kind, it seems to me. Let me mention two cases: Frederick Douglass and Abraham Lincoln. It would not be easy to decide
whether these men were conservatives or radicals. Douglass, a former
slave and an abolitionist, could not but despise the hypocrisy of those
who professed a faith in the principles of the Declaration of Independence
and the Constitution while remaining indifferent to the evident injustice of slavery; and yet, during most of his public life he was a vigorous
partisan of the Constitution, and he argued (against many of his abolitionist friends) that fidelity to the Constitution was the ground on which
those animated by an honorable and patriotic aspiration to abolish slavery must stand. Or consider his splendid oration in memory of Lincoln,
or his speech on "The Meaning of July Fourth for the Negro": in these
places, and elsewhere, Douglass speaks as both a citizen and a philosopher, a patriotic American and a radical critic of what Americans had
done, an angry friend of his fellow citizens and a bitter enemy who loves

---

[12] Michael Walzer, *Interpretation and Social Criticism* (Cambridge: Harvard University
Press, 1987).

justice.[13] So too, Lincoln's speeches reveal a mind at once conservative and radical: the Gettysburg Address and, in a more prosaic mode, the Peoria and Cooper Institute speeches are masterly expositions of the principles of the American regime; the Second Inaugural and the Lyceum speech, and many remarks scattered throughout his more ordinary speeches, are radical expressions of doubt regarding the justice and health of American institutions. Each man was at ease speaking both of our duties as American citizens and of our essential humanity; and this broadmindedness, among other virtues (the capacity to temper justice with mercy, indignation with charity; to resist both blind love and foolish moralism), enabled these statesmen to raise their community above itself, so to speak, for a time.

I argue, next, that our inability to imitate or even to recognize such virtues has its roots in the postmodernist reinterpretation of freedom and community.

III. COMMUNITY AND THE POSTMODERN SELF

Postmodernist liberals stand apart from this quarrel between radicals and conservatives regarding liberal education, just as they stand apart from quarrels between, say, classical liberals and Marxist radicals regarding liberalism itself. As Rorty and Bloom agree, postmodernism today has more in common with Nietzsche than with either Locke or Marx. Thus, radical and conservative partisans of old-fashioned liberal education are united by a certain aspiration, says Rorty: both accept the "distinctions between nature and convention and between what is essentially human and what is inhuman," and strive to enable human beings to realize their "essential humanity"; both recognize that there is a horizon beyond the community itself, in the light of which one must distinguish between the best ways of life and inferior ways. Conservatives affirm that the prevailing principles and practices of liberal democratic polities (or at least the ideals of Western civilization on which these are based) are, all things considered, superior to imaginable alternatives, and that the "familiar and self-evident truths" of our particular tradition are founded on human nature. So we must now defend these embattled "old-fashioned modes of thought" against fashionable enemies. Radicals deny this, of course, arguing that our particular (Western) way of life is "alienating and repressive," thus "depriving the young of their freedom and of their essential humanity"; and so they "regard the conservative's 'fundamental truths' as what Foucault calls 'the discourse of power.' " But this dispute does

---

[13] See Frederick Douglass, "The Constitution of the United States: Is It Pro-Slavery or Anti-Slavery?" (March 26, 1860), "Oration in Memory of Abraham Lincoln" (April 14, 1876), and "The Meaning of July Fourth for the Negro" (July 5, 1852), in *The Life and Writings of Frederick Douglass*, ed. Philip S. Foner (New York: International Publishers, 1955).

not reach fundamentals, says Rorty, because neither party questions the Enlightenment or Socratic account of the self upon which the idea of liberal education as an ascent from conventional opinion to knowledge of our essential humanity is founded. Because of this fundamental agreement, it is sometimes possible for old-fashioned conservatives ("Platonists") and old-fashioned radicals ("inverted Platonists") to get together against postmodernists in defense of a certain understanding of the universities.[14]

Postmodernism is different, because it is founded on a new account of the self. Here is the doctrine, from "Education without Dogma":

> There is no such thing as human nature, in the deep sense in which Plato and Strauss use this term. Nor is there such a thing as alienation from one's essential humanity due to societal repression, in the deep sense made familiar by Rousseau and the Marxists. There is only the shaping of an animal into a human being by a process of socialization, followed (with luck) by the self-individualization and self-creation of that human being through his or her own later revolt against that very process. . . . The point of . . . higher education is . . . to help students realize that they can reshape themselves—that they can rework the self-image foisted on them by their past, the self-image that makes them competent citizens, into a new self-image, one that they themselves have helped to create.

Or again: "If precollege education produces literate citizens and college education produces self-creating individuals, then questions about whether students are being taught the truth can be safely neglected."[15] Both left and right, so to speak (though perhaps this way of speaking is as misleading in the new dispensation as it was in the old), are transformed by the postmodernist reinterpretation of the self. At any rate, our understanding of "community," and of "freedom," is transformed. Let me now outline, in very broad terms, Rorty's version of this postmodernist account of the self.[16]

Here is a notable peculiarity of our moral experience: we love our privacy, our individuality, our uniqueness—and yet we long for community. We have been driven by some mysterious force to embrace, in speech, ever more unbounded modes of *idiosyncratic privacy*, on one hand, and *constitutive community*, on the other. In *Contingency, Irony, and Solidarity*, Rorty shows how these apparently disparate aspects of our moral experience can be traced to a fundamental common root: the postmodern

---

[14] Rorty, "Education without Dogma," pp. 198–99.

[15] *Ibid.*, p. 200.

[16] I also discuss this question in my essay "Privacy and Community," in *The Legacy of Rousseau*, ed. Nathan Tarcov and Clifford Orwin (Chicago: University of Chicago Press, 1996).

embrace of "contingency." Recall the liberal ironist, "who faces up to the contingency of his or her own most central beliefs and desires." How does the liberal ironist understand "community"? And how does he understand "freedom"?

Begin with the "contingency of community." Rorty insists that "socialization, and thus historical circumstance, goes all the way down"; "there is nothing 'beneath' socialization or prior to history which is definatory of the human." Again: "[T]here is nothing deep inside each of us, no common human nature, no built-in human solidarity, to use as a moral reference point. There is nothing to people except what has been socialized into them." Once more, most bluntly: "Socialization, to repeat, goes all the way down, and who gets to do the socializing is often a matter of who manages to kill whom first."[17] Beyond this, "morality" is no more than "the interest of a historically conditioned community," and "human dignity" is similarly "derivative from the dignity of some specific community": "loyalty to [our society] is morality enough." Morality is "the voice of ourselves as members of a community" (as opposed to the voice of "our own, possibly conflicting, private interests"), not "the voice of a divinized portion of our soul." It is therefore "impossible to ask the question 'Is ours a moral society?' ": there is no "larger community called 'humanity' which has an intrinsic nature" and which "stands to my community as my community stands to me."[18] Postmodernism, for Rorty, is distinguished above all by the courage to "face up" to this "contingency"; such courage enables the ironist to refuse to indulge the philosopher's cowardly temptation to seek an escape from time and chance, a temptation that has its origins in the need for a certain "metaphysical comfort," the "religious need" to "find something ahistorical and necessary to cling to." The ironist can "face up" to the hard truth (or anyway Rorty's "redescription") that nature "teaches no moral lesson, offers no spiritual comfort," something the philosopher cannot face.[19]

Now, it follows from all of this that postmodern communitarianism is much more thoroughgoing than the sort of conservatism that I described earlier. For, to repeat, such conservatives claim to know the "truth" that our particular civilization—say, the traditions, principles, and practices of the West as now realized, more or less, in liberal-democratic polities—is a good or even the best civilization; they thereby at least implicitly look to something beyond the community, something beyond "time and chance," as the measure of our virtues.[20] For such conservatives, and

---

[17] Rorty, *Contingency, Irony, and Solidarity*, pp. xiii, 177, 185.

[18] Rorty, *Objectivity, Relativism, and Truth*, pp. 197–99; Rorty, *Contingency, Irony, and Solidarity*, pp. 59–60.

[19] Richard Rorty, *Consequences of Pragmatism* (Minneapolis: University of Minnesota Press, 1982), pp. 165–66; Rorty, *Contingency, Irony, and Solidarity*, pp. 3, 52.

[20] Perhaps I should acknowledge that there are differences between the sort of conservatism that has made its peace with liberalism, which has been at issue here, and the more

especially those modern conservatives who have made their peace with liberalism, one's own community is not only treasured for its own sake but as the embodiment of something truly good. So far as conservatives admit this distinction between "the good" and "one's own" (as Rorty cannot), their position is marked by a kind of dignity, or even courage, that Rorty's postmodern communitarianism lacks. Consider the courage of Polemarchus, who cannot abide the political consequence of his conservatism, that he must harm good men who happen to be his enemies, and who is therefore willing to undertake a journey with Socrates toward a more reasonable (if still not wholly satisfactory) conservatism.[21] The second face of the ironist's courage, his ability to "face up" to contingency, is a certain cowardice: a refusal to permit the question "Is ours a moral society?" to be asked, a refusal that may easily slide into the ugly and thuggish self-satisfaction of those who suppose that they already know what they need to know — we do not need any advice from outsiders, thank you, we're doing just fine without your help. Here is the dark side of the ironist's courage, in Rorty's words: "[W]hat matters is our loyalty to other human beings clinging together against the dark, not our hope of getting things right."[22] What is the politics of *this* search for "spiritual comfort"?

Rorty's praise of community is, of course, praise of democratic community in particular. Indeed, it is an "exaltation of democracy for its own sake"; we now discover our "moral identity in membership in a democratic community."[23] But the postmodernist or ironist account of democracy has little in common with the honorable tradition of democratic thought that runs from Locke to the Declaration of Independence, *The Federalist Papers*, and Lincoln. "Instead of justifying democratic freedoms by reference to an account of human nature and the nature of reason," Rorty says, we should now embrace these freedoms as the "starting point — something we need not look behind." In the absence of such philosophical foundations, democracy must be understood in a new way: (liberal) democracy is nothing more than the regime where citizens are prepared to "call 'true' whatever belief results from a free and open encounter of opinions, without asking whether this result agrees with something beyond that encounter." Here, "in respect to words as

---

classical conservatism that preceded liberalism or now opposes it. Whatever these may be, they do not reach the issue here, since even the oldest conservatism affirms that "one's own" community is a "good" community, thereby opening the door to Socratic rationalism. For a notable example of the Socratic strategy in dealing with conservatism that this moral posture invites, see the Polemarchus section in the *Republic* (331e–336a). But Rorty and the postmodernists slam this door shut.

[21] Plato, *Republic*, 334d.

[22] Rorty, *Consequences of Pragmatism*, p. 166.

[23] Rorty, "Education without Dogma," p. 204; and Richard Rorty, "That Old-Time Philosophy," *New Republic*, April 4, 1988, p. 28.

opposed to deeds, persuasion as opposed to force, anything goes": and this despite the fact that, on the ironist view, "there is . . . no neat way" (is there any way?) "to draw the line between persuasion and force," "between a cause of changed belief which was also a reason and one which was a 'mere' cause"; and then there are the "messier cases: brain-washing, media hype, and what Marxists call 'false consciousness.' "[24] Thus, there is nothing behind liberal-democratic freedoms (and therefore no limit to be placed upon them), says Rorty: there is only the democratic conversation, and the agreement to embrace its results as " 'true.' " In the face of reasonable doubts regarding the ordinary vices of democracy, doubts of the sort expressed even by such democrats as the authors of *The Federalist Papers*—for example, that democrats too often agree to "call 'true' " opinions that are silly or wicked—Rorty can offer only "utopian hope," indeed "criterionless hope": "Hope—the ability to believe that the future will be unspecifiably different from, and unspecifiably freer than, the past." In short, Rorty's defense of liberal-democratic freedoms is founded on the admittedly groundless hope that "if we take care of polit-ical freedom, truth and goodness will take care of themselves."[25] This is the democratic version of "facing up" to contingency, "clinging together against the dark," refusing to look beyond one's own community in search of a way to measure its virtues and vices. Here there is a risk not only of conformism but also of irresponsible democratic partisanship.

Enough on postmodern democratic community, for that is only half of this story. What about postmodern "freedom"? Just as human beings must learn to embrace the contingency of community, so we must also face up to "the contingency of the self." Old-fashioned radicals are wrong, says Rorty, about the nature of liberation, just as old-fashioned conservatives are wrong about the nature of community. There is no "true self" to be awakened by stripping away the alienating and repres-sive prejudices of one's community; and so liberation cannot be, what it was for Glaucon, the quest for "what any nature naturally pursues as good." So what is freedom?

Begin where Rorty begins, with the fear of death. We do not fear extinction as such, but some concrete loss, says Rorty. We fear, or rather the ironist fears, the loss of "what made his I different from all the other I's." If there is nothing novel or distinctive about one's words or deeds, then one "will have spent one's life shoving about already coined pieces. So one will not really have had an I at all." Rorty goes so far as to say that " 'death' " *is* "the failure to have created." Following Nietzsche, we must

[24] Rorty, "Education without Dogma," pp. 200–201; Rorty, *Contingency, Irony, and Soli-darity*, pp. 52, 84–85, 48.

[25] Rorty, "Education without Dogma," p. 201; Rorty, *Contingency, Irony, and Solidarity*, p. 84. On the ordinary vices of democracy, see Alexander Hamilton, James Madison, and John Jay, *The Federalist Papers*, ed. Clinton Rossiter (New York: New American Library, 1961), "Federalist No. 10," pp. 81–84, and "Federalist No. 63," pp. 384–87.

learn to see "freedom as the recognition of contingency" and "self-knowledge as self-creation"; to know oneself is to know "one's contingency" (not one's essential humanity), and this knowledge is possible only for those who somehow liberate themselves by creating themselves anew (we know only what we make). (Freedom and self-knowledge are good, though it is not clear, on this account, why that is so.) Here is a reprise, says Rorty, of the "quarrel between poetry and philosophy, the tension between an effort to achieve self-creation by the recognition of contingency and an effort to achieve universality by the transcendence of contingency." Not the philosopher but the "strong poet, the maker, [is] humanity's hero."[26]

This account of the fear of death and the meaning of freedom is intelligible on the basis of the postmodernist understanding of the "contingency of the self." The "strong maker, the person who uses words as they have never before been used, is best able to appreciate her own contingency"; the philosophers, on the other hand, "are doomed to spend [their] conscious lives trying to escape from contingency rather than, like the strong poet, acknowledging and appropriating contingency." The philosophical quest to transcend contingency ("to see life steadily and see it whole," to discover "the universal conditions of human existence, the great continuities—the permanent, ahistorical, context of human life") can be defended only if there is such a thing as the true self, "an at least potentially well-ordered system of faculties" hidden inside every human being, awaiting discovery once the accidents of one's time and place have been torn away. But these "traditional distinctions between the higher and the lower, the essential and the accidental, the central and the peripheral" can no longer be sustained. Nietzsche and Freud have taught us that there is no true self—no Kantian moral self, no Socratic rational self—but only "the sheer contingency of individual existence," the "self which is a tissue of contingencies." Each human self is utterly idiosyncratic, constituted by countless contingencies, often trivial or freakish or mysterious. Thus, we each possess "our own private vocabulary of moral deliberation."[27]

Are we not then enslaved, creatures of our idiosyncratic and often mysterious pasts, with no prospect of spiritual freedom? (How are we to liberate ourselves from characters that are "the products of countless contingencies that never enter experience"?)[28] Indeed, if we recall the communitarian dimension of Rorty's account of the self, the appearance of slavery is still more troubling. "Human beings are centerless networks of beliefs and desires," says Rorty; there is no essential self behind the attributes. But these networks are, in the first place, the creation of the

---

[26] Rorty, *Contingency, Irony, and Solidarity*, pp. 23–27.
[27] *Ibid.*, pp. 26–32.
[28] *Ibid.*, p. 31.

community; Rorty argues that "there is nothing much to 'man' except one more animal, until culture, the meshes of power, begin to shape him into something else." Yet, to repeat, "who gets to do the socializing is often a matter of who manages to kill whom first," and therefore this account of the self might seem to justify the spiritual enslavement of all human beings to their community, and even to those in the community who most effectively use force or fraud to impose their idiosyncratic ways of thinking and acting on the rest of us — perhaps the so-called "strong poets."[29]

Rorty writes: "To fail as a poet — and thus, for Nietzsche, to fail as a human being — is to accept somebody else's description of oneself." That is a kind of slavery. Thinking itself has its origins in "terror" at this experience of slavery: "the fear that one might end one's days in such a world, a world one never made, an inherited world"; and a human life is "triumphant just insofar as it escapes from inherited descriptions of the contingencies of its existence and finds new descriptions." Freedom, in other words, is self-creation, self-overcoming; indeed, it is "the enterprise of saying 'Thus I willed it' to the past." So "we praise ourselves by weaving idiosyncratic narratives — case histories, as it were — of our success in self-creation, our ability to break free from an idiosyncratic past."[30] One final point: for postmodernist democrats it is possible (perhaps even necessary) to see "every human life as a poem," even the life of the *"bien-pensant* conformist, if we get him on the couch"; and thus we democrats must count not only the creations of "genius" but also those of "eccentricity or perversity" as instances of poetic self-creation. Thus, Freud and others help

> us overcome particularly intractable cases of blindness by letting us see the "peculiar ideality" of events which exemplify, for example, sexual perversion, extreme cruelty, ludicrous obsession, and manic delusion. He let us see each of these as the private poem of the pervert, the sadist, or the lunatic: each as richly textured and "redolent of moral memories" as our own life. He lets us see what moral philosophy describes as extreme, inhuman, and unnatural, as continuous with our own activity.[31]

What, then, is the business of a liberal education? For Rorty, as on the traditional view, a liberal education has two dimensions, a conservative (or socializing) dimension and a radical (or liberating) dimension. But, says Rorty: "I have been trying to separate both the conservative's insistence on community and the radical's insistence on individuality from

[29] Rorty, *Objectivity, Relativism, and Truth*, p. 191; Rorty, *Consequences of Pragmatism*, p. 208.
[30] Rorty, *Contingency, Irony, and Solidarity*, pp. 28–29, 33.
[31] *Ibid.*, pp. 35–38.

philosophical theories about human nature and about the foundations of
democratic society." In so doing, Rorty transforms both dimensions of liberal education. For the "socializing" dimension of liberal education (which
belongs to primary and secondary schools, supplemented today by the
"remedial" work "that Great Books curricula are typically invented to
carry out"), Rorty proposes an "exaltation of democracy for its own sake"
as an alternative to contemporary conservatism. I have already expressed
some reservations about this proposal, about which I shall have more to
say later. The transformation of the radical dimension of liberal education
is perhaps more fundamental, however: Rorty suggests that the "proper
business" of the colleges is not philosophical radicalism but rather "prov-
ocation to self-creation": "students need to have freedom enacted before
their eyes by actual human beings," where freedom is achieved by
"strong poetry" in the ways that I have described.[32] Postmodernist
higher education is for this reason more than a little self-obsessed, lacking both old-fashioned conservative patriotism and old-fashioned radical
love of justice.[33] What have been the psychological consequences, for
our students, of the transformation in our understanding of liberal education that has been wrought by postmodernism?

IV. POSTMODERN PATHOLOGIES

Here are a few of the pathologies of postmodernism—psychological ills
that have their roots in the postmodern embrace of "contingency." In putting together this catalogue, I think first about liberal education: What
have been the effects of Rortyian ideas about the "self," and about the
relation between the contingent individual self and the contingent liberal
community, on the souls of students? As before, however, I want to suggest that these pathologies may be observed more widely in the postmodern liberal world. Rorty (and kindred ironist theorists) are in the business
of inventing a new liberal human being.[34] I raise doubts here about this
liberal moral psychology, by pointing to certain ordinary ills that everyone will, I suppose, recognize. I hope that the argument here and earlier
reveals that these pathologies have their origins in the rise of what Rorty
calls "ironism"—that is, in the habitual pose of the sort of human being

---

[32] Rorty, "Education without Dogma," pp. 203–4.

[33] I should add that Rorty does affirm a connection between the two dimensions of his
account of liberal education: in the best cases, "enactments of freedoms" can connect student and teacher

> in a relationship that has little to do with socialization but much to do with self-
> creation. . . . Unless some such relationships are formed, the students will never real-
> ize what democratic institutions are good for: namely, making possible the invention
> of new forms of human freedom, taking liberties never taken before. (Rorty, "Educa-
> tion without Dogma," p. 204)

[34] See Rorty, *Contingency, Irony, and Solidarity*, chs. 2 and 4.

who "faces up to the contingency of his or her most central beliefs and desires."

Let me be clear: I do not speak here of philosophical necessities but of psychological probabilities; perhaps there are subtle philosophical moves that enable human beings to embrace contingency without succumbing to one or another of these temptations, but it can hardly be denied that the two human types I shall discuss are very ordinary ones today, among our students and more generally. Rorty himself acknowledges the propriety of this sort of psychological inquiry. For it may be that ironism is in some sense true, whatever that could mean on the ironist view, but that it is not possible to imagine a *liberal* ironist, which is the issue here. Thus, Rorty entertains the objection that "it is psychologically impossible to be a liberal ironist – to be someone for whom 'cruelty is the worst thing we do,' and to have no metaphysical beliefs about what all human beings have in common." This formulation surely makes the problem too easy: what we need to know is whether it is reasonable to suppose that a liberal polity can be sustained on this basis, not only whether it is "possible" for one human being to "be, in alternate moments, Nietzsche and J. S. Mill." And that requires an effort to understand the psychological consequences of such a liberal culture not only or primarily for the "intellectuals" who are "ironists," but also for the ordinary folks who are "commonsensically nominalist and historicist" and who "see themselves as contingent through and through, without feeling any particular doubts about the contingencies they happened to be." [35] My purpose here is to begin to raise doubts about this aspect of Rorty's project by describing certain pathologies associated with that sort of commonsensical historicism, the tamed or thoughtless ironism that knows no doubts regarding the particular contingencies that govern our lives here and now. These pathologies manifest themselves in at least two distinct postmodern personalities, which I shall call the "thuggish conservative" and the "complacent democrat."

Everyone knows the thuggish conservative student. In a splendid piece on toleration, Arthur Melzer describes students who grow up in a Rortyian culture that teaches them to "face up" to contingency:

> People who grow up in a world of great skepticism and diversity, instead of learning to question and think for themselves, often learn not to think at all. For what is the point of seriously doubting the beliefs you already feel comfortable with – an arduous and painful process – when you are constantly taught that there are many such beliefs, all equally good, and all "just a matter of opinion" anyway? In such a world, the whole phenomenon of conscientious self-scrutiny and principled openness tends to lose its raison d'être. . . .

---

[35] ibid., pp. 85, 87.

Self-criticism turns to self-satisfaction. And that is how diversity itself has become a force for complacency and prejudice.

. . . Students today believe as a matter of course that "everyone is different," but precisely for this reason they are too morally mellowed out to object to racist jokes on the university radio, mock slave auctions at a fraternity party, or the abusive lyrics of 2 Live Crew and Andrew Dice Clay. Can't a guy have fun anymore? They have less of the crusading, idealistic, dogmatic type of intolerance, but more of the visceral, nihilistic, self-indulgent kind. One can try to preach to them the importance of greater "sensitivity," but they are weary of this old sermon, which often only succeeds in convincing them that they are the ones being persecuted. In short, this new breed of intolerance—a lazy, easygoing loutishness—thrives on "diversity" and will not be dispelled by more of it.[36]

It is hard to imagine that students (and others) will resist Rorty's open invitation to crush "any particular doubts about the contingencies they happened to be"; many of these will not resist the further temptation to indulge their distaste for aliens of every description. Why should we hope, as Rorty does, that a habit of trying to "extend our sense of 'we' to people whom we have previously thought of as 'they' " will emerge and endure in liberal societies or even among our students—rather than indifference toward moral strangers to the community, or worse?[37] We all know that too many students (and others) take the easier path, toward thuggish self-satisfaction. What is most distressing, in my view, is that the postmodernist styles of thought that now prevail in the academy empower such students by enabling them to close their minds with a good conscience.

Among nicer students we confront another sort of vice, not as immediately threatening but still dangerous. Here is its simplest expression: We are democrats; therefore democracy is good. Silly dogmatism, to be sure: but who would deny that most of our students can approach no closer to an argument for their democratic prejudices than this? Even faithful friends of democratic politics must be troubled by this emerging habit of thoughtlessness regarding the nature of our political regime. For students of democracy, including its fondest admirers, have always known that democrats have vices too. Rousseau's *Social Contract*, *The Federalist Papers*, Jefferson's correspondence with Adams, Lincoln's speeches—all of these are serious meditations on the nature of democracy, its ordinary virtues and ordinary vices. In a democratic nation that has known slavery and its legacy, one might think that it would not be difficult to persuade students to respect arguments like these, whose aim is to secure a "republican rem-

[36] Arthur M. Melzer, "Tolerance 101," *New Republic*, July 1, 1991, p. 11.
[37] Rorty, *Contingency, Irony, and Solidarity*, pp. 87, 192.

edy for the diseases most incident to republican government."[38] I say again, however: Is it not true that many of our students, and many citizens, today embrace their democratic faith with such apathy and complacency that it has now become difficult to awaken healthy doubts regarding democracy? I do not here enter into the dispute between strong participatory democrats and thin liberal democrats, for this seems to me at least in part a dispute regarding the best means to cure the ordinary vices of democracy, or of our democracy. The present point is, again, that the whole inquiry is closed by Rortyian habits of thought; for Rorty teaches, to repeat, "exaltation of democracy for its own sake" and understands by democracy nothing more than a certain kind of conversation, an agreement to "call 'true' whatever belief results from a free and open encounter of opinions." How far is this from Stephen Douglas's "popular sovereignty," especially since (as Rorty also says) "when we surrender an old platitude (e.g., . . . 'Blacks have no rights which whites are bound to respect'), we have made a change rather than discovered a fact"?[39]

In an exchange between Rorty and Harvey Mansfield regarding Bloom's *The Closing of the American Mind*, Mansfield chides Rorty for "sav[ing] all his love for democracy" and for neglecting the duty of the "responsible democrat" to "care for the things majorities ignore or neglect." For Rorty's love is admittedly just another ungroundable desire, and as such it is more than ordinarily blind to the deformities of its object.[40] As students and citizens adopt Rorty's view that our belief in democracy is a "contingent" accident and not the product of "reflection and choice," it is hard to see how they will escape from the temptation to choose, to understand, and to defend their democratic habits thoughtlessly, as if these were merely matters of taste (as one might prefer carrots to peas) and not the reasonable practices of men and women who follow an argument and know themselves well. It will not be long before such democrats will find themselves easy prey for their enemies.[41]

---

[38] Hamilton, Madison, and Jay, *The Federalist Papers*, "Federalist No. 10," p. 84.

[39] Rorty, *Contingency, Irony, and Solidarity*, p. 77. For Stephen Douglas, Lincoln's great opponent during the 1850s, see *The Lincoln-Douglas Debates*, ed. Robert W. Johannsen (New York: Oxford University Press, 1965), esp. pp. 22–36. See also *Scott v. Sanford*, 60 U.S. (19 How.) 393, 407 (1857).

[40] Harvey C. Mansfield, Jr., "Democracy and the Great Books," *New Republic*, April 4, 1988, p. 35; cf. Rorty, *Contingency, Irony, and Solidarity*, p. xv.

[41] Let me add two further remarks here. Regarding conservatism: the postmodern embrace of contingency deprives conservatism of its traditional nobility or dignity, because it lacks a sense of honor—the conviction that we today are given the task of living up to an honorable way of life established by our "founders"; that our tradition embodies something, some grand way of life, that may be lost in time; and that such a loss would be a great tragedy rather than a contingent accident not especially to be lamented. Regarding liberal reformism: the postmodern embrace of contingency takes the wind out of its sails, in two ways. First, it deprives the reformer of a coherent idea of progress and reduces reform to the honorable but limited task of encouraging peoples to live up to existing ideals. Thus, Rorty has often been criticized from the social democratic (and also from the more extreme) left for

One final political pathology is worth mentioning. For those who are less at home in contemporary liberal society than thuggish conservatives and complacent democrats, the postmodern vocabulary of contingency gives rise to a new and more insular radicalism. Certainly there are those in our community who will not be able to "find" their "moral identity in membership in a democratic community" — the very community that has for so long oppressed them. But the postmodern dispensation deprives such students and citizens of the resources of liberal individualism: "there is no such thing as *inner freedom*, no such thing as an 'autonomous individual.'" [42] In repudiating the democratic community, the postmodern radical can no longer turn inward in search of "inner freedom," or turn toward the community in righteous defense of individual rights against the community. One must, then, search for one's true "home," or perhaps even an altogether new home, a place to stand in community with others of the same kind against the democratic community with which one cannot "identify," which is not one's "home." This is the postmodern root of what is sometimes called the "politics of difference": thus, for example, we "identify" with the "black community" or with the "gay community," to mention two paradigmatic cases, rather than with the "democratic community." Everyone knows the absurd lengths to which this process of balkanization can sometimes be taken; still, this seems to me the natural consequence of Rortyian talk about the "contingency of community" for those who are somehow outsiders, or moral strangers, in the democratic community itself. I do not mean to suggest that this impulse is not respectable; it is. Perhaps it is even misleading to count this among the "pathologies" of postmodernism without saying more than I will be able to say here; but let me suggest a few reasons for thinking that this is a distressing and dangerous development.

---

undermining efforts to sustain more-radical criticism of prevailing principles and practices. In the text, I present a conservative account of democratic self-satisfaction, but the argument can just as easily be made from the left, and has been. It must be admitted that Rorty's own remarks regarding liberal democracy are sometimes wonderfully smug, as in the passage on the North Atlantic democracies cited at the beginning of this essay, and as here:

> Indeed, my hunch is that Western social and political thought may have had the last *conceptual* revolution it needs. J. S. Mill's suggestion that governments devote themselves to optimizing the balance between leaving people's private lives alone and preventing suffering seems to me pretty much the last word. (Rorty, *Contingency, Irony, and Solidarity*, p. 63)

Second, and on the other hand, there is a hidden pessimism in Rorty's account of the history of social and political "progress" (whatever that might be) that diminishes liberal reformism. What is the point of such political undertakings if "what our future rulers will be like will not be determined by any large necessary truths about human nature and its relation to truth and justice, but by a lot of small contingent facts" (*ibid.*, p. 188)? In any case, Rorty sometimes speaks in a way that diminishes what he calls "social hope," as in the chapter on Orwell in *ibid.* (cf. p. 94). But this is a long story.

[42] *Ibid.*, p. 177.

Consider the radical insularity of such communities, when constituted on the new postmodern grounds. Of course, these communities existed before, in attenuated forms, as voluntary associations of aggrieved individuals uniting in order to bring more forceful claims against an unjust democratic community—in defense of universal human rights, say. Today, to repeat, liberal individualism is discredited and the idea of common humanity abandoned; therefore, these postmodern communities must be founded on more radical grounds. That is, such communities are not founded on principles that are available to all human beings qua human beings; they are founded on "difference," on what distinguishes one group of human beings from another group (though even the name "human beings" is here misleading, so far as it suggests that "human being" is the name of a natural kind whose members share more than biological traits in common). We face here the prospect of the endless balkanization of our political world, since there is no principle to help us distinguish true or natural communities from frivolous ones that do not name any real "we" (after all, what constitutes a "we" is contingent, the product of innumerable idiosyncrasies). But even if one could halt the balkanization, either in theory or in practice, one would nevertheless face the prospect of a political world consisting of communities at war, in principle at least; for such communities do not share "vocabularies," or any "neutral" tools for mediating differences, once one abandons the idea of a common humanity.[43] As the smaller communities that thus constitute human beings are multiplied, thereby respecting "difference," the prospects for building one community from this diversity are greatly diminished.

I turn finally to the "contingency of the self," and to the psychological pathologies that have their origins in this aspect of postmodern ironism.

Consider the problem of self-esteem. Almost all human beings praise themselves both for their loyalty to "home" (to family, to friends, to country) and for their longing for "freedom" from the unnatural bonds, the prejudices and orthodoxies, that confine human beings in every such home. Perhaps the radical has a greater taste for freedom; perhaps the conservative has a greater taste for loyalty: but it is hard to imagine a human being wholly free of either the love of the "good" or the love of "one's own." Thus, a noble way of life must somehow comprise both ideas or loves; and it is one of the tasks of a liberal education to enable us to achieve some measure of peace between these parts of our souls (or to show why, in a particular here and now, that peace cannot be achieved honorably). Who would choose to be either a traitor or a slave to one's own community (even in thought, much less in deed)? This is the dilemma that is on display in the conversation between Polemarchus and Socrates in the *Republic*, where Polemarchus is reduced to the silly (but somehow honorable) expedient of splitting the difference (" 'the man who

---

[43] *Ibid.*

seems to be, and is, good, is a friend,' he said, 'while the man who seems good and is not, seems to be but is not a friend' ").[44] The postmodernist too praises himself for loyalty ("what matters is our loyalty to other human beings clinging together against the dark") and for freedom ("we praise ourselves by weaving idiosyncratic narratives—case histories, as it were—of our success in self-creation, our ability to break free from an idiosyncratic past"), but the new postmodernist account of the self transforms loyalty and freedom in the ways that I have described, with certain consequences that I now wish to consider for our ways of thinking about self-esteem.[45]

As for the new loyalty, there is perhaps not much more to be said. I have cited Rorty on "clinging together against the dark," because this remark suggests that Rorty's democratic humanism sometimes approaches despair. The postmodernist knows, above all, that nature "teaches no moral lesson, offers no spiritual comfort": that is what it means to face up to contingency. Human beings are by nature homeless, and clinging together against the dark offers a respite from the deracinating quality of modernity—from meaninglessness, alienation, anomie, and the rest. Solitude is not bearable; we seek warmth. Philosophers are, of course, no better than communitarians in this respect, says Rorty: the philosopher is animated by the "neurotic" need for a certain " 'metaphysical comfort,' " "to find something necessary and ahistorical *to cling to*"; the postmodernist, on the contrary, seeks "spiritual comfort" in an embrace of one's own community, now recognized as "*ours* rather than *nature's, shaped* rather than *found*." [46] The philosophic quest for a natural home is now known to be hopeless, however; so we now have no choice but to seek solace in the embrace of our neighbors, clinging together against the dark.

And yet, we also know that community is contingent, that who "we" are is sheer accident, the product of "countless contingencies"; the notion that any particular community is distinguished by a humane tradition, by fitful progress toward a kind of "humanity," must be a myth (since "there is no human dignity that is not derivative from the dignity of some specific community"; there is no "humanity").[47] Thus, the postmodernist is not only opposed to the philosopher, but also to the citizen—who says, to repeat, that he is loyal to a community that embodies something noble, for this is what he believes. Citizens look to the past in order to honor heroes who earn their respect (like, say, Lincoln and Douglass). The citizen's loyalty, then, is potentially ennobling, as well as humbling; in the best case, it enables him to rise above petty private concerns in the service of a greater good that he identifies with the common good of his

---

[44] Plato, *Republic*, 334e–335a.

[45] Rorty, *Consequences of Pragmatism*, p. 166; Rorty, *Contingency, Irony, and Solidarity*, p. 33.

[46] Rorty, *Consequences of Pragmatism*, pp. 161, 165–66, first emphasis added.

[47] Rorty, *Objectivity, Relativism, and Truth*, p. 197.

community. (Of course, citizens may be mistaken, since what counts as noble in any particular community may not in truth mark progress toward greater humanity. But the aspiration makes a difference.) For the postmodernist, our needs are deeper, but our hopes are chastened. Postmodern loyalty is more willful ("creative") but also more desperate than the loyalty of the old-fashioned patriot: what counts is having others to cling to, not the beauty or goodness of the objects of our love. Here is the origin of a certain cultish dogmatism, manifested in unreflective blindness, or even in willful disregard of the evident vices of the objects of one's love. It is better not to know: if we cannot find companions against the dark, or in the face of the "inconsolable coldness of modernity," we will be utterly homeless.[48] For we are now deprived of the consolation available to the philosopher (or to the disillusioned citizen), who can find a place to stand, a home, outside the cave. The psychological consequence of facing up to the contingency of community is, for some human beings at least, some combination of (willful, self-conscious) dogmatism and (nihilistic) self-pity. Here is another aspect of the thuggishness described above, though now it is clear that there is no particular reason to suppose, as I did there, that this thuggishness is more characteristic of the right than of the left. But can we really esteem ourselves for rushing headlong into the embrace of our fellows, whoever they might be, in search of a cure for our postmodern despair? In any case, postmodern loyalty surely lacks the dignity of traditional citizenship, for there is, in such loyalty, none of the self-transcendence and self-sacrifice that marks the ways of life of citizens who rise above their petty private needs to serve a common good.

There is of course a cheerful (or, as Rorty sometimes says, "playful") version of postmodern loyalty, what Allan Bloom called "easygoing" nihilism, a *Don't Worry, Be Happy* posture toward one's way of life. It is hard to know how far to credit this aspect of Rorty's postmodernism, not only because it is hard to square with "clinging together against the dark," but also because it is hard to square with the strong poet's "fear" and even "terror" that "one might end one's days in . . . a world one never made, an inherited world." Here is another impressive example of this remarkable good humor in the face of distressing news, from that postmodernist Bruce Ackerman's *Social Justice in the Liberal State*:

> The hard truth is this: There is no moral meaning hidden in the bowels of the universe. All there is is you and I struggling in a world that neither we, nor any other thing, created.
>
> Yet there is not need to be overwhelmed by the void. We may create our own meanings, you and I; however transient or superficial,

---

[48] Benjamin R. Barber, *The Conquest of Politics* (Princeton: Princeton University Press, 1988), p. 179.

these are the only meanings we will ever know. And the first meaningful reality we must create—one presupposed by all other acts of
meaningful communication—is the idea that you and I are persons
capable of giving meanings to the world.

Yet this is just the achievement of a Neutral conversation.[49]

Such cheerfulness, however, surely depends on finding or creating
human beings who are "never quite able to take themselves seriously,"
as Rorty says.[50] There is something frivolous, or so it has appeared to a
number of Rorty's critics, about this sunny disposition in the face of the
loss of permanent sources of meaning.[51] (At least, "facing up" to contingency should be hard.) From the perspective of critics on the left, it
appears that Rorty's playful ironist is content to give up his love of justice and of humanity, and to become the easygoing tool of the prevailing
authorities in a community. From the perspective of critics on the right,
it appears that the ironist is content to trivialize community, treating it as
an "experiment," an arena for play, and not as the deepest ground of the
duties, loyalties, and aspirations that ennoble the lives of human
beings.[52] These are real losses, and thus it is hard to know what to make
of the cheerful, not-to-worry pose that Rorty and other partisans of contingency sometimes adopt. In any case, it can hardly be denied that the
"death of God"—for that is what is at stake here, the loss of what most
human beings have always held most dear—must soon diminish humanity (consider Nietzsche's account of the so-called "last man" in *Thus Spoke
Zarathustra*).

I turn, finally, to the new freedom. To begin, it is worth recalling
Rorty's own distinction between "ironists" and "commonsensical histor-
icists," between (as he says in another place) "oddballs" and "ordinary
persons." Poetry is surely an acquired taste. Even in the postmodern liberal community, there will be few supermen, few strong poets, and many
"dull" but "decent" folks who will absorb the new orthodoxies regarding
contingency without becoming oddballs who seek to recreate themselves.[53]

---

[49] Allan Bloom, *The Closing of the American Mind* (New York: Simon and Schuster, 1987),
pp. 141–240; Bruce Ackerman, *Social Justice in the Liberal State* (New Haven: Yale University
Press, 1980), p. 368.

[50] Rorty, *Contingency, Irony, and Solidarity*, p. 73.

[51] See, for example, Jean Bethke Elshtain, "Don't Be Cruel: Reflections on Rortyian Liberalism," in *The Politics of Irony*, ed. Daniel W. Conway and John Evan Seery (New York:
St. Martin's Press, 1992), together with Rorty's "Robustness: A Reply to Jean Bethke
Elshtain," in *ibid.*; and Richard J. Bernstein, "One Step Forward, Two Steps Backward: Richard Rorty on Liberal Democracy and Philosophy," *Political Theory*, vol. 15, no. 4 (November 1987), together with Rorty's "Thugs and Theorists: A Reply to Bernstein," in *ibid.*

[52] Rorty, *Contingency, Irony, and Solidarity*, p. 45.

[53] Rorty, *Contingency, Irony, and Solidarity*, p. 87; Richard Rorty, "The Philosophy of the
Oddball" (review of Stanley Cavell, *In Quest of the Ordinary*), *New Republic*, June 19, 1989,
p. 41. On the dull but decent folks, see Rorty, *Contingency, Irony, and Solidarity*, p. 35.

Here, I consider the effects of the new doctrines on these "ordinary" folks. That is, how will democrats (not elite ironists) experience the new freedom of self-creation?

The democratic meaning of the new account of freedom as self-creation is the discovery of something like Ronald Dworkin's "right to equal respect."[54] In a world where idiosyncratic self-creation is celebrated, every way of life (however bizarre or distasteful or perverse or even wicked it might appear) is worthy of the equal respect of the community. It follows that my way of life, in particular, merits the respect of my fellow citizens. (Recall Rorty on the "private poem of the pervert, the sadist, or the lunatic.")[55] Moreover, on the postmodernist view, the roots of self-esteem are communal or social ("there is no such thing as *inner freedom*, no such thing as an 'autonomous individual' "): there is no reasonable ground of self-esteem beyond the community, as liberal rationalists once supposed; the old idea of a proud, "rugged individualist" is a myth. It follows that the liberal ironist demands not only permission or tolerance, but also praise or respect, for these idiosyncratic acts of self-creation and the ways of life that then come into being. Thus, it is now official liberal doctrine, more or less, that it is the business of the liberal community, perhaps even its main business, to provide communal supports for self-esteem by recognizing the equal worth of idiosyncratic, self-creative private choices or ways of life. That is a novel way of bringing together idiosyncratic privacy and constitutive community, while striving to maintain a liberal commitment to tolerance and diversity: on one hand, the new liberal orthodoxy affirms a right to equal respect for every private way of life, however idiosyncratic and whatever its quality, since judgments regarding the quality of private choices are now thought by such liberals to be illicit in principle; on the other hand, the new liberals admit that there is no reasonable ground of self-esteem beyond the community, so that a failure to "recognize" or esteem alien private choices "can inflict harm, can be a form of oppression."[56]

I have discussed elsewhere the idea of a right to equal respect, its relation to Rorty's account of the contingency of the self and the contingency of community, and the political consequences of these doctrines for liberalism. I argue that this account of freedom does not advance but rather

---

[54] Ronald Dworkin, *A Matter of Principle* (Cambridge: Harvard University Press, 1985), pp. 181–213, 335–72. See note 57 below.

[55] Rorty, *Contingency, Irony, and Solidarity*, p. 38; see the discussion near the end of Section III above. See also Rorty, *Objectivity, Relativism, and Truth*, pp. 203–10.

[56] Charles Taylor, *Multiculturalism and "The Politics of Recognition"* (Princeton: Princeton University Press, 1992), p. 25. Consider Taylor's account of the "politics of recognition": on one hand, "[o]ur moral salvation comes from recovering authentic moral contact with ourselves" (*ibid.*, p. 29); on the other hand, "[d]ue recognition is not just a courtesy we owe people. It is a vital human need" (*ibid.*, p. 26). See, generally, *ibid.*, pp. 25–44.

undermines the case for toleration.[57] Here, I have tried to focus on the psychological consequences of postmodern liberal doctrines, rather than their political consequences. The combination of the two fundamental postmodern dispositions (toward the self and toward community) produces a remarkable transformation of liberal moral psychology: from a doctrine of proud individualists who insist on the right to be left alone, to a doctrine more suitable for the desperately lonely, "clinging together against the dark." "Mind your own business" has become "I'm OK! You're OK!" Consider the effects of these doctrines on our students, and on liberal citizens generally. No one should be surprised that the ordinary response to the Rortyian celebration of contingency is not strong poetry, but rather self-satisfaction. Those students (and other "commonsensical historicist" citizens) who do not share the poet's "terror" ("the fear that one might end one's days in such a world, a world one never made, an inherited world") are simply excused from the business of self-criticism, the very heart of old-fashioned liberal education. (Here the issue is not criticism of one's own community, but criticism of one's private self and way of life.) Beyond this, such students are invited to plead for applause, to demand the right not to be scowled at: for it is a kind of cruelty for the community to display contempt when the object of that contempt has no other place to turn, beyond the community, for the praise that alone makes possible self-esteem.[58] Warmth is the fundamental political good.

But of course, this longing for reassurance is the mark of a certain desperation, at least for more thoughtful students. Is the applause of the community enough to compensate for the anxious suspicion that one's way of life is an enormous folly? That is the suspicion that is the origin of liberal education, but if there is no path out of the cave, and if, further, the hugs of one's neighbors do not quiet these doubts, then the psychological consequence of embracing contingency will be not-so-quiet desperation. It is hardly surprising, then, that when we speak about privacy today, our talk is commonly empty, formal, restless, self-indulgent, sometimes angry. We love our privacy, but we are not especially confident that we know very well what to do with it. What counts is the liberating experience, the rebellion, not the chosen way of life: we are always in search of something new and exotic, never altogether at home in a private way of life. We lack both self-confidence in our chosen ways and resources for autonomous self-criticism of those ways.

---

[57] Steven Kautz, "Liberalism and the Idea of Toleration," *American Journal of Political Science*, vol. 37, no. 2 (May 1993). In that essay, I also put forward a case for toleration that suits the proud individualism of classical liberalism (though I might be inclined to draw the line this side of lunacy and sadism). What is at issue here is not whether toleration is a liberal good, but whether the postmodern liberal mode of thinking about toleration is reasonable.

[58] Rorty, *Contingency, Irony, and Solidarity*, p. 29; and see *ibid.*, pp. 89–92; cf. pp. 141–68. See also the passages cited in note 56.

Who suffers? Perhaps we are so far in the habit of thinking of ourselves as "unique" individuals and (what might seem to be the opposite) as communal beings, that we have forgotten some of the joys of thinking about how to reconcile, in our own lives, the competing claims of the individual and the community (for there is no possible harmony between individual and community when these are conceived in the extreme postmodern manner described in this essay). These joys, it seems to me, are particularly available to those individuals who most chafe at the constraints of community, whose situations most invite thought: those who are somehow dissenters in their communities, marginalized but not wholly outside them. The tragedy of the new liberal education, and of the new liberalism itself, is that it so often turns such students so far inward—toward idiosyncratic reverie or a politics of insular radicalism—that no paths remain open in the direction of a more humane reconciliation of our natural longings for "home" and for freedom.

Political Science, Emory University

WHAT LIBERALISM MEANS

By Ronald Beiner

Nietzsche is the one, I suppose, who has expressed what it is about modernity that makes life impossible.

— Hans-Georg Gadamer[1]

My purpose in this essay is to give an account of the kind of robust social criticism that I associate with the very enterprise of theory and to explain why the liberal philosophy that prevails in the contemporary academy is averse to this sort of social criticism. My purpose, then, is both to explore a certain conception of radical social theory and to defend this conception against familiar objections posed by those who represent the dominant liberal political philosophy.

I. The Liberal-Communitarian Debate

The so-called "liberal-communitarian debate" of the 1980s seems a good starting-point, since this debate focused attention on anxieties about the theoretical sufficiency of liberalism, and helped to keep alive theoretical challenges to the hegemony of liberalism that might not otherwise have survived the demise of Marxism. "Communitarian" critics of liberalism such as Charles Taylor, Michael Walzer, Alasdair MacIntyre, Michael Sandel, Robert Bellah, and Christopher Lasch put the problem of community on the theoretical agenda by addressing questions both to liberalism as a social philosophy and to the kind of society we think of as a liberal society.[2] These critics asked whether liberalism, as a basically individualistic creed, could do justice to the richly textured narrative histories and socially constituted practices by which individuals in any society come to acquire meaningful selves. And they asked, quite properly, whether liberal societies, which basically define and understand themselves within a frame-

---

[1] *Hans-Georg Gadamer on Education, Poetry, and History,* ed. Dieter Misgeld and Graeme Nicholson (Albany: State University of New York Press, 1992), p. 145.

[2] Charles Taylor, *Philosophical Papers,* vol. 2, *Philosophy and the Human Sciences* (Cambridge: Cambridge University Press, 1985); Michael Walzer, *Spheres of Justice* (New York: Basic Books, 1983); Alasdair MacIntyre, *After Virtue* (Notre Dame, IN: University of Notre Dame Press, 1981); Alasdair MacIntyre, *Whose Justice? Which Rationality?* (Notre Dame, IN: University of Notre Dame Press, 1988); Michael J. Sandel, *Liberalism and the Limits of Justice* (Cambridge: Cambridge University Press, 1982); Robert N. Bellah, Richard Madsen, William M. Sullivan, Ann Swidler, and Steven M. Tipton, *Habits of the Heart: Individualism and Commitment in American Life* (Berkeley: University of California Press, 1985); Christopher Lasch, *The Culture of Narcissism* (New York: W. W. Norton and Company, 1979).

   © 1996 Social Philosophy and Policy Foundation. Printed in the USA.

work of individualistic categories, can offer the rich experiences of mutual involvement that make for a meaningful human life. In order to assess whether these communitarian concerns pose a sufficiently radical challenge to liberal theory and the social reality it justifies, we need to probe more deeply into what is to be understood by the term "liberalism."

What is the basic character of the social order in which we live? From whence may we draw theoretically illuminating categories to make sense of our experience within this social order? Within what horizon of theoretical understanding can we become fully reflective about the shared way of life in which we participate? Questions of this sort are, surely, central to the enterprise of theory. Yet if we take our bearings by the dominant liberal philosophy of our day, we will discover, to our surprise, that such questions can barely even be formulated. For leading liberal theorists such as John Rawls, Ronald Dworkin, Bruce Ackerman, Charles Larmore, and Will Kymlicka, liberalism does not name a pervasive social order;[3] on the contrary, liberalism refers to a principle of political organization that accords individuals the freedom to navigate a course of their own design, constituted by self-elected plans and purposes. In the view of right liberals (such as F. A. Hayek, Robert Nozick, and Michael Oakeshott), this vision of individual self-government requires that the state intervene as little as possible in the social and economic life of the society;[4] for left liberals (including Rawls, Dworkin, Ackerman, and Kymlicka), considerable state intervention is required in order to distribute to every individual an equitable share of the total aggregate of social resources, in order to give each individual a fair opportunity to give play to his or her unique conception of his or her own personal good. But all of these theorists, whether right liberal or left liberal, agree that there is no overarching social order to which it would be reasonable to apply the name "liberalism." Rather, liberalism for them denotes an officially agnostic or "neutral" grid that allows self-governing individuals to coordinate their reciprocal relations in ways that maximize the attainment of their own individual purposes.[5]

---

[3] John Rawls, *A Theory of Justice* (Oxford: Oxford University Press, 1971); John Rawls, *Political Liberalism* (New York: Columbia University Press, 1993); Ronald Dworkin, *Taking Rights Seriously* (London: Duckworth, 1977); Ronald Dworkin, *A Matter of Principle* (Cambridge: Harvard University Press, 1985); Bruce A. Ackerman, *Social Justice in the Liberal State* (New Haven: Yale University Press, 1980); Charles Larmore, *Patterns of Moral Complexity* (Cambridge: Cambridge University Press, 1987); Will Kymlicka, *Liberalism, Community, and Culture* (Oxford: Clarendon Press, 1991).

[4] Friedrich A. Hayek, *The Constitution of Liberty* (Chicago: University of Chicago Press, 1960); Robert Nozick, *Anarchy, State, and Utopia* (New York: Basic Books, 1974); Michael Oakeshott, *On Human Conduct* (Oxford: Clarendon Press, 1975).

[5] It must be noted that not all contemporary liberals are "neutralist" liberals; indeed, the axiom of "neutralism" has been strongly contested by a group of authors who have come to be called "perfectionist" liberals. Among the important works in this category, see Joseph Raz, *The Morality of Freedom* (Oxford: Clarendon Press, 1986); Stephen Macedo, *Liberal Virtues: Citizenship, Virtue, and Community in Liberal Constitutionalism* (Oxford: Clarendon Press,

The kinds of social phenomena that are of concern to the critic of liberalism include the following: anemic citizenship, a brutalizing mass culture, the resort to hyper-individualistic fantasy and escapism, the increasing brittleness of basic social institutions like the family, the overwhelming of civic confidence by problems of scale and technological complexity in contemporary life, the mindless frenzy of modern consumerism, the world of therapy and self-preoccupation associated with Lasch's "culture of narcissism"—to say nothing of the attenuation, by market-based individualism, of that degree of civic solidarity needed to sustain even a minimally decent welfare state (e.g., universal health care). The liberal will maintain that these cultural-political concerns actually have very little to do with liberalism in a strict sense. Therefore, liberals, even if they grant that these are real problems in contemporary society, will want to contest the appropriateness of the term "liberalism" as a designation for the social order that tends to generate such social problems. The complaints about liberal society that I share with other critics of liberalism—liberal society's disorientation, tendency toward anomie, civic pathologies, and widespread soullessness—are, it will be said, a function of many things that, strictly speaking, are entirely distinct from liberalism: namely, capitalism, mass society, secularization, and so on. Liberalism, defined strictly, concerns the delimitation of the moral authority of the state in order to shield individuals from having what are for them indigestible moral beliefs and practices coercively thrust upon them. Or so it will be insisted by liberals made indignant by the effort to blame all the ills of the modern world on them and no one but them. I certainly accept that people describe themselves as liberals in a wide variety of ways and for a wide variety of reasons, and I am aware of the peril of getting too hung up on a quarrel about mere labels. However, I feel an urge nonetheless to defend my nomenclature, and to demonstrate to the liberal that what strikes him or her as a merely eccentric or perverse overenlargement of the scope of the term "liberal" actually does help to pinpoint a common core of moral commitments, reasonably described as liberal, that do in fact connect up with the range of supposedly distinct social pathologies that concern me.

II. THE MEANING OF LIBERALISM

One may distinguish three broad senses of the term "liberalism": (1) liberalism as a political doctrine, referring to the liberal urge to circum-

---

1990); William A. Galston, *Liberal Purposes: Goods, Virtues, and Diversity in the Liberal State* (Cambridge: Cambridge University Press, 1991); and Amy Gutmann, *Democratic Education* (Princeton, NJ: Princeton University Press, 1987). Needless to say, I have much greater sympathy for the antineutralist version of liberalism common to these works, although they still fall short of the horizon of critical reflection that I am demanding. It seems fair to say that perfectionist liberalism is situated somewhere midway between the liberal neutralism that is the primary focus of my critique, and the more ambitious vision of social criticism that is being defended in this essay. (Cf. Galston, *Liberal Purposes*, pp. 43–44.)

scribe the authority of the state as a legislator of morality; (2) liberalism as a social order, which I have elsewhere labeled "the regime of the modern bourgeoisie";[6] and (3) liberalism as a philosophical ranking of priorities, according to which intellectuals ought to be focusing more on the achievements than on the debilities of modern liberal societies; a liberal in this third sense typically disdains antibourgeois, antimodernist cultural criticism for its political irresponsibility. If it turns out that of these three definitions, only the first sense is a legitimate application of the term "liberal," one will be obliged to conclude that this essay is mistitled, and that much of what I want to subsume under the critique of liberalism is directed at a target that does not actually exist. Many of those who feel comfortable being philosophically classified as liberal will no doubt come to this very conclusion. Therefore, upholding my enterprise as a critique of *liberalism* (as opposed to its being a critique of something else about which I am fundamentally confused) requires an elaboration and defense of my threefold definition.

Let me start with the question of *why* liberals everywhere are so preoccupied with resisting threats posed by the state to the independence of individuals. As we pursue this most basic element of liberal conviction, we will be led ineluctably in the direction of larger, more encompassing moral commitments that, I hope, will show my employment of the term "liberal" to be less eccentric and less perverse than it may appear — and, perhaps, even to be reasonably plausible.

What I want to maintain is that *depoliticizing moral life*, ejecting the state from the business of tampering with the soul, is but one aspect of a larger moral vision. The basic liberal idea is that the individual ought to be given the space in which to make something of his or her life, over which the individual exercises ultimate moral responsibility. According to liberalism, the state, in effect, says to the individual: "Okay, Bud, it's your life. Do something with it." (This vision is not necessarily biased toward individualism, since if individuals freely opt for communalist commitments, this is certainly fine with the liberal; but nothing in liberal philosophy *requires* individuals to embrace such commitments.)

The fundamental anxiety underlying all my critical reflections on liberalism is the thought that, once we have given individuals this moral space, they might then proceed to unfold a shared way of life that is spiritually empty, with only a minimum of humanly meaningful moral substance. The question then will be whether liberal political philosophy will have left itself the intellectual resources with which to pass judgment on this outcome.

The basic liberal idea I have described is captured quite nicely in MacIntyre's helpful phrase "the privatization of good."[7] To this will come the

---

[6] Ronald Beiner, *What's the Matter with Liberalism?* (Berkeley: University of California Press, 1992), p. 8 n. 4.

[7] Alasdair MacIntyre, "The Privatization of Good: An Inaugural Lecture," *Review of Politics*, vol. 52, no. 3 (Summer 1990), pp. 344–61.

liberal's objection that rather than "privatizing" the good, liberal politics seeks to "socialize" it, as opposed to "politicizing" it.[8] While it is illegitimate for the *state* to shape moral character, it is perfectly acceptable for character to be shaped within the moral agencies of civil society: family, church, neighborhood, and so on. I certainly agree that liberals by and large are more sympathetic to civil society as a locus of moral life than they are to the idea of the state as a moral authority. I do not, however, think that this formulation fully captures the moral thrust of liberalism. Why should the liberal be any more comfortable with citizens being morally bullied by preachers from the pulpit or by community leaders within the neighborhood than with bullying by politicians holding public office at the level of the state? (Admittedly, the state possesses powers of coercion that are unavailable to civil society; but there are other ways of orchestrating people's lives than by applying direct coercion.) Liberals want individuals to think for themselves, to choose for themselves. *Social* pressure that locks individuals into preappointed roles and expectations is as objectionable, from the point of view of this ideal of moral self-government, as political pressure. As John Stuart Mill's *On Liberty* makes clear, if liberals want to fortify individuals against pressures to conform, civil society can be just as oppressive as the state.[9]

If the basic liberal goal is to defend individuals against the prospect of outside interference in the formation of their moral convictions and moral commitments (and this, after all, is the *point* of liberal anxiety about the state), then the moral ideal here is indeed "the privatization of good." This brings me back to my bedrock objection—that it is unclear whether, having privatized the good, we are still permitted the possibility of rendering critical judgments on the global way of life in which these putatively "self-governing" individuals nonetheless participate. The basic question, as I see it, is whether we are willing, as theorists, to be bold enough, *illiberal* enough, to admit that taken as a whole, the moral civilization that defines contemporary liberal society is not terribly impressive; my claim is that you can tell a liberal every time by the aversion to being so presumptuous.

I know what the liberal will say to all this. The liberal will say that this insistence on passing judgment on the moral substance of a way of life

---

[8] I owe this formulation to Stephen Newman.

[9] An extreme illustration of this point is the fact that the prime agent of the Islamic persecution of Salman Rushdie is (at least officially) not the Iranian state, but an institution within "civil society," namely, the 15 Khordad Foundation, which put up the bounty for Rushdie's execution. For Mill's views, see, for instance, John Stuart Mill, *On Liberty*, ed. David Spitz (New York: W. W. Norton and Company, 1975), p. 15, where he writes that what concerns him is the "disposition of mankind, whether as rulers *or as fellow-citizens*, to impose their own opinions and inclinations as a rule of conduct on others" (my italics). The tendency that worries Mill is advanced, he says, both by legislation and "by force of opinion."

violates the overwhelming "fact of pluralism" that surrounds us.[10] For liberals, pluralism—the condition whereby individuals are committed to irreconcilably different moral ideals, personal aspirations, visions of the good life—is a sociological given in all modern societies. My response is that, once again, we require the moral and intellectual resources to distinguish phony pluralism from real pluralism—resources that are missing in contemporary liberal philosophy. One has less true pluralism in a hundred different trashy tabloids than one has in one or two quality newspapers, but in order to say this, one has to be prepared to offer substantive judgments that theorists of a liberal disposition are reluctant to make available.

Here, as elsewhere, we may take Isaiah Berlin as a paradigmatic liberal. Berlin defines the liberal tradition in terms of its recognition of the absoluteness of rights and the idea that "there are frontiers . . . within which men should be inviolable."[11] Presumably, it is impermissible for these frontiers to be violated by civil society any more than by the state. My *main* point is that liberals are averse to any very penetrating social criticism for fear of impugning or casting into question this inviolability of frontiers. This comes out very well in the following statement of principle by Berlin:

> Most modern liberals, at their most consistent, want a situation in which as many individuals as possible can realize as many of their ends as possible, without assessment of the value of these ends as such, save in so far as they may frustrate the purposes of others. They wish the frontiers between individuals or groups of men to be drawn solely with a view to preventing collisions between human purposes, all of which must be considered to be equally ultimate, uncriticizable ends in themselves.[12]

Once again, the concern with the state's power over individuals appears merely derivative; what is primary is a certain moral vision. Liberals are fearful of state power on account of a certain understanding of what it is to respect individuals, not vice versa.

It might be thought that the proper label for what I am criticizing under the heading of "liberalism" is: "capitalism." I don't think so. Capitalism is the name of an economic system for the relatively efficient production of commodities and services involving the free disposal of capital. Liberalism, at least according to the broader definition that I am trying to render plausible, is a philosophy of life that seeks to liberate individuals from

---

[10] The "fact of pluralism" is John Rawls's phrase: see Rawls, "The Priority of Right and Ideas of the Good," *Philosophy and Public Affairs*, vol. 17, no. 4 (Fall 1988), pp. 259, 275.

[11] Isaiah Berlin, *Four Essays on Liberty* (London: Oxford University Press, 1969), p. 165.

[12] *Ibid.*, p. 153n.

the shackles of predefined social roles and stations in life. Let us be clear
about which of these two categories has logical priority. Morally speaking, it can be presumed that one opts for a capitalist economic system
with a view to securing a wider play for individual liberty; one does not
embrace liberalism in order to serve an antecedent commitment to capitalism. It is true enough that a given society (say China) might be induced
to liberalize itself over time in pursuit of the material benefits dangled in
front of it by a free-market economy. But I do not think this affects my
point here, which is as follows: if political philosophy is concerned with
the grounds for embracing one moral-political world rather than another,
then the question of liberalism "trumps" the question of capitalism. Capitalism denotes merely an *economic* alternative to feudalism, whereas liberalism denotes a *moral* alternative to feudalism. I am not suggesting that
political philosophy should not concern itself with choosing between
alternative economic systems. Nor am I suggesting that the choice of an
economic system is unrelated to a comprehensive choice of a way of life—
quite the contrary! What I am suggesting is that the choice of one economic system rather than another is logically subordinate to the choice
between alternative visions of moral order.[13]

I have discussed the relation between capitalism and liberalism; let me
now turn to a brief discussion of the relation between democracy and liberalism. Some will charge that to criticize liberalism in the context of a
liberal-democratic society is really to criticize democracy, or to use criticism of liberalism as a cloak for criticizing democracy. In response, I
would say that my own inclination is to criticize liberal democracy from
the perspective that it is not democratic enough, not that it is too democratic. My intention as a critic of liberalism is to criticize liberalism in the
name of democracy, but at the same time to elevate democracy to a rather
demanding standard. My criticism of liberal democracy is that it neither
encourages nor requires its citizens to be more active or more knowledge-
able in their command of public affairs. However, there is an opposed
conception of democracy which consists in deferring to whatever happen
to be the current standards of public participation, whether high or low
(more likely low, or extremely low). According to this conception, talk
about elevation of the standards of democratic participation is itself antidemocratic. Invoking the banner of democracy simply as a way of legit-
imizing the acceptance of a descent to the lowest common denominator

---

[13] It is not uncommon for liberals to argue that the philosophical rationale for the market economy is a moral conception, namely, a certain kind of egalitarianism that sees market society as having emancipated individuals from the hierarchical ascriptive roles and
relationships characteristic of a preliberal, premodern social order. One such argument is
offered in William James Booth, *Households: On the Moral Architecture of the Economy* (Ithaca:
Cornell University Press, 1993), Part 2. This is consistent with my argument above in regard
to the logical priority of liberalism as a moral vision over capitalism as a vision of the
economy.

with respect to standards of cultural and political life is another expression of precisely what I understand by liberalism.

Thus far, I have tried to suggest some reasons for preferring a broader rather than a narrower definition of what it means to be a liberal. Another advantage of the broader definition is that the narrower definitions fail to cover adequately the full range of contemporary liberal thought. According to the narrowest definition, a liberal is someone whose central anxiety is the possibility of abuses of state power, and whose defining preoccupation is to devise institutional means for coping with this anxiety. Yet when we look at the huge span of opinion among self-defined liberals with respect to the legitimate exercise of state power – the gulf between, say, the welfare liberalism of Rawls and the antiwelfare liberalism of Nozick – we realize that this is not a terribly helpful way of pinpointing what a commitment to liberalism entails. Even when we consider less narrow definitions, however, we encounter similar problems. Suppose we define the liberal as someone who believes that the raison d'être of a society is its furnishing individuals with the best possible opportunity to develop their own unique personalities. Without question, this is what defined the political vision of certain nineteenth-century liberals, including John Stuart Mill. Again, however, this definition is betrayed by what leading liberals today profess. For some of the most influential contemporary formulations of liberal philosophy (those of Rawls and Larmore, to name two) consider individual autonomy as merely one moral view among a plurality of competing moral conceptions, and think it would be morally and politically illegitimate to privilege the ideal of individual self-development, rather than allowing this ideal its place among other ideals in a larger "overlapping consensus," or alternatively, in a *"modus vivendi"* among moral views.[14]

These definitions therefore fail the test of all-inclusiveness. This gives us a reason to opt for my much more encompassing definition, namely: a liberal is someone who sees nothing *fundamentally* questionable, morally or metaphysically, in the kind of social order that has currently been developed in the United States of America, a society devoted to guarding the rights, freedom, and well-being of individuals, and who finds nothing questionable in applying this social order as a standard of judging social progress in other parts of the world. According to this definition, the liberal restricts the function of social theory to suggesting piecemeal reforms – perhaps, in order to render such a society somewhat fairer, more open, more democratic, more generous than it presently is. I take the ameliorative liberalism defended by Richard Rorty (notwith-

---

[14] This is the basic structure of argument in Rawls, *Political Liberalism*; Larmore, *Patterns of Moral Complexity*; and Charles Larmore, "Political Liberalism," *Political Theory*, vol. 18, no. 3 (August 1990), pp. 339–60. However, Rawls insists that his "overlapping consensus" theory is not a *"modus vivendi"* conception, and to this extent would want to distance himself somewhat from Larmore's version of liberalism.

standing certain idiosyncrasies bound up with his own philosophical project) as representative of what I understand by liberalism in this very broad sense.[15] I think that my definition captures what is distinctive about contemporary proponents of liberal philosophy better and more inclusively than other, narrower alternative definitions. A liberal is someone who feels quite comfortable, metaphysically speaking, with the kind of social order made available by contemporary American society, and whose moral and philosophical concerns are exhausted by an urge to make such societies incrementally less unjust. For Canadians, the vision of liberalism that I am trying to sketch gains clarity through a contrast between the unbridled social dynamism at work south of the border and the residual preliberal traditions that we see being swallowed up in contemporary Canada; and therefore, my sense of the term "liberalism" should be reasonably familiar to readers of George Grant's book *Lament for a Nation*.[16] Likewise, in all those countries around the world where the struggle between modernity and premodernity is still being fought, the stakes involved in the cultural triumph of liberalism ought to be pretty clear, both positively and negatively. (To mention examples: positively, it means an end, thankfully, to practices such as female circumcision in the Sudan; negatively, it means the growing hegemony of certain imperialistic languages — notably English — that serve as the agents of the liberal way of life, and correspondingly, the tragic withering of languages that are marginal to the liberal empire.)[17]

Many liberals will deny that liberalism has anything to do with cultural judgments about modernity; they will assert that liberalism has to do with the extent to which the state does or does not impinge upon the citizen. But liberalism has everything to do with cultural judgments about modernity. A liberal is someone who celebrates modernity wholeheartedly as emancipatory. An antiliberal is someone who is at least somewhat anxious about the quality of this emancipation, and who worries about the price we have to pay for being culturally "emancipated." Let me offer an

---

[15] Richard Rorty, *Contingency, Irony, and Solidarity* (Cambridge: Cambridge University Press, 1989); Richard Rorty, "The Priority of Democracy to Philosophy," in Rorty, *Philosophical Papers*, vol. 1, *Objectivity, Relativism, and Truth* (Cambridge: Cambridge University Press, 1991), pp. 175–96. See the criticisms of Rorty's political philosophy elaborated in my article, "Richard Rorty's Liberalism," *Critical Review*, vol. 7, no. 1 (Winter 1993), pp. 15–31.

[16] George Grant, *Lament for a Nation: The Defeat of Canadian Nationalism* (Toronto: McClelland and Stewart, 1965); see esp. ch. 5. Grant's book was a major theoretical manifesto for Canadian nationalism in the 1960s. Although Grant himself conceived his argument on behalf of nationalism as an expression of his commitment to conservatism, or more strictly Anglo-Canadian Toryism, the book also had a very large impact upon Canadian nationalists on the Left, who of course had their own reasons for hostility to the imperialistic thrust of Americanism.

[17] Consider, here, Leszek Kolakowski's acute remarks concerning the looming extinction of the Celtic languages; see his *Modernity on Endless Trial* (Chicago: University of Chicago Press, 1990), p. 23. See also my commentary on Kolakowski: "Thin Ice," *History of the Human Sciences*, vol. 5, no. 3 (August 1992), pp. 65–70, where I discuss the complexities of judgment concerning modernity and antimodernity.

illustration that goes to the heart of the *Kulturkampf* being fought by liberals. On February 14, 1989, to the horror of liberals throughout the West (a horror I certainly share to the fullest), Ayatollah Ruholla Khomeini issued a *fatwa* against Salman Rushdie for having written *The Satanic Verses*. In his 1990 Herbert Read Memorial Lecture, however, Rushdie himself tells us that this same Islamic culture that ultimately condemned him as an author instilled in him a capacity to *cherish* books, to treat *all* books as holy — a disposition that is not unrelated, I think, to the *fatwa*. His Islamic upbringing taught him to kiss any book that had been dropped in order to repair the disrespect shown to the book, whatever it happened to be (whether a novel or a comic book).[18] For such a non-liberal culture, books *matter*, and because they matter, one either kisses them or burns them.[19] A liberal society is a society that does not take books seriously enough either to kiss them *or* to burn them. A liberal celebrates this. An antiliberal, as I mentioned above, worries about it. It seems to me, moreover, that an analogous point applies across a wide swath of cultural experience (including sexual life).[20]

III. INDIVIDUALS AND SOCIETY

In order to discover what liberalism really means, we must look not just to the mechanical politics of the liberal state, but to the spiritual politics of the liberal soul. We must, as Plato insisted in *The Republic*, draw the connection between the polis and the psyche, and see that a liberal political order does not guard the individual against governance by larger forces, but rather, shapes that governance in a particular fashion. Here, it is well to observe the paradoxical character of MacIntyre's definition of liberalism in terms of its attempt to privatize the good. While it is indeed true that liberalism aspires to privatize the good, it really cannot be done, because this very attempt at privatization already expresses a larger, global conception of what the good is (for instance, the conception of the good as something that admits of private stipulation — which is itself a global, not a private, conception).

Saying that we inhabit a *liberal* civilization is therefore different from saying that we inhabit a capitalist civilization, a democratic civilization, a civilization of mass culture or mass society, and so on. The most dis-

---

[18] Salman Rushdie, "Is Nothing Sacred?" in Rushdie, *Imaginary Homelands* (New York: Penguin, 1991), p. 415.

[19] Cf. *ibid.*, p. 261 (Rushdie quoting Italo Calvino): "Nobody these days holds the written word in such high esteem as police states do."

[20] As concerns sexual life: in an unpublished essay entitled "Borrowed Truths: Sexuality, Authenticity, and Modernity," Leslie Green argues that it is to the credit of liberal society that it takes sex "off the high-tension wires," and turns decisions about sexual life into matters of taste and mere preference, stripping them of any "cosmic" meaning. Here too, it may be replied, one pays a price for this banalization of sexuality.

cerning liberals have been able to appreciate this very well. Let me cite
the statements of three liberals on this point:

1. Stephen Macedo has written: "Liberalism holds out the promise, or
the threat, of making all the world like California."[21]

2. According to John Gray: "Liberalism . . . is the political theory of
modernity."[22]

3. Finally, Richard Rorty acknowledges that the liberal order is not neutral on the question of how human beings should live, but on the contrary, embodies a decision that human beings be "bland, calculating,
petty and unheroic," because this is the necessary price that one pays for
a society that cherishes individual liberty.[23]

These three liberals here give expression to an insight about the relation between the individual and society that has eluded most contemporary liberal philosophers. What distinguishes the majority of liberal
theorists today is the philosophical assumption that we start with individuals and then ask how we can design social institutions that allow these
individuals, in a fashion that best suits them without prejudicing the welfare of others, to define and redefine their own needs, wants, interests,
and preferences. This runs directly counter to the philosophical assumption shared by almost all the great political philosophers running from
Plato to Nietzsche (and shared even by nineteenth-century *liberals* like
Alexis de Tocqueville and Mill) that, by contrast, we rightly start with a
social order and ask how that social order shapes individuals of a particular cast. If we opt for the latter brand of political philosophy, then in
judging liberal society philosophically, we begin by asking what kind of
human beings it characteristically churns out.[24]

Does it make sense to speak of modern, individualistic societies as animated by a shared way of life? And is it fair to highlight the adjective "liberal" in order to characterize the global ordering principle at work in
contemporary liberal societies? To address these difficult questions, I want
to make a little detour into art criticism. Although it might seem odd (to
the liberal it will seem *very* odd) to conceptualize my understanding of liberalism by offering a commentary on a cultural artifact, as opposed to
inquiring into structures of government or institutional power, it should
already be clear that the questions I want to pose require cultural exploration. In thinking of what liberalism means, the image that comes to my
mind is an exceptionally striking painting by David Hockney entitled

---

[21] Macedo, *Liberal Virtues*, p. 278.

[22] John Gray, *Liberalism* (Minneapolis: University of Minnesota Press, 1986), p. 82.

[23] Rorty, *Objectivity, Relativism, and Truth*, p. 190.

[24] Here I can actually cite the authority of John Stuart Mill, who *agrees* that this is the
proper function of theory: "The first question in respect to any political institutions is, how
far they tend to foster in the members of the community the various desirable qualities, moral
and intellectual" (Mill, *Considerations on Representative Government*, ch. 2).

"Mr. and Mrs. Clark and Percy," which was executed in 1970–71. Anyone who has seen the painting hanging in the Tate Gallery in London would, I think, have trouble forgetting it. It is a portrait of two nearly life-size figures, a man seated and a woman standing, in a typically barren sixties domestic landscape. "Mr. and Mrs. Clark and Percy" portrays two close friends of Hockney, Ossie Clark and Celia Birtwell, both successful and quite well-known London fashion designers, who were married in 1969. The painting was intended as a marriage portrait, and is set in the living room of their flat in Notting Hill Gate, London. Everything in the painting bespeaks emptiness: the insipid pastel colors throughout; the soulless sixties furniture; the blank walls, adorned only by a Hockney print off to the left side; the white cat on Ossie's lap ("Percy" in the painting's title refers to the cat) and the tasteless sixties carpet into which Ossie's bare feet are sunk; the sterile white lilies on a sterile white coffee table; the telephone and lamp deposited forlornly on the floor to the right. The characters themselves, Celia and Ossie, look as if they have been deposited in a spiritual void; they appear utterly lost, uncomfortable, totally ill-at-ease with themselves, and seem in some strange way to be separated by an immeasurable distance, several hundred miles apart. It seems entirely fitting that the marriage celebrated in this strange painting was to end subsequently in divorce.[25]

How is this painting relevant to an understanding of liberalism? Let me try to translate my commentary into more theoretical terms. Liberalism as I understand it does not merely refer to a particular relation between the state and the individual, but expresses an encompassing view of human life, one that aspires to leave individuals as much as possible free to shape their lives according to their own notions, so that the society offers no official guidance on how people are to conduct their lives in a meaningful direction. What Hockney's painting conveys is that this vision of things has the consequence that the furniture of our world, as it were, is reduced to the bare minimum. In short, I think that the painting offers a visual answer to the question that concerns me here — namely, that the liberal preoccupation with formal freedoms obscures the issue of the political-moral-spiritual matter or substance of a particular way of life.

At this point the philosophical liberal is bound to leap up and cry: "Aha! Just as I suspected! Cultural criticism masquerading as political analysis!" What is my rejoinder? Well, to be honest, I have real trouble seeing why political philosophers should be required to abstain from cultural criticism, and I find considerable comfort in the fact that the most ambitious theorists of the tradition — Plato, Rousseau, Tocqueville,

---

[25] My source for biographical information concerning the painting is Peter Webb, *Portrait of David Hockney* (New York: E. P. Dutton, 1988), pp. 109–10. For reproductions of the painting and preliminary studies, see *ibid.*, plates 87–90 and 112.

Nietzsche — had no reluctance about placing cultural critique at the heart of their enterprise. Indeed, it is my chief complaint against contemporary liberal political philosophers (as distinct from nineteenth-century liberals, who did *not* feel obliged to observe maxims of intellectual parsimony) that they have abandoned this essential critical dimension of theory — and therefore limit themselves to pursuing, at most, a modest reformist agenda. Relative to the great tradition of theory from Plato to Nietzsche, this amounts to chopping political philosophy off at the knees.

Contemporary theorists should strenuously resist this constricted agenda. For instance, in order to reflect properly on the character of liberalism as a regime devoted to comfortable bourgeois existence, one would be required to give some account of why a significant proportion of individuals in modern society feel driven to experience life through the mediation of opiates and hallucinogens. This would be less of a problem if drug use were confined to members of a deprived underclass, since it could then be interpreted as an intelligible response to the hopelessness of their social condition. However, it is clearly a quite different matter where what calls for explanation is a situation in which, say, cocaine use by lawyers, doctors, teachers, and civil servants (i.e., by the privileged middle class) becomes commonplace. To characterize it philosophically, I would say that it is a symptom of nihilism as diagnosed by Nietzsche, that is, as the drying up of the narrative possibilities of our civilization, of our capacity to project civilizational purposes in which we ourselves still believe, to sustain narratives that make these purposes credible to ourselves. A public void is then compensated for by a retreat to hypersubjectivity. Yet if the liberal parameters of theorizing prevail, then this never even arises as a topic for philosophic reflection.

A liberal society is a society chiefly dedicated to the protection of individual rights and liberties. A liberal theorist is an intellectual who is reluctant to cause liberal society to feel uneasy with itself by posing radical (i.e., tactless) questions about the real worth of the activities to which individuals within such societies devote their main energies.[26] If my reading of Hockney's painting is more or less on the mark, what it communicates is that a liberal world is a world without furniture. We purge our dwelling-place of furniture because its presence would derogate from the moral imperative resting upon individuals to create every bit of spiritual furniture from out of themselves. (In this sense, liberalism begins with the Protestant Reformation.) The liberal impulse is an adventure in

---

[26] It is a central aspect of my argument in this essay that the decisive measure of one's liberalism is the extent of one's philosophical commitment to modernity. This will have what will appear to many to be a paradoxical consequence (but one that I willingly embrace), namely, that authors like Charles Taylor and Jürgen Habermas who offer strong defenses of modernity in their recent work are to that extent to be categorized as liberals — in contrast with, say, Hannah Arendt and Alasdair MacIntyre, who throughout their work are consistent critics of modernity.

spiritual self-creation, and it transfers what the greatest poets and artists have been able to accomplish onto the shoulders of "Everyman." This is liberalism's most primal egalitarianism.

A liberal is someone who says that the present social order in contemporary Western, democratic, individualistic, and pluralistic societies is basically okay, apart from a need for improvements in equality of opportunity and more equitable social distribution. A critic of liberalism like myself will say this is nonsense. To this, the liberal will reply: "Okay, this isn't good enough; what's your alternative?" It is both necessary and legitimate for me to claim that I don't need to answer this question. I don't see myself in the business of designing an alternative social order. People who do that always end up making fools of themselves. That's not my job. My job as a theorist is to criticize the prevailing social order, and to draw upon the great traditions of Western political philosophy in order to puncture liberal complacency. The rhetorical trademark of the liberal, by contrast, is the readiness to denounce as "romantic nostalgia" any effort at a more ambitious social criticism.

Relative to this standard of a more ambitious social criticism, I fear that exactly the wrong lessons have been drawn from the so-called "liberal-communitarian debate," and that communitarianism, rather than inducing contemporary liberalism to become more robustly self-critical, has actually done the opposite. Rorty, for instance, thinks that the post-communitarian Rawls is preferable to the pre-communitarian Rawls because communitarianism teaches liberals to historicize and relativize their liberalism. This means that liberalism meets the communitarian standard simply by relating liberal principles to the existing practices and self-understanding of liberal societies as they have unfolded historically. In my opinion, this is exactly the wrong influence for communitarianism to have had upon liberalism, because what was welcome about the communitarian challenge was that it was a *challenge*: it required another look at fundamental issues concerning the adequacy of liberal society in satisfying profound human needs for rootedness, common purpose, and meaningful traditions. But what has happened, unfortunately, is that this challenge has been turned around so that it functions as a rationale for greater complacency with our own historically evolved liberal way of life. Since the communitarians demand appeals to tradition and historically rooted practices, the liberals reply, it suffices to point out liberal society's own rootedness in a historical community of self-interpretation in order to meet the communitarian challenge.[27] The net effect of the liberal-communitarian encounter, then, is not a more probing examination of lib-

---

[27] For notable examples of works representing this tendency, see Rawls, *Political Liberalism*; Ronald Dworkin, *Law's Empire* (Cambridge, MA: Belknap Press, 1986), ch. 6; Ronald Dworkin, "Liberal Community," *California Law Review*, vol. 77, no. 3 (May 1989), pp. 479–504; Rorty, *Contingency, Irony, and Solidarity*; and Rorty, "The Priority of Democracy to Philosophy."

eral practice, but one which is, precisely because it has been "communitarianized" and therefore historicized, *less* probing, less radical. The consequence of the debate is therefore the opposite of what, I think, theorists like MacIntyre, Taylor, and Sandel had intended. It is as if one thought one could accommodate Simone Weil's analysis of our "need for roots" by asking people who are products of modern suburbia to appreciate the communal constitution of their selfhood by embarking on an exploration of their suburban roots! (I take this to be a *reductio ad absurdum* of the communitarian liberalism celebrated by Rorty.)[28].

IV. CONCLUSION

Let me sum up my position regarding liberalism, in order to make my standpoint as clear as it can be made: First of all, philosophical antiliberalism does not require that one embrace some militantly illiberal or antiliberal creed. For myself, I am sure that my politics differ hardly at all from those left liberals I criticize. As I have discussed elsewhere, liberals and their critics commonly embrace identical policy commitments in practice.[29] What the debate concerns, rather, is the underlying philosophic visions that furnish the *grounds* for convergent policy commitments (since opposing theoretical premises can yield the same practical conclusions);[30] it also concerns the enveloping cultural attitudes that are often

---

[28] In its least penetrating version, the communitarian critique of liberalism seems to issue in the suggestion that the failings of liberalism can be remedied by a heightened collectivist consciousness; for me, the demand for a heightened collectivist consciousness does not pose a sufficiently radical challenge to liberalism. Hannah Arendt once remarked that "just as socialism is no remedy for capitalism, capitalism cannot be a remedy or an alternative for socialism" (Arendt, *Crises of the Republic* [New York: Harcourt Brace Jovanovich, 1972], p. 220); and I am tempted to say that the same applies to the quarrel between liberals and communitarians.

[29] Beiner, *What's the Matter with Liberalism?* p. 15. In chapters 1 and 7 of the book, I try to make the case that it is not the chief purpose of theorists to offer immediate guidance on questions of policy. Rather, the aim of theory at its best is to offer grand visions of moral and political order in the light of which we can engage in ambitiously critical self-reflection about the character of our society. It is *not* the purpose of this essay to argue that the standard by which contemporary political philosophies should be judged is the ambitiousness with which they presume to legislate political practice from the heights of philosophical insight; the purpose, rather, is to argue that they should be judged according to their ambitiousness in enlarging the space of critical reflection (which is certainly not the same thing as presuming to direct political practice). Therefore, I cannot agree with John Dunn that "[t]he purpose of political theory is to diagnose practical predicaments and to show us how best to confront them" (Dunn, *Interpreting Political Responsibility* [Princeton, NJ: Princeton University Press, 1990], p. 193). I do agree with him, however, that political philosophy as it is dominantly practiced today reflects "its radical domestication, its complete subordination to the dynamics of an existing ideological field" (*ibid.*, p. 195).

[30] To cite one example: in "Do We Have a Right to Pornography?" (in *A Matter of Principle*, pp. 335–72), Ronald Dworkin severely criticizes Bernard Williams's philosophical premises, yet he has no desire at all to contest the validity of the practical recommendations that Williams seeks to draw from these premises.

the chief mark of liberal or antiliberal sympathies. Liberals typically regard these cultural attitudes as politically irrelevant, whereas their critics hold that if a people is culturally anomic, rootless, and dislocated, this will inevitably give rise, sooner or later, to political pathologies such as civic apathy and alienation from the state, contributing to what has come to be called a "legitimation crisis."[31]

Secondly, if we are to consider ourselves heirs of a Socratic tradition (i.e., a tradition devoted to mental liberation from the imprisoning assumptions of one's own society), then as members of a *liberal* civilization, fidelity to that Socratic tradition requires us to submit liberal assumptions about social life to radical self-criticism. My problem here is that I find it hard to see how a theorist committed simply to the articulation of liberal principles can be much of a gadfly in the context of a liberal society. To be sure, I fully recognize that such a liberal theorist can be a most effective gadfly in the context of *il*liberal societies, and of course I do not dispute that in illiberal societies, liberal gadflies are not merely desirable but indispensable. (Indeed, I am really not sure whether Socrates counts as a liberal gadfly in an illiberal society, or an illiberal gadfly in a liberal society. It seems likely that in some respects he was each of these things.)

Finally, and perhaps most importantly, we owe it to ourselves as intellectuals to make sure that we do not bore ourselves to death by reducing the grand tradition of Western theory to ridiculously modest proportions, namely, mere tinkering with the economic and political details of the liberal order while leaving its grounding assumptions fundamentally unquestioned. If we convince ourselves that our sole task as theorists is to write uplifting treatises explaining why liberal citizens should be decent and tolerant toward each other, the whole enterprise of theory is sure to become a big yawn — whereas lunatics like Nietzsche and Heidegger, precisely because they conceive the task of philosophy far more ambitiously, remain genuinely challenging and profound. But again, one can find one's philosophical reflection richly stimulated by a thinker like Heidegger without being obliged to embrace his odiously illiberal politics. It must be conceded to liberals that as good citizens, we have an obligation to be

---

[31] An instructive case is Judith Shklar's "liberalism of fear" (see, for instance, her article of that title in *Liberalism and the Moral Life*, ed. Nancy L. Rosenblum [Cambridge: Harvard University Press, 1989], pp. 21–38), since Shklar's liberalism, even though it is richer and more interesting than the neo-Kantian liberalisms that have been so influential, shares the decisive flaw common to all contemporary liberalisms. For Shklar, a society that does not torture, maim, oppress, degrade, or humiliate its members, or particular groups within it, meets the only relevant standard of political desirability. It is true that even this minimalist standard offers some scope for criticizing existing liberal regimes; yet it is very easy to think of societies that meet this standard and nonetheless embody in their social order a pretty crummy way of life. Shklar's conception of what it is to do political theory discourages her from passing judgment on these "cultural" concerns. Exactly the same considerations apply to Isaiah Berlin.

sensible enough not to be Stalinists, nostalgic conservatives, evangelical moral-majoritarians, or Islamic fundamentalists. As intellectuals, however, we also have an obligation to keep the space of intellectual life as rich and open as possible, and in practice we can only fulfill this duty by blasting away at liberal orthodoxy.

Political Science, University of Toronto

AGAINST TRADITION

By Cass R. Sunstein

I. Introduction

In recent years many people have suggested that rights come from traditions. More particularly, many people interested in American constitutional law have said that constitutional rights should be developed with close reference to American traditions.[1] In this essay, I mean to challenge these claims. I argue that the enterprise of defining rights, including constitutional rights, should not be founded on an inquiry into tradition. Traditions should be assessed, not replicated. I also try to unpack some of the complexities in the idea that rights should be based on traditions.

The topic is highly relevant to the debate over "communitarianism." Many communitarians appear to be traditionalists, at least implicitly; they are concerned to defend social practices against abstract, acontextual claims about what is to be done, or about "rights."[2] It is important to ask why and when communitarians believe that a community's practices deserve insulation from rights-based claims. Often the best or most interesting answer has a Burkean dimension. It involves the extent to which a community — perhaps a local community resisting national efforts, perhaps a nation resisting international goals — owes its practices to long traditions that, precisely because of their longevity, might seem to make special sense. Ideas of this sort might be thought to have special strength when we think about rights in general or about constitutional rights in particular.

Constitutional traditionalists do insist on some important truths. It is correct to say that people (and especially judges) should be cautious before rejecting judgments that have been made by many people in many periods. It is also true that rights ought to come from traditions in the sense that any rights, to qualify as such, should be intelligible to the human beings who are said to have rights, and rights without sources in any recognizable tradition will not be intelligible to the human beings who enjoy them.[3] But these (obvious) truths do not suggest that tradi-

---

[1] See the discussion of Antonin Scalia in Section V below.

[2] See Mary Ann Glendon, *Rights-Talk* (New York: The Free Press, 1991).

[3] There are complex issues in the background here. It may well be correct to grant rights to people who do not understand those particular rights, or even rights in general. People accustomed to systematic deprivation because of (for example) sex inequality should still have a right to sex equality, even if the notion of sex equality seems unintelligible to them.

© 1996 Social Philosophy and Policy Foundation. Printed in the USA.

tion is the best source of rights or of constitutional rights. Traditions in America and elsewhere include much that is bad as well as much that is good, and it is an appropriate democratic and constitutional task to evaluate traditions on their merits, rather than to embody them in law.

Moreover, traditions do not come prepackaged for easy identification. They lack labels. The task of identifying traditions is evaluative and therefore interpretive, not merely descriptive. If traditions are to be used as a source of rights, it is inevitably the task of the aspiring traditionalist to engage in evaluation. This task is often unself-conscious, or sometimes even masked, and the masking tends to mark traditionalists as legal formalists, making evaluative judgments that they simultaneously disavow.[4] I conclude that courts thinking about what the Constitution requires should be cautious about disrupting long-standing practices, but that apart from this simple cautionary note, traditionalism has nothing to offer to those thinking about the appropriate content of rights or the mandates of the American Constitution.

II. THE PROBLEM

Where do constitutional rights come from? Once a constitution is in place, the usual answer is: From the words of the Constitution. The answer is right so far as it goes, but it is ludicrously incomplete. The rights-conferring provisions[5] of the American Constitution are vague and apparently open-ended; they are hardly self-interpreting. What is "the freedom of speech"? When have people been deprived of "the equal protection of the laws"? When has government "taken private property"? And what counts as liberty within the meaning of the Fifth and Fourteenth Amendments? A familiar kind of legal formalism consists of the effort to treat legal texts as self-defining; it is embodied in the claim that ambiguous abstract terms can be understood to have a single meaning without the aid of controversial supplemental interpretive claims. Formalism exerts a continuing hold on the legal mind, but it ought not to; in fact, formalism should be ranked one of the two or three truly mortal sins of constitutional interpretation.[6]

The lawyer's conventional tools include not just text, but also constitutional structure and history. From constitutional structure, for example,

---

[4] I am dealing here with a particular species of formalism; some species are quite honorable. See Frederick Schauer, *Playing by the Rules* (Oxford: Oxford University Press, 1992).

[5] In using the term "rights-conferring," I do not mean to deny that some people in the founding period thought that the Constitution acknowledged preexisting rights. See in this regard the Ninth Amendment, which says that "[t]he enumeration in the Constitution, of certain rights, shall not be construed to deny or disparage others retained by the people." There is a sharp dispute over how to interpret this amendment. See Geoffrey R. Stone et al., *Constitutional Law*, 2d ed. (Boston: Little, Brown and Co., 1991), ch. 6.

[6] I think that formalism underlies, e.g., Robert Bork, *The Tempting of America* (New York: The Free Press, 1989); see Cass R. Sunstein, *The Partial Constitution* (Cambridge: Harvard University Press, 1993), ch. 4.

we might conclude that there is a right to travel. After all, the system of federalism might well be defeated without a right of interstate mobility. And in discerning the meaning of an ambiguous constitutional provision, we should probably attend to the history behind it, so as to discipline the judges and respect past democratic judgments. For example, the equal protection clause was an outgrowth of a belief that the states were not protecting the newly freed slaves from public and private violence. Judges should probably use this history to limit and shape current interpretations of the equal protection clause.

Sometimes, however, these conventional sources of interpretation run out, in the sense that they leave conspicuous gaps and ambiguities. Constitutional structure hardly tells us whether commercial speech is protected by the First Amendment, whether discrimination against homosexuals is forbidden by the equal protection clause, or whether the Fourteenth Amendment protects the right to die. Pre-ratification history leaves equally hard issues. Should the historical understanding be described narrowly or broadly? If defined narrowly, why should it be binding? How do we deal with changed circumstances?

The conventional sources of interpretation therefore yield a number of open questions. Perhaps political philosophy can help us; certainly political philosophy has played a role in decisions about the content of constitutional rights. But in a famous opinion Justice Oliver Wendell Holmes said that "the Constitution does not enact Mr. Herbert Spencer's Social Statics,"[7] and the same might be said for any effort to invoke the works of John Stuart Mill or John Rawls. Holmes's point seems to be twofold. First, the Constitution is best understood to allow majorities to choose among a range of political philosophies, rather than to require the nation to select any particular one (though this very understanding is a kind of political philosophy and of course requires an independent defense). Second, those of us who live in a heterogeneous society should distrust our judges, who may well be unresponsive, ignorant, parochial, or confused; we should therefore seek to disable them from invalidating statutes on the basis of the political philosophy that they find most congenial.

In the history of American constitutionalism, tradition has sometimes been invoked to fill the gaps left by text, structure, history, and moral argument.[8] In judge-made constitutional law, tradition has very recently emerged as an extraordinarily important source of constitutional rights, especially in the interpretation of the due process clause of the Fourteenth Amendment. For example, the Supreme Court held in *Griswold v. Connecticut* (1965) that married people had a right to use contraceptives,[9] thus invalidating a Connecticut law forbidding such use. In doing this,

[7] *Lochner v. New York*, 198 U.S. 45, 56 (1905) (Holmes, J., dissenting).
[8] See, e.g., *Palko v. Connecticut*, 302 U.S. 319 (1937).
[9] *Griswold v. Connecticut*, 381 U.S. 479 (1965).

the Court relied heavily on what it saw as the tradition of marital privacy. Some justices stressed the novelty of the ban on use of contraceptives; for them it was critical that in Anglo-American history, there had never been bans on use of contraceptives within marriage. When the right of privacy was established in *Griswold*, tradition was a notably large ingredient in the Court's analysis. The barrier protecting the individual from the state was defined in large part by traditional practices.

The use of tradition was far more attenuated in the next major privacy case, *Eisenstadt v. Baird* (1972),[10] where the Court invalidated, as "irrational" under the equal protection clause, the prohibition on the distribution of contraceptives to unmarried people. Here tradition did not support those who sought to attack the law. Surely unmarried people have no traditional right to purchase contraceptives. In invalidating the law, the *Eisenstadt* Court began the process of judicial definition of fundamental rights not by reference to tradition, but by reference to something like an account of what sorts of rights are most important to individual self-definition. Some such account underlay the conception of privacy in *Roe v. Wade* (1973),[11] the famous (or infamous) case establishing the abortion right. This case was not fundamentally a case about tradition. Instead, *Roe* depended above all on a conception (controversial to be sure) of what individual liberty properly included, and about the boundaries that communities could not legitimately cross.

But the life of tradition, as a source of constitutional rights, was hardly over. Tradition reemerged as a defining idea in *Bowers v. Hardwick* (1986),[12] where the Court upheld a ban on same-sex sodomy. There the Court emphasized that sodomy was a criminal offense at common law, and that thirty-two of the thirty-seven states outlawed sodomy in 1868, when the Fourteenth Amendment was ratified. "Against this background, to claim that a right to engage in such conduct is 'deeply rooted in this Nation's history and tradition' or 'implicit in the concept of ordered liberty' is, at best, facetious." Chief Justice Warren Burger underlined the importance of tradition in his separate opinion, as he wrote in concurrence that "[d]ecisions of individuals relating to homosexual conduct have been subject to state intervention throughout the history of Western Civilization."

Perhaps the most important recent use of tradition occurred in *Michael H. v. Gerald D.* (1989),[13] in which the Court denied an adulterous father's claim of a constitutional right to visit his child, who had been conceived by a woman who was married to someone else. There the plurality of the Court relied heavily on the absence of any such right in tradition. The plurality emphasized "the historic respect—indeed, sanctity would not be

---

[10] *Eisenstadt v. Baird*, 405 U.S. 438 (1972).
[11] *Roe v. Wade*, 410 U.S. 113 (1973).
[12] *Bowers v. Hardwick*, 478 U.S. 186 (1986).
[13] *Michael H. v. Gerald D.*, 109 S.Ct. 1333 (1989).

too strong a term—traditionally accorded to the relationships that develop within the unitary family." Writing in dissent, Justice William Brennan argued that the relevant tradition should be construed as a general respect for parental rights, that the privacy cases involved general aspirations rather than concrete practices, and that the plurality's approach would unravel the Constitution's protection of liberty. In a key and much-discussed footnote offered in response to Justice Brennan, the plurality defended its reliance on "historical traditions specifically relating to the rights of an adulterous natural father, rather than inquiring more generally 'whether parenthood is an interest that traditionally has received our attention and protection.' " The plurality said:

> Why should the relevant category not be even more general — perhaps "family relationships"; or "personal relationships"; or even "emotional attachments in general"? Though Justice Brennan has no basis for the level of generality he would select, we do: We refer to the most specific level at which a relevant tradition protecting, or denying protection to, the asserted right can be identified. . . . Because general traditions provide such imprecise guidance, they permit judges to dictate rather than discern the society's views. Although assuredly having the virtue (if it be that) of leaving judges free to decide as they think best when the unanticipated occurs, a rule of law that binds neither by text nor by any particular, identifiable tradition, is no rule of law at all.

Tradition has reemerged as a key issue in cases involving a patient's right to refuse lifesaving medical treatment and the right to die. Suicide has been banned by tradition. Should this count decisively against the alleged right to die? So Justice Antonin Scalia argued, in a separate opinion concluding that the Constitution does not constrain the state's power over individual choice in this area.[14] Some justices have claimed that tradition has guarded against "state incursions into the body," and that therefore people have a right to resist invasive medical treatment even when such treatment is necessary to save their lives.[15] The role of tradition promises to be one of the most important issues in ascertaining the reach of the Constitution's basic liberty guarantee.

III. Tradition and the Puzzling Search for an Antonym

Suppose we think that tradition is a good source of rights — even constitutional rights. To get a fix on this idea, we need to know to what sources of rights tradition is designed as an alternative.

---

[14] See *Cruzan v. Director*, 110 S.Ct. 2841 (1990).
[15] *Ibid.*, p. 2849 (O'Connor, J., concurring).

At first glance, it might seem trivial to suggest that traditions are a source of rights. To decide on the appropriate category of rights, human beings usually must rely on what other human beings think or have thought. For people in a particular nation, it is natural to ask about the present and past judgments of other people, in that nation or elsewhere. If traditionalism is meant as a reminder that wholly external evaluations of human practices are not possible, traditionalism seems right; but against whom is it directed?

Perhaps the answer is *metaphysical realists* — people who believe that with respect to rights (or anything else), human beings can have access to something wholly external to human judgment and cognition. To say the least, the issues underlying metaphysical realism are extremely complex.[16] Fortunately, we do not have to resolve those issues here. Some people believe in natural rights; but few people seriously believe that constitutional rights should be identified by exploring a point of view that is external to human perceptions, needs, and interests. If traditionalists are concerned to emphasize the human basis of constitutional rights, they are not offering anything really distinctive. Those who reject constitutional traditionalism are not claiming to be metaphysical realists.

Perhaps traditionalism has other targets. Perhaps traditionalists are concerned not to emphasize the origins of rights in human practices, but instead to oppose *cosmopolitanism*. Some people think that any community should decide on rights by reference to its own particular practices, rather than by reference to claims that come from elsewhere. (The notion of a "community" is not self-defining, but perhaps we can bracket the obvious difficulties here.) On this view, Chinese traditionalism is good for China, South African traditionalism is good for South Africa, Russian traditionalism makes sense for Russia, American traditionalism is good for America, and so on. Constitution-making and constitutional interpretation should be done with close reference to local traditions. Certainly ideas of this kind are playing a role in current processes of constitution-making in Eastern Europe, where documents are being drawn up with close reference to national traditions and values, historically defined. Thus, it appears that precommunist traditions, defined nationally, are playing a large role in current debates. Those traditions are an important source of constitutional commitments.

What implications might anticosmopolitan traditionalism have for the United States? In the American constitutional order, traditionalism might be opposed to *nationalism*, in favor of respect for the judgments of localities and small communities. Opposition to nationalism in favor of local traditions has a distinguished history in American federalism. Some

---

[16] See Hilary Putnam, *Renewing Philosophy* (Cambridge: Harvard University Press, 1992); and John Searle, *The Construction of Social Reality* (New York: The Free Press, 1995).

forms of modern communitarianism are localist in character. They stem from the concern that rights, imposed by the central government, will be unresponsive to local traditions and practices. In the constitutional context, we might think that the Supreme Court should be reluctant to impose national norms on a large nation having heterogeneous subunits.

On one view, for example, we should reassess the "incorporation" movement, which applied the Bill of Rights to the states on the same terms as it applied to the national government.[17] Perhaps the incorporation of the Bill of Rights was a mistake. Perhaps some rights should not have been incorporated at all; perhaps they should have been incorporated, but in more modest form, setting basic floors for rights without making the bill of rights, as applied to the states, equivalent to the bill of rights guaranteed against the more remote and less accountable national government. Whether or not incorporation makes sense, perhaps the Supreme Court should be more respectful than it now is of local traditions, refusing to impose national rights unless they are a clear or unmistakable inference from constitutional structure.

There is much to be said on behalf of this view, at least in the abstract. Certainly local governmental units face constraints that can make some rights a bit less urgent. If there is free mobility, people who are unhappy with the governance of a local unit have the ability to leave. The power of exit creates an *ex ante* deterrent and an *ex post* corrective to oppression. In addition, democratic processes are reinforced by allowing a large degree of local self-determination. Because localities are more highly responsive to democratic will, they might have less need for external safeguards in the form of judicially enforceable rights. There are, of course, countervailing considerations. But we might well think that localities should be permitted to impose, for example, more stringent regulations on obscene materials if this is their choice. There is no reason to have the same rules for obscenity in New York as in Utah.

So far so good. But it is equally correct to say that many norms involving rights are properly taken as national, because they represent basic minima of national citizenship, or basic goods that all people deserve to have. The relation between basic minima and basic goods on the one hand, and constitutional rights on the other, is a complex business. Constitutional rights are practical instruments, with concrete purposes; and for this reason they might not match the set of minima and goods that would be identified by the best political theory.[18] But some constitutional rights are rightly taken to embody national norms. The prohibition on governmental race discrimination in the Fourteenth Amendment is a core example; another is the protection of rights of political speech.

---

[17] See Stone et al., *Constitutional Law*, ch. 6.

[18] For some notes, see Cass R. Sunstein, "Liberal Constitutionalism and Liberal Justice," *Texas Law Review*, vol. 72 (1993), p. 305.

In this light, the problem with constitutional traditionalism—if it is intended as an antonym to cosmopolitanism or nationalism—is not that it is wrong but that it is too vague and broad-gauged. It does not offer the resources with which to make necessary distinctions between national rights and local self-determination. To make such distinctions, we have to say much more, and the more that must be said will involve distinctions between goods and rights that all people should have, on the one hand, and appropriate local and national distinctions, on the other. To make these distinctions, we must invoke criteria about the proper mix between universal and local rights. The mere notion of "tradition" is unhelpful in supplying those criteria. What has been done in the past need not be a secure guide.

Perhaps the target of traditionalism is not cosmopolitanism or nationalism, but *independent moral argument*. Traditionalism is thus opposed to one form of *rationalism*.[19] We might think that human beings (or at least judges) have inadequate capacities to think through our practices, and that our practices are themselves the best guide to what is to be done. If a practice has endured, then many people have endorsed it, or at least not seen fit to change it. If a practice has endured, then it has been found acceptable by numerous people over long periods, which is itself a reason to think that it is good. The tradition is therefore likely to serve important social functions that people at a particular time may not be able to perceive.

In this form, the inspiration for traditionalism can be found in the writings of Edmund Burke, and in particular in his enthusiasm for common-law processes of incremental development over thinking on the basis of first principles. As a creed for constitutional law, traditionalism respects common-law processes, and perceives them as a model for legal and even social development. It finds its antonym in the (liberal?) belief that human beings should try to evaluate their practices by reference to criteria of freedom and equality that give us an independent, critical purchase on what we have done.

To the extent that traditionalism is designed to offer a cautionary note about the potentially harmful consequences of social change, it makes a lot of sense. It is a familiar but often overlooked point that particular social changes—minimum-wage increases, health-care laws, environmental protection—may have unanticipated systemic effects. A society is certainly not an ecological system; but a change in a particular aspect of society may well have effects on other parts of the system, and those effects may be both hard to anticipate and harmful. It is also important for people to be humble about their ability to evaluate long-standing practices.

---

[19] An excellent, moderate discussion is David Strauss, *Common Law Constitutionalism* (forthcoming).

Those practices may well have virtues that particular people are unable to see, or they may fit with a range of other practices in a complex way.

These considerations give us some important reasons for exercising caution in constitutional law and elsewhere. The political and legal virtue of prudence embodies an appreciation of those reasons.[20] It is important, however, to stress that prudence is a limited virtue, and that constitutional law is sometimes based on the judgment that our practices may offend our own aspirations and commitments. We do and should use our aspirations as the basis for moral argument. The attack on chattel slavery is perhaps the most vivid example, but there are many others. Consider the challenge to sex discrimination, to restrictions on political speech, to violations of religious liberty (including compulsory school prayer), to maldistributions of political power, as through the poll tax and apportionment schemes that allocate votes on a discriminatory basis.

Moral argument frequently takes the form of a search for "reflective equilibrium," in which we try to align our various moral judgments at levels of both generality and specificity.[21] In this process, some traditional practices, and some particular convictions, may not survive reflection. This point jeopardizes traditions as a source of rights, because many traditions cannot be shown to cohere with our considered judgments about much that we believe.

To be sure, constitutional argument is not a search for reflective equilibrium. Text, structure, and history discipline the process of legal argument, creating "fixed points" that have no clear analogue in the search for reflective equilibrium. Moreover, judges must take precedents as fixed or relatively fixed points even if they disagree with them. There are thus large differences between the search for reflective equilibrium and the process of constitutional argument.[22]

But the differences do not mean that traditions are immune from attack in the process of constitutional argument; and there are similarities as well as differences. For the antitraditionalist lawyer or judge (or citizen), constitutional argument is disciplined and constrained by sources of law that are not themselves the same as moral judgments (even though adverting to those sources requires a moral or political defense); but a large part of constitutional law involves the critical assessment of tradition by reference to sources of law and the moral arguments to which such sources, properly interpreted, draw attention. Thus, for example, the equal protection clause might be understood to embody a norm of

---

[20] See Alexander Bickel, *The Least Dangerous Branch* (New Haven: Yale University Press, 1965).

[21] John Rawls, *A Theory of Justice* (Cambridge: Harvard University Press, 1971).

[22] See Cass R. Sunstein, "On Analogical Reasoning," *Harvard Law Review*, vol. 106 (1993), p. 421; and Cass R. Sunstein, "Political Conflict and Legal Agreement," *The Tanner Lectures in Human Values* (forthcoming in 1996).

equality that forbids sex discrimination; the First Amendment might embody a principle of popular sovereignty that requires government to allow and perhaps to encourage political deliberation. The norm and the principle will have more weight if they can be found in the history behind the clauses, and if they are reflected in previous judicial precedents; but they need not be justified by reference to traditional practices. Indeed, they may operate as a sharp critique of traditional practices, as in fact they have done in the law of sex equality and the law of libel, and increasingly in the law governing discrimination on the basis of sexual orientation, an area where liberal norms of equality are increasingly jeopardizing traditional community practices.

Now it may well be that we should be cautious in attempting to change practices merely because they do not survive critical reflection. Perhaps we have overlooked something. Perhaps change would be futile or counterproductive. Points of this kind suggest a mood of caution;[23] but they hardly make tradition a good foundation for rights, constitutional or otherwise. If we are trying to figure out what rights people have, some traditions will have to yield because they cannot survive moral or legal scrutiny. Of course, it is true that for many people, the search for reflective equilibrium will include, as fixed points, many traditional practices, and it may therefore be quite difficult to dislodge their (or our) approval of much that is long-standing.

IV. TRADITION AS A SOURCE OF LAW

Thus far I have attempted to criticize the view that tradition is an appropriate source of rights, by suggesting that it is hard to figure out what traditionalists are seeking to oppose, and that once we disentangle their possible targets, we will uncover the virtue of prudence and little else. Certainly we have no good reason to challenge the view that rights, discovered on grounds independent of tradition, ought to be enjoyed nationally or universally. It is now time to turn to some particulars, and especially to the suggestion that tradition should have an honored place in the interpretation of the Constitution.

First some background. The current emphasis on tradition has a particular source in history and indeed in tradition: the Supreme Court's unfortunate experience with "economic liberties" in the first third of the twentieth century. In this period, the Court held that the due process clause of the Fourteenth Amendment created a right to freedom of contract, subject to interference only under special and highly limited conditions. The great case of the period was *Lochner v. New York* (1905),[24] where the Court invalidated a law limiting the number of hours an

---

[23] See Strauss, *Common Law Constitutionalism.*
[24] *Lochner v. New York*, 198 U.S. 45 (1905).

employee could work each week. Writing in dissent, Justice Holmes said that the due process clause would not be violated "unless it can be said that a rational and fair man necessarily would admit that the statute proposed would infringe fundamental principles as they have been understood by the traditions of our people and our law." (Note Holmes's emphasis not only on judicial restraint, but also, and in his view equivalently, on tradition as a source of rights.) For many decades the Court rejected Holmes's counsel, instead concluding that contractual freedom, as part of the liberty protected by the due process clause, should be presumed immune from governmental interference (though of course the presumption could be rebutted with a particular demonstration that the law fell within the government's "police power").

Many things contributed to the demise, in the New Deal period, of the *Lochner* era understanding, and *Lochner*'s legacy remains sharply contested.[25] Some people think that there is no room at all for "substantive due process," that is, for the idea that the due process clause imposes substantive limits on governmental power. The Court has never accepted this view. Eventually, however, the Court concluded that it had indeed exceeded its authority and abused its constitutional role.[26] It held that so long as the government behaved "rationally," the government behaved constitutionally; and in the economic arena, almost everything counts as rational.

The shadows of the *Lochner* era, and of Holmes's famous dissent, loom over current constitutional law, especially over cases decided under the due process clause. *Griswold v. Connecticut* itself purported not to be an interpretation of the due process clause at all, but instead of "penumbras" from other provisions. The right of privacy is now thought to be an inference from the due process clause, and in retrospect, *Griswold* is understood in terms of due process. The current Court speaks of *Griswold* as a due process case rather than as one of penumbras. But the textual basis of "substantive" due process is dubious; the text seems to refer to procedure, and not to call for judicial oversight of the reasonableness of laws. In any case the textual awkwardness, and the perceived disaster of the *Lochner* era, threaten the legitimacy of all the privacy cases and indeed of all substantive liberty cases. I think that it is right to question substantive due process as a matter of first principles; and the problems with the legitimacy of substantive due process should push us to limit its reach so long as it exists.[27]

---

[25] See Sunstein, *The Partial Constitution* (*supra* note 6), ch. 2; Ronald Dworkin, *Taking Rights Seriously* (Cambridge: Harvard University Press, 1976); and John Hart Ely, *Democracy and Distrust* (Cambridge: Harvard University Press, 1981).

[26] See *Ferguson v. Scrupa*, 372 U.S. 726 (1963).

[27] More specifically: Substantive due process is a linguistically difficult notion. By an ordinary reading of its terms, the due process clause is procedural, not substantive. That is, the clause seems to require procedures of a certain kind, rather than a judicial evalua-

Justice Scalia's emphasis on tradition, read at a level of great specificity, must be understood in this light. Justice Scalia, and to some extent the Court as a whole, are using tradition as a means of limiting national judicial interference with democratic processes at the state and local levels. We might speculate that Justice Scalia believes that substantive due process is itself illegitimate, and that his understanding of tradition, as a source of rights, is designed to minimize the harm done by substantive due process — not by eliminating it altogether, but by understanding it in an exceedingly narrow way, so as to limit the interference with the Court's legitimacy that some perceive whenever the Court invalidates legislation on substantive due process grounds. Under Justice Scalia's criteria, *Griswold* may be the only substantive due process case that rightly invalidated a law, because *Griswold* was the only case in which the outcome was grounded on tradition. The resort to tradition is therefore a second-best strategy, designed to minimize the problem of having due process at all. For other justices using tradition, substantive due process is not itself anathema, but the *Lochner* era shows that it should be deployed cautiously. The value of tradition is that it operates to confine judicial discretion and to limit the occasions for invalidation of democratically enacted measures.

In the view of some of *Lochner*'s critics — and they could be liberal, conservative, or somewhere in between — tradition therefore plays a defining role under the due process clause; but it may not be the appropriate source of rights under (say) the equal protection and free speech clauses. Tradition has a particular constitutional role, designed for a particular provision with a particular history. Tradition deserves a place under the due process clause as a way of preventing abuses under that otherwise open-ended clause, or because that clause is best understood as having been designed to safeguard old practices from myopic or ill-considered practices. But tradition is not an all-purpose source of rights. It is not, for example, a good guide to the meaning of the equal protection clause, which was specifically designed as a check on traditions, most notably the tradition of racial inequality.

The main question remains: What can be said on behalf of invoking tradition as the foundation of constitutional rights under the due process clause if not elsewhere? Several possibilities come to mind.

---

tion of the substance of legislation. A better constitutional foundation for substantive protection of important interests would have been the privileges and immunities clause, also found in the Fourteenth Amendment. The Supreme Court concluded in an early case that this clause added nothing to the original Constitution. See *The Slaughterhouse Cases*, 83 U.S. 36 (1873). This conclusion is most doubtful; but aggressive use of the privileges and immunities clause would have left open many of the issues discussed here: How do we know what interests count as "privileges and immunities"? Perhaps tradition would have been a key way of answering this question. I cannot discuss these complex issues here. I am attempting to explain the origins of the use of tradition under the due process clause, rather than to reach a final judgment on the legitimacy of substantive due process or what might have been, in a different form, "substantive privileges and immunities."

First, tradition might be a good source of constitutional rights simply because our particular traditions are good. We might think, for example, that Anglo-American traditions of liberty can be defended as a matter of political philosophy; these are wonderful traditions. Or we might think that Anglo-American traditions promote general well-being. Use of traditions to define rights—by the Supreme Court or others—is good not because traditions are good as such, but because our traditions warrant independent defense. Traditionalism might even be urged on rule-utilitarian grounds. Even if our traditions are imperfect, a general use of traditions to define rights might be best because it produces better overall outcomes than any plausible alternative. This conclusion might not hold for, say, South Africa and China, which have had oppressive governments for long periods; but the conclusion does hold for Americans.

The problem with this view is that our own traditions are multiple, and that if we investigate them on their merits, we will find much that is bad as well as much that is good. This insight itself fits with American traditions. Indeed, a large part of our tradition is critical rather than celebratory. A problem with Burkeanism for America is that Burkeanism does not conform to American traditions, which have been punctuated by periods of critical self-consciousness, in which even widespread practices are challenged on political and legal grounds, as failing to conform to our general aspirations.[28] In the areas of race and sex equality, protection of the environment, rights of workers, and much more, our political and legal practices have been revised after inspection.

More particularly, our traditions include race and sex discrimination as well as (general respect for) freedom of political speech and religion. Once we conclude that traditions are a source of rights because they are defensible on independent grounds, why not move to those independent grounds, and eliminate the middleman? If traditions are a source of rights because our traditions are right or good, we might proceed directly to the right or the good, and put traditions to one side. This inquiry is subject to the general requirements of humility and prudence; but if those requirements are all there is to traditionalism, traditions become a simple cautionary note, and hardly a source of rights in any interesting sense.

These points leave open the possibility of a rule-utilitarian defense of traditionalism; but without a lot more detail, that defense seems highly speculative. To accept it, we would have to offer a great deal of information about the content of our various traditions and the capabilities of our judges. And once that detail is offered, the defense of traditionalism for law becomes more refined and quite different; it is to a defense of that sort that I now turn.

The second defense of relying on traditions as a source of rights rests on the proposition that for particular people occupying particular official positions, traditions are superior to the principal alternative—that is,

---

[28] See Bruce A. Ackerman, *We the People* (Cambridge: Harvard University Press, 1992), vol. 1.

independent moral theorizing. We might agree that our traditions are not perfectly correlated with the class of rights that would emerge from good theorizing, and we might also agree that traditions are inferior to good theorizing as a source of rights. But perhaps judges cannot theorize well, or cannot reach anything like a consensus on good theory. Use of traditions might therefore be justified on the ground that it is the best real-world source of rights, including decision costs as well as error rates in our judgments about what is best.

This argument also depends on some highly uncertain empirical claims. Its conclusion may be right, but we do not know whether it is right. Perhaps judges can theorize pretty well on such issues as the right to die, reproduction, and sexual privacy. Perhaps they can do this precisely because of their training, the mode of their selection, and their insulation from politics. Perhaps judges can engage in the requisite theorizing by proceeding on the basis of rules, analogies, and precedents, and without making high-level or complex philosophical arguments of their own. Perhaps our traditions are very hard to describe; perhaps too many of our traditions, insofar as they bear on hard cases of this sort, contain injustice. The rule-utilitarian argument for constitutional traditionalism as a guide for judges is not implausible; but it is based on assumptions that are far from self-evident.

There is a third argument on behalf of constitutional traditionalism. I have suggested that traditions may be a good source of rights because any practice that has lasted for a long time must have something to offer. If people have done a certain thing for a long period, their practice probably serves some important social function, hard as it may be for outsiders (or even insiders) to see what that function is. On this view, the real reason for constitutional traditionalism is that traditions are good, but not because we usually have an independent argument on their behalf. The whole point is that we may well lack any such argument — and that this does not mean that traditions are not good.

This argument has something to offer, but it too rests on fragile ground. Undoubtedly it is true that some practices have lasted because they serve desirable social goals, and undoubtedly it is also true that it is often hard to figure out how they do this. Here too we have a reason for prudence, humility, and caution. But some practices persist not because of their salutary functions, but because of inertia, myopia, bias, power, confusion, or indeed far from salutary functions. The functionalist defense of traditions is too coarse-grained; it verges on a form of sentimentalist political philosophy. It approves of traditions without giving an adequate sense of what sorts of traditions warrant approval.

V. AGAINST TRADITION

Thus far I have tried to identify the grounds for basing constitutional law on tradition, and I have tried to challenge those grounds. The argument has been largely defensive. In this section, I take the offensive, arguing that tradition is not an appropriate source of constitutional rights. There are three basic problems.

The first problem has to do with the existence of changed circumstances. Sometimes the facts change. Sometimes values, or perceptions of facts, change as well. (Of course, these are not easily severable phenomena.) If they do, the role of tradition becomes far less clear. When facts and values change, it seems sensible to insist that traditions have to be characterized and hence evaluated, rather than simply "applied." The category of changed facts and values is a large one. It severely complicates the enterprise of constitutional traditionalism.

Return, for example, to the *Michael H. v. Gerald D.* case, and suppose that the question arises whether the father of a child conceived in an adulterous relationship has a constitutional right to see the child on some regular basis. As the plurality of the Court said, there is no specific tradition to support the father, at least if we ask whether rights of the sort he seeks to vindicate have been recognized in the past. Children of a mother in an intact marriage were conclusively presumed to be the children of the husband and wife. But the reasons for the tradition may be obsolete. Both facts and values have changed.

Facts first: An important basis of the conclusive presumption was the state of technology. It was impossible to know whether someone alleging that he was the father of a child was in fact the father of the child. Human beings lacked the means to find out. In light of that fact, the tradition made a lot of sense. If science could not tell us whether someone alleging that he was the father was in fact the father, it would probably be best to presume that he was not, so as to protect intact families from external assaults when the legal system lacked the means to distinguish true allegations from false ones. But the facts have changed: we can now figure out whether the alleged father is really the father. Must the old tradition be binding if it rested on assumptions that fail to hold? If the foundations of the tradition are missing, does the tradition still bind? How should the tradition be conceived under present conditions? To answer such questions, we cannot simply identify past practices. We have to engage in an act of constructive interpretation.

Now for values, or perhaps better, the interaction between facts and values: It used to be the case that children conceived out of wedlock were subject to extreme social opprobrium and to a series of legal disabilities as well. Both the opprobrium and the disabilities have diminished—in part because of the perceived mandate of the equal protection clause, which is taken to forbid most discrimination on the basis of illegitimacy. This change means that another of the foundations of the tradition is absent: the old conclusive presumption may have made sense as a way of protecting the child against social hostility, but the need for the protection is sharply diminished.

Perhaps the changing norm should make us revisit or recharacterize the tradition, whose founding assumption has become obsolete. It may make sense to have a conclusive presumption of the old kind when the consequences of conception in adultery would be so damaging for the child.[29] But if the consequences are no longer so damaging, should the tradition remain?

The problem is not limited to the *Michael H.* case. Changing facts and values can be found in debates over contraception, abortion, the right to withdraw lifesaving equipment, and euthanasia. In each of these areas, we could identify changes quite similar to those in *Michael H.* itself. The right to abortion now involves new, safer medical procedures, and it is urged in the context of sharply changed understandings about the relation between men and women. Medical technologies have changed so rapidly, and the availability of invasive life-prolonging equipment is so novel, that past traditions about euthanasia rest on palpably anachronistic assumptions. It should be unnecessary to belabor the fact that the assumptions that underlie traditions often become obsolete.

There is a second (related) problem for constitutional traditionalists: How do we describe the tradition? Traditions do not come in neat packages; it is not simple to identify them. In the United States, there are of course multiple traditions with respect to everything that matters, including free speech, sexual privacy, and individual choices about whether to live or to die. As I have noted, traditions can be described at many different levels of generality. We might think, for example, that there is a tradition of respect for freedom of contract, and that laws forbidding the sale of marijuana violate that tradition. Or we might think that there is a tradition of respect for sexual privacy, and that laws forbidding heterosexual sodomy offend that tradition. How specifically do we characterize a tradition?

Justice Scalia is quite alert to this problem, and he explicitly attempts to overcome the problems of multiplicity of traditions and conflicting levels of generality. A tradition that includes inconsistency and multiplicity is not, on his view, usable for constitutional purposes. To be usable, a tradition must be both consistent and unitary. Moreover, traditions should be described at a very specific level. This is so for several reasons. If traditions are described at a high level of generality, the judge's use of tradition is fraudulent. Described broadly, traditions do not exist as such. There is no tradition of respect for freedom of contract or sexual privacy. If we look at the details, we will see that no such traditions exist.

In addition, if tradition is relevant because traditions are good and because their use disciplines the judges, it seems silly to read traditions at high levels of generality. At such levels, the discipline is removed, and

---

[29] Perhaps the consequences remain damaging even today. I do not mean to deny this possibility, but simply to point to the complexity of traditionalism in the context of changed norms.

we have no (real) long-standing practice on which we can rely. The basic defense of constitutional traditionalism thus calls for highly specific readings of tradition. Specific readings tend to discipline judges. Specific readings also tend to draw on actual practices that have persisted over time.

Especially for critics of substantive due process, Justice Scalia's argument has much to be said in its favor. If we are seeking to control the damage of having any substantive due process at all, Justice Scalia's route seems as good an approach as any;[30] but there are problems with his approach as well. As we have seen, changed circumstances may complicate the use of tradition, because specific old practices may rest on assumptions that no longer hold, and changes may argue both for and against constitutional protection if we attend to what the specific past practices really represented. Perhaps an old right was based on grounds that no longer make sense.

Moreover, the notion of a "most specific" understanding of tradition is ambiguous. Defined at the highest level of specificity, every case is one of first impression and sui generis.[31] No case is exactly like a case that has come before. We can always identify features of a current case that distinguish it from the specific tradition invoked on the plaintiff's behalf. Justice Scalia seems to think that we can identify a "most specific" tradition without making evaluations of any sort, and that we can "read" traditions off practices without indulging in interpretative assumptions. But any reading of a tradition is constructive and to that extent evaluative. When we say that there is a tradition of banning suicide, we are not simply reporting on the facts, but also reading the past in a certain way. Sometimes suicides were not banned in practice. Sometimes extenuating circumstances were found, at least as a practical matter. Certainly Justice Scalia has some good arguments against purported traditionalists who actually invoke broad aspirations ("marital privacy," "freedom of contract," "right to control the body") that were not in fact respected in all contexts; but references to the "most specific" understanding of tradition do not escape the problem of definition.

In addition, Justice Scalia may be a bit too skeptical about the reasoning capacities of judges, disciplined as they will inevitably be by the system of precedent, the need to think analogically, and the judges' own awareness of their limited institutional role. We do not know enough to know whether Justice Scalia's approach to the definition of traditions would be better, all things considered, than a more general understanding of traditions. On that more general understanding, traditions would be treated as broad aspirations that defeat particular practices once those

---

[30] Hence the various criticisms put forward by Laurence Tribe and Michael Dorf seem to me far from decisive; see Tribe and Dorf, *Reading the Constitution* (Cambridge: Harvard University Press, 1990).

[31] See Jack Balkin, "Tradition, Betrayal, and the Politics of Deconstruction," *Cardozo Law Review*, vol. 11 (1993), p. 1613.

practices stand revealed, on reflection, as products of ignorance or big-otry. In *Bowers v. Hardwick*, for example, we might read from our tradi-tion a general respect for consensual sexual activity, and carefully assess any specific departure from that tradition, to make sure that it is based on something legitimate and reasonable. I do not believe that this is the best approach to *Bowers v. Hardwick* (see below), but it remains for con-stitutional traditionalists to explain why this approach is inferior to Jus-tice Scalia's.

The third problem facing constitutional traditionalists is the largest. We have seen that American traditions contain both good and bad elements. By itself, the fact that some practice is long-standing is an insufficient rea-son to allow it to guide us. For example, no one thinks that tradition is a good guide to the meaning of the equal protection clause. Old traditions of race and sex discrimination cannot plausibly be invoked in defense of current practices of race and sex discrimination. Nor is the problem lim-ited to these contexts of inequality. Specific intrusions on private auton-omy (understood as actual choices), or indeed specific protections of autonomy (similarly understood), may depend on bias or prejudice or simple confusion. We cannot know whether this is so until we have done some investigating. Constitutional traditionalism truncates the analysis much too quickly.

Nothing in these notions justifies the idea that courts should feel free to overrule practices with which they disagree, or that they should invoke their own conceptions of the good and the right in order to test legisla-tion. Indeed, I will shortly urge approaches to the privacy cases that are quite narrow, and that allow the Court to avoid large-scale pronounce-ments about "privacy" or "liberty." But I hope I have said enough to ex-plain why tradition is an unpromising source of rights, constitutional or otherwise.

VI. The Privacy Cases Revisited

The Supreme Court's privacy cases are notoriously difficult, and the Court's own analysis has been notoriously incomplete. I cannot analyze the cases in detail here. Instead, I want to present two narrower argu-ments, each applicable to several of the relevant cases. The two arguments are designed to show how constitutional rights might be founded on something other than traditional practice without fundamentally threat-ening democratic values.

The first argument invokes the old notion of desuetude.[32] If a law is founded on a social norm that no longer has much support, we might expect it to be enforced not at all, or only on rare occasions. It is there-

---

[32] See Bickel, *The Least Dangerous Branch*. I am grateful to Michael McConnell for help-ful discussion of this point.

fore a tool for harassment, and not an ordinary law at all. The rare enforcement occasions might well involve arbitrary or discriminatory factors. They might result from a police officer's mood, or personal animus, or bias of some kind. A prosecution for fornication, brought in 1996, might well have such features. In my view, the prosecution would be unconstitutional for procedural reasons having to do with the rule of law, not (necessarily) for substantive reasons having to do with the right to do as one chooses with one's body. The prosecution would thus be unconstitutional not because there is any general right to privacy, but because the state may not enforce a law unsupported by public judgments — and no longer taken seriously as a law — in a few, randomly selected cases. In a world in which prosecutions for fornication were common and accepted, perhaps no privacy right would be at stake, and hence there might well be no constitutional violation. But in a world in which such prosecutions cannot meet with public approval, an arrest or indictment would be the occasion for invalidation on procedural grounds.

Griswold might well be understood in this way. The ban on contraception within marriage was not enforced by prosecutors. It served principally to deter clinics from dispensing contraceptives to poor people. The problem with the ban was not that it was unsupported by old traditions but that it had no basis in modern convictions. Few people believed that sex within marriage was legitimate only if engaged in for purposes of procreation, and those people could not possibly have commanded a legislative majority, or even made it possible to bring many actual prosecutions against married couples. Notably, the law was not defended on its obvious foundational ground: a quasi-religious judgment about when sexual activity is appropriate. It was defended instead as a means of preventing extramarital relations. So defended, the law made at best a little sense, for it remained to be explained why the prohibition applied to the *use* of contraceptives by married people, and not just to the distribution of contraceptives. Because of its lack of real enforcement, and its lack of foundation in anything like common public sentiment, the law offended a form of procedural due process, not substantive due process. *Griswold* should have been decided on this basis, which is narrower, more plausible as a textual matter, and more democratic; and as we will soon see, the notion of desuetude covers several other cases as well.

Alternatively, we might see the privacy cases as not principally or only about privacy, but as closely connected with sex equality. The advantage of the equality approach is that it builds on a genuine constitutional commitment and provides a clearer focus for judicial work. Instead of asking whether a right is fundamental — a question on which the due process clause is not helpful — courts might ask whether discrimination has been adequately justified, an inquiry that can be anchored in some of the purposes of the Civil War Amendments. All of the privacy cases were concerned to prevent the state from turning women's reproductive capacities into a basis for inequality, especially if the state was doing so on the basis of outmoded stereotypes about the appropriate role of women, or if the relevant laws could not have been enacted without the assistance of those stereotypes. On this view, the cases were about equality, not simply about a right to do as one wishes. Of course, all of the justices were well aware that the burdens of unwanted pregnancies are borne disproportionately by women. Perhaps all of the justices believed as well that bans on the use or distribution of contraceptives would not have been likely if the consequences of unwanted pregnancies would be borne by men. In any case, issues of sex equality come to the foreground once it is clear that the burdens of legal barriers to the use of contraception—as well as to abortion—are faced disproportionately by women. The Court spoke in terms of privacy, but its subtext was equality.

Thus far my point is a bit abstract; let me bring it down to earth. The relevant laws were defended as means of protecting against extramarital relations. The state's allegedly basic fear was that if contraception were available, adultery and fornication would be facilitated. As I have said, this is not an implausible suggestion. Nor did the Court say that the laws forbidding adultery and fornication were unconstitutional; on the contrary, it went out of its way to say that they might well be legitimate.

We might therefore understand the Court in the following way. The state might legitimately punish extramarital sexual activity directly (so long as the public will permit it to do so). But the state may not take the step of punishing extramarital sexual activity through the indirect, far less accountable, and discriminatory means of foreclosing access to contraception. It may not choose this route, because the indirect route is not very well connected with achievement of the relevant goal; because that route harms children (many of whom will be unwanted); and because that route imposes disproportionate burdens on women, who must bring children to term (or face the prospect of abortion if it is available). If the state is really concerned about extramarital relations, it must proceed through an adultery or fornication prosecution, which has the comparative advantage of sex neutrality, of refusing to create unwanted children as a punishment, and of exposing to public scrutiny and review the real interest at stake. The Court was telling the states: If you are really invoking public morality, your remedy is to invoke public morality directly in favor of the interest at stake, through punishing extramarital sexual relations. We doubt that you yourselves take this interest seriously enough to prosecute anybody.

The privacy cases might, then, be approached most narrowly as cases about desuetude, and more ambitiously as cases about sex discrimination; various combinations of the two ideas are easily imaginable. On this view, tradition would be irrelevant. It is with these foundations that we might understand the subsequent decisions. Here as well it would be unnecessary to speak of tradition. *Bowers v. Hardwick* was a repeat of

Griswold, and for this reason, it was wrongly decided. The ban on homosexual sodomy is rarely enforced against consenting adults. Prosecutors simply do not initiate proceedings, since prevailing social norms would not permit many prosecutions of this kind. Realistically speaking, the ban on consensual homosexual sodomy is instead a weapon by which police officers and others might harass people on invidious grounds. The existence of unenforced and unenforceable sodomy laws, used for purposes of harassment, is an affront to the rule of law, and objectionable for that reason, whatever we may think of privacy.

Alternatively, and more ambitiously, we might approach *Bowers v. Hardwick* as an equality case, in which the state was proceeding against homosexuals rather than heterosexuals. The state does not in fact challenge heterosexual sodomy, even when the law does so as a technical matter. The relevant inequality consists of enforcement policies through which the police (and not the prosecution, which refuses to act at all) harass homosexuals and leave heterosexuals alone. Although I cannot establish the point here, I think that this form of discrimination is objectionable, because discrimination on grounds of sexual orientation is usually illegitimate, and because such discrimination is a form of sex discrimination.

What of *Roe v. Wade*, sometimes taken to establish a general right to "control one's body" under the due process clause? So understood, the decision in the case was wrong. If it was right, it is because of sex equality. Bans on abortion discriminate on their face on the basis of sex; they are targeted at women. Moreover, men are not generally required to devote their bodies to the protection of others, even when the lives of innocent third parties are at stake — indeed, even when the lives at stake are those of innocent third parties for whose existence they are responsible. (Fathers are not compelled to give up kidneys or even blood when the lives of their children are at stake.) There is at least apparently impermissible selectivity in the imposition of this burden on women alone. Moreover, the ban on abortion is closely entangled in the real world with the desire to maintain traditional gender roles. There is certainly no logical connection between opposition to abortion and commitment to those traditional roles; but such restrictions on abortions as are enacted owe their existence to that commitment, and this dooms the restrictions as a constitutional matter. A literacy test motivated by a discriminatory purpose is invalid, even though a literacy test need not be motivated by a discriminatory purpose.[33]

These are inadequate and brief remarks on some complex issues. Of course, constitutional argument as I have understood it leaves room for discretion, and traditionalists may not be happy to see that a range of principles might be invoked in different contexts. I offer these remarks here not to resolve the relevant issues, but to suggest the possibility of

---

[33] See Sunstein, *The Partial Constitution*, ch. 9, for more detail.

sources of constitutional rights, useful for the so-called privacy cases, and not relying on tradition or substantive due process at all. One of the most appealing arguments for traditionalism involves the apparent inadequacy of the alternatives: If not tradition, then what? I hope that these remarks are enough to show that this is hardly a rhetorical question.

VII. CONCLUSION

Traditionalism often lies at the heart of communitarianism. Many communitarians are fearful that rights-based thinking or even liberalism will be insufficiently respectful of past practices, often at the local level, which have been developed over long periods of time. In a sense, moreover, all rights are grounded in tradition. Rights are a product of human thought and activity, and no right is likely to have appeal unless it has resonances in public convictions as these have been understood over time. Certainly traditions are a source of constitutional rights in the sense that the Constitution itself is a product of history, and also in the sense that judicial interpretation of a constitution will and should pay attention to both precedents and past practices. These are unexceptionable points, and I have said nothing to challenge them.

But if constitutional traditionalism — perhaps understood as part of a communitarian project — is meant more ambitiously, it is a poor source of rights. For democratic reasons, judges should approach Fourteenth Amendment safeguards with some caution, but those safeguards should not be defined by reference to traditions. Instead of searching in an insufficiently disciplined way for "fundamental" interests when interpreting the Fourteenth Amendment, the Court should concern itself principally with unjustified inequality and with procedural failures, of which desuetude is an important illustration. More generally, a large part of human (and judicial) reflection involves critical assessment of traditions, some of which are products of confusion, happenstance, inequality, myopia, or self-interest. American political and legal traditions have been pervaded by such critical assessment, and in this sense constitutional traditionalism of the Burkean sort fits poorly with American traditions. A principal point of constitutionalism is to subject past practices to critical assessment.

Of course, there is much to be said on behalf of constraining judges, whose role in society should be modest. But it is revealing that the case for a modest judiciary itself depends not on tradition, but on considerations of democracy, and hence of judgments about the rights that the people have, all things considered. When constitutionalism is working well, rights are a product of a search for reflective equilibrium, suitably disciplined and constrained in the way that a legal system requires. Rights are not a product of a search for tradition.

Law and Political Science, University of Chicago

THE CASE FOR TOLERANCE

By George P. Fletcher

For people to live together in pluralistic communities, they must find some way to cope with the practices of others that they abhor. For that reason, tolerance has always seemed an appealing medium of accommodation. But tolerance also has its critics. One wing charges that the tolerant are too easygoing. They are insensitive to evil in their midst. At the same time, another wing attacks the (merely) tolerant for being too weak in their sentiments of respect. "The Christian does not wish to be tolerated," as T. S. Eliot said; and by this he meant to claim, presumably, that the Christian desires respect and acceptance, and not merely the forbearance suggested by "tolerance."

To make the case for tolerance, we must engage in a three-front campaign: first, against intolerance; second, against the moral failing of indifference; and third, against the desirability of respecting and accepting everyone. The central claim in making this case will be that unlike these three competing sentiments, tolerance is a complex attitude toward the behavior and beliefs of others. Its complexity consists in both moral disapproval (or at least cultural rejection) and the avoidance of interference. If there is a case to be made for tolerance, it must derive from this peculiar complexity. After surveying its alternatives, I will argue that the complex sentiment of tolerance is more readily praised than its alternatives.

I. Against Intolerance

Although there are particular evils we should not tolerate, a generalized charge of intolerance carries a special sting. An intolerant person is one who recoils at the presence of persons or things that are different from the local and the ordinary. The difference may be in the realm of physical appearance, of dress, of religious beliefs, or in some other dimension of similarity and difference. Intolerance in this sense reflects a zeal for homogeneity. The intolerant have no play in the joints. When a cylinder has no tolerance for error, its piston must fit perfectly. Similarly, when an individual has no tolerance for difference, the people he meets must reflect the contours of his own personality.

By contrast with the general attribute of intolerance, a specific intolerance might well be acceptable. Newspapers reported that in the summer of 1994, many German citizens protested against neo-Nazi rampages by German youth. Reuters quoted an organizer of the protest as saying that "the majority of Germans deplored far-right rowdiness and would no lon-

© 1996 Social Philosophy and Policy Foundation. Printed in the USA.

ger tolerate it."[1] The far-right toughs (or "skinheads") who give the Nazi salute and express hatred for foreigners are readily labeled "intolerant" in the unacceptable sense. Interestingly, however, those who say that they will no longer tolerate the skinheads are not called intolerant with the same negative connotations. That they cannot and will not tolerate a specific form of antisocial behavior does not visit upon them the general quality of having no play in the joints. They may have no play — but only in the particular direction of specifically defined harmful behavior.

We can distinguish, then, between the *general* intolerance of the skinheads and the *specific* intolerance of those who will not tolerate their objectionable behavior. The skinheads are generally intolerant of all foreigners, all people who differ from some perceived standard of normalcy. Those who are intolerant of skinheads direct their sentiments toward one specific activity. It seems, then, that general intolerance is always problematic, but that the propriety of specific intolerance depends on the activity that will not be tolerated. It is all right — even imperative — not to tolerate behavior that patently harms others, but it is more questionable not to tolerate, let us say, intermarriage between Jews and Christians. Whether tolerance of the latter is good or bad depends, in the end, on whether the activity in question is good or bad.

The general distinction between general and specific intolerance resolves the old conundrum about whether it is proper to be intolerant of the intolerant. In the example of not tolerating skinheads, the object of the specific rejection is general intolerance, and because we assume the latter to be wrong, there is nothing untoward about not (specifically) tolerating it. Indeed, there is something odd about describing the rejection and disapproval of the skinheads as intolerance. The verb "not tolerating" applies, but the notion "intolerance" seems better reserved for general intolerance. Yet this sharp distinction between specific rejection and general intolerance leaves us with the question: Why is general intolerance so bad?

It is tempting to rest our critique of general intolerance on the ground that it is harmful to others, namely, to those who bear the brunt of scorn and derision; but this account strikes me as unpersuasive. We could readily imagine that the intolerant keep their opinions to themselves or confide them in private only to like-minded people. There is something wrong about hating those who are different that is not quite captured by our solicitude for those who are hated.

The intolerant resemble a taut string. Unusual surroundings and encounters with people produce vibrations that disturb their inner harmony. The source of an intolerant reaction might not be people but an irritating physical phenomenon, such as noise. Immanuel Kant was reputedly so intolerant of noise that he sold his home and moved across

---

[1] *International Herald-Tribune*, August 8, 1994, p. A5.

town in order to escape his neighbor's quacking hen. In this respect, intolerance seems to resemble more a psychological condition than a moral failing. It might have been better for Kant to be more tolerant of noise, but no one could say that it was wrong for the Königsberg genius to insist on certain working conditions.

When the intolerance is about people, however, a moral dimension seems to enter the argument. If Kant had moved across town because his neighbor was a Catholic or a foreigner, it would be hard not to see in this reaction a moral failing as well as a psychological one. The reason for this, I suppose, is that we think that the neighbor (unlike his hen) would suffer if he knew he was the subject of avoidance. Even apart from this possible harm to the neighbor, however, the question is whether there is a moral failing in moving away — or avoiding the initial move in — in order to avoid people one does not like. The matter is not so simple. People should be able to follow their aesthetic preferences for those who share their interests, speak their language, and share their deepest moral and religious convictions. Yet these preferences that define people as knowing what they want are likely to lead them toward intolerance for those who are different.

It is true that, by definition, tolerance increases one's level of comfort with the varieties of human existence. Perhaps this added comfort — when joined with the benefits that accrue to those who are no longer rejected — constitutes the only case that can be made for generalized tolerance. We should note, however, that generalized tolerance carries with it a measure of indifference. Not hating the other often derives from simply not caring about what he or she thinks or does. Tolerance for noise or dirt does not always mean that one prefers it that way; often the point is that the tolerant do not care much about their surroundings. The tolerant achieve with a modicum of indifference what the intolerant gain by controlling their environment.

As for specialized intolerance, we should distinguish between public (or governmental) and private sanctions. The discussion of the former typically begins with John Stuart Mill's maxim — namely, that the government should intervene only to prevent one person from harming another. The difficulties of sorting out degrees of harm are well known. For a nice case in the borderland of harm, think of the dispute, recently resolved by the U.S. Supreme Court, over whether devotees of the Santeria religion had a constitutional right to engage in animal sacrifice.[2] The Santeria religion coalesced in Cuba as a fusion of native East African beliefs and Catholicism; its adherents sacrifice small animals, such as chickens and turtles, in order to nourish the "orishas" that guide their personal destinies. When the residents of Hialeah, Florida, learned that practitioners of the Santeria rites had immigrated from Cuba, they enacted a special ordi-

[2] See *Church of Lukumi Babalu Aye v. Hialeah*, 113 S.Ct. 2217 (1993).

nance to suppress the "ritual sacrifice" of animals. The problem under Mill's principle is whether the unnecessary killing of animals (i.e., not for food consumption) represents a harm to other individuals in Hialeah or elsewhere.

It is obviously not enough that the local residents were offended by the practice of killing chickens and turtles in church. If being offended by thinking about others' engaging in the practice constituted a harm, anything might qualify as harm to others. The best argument for the city of Hialeah was that the unnecessary killing of animals created a danger to public health. Creating a risk of disease would be sufficient to justify official intolerance toward animal sacrifice. This argument persuaded the two lower courts that the city had a sufficiently strong interest to justify the apparent restriction on official freedom. But the same argument failed at the level of the Supreme Court, where the justices were impressed by the apparent failure of the city of Hialeah to address other equally urgent risks to public health, such as the restaurants' disposing of organic waste and hunters' bringing home dead carcasses. The selective nature of the local ordinance convinced the Court that the motive for legislative intervention was not the public good but discriminatory intolerance. That the ordinance targeted one religious group and its practices made it constitutionally unacceptable.

The Santeria problem poses a nice test for theories of tolerance and pluralism. But it is not readily solved by consulting the work of philosophers who have sought to demarcate the permissible realm of public legislation. For John Locke, the question would have been whether the legislation falls under the jurisdiction of the "magistrate," authorized to use force to protect civil interests such as life, liberty, health, and property.[3] John Rawls agrees that liberty of conscience is limited by the "common interest in public order and security."[4] These vague terms carry us no further than Mill's threshold of harm to others.[5]

Another borderline form of official intolerance occurs in the realm of language politics. The French have acquired a reputation for reacting intolerantly to the use of English in the public sphere. In Quebec and in France itself, cultural conservatives are willing to use legal instruments to prevent people from reading advertising in English and thereby being influenced toward speaking the idiom of the American fast-food culture. There is something slightly ludicrous about sanctioning a Parisian restaurant for writing "cheeseburger" on the menu. But for those seeking to preserve the uniqueness of French culture, the line must be drawn somewhere.

---

[3] John Locke, *A Letter Concerning Toleration*, ed. John Horton and Susan Mendus (London: Routledge, 1991), p. 17.

[4] John Rawls, *A Theory of Justice* (Cambridge: Harvard University Press, 1971), p. 212.

[5] For a general study of the problem, see Joel Feinberg, *Harm to Others* (Oxford: Oxford University Press, 1984).

Americans should hardly laugh at the French preoccupation with using *le mot juste*, for the French-only movement bears strong resemblance to the forms of censorship that pass under the name of "political correctness" in the United States. Whether one says "woman," "girl," "lady," or something else (not to mention "colored," "black," "African American," etc.) is a matter of deadly earnest in many circles in the U.S. (mainly in universities and the media), and very few academics have the distance to laugh at the American search for *le mot juste*. The difference between P.C. censorship and the French defense of their language is that the former takes place informally, with at most unofficial means of control. Yet the notions here of "official" and "unofficial" intersect in their impact on people's lives. If a journalist or a professor persists in politically incorrect speech, his or her job might be at stake. The sanctions against nominally racist, sexist, or homophobic speech in the U.S. are surely greater than the French government would dare impose for anti-Gallic linguistic behavior.

While the problem in the Santeria case is quickly categorized as an issue of tolerance, the same label is not likely to haunt those who censor English in Quebec or ethnic jokes in the United States. Our notions of required tolerance run in certain channels—race, religion, national origin, gender, sexual orientation—and we are not inclined to think of the new taboos on speech as matters of intolerance. An analogous case is smoking cigarettes, an activity fervently enjoyed by a good quarter of the population but treated with disdain by the educated elite. Because I have always disliked the smell of cigarette smoke, I share in the pleasures of curtailing this form of pollution. Yet I am also appalled and ashamed at the sight of a retired colleague, a distinguished scholar of constitutional law, sitting on a brick trash-can container in front of the Columbia Law School—the only place he can enjoy an unharassed smoke.

If we were more candid about the taboos placed on speech and smoking, we would recognize both forms of control as raising issues of tolerance. And indeed, for all the tolerance expressed today toward, say, sexual orientation and intermarriage, we are becoming increasingly intolerant of activities that we collectively deem to be wrong. It is not far-fetched to refer to this movement as the "new intolerance" in American life.

Health concerns play an amusing and mildly hypocritical role in shaping and masking the new intolerance. In a society that breathes polluted air because everyone insists on driving automobiles, no one can tolerate the possible injury to his health posed by a coworker taking a smoke break. Health is supposedly an absolute; there is not even room to discuss whether one person's pleasure warrants the compromise of another person's health. Intriguingly, the same gambit figures in the informal censorship exercised in the name of protecting the sensibilities of "disadvantaged" groups. Using the wrong words supposedly injures blacks, gays, and women in their self-esteem. The injuries affect not their physical health but their mental well-being. Thus, health — because it is the absolute of our time — conceals the intolerance that we now readily express toward both smokers and those who use the wrong words at the wrong times.

Also concealed in the new intolerance is the class dimension implicit in the relationship between intolerant critics and the objects of their contempt. The critics are, by and large, members of the educated elite. The objects of criticism are typically working-class men and women. What members of the working class do in the United States is no longer *salonfähig* (i.e., respectable in bourgeois circles). The remaining smokers are likely to be found among them. They put pinups on their walls. They tell jokes that invariably embarrass someone. So far as I know, they still believe in traditional marriages. This kind of behavior has become intolerable to the leaders of the "chattering class." They simply cannot stand the "false consciousness" of the uneducated. It would never occur to them that, with their cleverly concealed intolerance, they are participating in a system of class oppression. My argument, then, is that a broader and more sophisticated version of tolerance might make a difference in our approaches to free speech, smoking, and other forms of interaction that arguably harm someone.

II. AGAINST INDIFFERENCE

If there is plenty of room for increased tolerance in the United States, there is also the danger of veering in some areas too far to the opposite extreme of indifference. Among intellectuals in the West, the dominant attitude seems to be not tolerance, but a profound sense that none of it really matters anyway — provided religious practices take the conventional forms of prayer, singing, drinking wine, and consuming lawful foods charged with magic significance. It is hard to find people who really care about the issues that fueled the religious wars of the seventeenth century. Not many people even know what the transubstantiation debates were about, much less care whether the wafer of the Eucharist is or is not the body of the Savior. (Just think how often even educated people confuse the Immaculate Conception with the Virgin Birth.)[6] Religious beliefs are considered private matters, with as much relevance to others as private reading and eating habits. Indeed, very few people seem to care what their friends think about matters such as the afterlife and the purpose of human existence. They would probably be too embarrassed to raise these topics.

---

[6] The doctrine of the Immaculate Conception holds that Mary, the mother of Jesus, was born without original sin.

All of this is a long and painful way from the wars that bred the imperative of religious tolerance. In order to understand Locke's letter on religious toleration,[7] we have to place ourselves in a frame of mind that regards salvation or permanent union with God as a serious possibility open to everyone. In most Protestant conceptions of salvation, whether this eternal union is realized depends not on what the individual does (or what God does) but on his or her inner spiritual quest. What people believe about church teachings carries, therefore, ultimate significance. If they hold the wrong theological position on the nature of the Trinity or the Eucharist, their inner quest becomes distorted and salvation is closed to them.

In the religious culture in which Locke wrote, loving one's neighbor meant, above all, helping the object of one's love to achieve salvation. This was more important, I dare say, than helping him or her to achieve good health in this world. Nothing could be more important than eternal bliss, and nothing could be higher on the agenda of loving relationships. Christians taught universal love, and therefore every Christian became responsible for the salvation of everyone — by coercion and war if necessary. If indeed some particular Christian sect was right about salvation and how to achieve it, one would not fault its members for spilling a little blood to bring this priceless gift to their neighbors. No one could imagine a greater act of fraternity.

Today we assume that all this bloodshed in the name of religious truth was irrelevant — a giant mistake. But this perspective of modernity misses the point about the conditions that gave rise to tolerance as virtue. You must assume that you love your neighbor and further that you know something vital for your neighbor's life that she refuses to accept. The closest examples from contemporary culture would be drawn from our obsession with health and longevity, the values that have replaced the quest for eternal life in the structure of modern thinking. Suppose your neighbor refuses to stop smoking and to lose weight. The question is whether you should intervene to force her. If you truly loved her, you would surely want to help her. You could bring it up once or twice, but carrying on a campaign — say, by slipping notes under her door and leaving messages on her answering machine — would be thought overaggressive. In the modern idiom, it would be a violation of her privacy. Admittedly, health is only one value to be balanced against others, such as privacy and pleasure. No one would want to live in a society that so devalued these competing elements of the good life that smokers had to sneak their puffs in the closet and meat eaters had to go beyond the three-mile limit to have a good steak.

If this were the way seventeenth-century Christians thought about the salvation of their neighbors, there would never have been a need for a

---

[7] See Locke, *A Letter Concerning Toleration*, p. 23.

principle of tolerance. As we now let others smoke themselves to their graves, Christians would have allowed their neighbors to go to hell with their incorrect vision of God. It is only when saving the souls of others becomes our mission and duty that we encounter a problem of tolerance. For passionate Jews today, the problem of tolerance is particularly acute, for the religion holds that all Jews are responsible for each other and further that the Messiah will come (the Jewish version of salvation) only when all Jews observe all the *mitzvoth* or commandments. When an observant Jew encounters one who refuses to follow the commandments, he can only feel pain and the yearning to find a way to induce his fellow Jew to comply with what he takes to be God's law.

The nature of Protestant belief provided John Locke with an opening for a knock-down argument to show why intervention against those following the false religion would be counterproductive. Salvation, he reasoned, requires a personal quest, a self-actuated identification with the beliefs and practices that bring about the state of grace. State coercion, intervention "by the magistrate," prevents this personal quest from taking place. Tolerance is required of other Protestant sects because it is the only way to permit individuals to pursue and achieve their own salvation.

The argument works so far as Protestant salvation by faith alone is our concern. The argument works less well for Catholics (salvation by works rather than faith) and seemingly not at all for Jews relative to other Jews (non-Jews not being their concern). The internal Jewish position appears, at first blush, to be the opposite of Locke's. A long tradition supports the view that it is not intention but external compliance with the *mitzvoth* that counts. So long as *matzah* passes over his lips during Passover, a Jew fulfills the commandment of eating *matzah*. Whether he wants to eat unleavened bread is supposedly irrelevant.

Yet a version of Locke's argument applies as well in the Jewish context. According to the late, revered Jewish theologian Yeshayahu Leibowitz, the proper posture of the Jew in fulfilling the commandments is submission to God's authority.[8] Doing the same act without being commanded to do so is less worthy, for it does not testify to God's sovereignty as lawgiver. Now, if a Jew observes the commandments solely because the magistrate has commanded him to do so, his actions do not testify to God's supremacy over all other lawgivers. He acts for fear of secular sanction rather than out of respect for God's command.[9] He does the right deed for the wrong reason. It is good that he does it, but less holy than if the state had not coerced it. Not surprisingly, Leibowitz regarded the state as the primary enemy of the religious life.

---

[8] See Yeshayahu Leibowitz, *Judaism, Human Values, and the Jewish State*, ed. and trans. Eliezer Goldman (Cambridge: Harvard University Press, 1992).

[9] On this point, see Meir Dan-Cohen, "In Defense of Defiance" (unpublished manuscript).

There is a general argument, then, of the form: Neither the state nor other coercive bodies can intervene to bring about desired behavior because, in the nature of things, the individual must do it on her own, and coercive threats—from the state or anybody—prevent (or tend to prevent) the individual from acting with internal motivation. Call this the logical argument against intervention. Locke uses the argument.[10] Kant uses it.[11] Leibowitz uses it. It is probably the most ingenious argument ever devised to curtail the power of the state. The argument forces us to stand back and recognize the limits of our collective power over dissenters. We cannot intervene and force them to do the right thing; nor can we get the magistrate to do it for us.

Of course, the logical argument for nonintervention works only if we take seriously ultimate values such as salvation (Locke), transcendent reason (Kant), and the Kingship of God (Leibowitz). These are the ideas that generate our need to defer to the individual's acting on his or her own internal springs of action. Without these ultimate values, the reasons for nonintervention and the basis for tolerance both collapse.

The element of suffering distinguishes tolerance from indifference. The tolerant suffer because they yearn to intervene and they cannot. They are blocked by Locke's logical argument against intervention or by the shield of modern values, like privacy, that permit people space to do what they want to do. The element of suffering in tolerance comes through clearly in the closely related virtue of patience.[12] Medical patients suffer (because of their illness, not because they must wait to see their physicians). And so does young Tybalt when after Romeo sneaks into the Capulet ball to catch a glimpse of Juliet, Tybalt desires to kill him on the spot. Capulet responds, "Young Romeo, is it? . . . I would not for wealth of all this town here in my house do him disparagement. Therefore be patient. Take no note of him." Tybalt is instructed to be patient, tolerant, and therefore to suffer the presence of his enemy.

Where tolerance is based on loving concern, the nonrealizable impulse to correct the lives of others expresses social solidarity. People care enough to be tolerant rather than indifferent. Even when the tolerance is based on moral disapproval, the impulse to intervene expresses the vibrancy of moral concerns. It is better that people condemn and then stay their intervention, rather than develop a posture of alienated nonconcern. Yet not all cases are of this sort. In some situations, tolerance derives from the assertion of a hegemonic culture. In most European societies, and indeed in most of the world outside the United States, the

---

[10] See Locke, *A Letter Concerning Toleration*.

[11] Immanuel Kant, *Fundamental Principles of the Metaphysics of Morals*, trans. Thomas K. Abbott (New York: Liberal Arts Press, 1949).

[12] This connection is more obvious in other languages. The same root generates both tolerance and patience in German (*Geduldsamkeit* and *Geduld*), Hebrew (*sovlanut* and *savlanut*), and Russian (*terpimost'* and *terpenie*).

dominant language and religion entrench themselves as the norm; all others are merely tolerated. In these situations, the attitude toward non-conforming minorities is not exactly indifference. Romanians are not indifferent to their Hungarian minority; nor are Israeli Jews nonchalant about the Arab citizens in their midst. Allowing these minority cultures to survive in their own schools and religious institutions is a sound expression of tolerance.

III. Doubts about Respect

Where tolerance is based on moral disapproval or religious rejection, one could hardly maintain that the tolerated are entitled to equal respect. Those who engage in hate speech may not be subjected to censorship, but that is not the same as approving what they have to say. The more difficult case is the assertion of cultural hegemony without moral pretensions. One might say that a minority culture is entitled to more than tolerance. The minority's language, religion, and lifestyle should be accepted and respected. It is not clear, however, what the operative significance of this respect would be. To some extent, noninterference with cultural autonomy betokens respect. And yet the maintenance of an official language or state religion stands in the way of full acceptance. After all, not every minority can have the right to use its native language in the national parliament.

A sharper illustration of the distinction between tolerance and respect is the "don't ask, don't tell" policy toward gays and lesbians in the U.S. military. This is an expression of tolerance. Respect for gays would permit them to act openly with pride. The policy resembles the self-imposed tolerance of Moses Mendelssohn toward his own Jewishness. He claimed that Jews in Germany should be Germans in public and Jews in private. Similarly, under the "don't ask, don't tell" policy, gays in uniform must appear to be straight in public, whatever they may do in private. Using the public/private distinction in this context is a way of affirming the legitimacy of a hegemonic culture. Military leaders have no doubts about the heterosexual nature of their culture. Those who deviate from it can be tolerated but not respected.

When tolerance is born of moral disapproval, one cannot expect the perceived moral order to yield pluralistic respect. Even if right-to-life groups were to become more tolerant toward abortion, they could not be expected to approve of the practice. But what should we say of tolerance (as opposed to respect) when it derives from the nonmoral hegemony of a particular culture? This is not a form of tolerance that sits well with the American commitment to equality. All groups and their customs — so far as they are not harmful to others — seemingly warrant equal respect. The "don't ask, don't tell" policy appears to be the exception that highlights the rule.

I confess that I have greater sympathy than my liberal academic colleagues toward the inherent right of hegemonic cultures to defend themselves. A good example is the position of the English language in the United States. There is no moral value to speaking one language over another, and multilingualism is a virtue that, in my view, every educated person should cultivate. Yet if a language does happen to be dominant in a particular culture, as English is in the United States, then those who read their history, literature, and law in that language are, I believe, entitled to defend their culture against erosion from the outside. Accordingly, other languages are entitled not to equal respect but merely to tolerance.

Yet the concepts of tolerance and respect may fail us in coming to grips with the language issue. It is not entirely clear what the operational content of "respect" is in this context. One could respect a foreign language, as the Northern Europeans respect the use of English, without proposing that the language become official in the culture. And a language might be official, as Arabic is in Israel, without a commitment to teaching the language to every schoolchild.

Tolerance and respect may also lose their sharp edges when applied to the issue of religion. One can respect Christians or Jews without thinking of becoming one. Or does respect—in the context of both language and religion—mean that one wants to adopt the practice for oneself?

The ambiguity of respect in these cases only strengthens the case for tolerance. The notions of acceptance and respect are simply too vague in most cases to undercut the virtue of disapproving or distancing oneself from the behavior of others without trying to suppress what they are doing.

The case for tolerance turns, in the end, on its being the least problematic way for individuals to live together in a pluralistic society. Indifference carries a moral cost. Respect is too vague a concept to enable us to maintain a culture that unifies us across our pluralistic ways. Tolerance is not perfect, but it is the best way to live with neither indifference toward the moral shortcomings of others nor total acceptance of contrary ways of life.

Jurisprudence, Columbia University School of Law

COMMUNITY, DIVERSITY, AND CIVIC EDUCATION: TOWARD A LIBERAL POLITICAL SCIENCE OF GROUP LIFE*

By Stephen Macedo

I. Introduction

Although liberals too often forget it, the health of the liberal public order depends on our ability to constitute not only political institutions and limits on power, but appropriate patterns of social life and citizen character. Liberal character traits and political virtues do not, after all, come about "naturally" or by the deliverance of an "invisible hand." Even Adam Smith did not think that, as we will see below. Harry Eckstein gets closer to the mark by suggesting that "stable governments . . . are the product of 'accidental' (extremely improbable) conjunctions of conditions which do sometimes, but rarely, occur in actual societies."[1]

Liberalism makes the protection of individual freedom its central aim, and it is not as demanding with respect to civic virtue as some other forms of government, such as the republican ideals described by Plato and Rousseau. Nevertheless, sensible liberals will allow that freedom may be constrained in various ways to help promote a stable system of decent and orderly freedom. Among the reasonable constraints are measures that help insure that citizens are educated toward liberal values and virtues. Liberals need to think about political education in order to plan for their own survival.[2]

The liberal need to plan for civic education may be in some tension with certain freedoms—such as the free exercise of religion, as some people understand it—but that tension can be allayed somewhat if we think creatively about the indirect as well as the direct means of political education. Civic education is not undertaken only in the most direct and obvious ways: through schools, civics curricula, and direct political ped-

* For comments on an early draft of this essay I would like to thank Fred Miller, Barry Shain, Leif Wenar, and the other contributors to this volume. The essay benefited enormously from being worked over in the fellows seminar at the Center for Human Values, at which I was privileged to spend the academic year 1994–95. I owe a great debt to that wonderful institution, and especially to its director, Amy Gutmann, as well as to my fellow research fellows Daniel A. Bell, Christopher Bobonich, Hilary Bok, Samuel Fleischacker, Kent Greenawalt, and Yael Tamir.

[1] Harry Eckstein, *A Theory of Stable Democracy* (Princeton: Woodrow Wilson School of Public and International Affairs, Research Monograph No. 10, 1961), p. 47.

[2] Plato, *The Republic*, trans. Allan Bloom (New York: Basic Books, 1968); Jean-Jacques Rousseau, *On the Social Contract*, trans. and ed. Donald Cress (Indianapolis: Hackett, 1983).

© 1996 Social Philosophy and Policy Foundation. Printed in the USA.

agogy. People are educated indirectly in a host of ways: our social and political lives are themselves educative, not only for children but for adults as well. Indeed, liberal citizens can be encouraged to use their freedom — including their freedom to associate and cooperate — to contribute indirectly to the task of liberal civic education.

This essay will urge that a liberal political science of group life should be investigated as a tool of indirect civic education. It will address the question of how group life can be constituted and shaped so as to be of service to our liberal political order. I will largely bypass Alexis de Tocqueville's well-known argument about the importance of participation in local communities, and instead focus on Adam Smith's interesting and little-discussed account of the crucial role of religious communities in the Great Society.[3]

By drawing on Smith and the work of some subsequent social and political theorists, I also hope that this essay helps us move beyond the increasingly stale debate about whether liberalism is compatible with attractive forms of community life. Perceptive liberals have long recognized that liberalism and community are not only compatible, but that a particular pattern of community life is essential to sustaining free self-government in modern mass societies.

Exploring the educative side-effects of citizen participation in local communities, groups, and associations, will also help allay the worry that liberal conceptions of political virtue operate at too high a level of abstraction from the "self and parochial interests that conventionally draw citizens into politics," as Shelley Burtt puts it.[4] The practical realization of a liberal theory of justice (such as that of John Rawls) might appear to depend on unrealistic expectations about citizen virtue. The possibility of approximating liberal citizen virtue in practice will appear far more "realistic," I shall try to show, when we flesh out the ways such virtues might be generated by the right patterns of community life.

The picture of liberal community life to be sketched here should have another kind of purchase on contemporary political argument. There is a tendency nowadays to uncritically celebrate diversity and the "politics of difference." The argument advanced below strongly suggests that particularistic communities — including those oriented around religious, ethnic, and other forms of deep diversity — need to be constituted and shaped to be of use in a liberal regime.[5] While heavy-handed interventions in religious life or other "private" matters may be neither necessary

---

[3] Alexis de Tocqueville's well-known argument is found, of course, in *Democracy in America*, trans. George Lawrence, ed. J. P. Mayer (New York: Doubleday, 1969).

[4] Shelley Burtt, "The Politics of Virtue Today: A Critique and Proposal," *American Political Science Review*, vol. 87 (1993), p. 363.

[5] I have made this argument at greater length elsewhere; see my "Liberal Civic Education and Religious Fundamentalism: The Case of God v. John Rawls?" *Ethics*, vol. 105 (April 1995), pp. 468–96.

nor permissible, liberals should not shy away from the important work of shaping community life for civic ends.

II. Educational Statecraft in the Great Society: Adam Smith and the Uses of Sectarianism[6]

A. Smith on civic education

Let us begin with a theorist whose impeccable liberal credentials did not stop him from worrying about the moral and civic consequences of life under capitalism. Adam Smith did more, indeed, than simply worry about what might be thought of as the civic deficit of commercial societies, he also offered a subtle and suggestive plan of public response. My aim here is to suggest that while we should not mimic this plan, we can take from it some important lessons about the indirect means of liberal civic education.

Smith regarded the new commercial order as a monumental advance over previous social forms, but it was a flawed advance: economic development could, as we shall see, undermine many forms of civic competence and personal well-being. Smith's problem was not unlike our problem: how do we plan for a citizenry with civic competence while respecting individual freedom? Smith's answer was that through canny statecraft we can respect associative freedom while gently shaping particular communities to draw out the resources they provide for civic education.

Smith aptly depicted mass capitalistic markets as vast networks of people whose relations are fragmentary, indirect, and often quite distant. The progressive advance of capitalism depends on an ever more developed division of labor, which in turn depends on ever more extensive markets. Since mass production requires concentrations of labor, commercial society will also tend to be urban and cosmopolitan. Modern commercial society, for Smith, is a society of strangers: a dangerously anonymous society of people with distant and fragmentary relations, a society that poses a real danger of such severe demoralization and civic decline that free self-government could be rendered impossible.

Mass commercial societies stand in stark contrast with the village and small-town life which they increasingly supplant. The Great Society is anonymous and liberating, in part because people's conduct simply becomes so much harder to monitor as people uproot themselves and settle in expanding urban centers. While important forms of freedom become possible only in the Great Society, this new freedom is also dangerous: liberation from the thick texture of small-scale communities and

---

[6] This section is greatly indebted to Samuel Fleischacker's searching criticisms of two earlier drafts, for which I am extremely grateful.

social networks of traditional village life could lead to a dangerous slackening of interpersonal relationships.

While the division of labor was a critical engine of increasing productivity, Smith believed that it also threatened to transform the work of the laboring poor—"the great body of the people"—into an increasingly repetitive and narrow routine that would be as intellectually deadening as it was physically debilitating. Confined "to a few very simple operations," the worker would become "as stupid and ignorant as it is possible for a human creature to" become: incapable of "rational conversation," incapable of "forming any just judgment" concerning ordinary life, still less the "great and extensive interests of his country."[7] How could a free society survive, Smith worried, with a large segment of the populace benumbed by "gross ignorance and stupidity," prone to the "delusions of enthusiasm and superstition," and incapable of seeing through "the interested complaints of faction and sedition?"[8]

Far from taking a laissez-faire attitude toward the deleterious consequences of the commercial order for citizen character and competence, Smith advanced a subtle scheme for civic education. He argued, first of all, that public policy "can facilitate, can encourage, and can even impose upon almost the whole body of the people, the necessity of acquiring those most essential parts of education."[9] To *facilitate* the education of the common people, the state should partly fund schools so that every child could be provided with a basic minimum level of education in practical subjects: the capacity to "read, write, and account," and the rudiments of "geometry and mechanicks."[10] Smith would have had the public further *encourage* basic education by giving "small premiums and little badges of distinction, to the children of the common people who excel" in their studies. And he would have *imposed* the requirement that people should pass a public examination before being allowed to practice a trade in a town, or enjoy the privileges associated with membership in many forms of corporate life.[11]

For Smith, civic and moral education was not limited to the acquisition of basic intellectual tools. He also urged public attention to physical training, not simply for its own sake but as an important aspect of moral and civic education. While Smith regarded citizen militias as no longer crucial to national security (here as elsewhere, the division of labor would promote specialization), he nevertheless held cowardice to be a grave character flaw and a form of "mental mutilation" which deserves "the most

[7] Adam Smith, *An Inquiry into the Nature and Causes of the Wealth of Nations*, ed. R. H. Campbell, A. S. Skinner, and W. B. Todd (Oxford: Clarendon Press, 1979), vol. 2, V.i.f, pp. 782, 781.
[8] *Ibid.*, p. 788.
[9] *Ibid.*, p. 785.
[10] *Ibid.*
[11] *Ibid.*, p. 786; *ibid.*, vol. 2, V.i.g, p. 796.

serious attention of government." In order to combat this "loathsome and offensive disease" and instill a healthy measure of "martial spirit" and self-respect in the citizenry, Smith recommended public encouragement for widespread gymnastic and militia training.[12]

Smith advocated direct public support for a variety of educative measures, therefore, and hoped that in this way the vast bulk of the populace would acquire at least some basic intellectual tools, a degree of martial spirit, and a merited respectability. By combating both cowardice and "gross ignorance and stupidity" among the common people, Smith believed that public agencies could promote people's private well-being, as well as the free society's need for a "decent and orderly" populace: a citizenry able to resist "enthusiasm and superstition," and to judge public affairs with some degree of discernment.[13]

The more or less directly educative measures discussed so far did not exhaust Smith's educational plan. He also worried that the social structure of an increasingly urban, mass society would undermine moral character. The burgeoning commercial order would, Smith worried, pay a heavy price for the atrophy of the smaller social settings of towns and villages, for these social settings were, as we shall see, crucial features of the moral infrastructure of a healthy mass society.

A crucial part of Smith's educative plan, then, was his attempt to promote substitutes for the small-scale communities of the old regime. It was for this reason that Smith arrestingly described religious "sects" or churches as "Institutions for the Instruction of People of all Ages."[14] Smith's concerns were with the civic side-effects of religious communities: the social, political, and moral benefits they could provide quite apart from their religious missions.

The religions of Smith's day could, for one thing, be counted on to help combat the "vices of levity" and the "liberal or loose" moral system, which is marked by "luxury, wanton and even disorderly mirth" and the intemperate pursuit of pleasure.[15] In place of the morality of self-indulgence, religion would promote an "austere" morality, one that promotes self-control, frugality, and prudent regard for the future. These character traits would be altogether essential to the "poor workman" and the "common people," whom "a single week's thoughtlessness and dissipation is often sufficient to undo" forever.[16]

Religious communities were effective moral educators because they did more than preach morality: the very nature of the small, face-to-face community was itself a crucial means for actually securing responsible con-

[12] *Ibid.*, vol. 2, V.i.f, pp. 786–88. ·
[13] *Ibid.*, p. 788.
[14] *Ibid.* Smith uses the term "sect" broadly to include "antient and established systems" (p. 789), as well as Anglicanism and Roman Catholicism.
[15] *Ibid.*, vol. 2, V.i.g, p. 794.
[16] *Ibid.*, pp. 794–95.

duct. The moral capital provided by these small communities was especially needed by those poorer people who lacked other social supports for good conduct.

The wealthy, Smith argued, do not have the same need as the rest of us to act responsibly: their wealth provides a cushion for irresponsible behavior. Even so, the social status and visibility of persons of wealth and distinction supply them with crucial incentives for responsible conduct. Wealth and social standing make people *visible* to others: the wealthy are "distinguished members of a great society." Observed "by all the world," the wealthy attend to every part of their own conduct.[17] This consciousness of being watched, of being visible to others, was for Smith a crucial bulwark of self-control: a crucial motive for caring about and looking after one's conduct. So while the wealthy did not need supports for responsible behavior to the same degree as the poor, they nevertheless had the motives for self-control provided by social visibility.

The poor, on the other hand, lack not only wealth but social status, and thus tend to be socially invisible. This invisibility breeds demoralization and irresponsible behavior: "Why should the man, whom nobody thinks it worth while to look at, be very anxious about the manner in which he holds up his head, or disposes of his arms while he walks through a room?"[18] Indeed, for Smith, the worst part of poverty appears not to be the material deprivation—bad as that may be—but rather the demoralization bred by social invisibility. "The poor man goes out and comes in unheeded," Smith poignantly remarks, "and when in the midst of a crowd is in the same obscurity as if shut up in his own hovel."[19]

The basic problem for the poor is not poverty per se, but the social invisibility, isolation, and consequent demoralization which are caused by poverty and which must make it hard or impossible to rise out of poverty. Without social supports for personal responsibility, self-control, initiative, and prudent regard for the future, invisible men will not only become slovenly and unkempt in their personal habits, but will also sink into broader forms of "slothful and sottish indifference."[20] "[A]s obscurity covers us from the daylight of honor and approbation, to feel that we are taken no notice of," Smith sadly observes, "necessarily damps the most agreeable hope, and disappoints the most ardent desire, of human nature."[21]

Luckily for most of us, great wealth and status are not the only sources of social visibility: these can also be provided by a peer group, by membership in a face-to-face community. The plight of the poor, as we have

[17] Adam Smith, *The Theory of Moral Sentiments*, ed. D. D. Raphael and A. L. Macfie (Oxford: Clarendon, 1979), I.iii.2.2, p. 51.

[18] *Ibid.*, p. 55.

[19] *Ibid.*

[20] *Ibid.*, I.iii.2.7, p. 57.

[21] *Ibid.*, I.iii.2.2, p. 51.

seen, is grounded less in material deprivation than in the decline of smaller social settings. The problem is that the

> man of low condition . . . is far from being a distinguished member of any great society. While he remains in a country village his conduct may be attended to, and he may be obliged to attend to it himself. In this situation . . . he may have what is called a character to lose. But as soon as he comes into a great city, he is sunk in obscurity and darkness. His conduct is observed and attended to by nobody, and he is therefore very likely to neglect it himself, and to abandon himself to every sort of low profligacy and vice.

Here, then, is where the benefits of religious communities really show themselves. Nothing can combat the invisibility, anonymity, and consequent hopelessness and irresponsibility of the commercial order, Smith argues, like face-to-face religious communities. The poor man "never emerges so effectually from this obscurity, his conduct never excites so much the attention of any respectable society, as by his becoming the member of a small religious sect."[22]

Popular religious communities provide moral resources greatly needed in the Great Society: not simply demanding codes of conduct, but peer groups that notice and care about the conduct of ordinary people, thereby giving them an incentive to attend to their own conduct, think about and plan for the future, and behave responsibly. Religious communities were a crucial part of the moral infrastructure of Smith's Great Society precisely because they helped provide substitutes for the social supports for responsible conduct once provided by small towns and villages. Membership in these face-to-face communities gave ordinary people a public character or reputation to lose — a social incentive to display prudent, responsible conduct.

It should be emphasized that Smith's plan for moral and civic education was not intended simply to produce a disciplined working class. He regarded self-control, personal responsibility, and a prudent regard for the future as important but fragile achievements for all. He opposed, for example, the practice of sending young gentlemen abroad for several years, because he believed that by placing young people "at a distance from the inspection and controul" of "parents and relations," wealthy families encouraged "frivolous dissipation" and weakened the good effects of early education undertaken (as he thought it should be) in the home and in schools near the home (rather than in boarding schools). Indeed, he felt that the proximity of children and parents would help to restrain the conduct of both.[23]

---

[22] Smith, *Wealth of Nations*, vol. 2, V.i.g, p. 795.
[23] *Ibid.*, pp. 773–74; Smith, *Theory of Moral Sentiments*, VI.ii.1.10, p. 222.

Likewise, the *economic* benefits of personal responsibility were important but not all-important to Smith. The economic importance of self-control and prudent regard for the future is obvious: the great mass of poor people were doomed to horrible poverty in the absence of economic growth. Not only frugality and economic growth, however, but all of the higher and nobler pursuits of human beings depend on the possession of the basic capacity for self-command. Smith did not rely on any narrow preoccupation with economic development, therefore, but instead stressed the intrinsic importance of intellectual and moral development. Communal memberships would, along with the other elements of Smith's civic education, help make people not simply more frugal, but more self-respecting and confident, more open to fellow-feeling and sympathy.

B. *Smith on religious morality and its limits*

Smith spoke very warmly of the habits of sober and tranquil prudence, and he regarded religious communities as crucial parts of the moral infrastructure of the Great Society. He also recognized that "austere" morals had the great advantage of being profoundly useful, even necessary, for the great bulk of common people: the working poor. Yet Smith neither opposed the virtue of liberality in the abstract, nor regarded the austere morality as altogether lovely. (Indeed, at one point he contrasts the "austerities and abasement of a monk" with the "liberal, generous, and spirited conduct of a man.")[24] Taken to extremes, austere self-command could lead to "disagreeably rigorous and unsocial" behavior.[25] A way was needed to temper the excessive rigor of religious communities.

Smith offered a political plan to blunt the potentially sharp edges of the austere moral system, and indirectly to shape these communities toward civic aims. He argued, first of all, that it is generally best to allow religious bodies to rely on private support. Here as elsewhere, competition will promote enterprise, and encourage the clergy to maintain "the fervour of the faith" by practicing all "the arts of popularity."[26] It should be for the clergy as for the hussars, he said: "no plunder, no pay."[27]

In this, Smith took direct exception to the view of his friend David Hume, who argued that

> this interested diligence of the clergy is what every wise legislator will study to prevent. . . . Each ghostly practitioner, in order to render himself more precious and sacred in the eyes of his retainers, will inspire them with the most violent abhorrence of all other sects, and

---

[24] Smith, *Wealth of Nations*, vol. 2, V.i.f., p. 771.

[25] *Ibid.*, vol. 2, V.i.g., p. 796; see also Smith, *Theory of Moral Sentiments*, VI.i.4, pp. 212–17.

[26] Smith, *Wealth of Nations*, vol. 2, V.i.g, p. 789.

[27] *Ibid.*, p. 790. The term "hussars" refers to members of European light cavalry units.

continually endeavor, by some novelty, to excite the languid devo-
tion of his audience. . . . Every tenet will be adopted that best suits
the disorderly affections of the human frame.[28]

Far better, Hume said, to provide a "fixed establishment [i.e., salary] for
priests," and thereby to "bribe their indolence."[29]

Smith certainly shared some of Hume's uneasiness about religious zeal,
passion, and fanaticism, and, as we shall see, he sought ways to temper
these unfortunate extremes.[30] He argued that it was, however, far-
fetched to think that salaries would be provided to clergy in anything like
an evenhanded manner. Subsidies would be guided by religious favor-
itism and party spirit, and that would inflame resentment. Far better,
Smith argued, for politics to resist relying on "the aid of religion," instead
dealing "equally and impartially with all the different sects," and allowing every individual to freely choose his own priest. Smith hoped that,
in this way, the state would not only respect religious freedom but also
promote civil peace: with free competition, the number of sects would
multiply, and the power of any one religious leader or community would
not be very great. The fragmentation and consequent weakness of sects
would encourage all to practice moderation and mutual respect. The law's
impartiality among contending religions would promote "philosophical
good temper and moderation," perhaps even mutual respect.[31] In these
ways, Smith both promoted religious freedom and channeled religious
communities toward public purposes, not by force — which he thought
would be not only illiberal but ineffective — but through "gentle usage."[32]

It is worth noting that Smith's argument that freedom for religious
groups in the Great Society will lead them to multiply, fragment, and
thence to moderate their opposition to one another, is an obvious precursor
to James Madison's argument, in "Federalist No. 10," that the embrace
of an "extended republic" would help "break and control the violence of
faction."[33] If a polity embraces many factions in a large territory, Madison
argued, no one faction will be able consistently to dominate the others,
and this "renders factious combinations less to be dreaded." Embracing
a "greater variety of parties" places a "greater variety of obstacles" before
"the secret wishes of an unjust and interested majority."[34] In a large pol-

---

[28] David Hume, *History of England* (1778), iii.30–31, quoted in *ibid.*, p. 791.

[29] *Ibid.*

[30] Smith, *Wealth of Nations*, vol. 2, V.i.g., p. 806.

[31] *Ibid.*, pp. 792–93.

[32] *Ibid.*, pp. 798–99.

[33] James Madison, "Federalist No. 10," in *The Federalist Papers*, ed. Clinton Rossiter (New
York: New American Library, 1961), p. 77.

[34] *Ibid.*, p. 84. Later in "Federalist No. 10," Madison hearkens back to Smith even more
closely (though I cannot say consciously) when he says that "a religious sect may degenerate into a political faction" in a small political unit, but a "variety of sects" dispersed across
a large nation are less to be feared (*ibid.*).

ity with many different interests—many minority factions—governing coalitions will have to be built, and the fact that people engage in fluid, open, and shifting political coalitions should also help to moderate their partisanships.

Interestingly, Smith avoids one shortcoming of *The Federalist Papers*, for while that insightful analysis of America's constitutional institutions counts on citizen virtue, it says little about where those virtues will come from. The embrace of many groups in a large political sphere remains, in Madison's hands, largely a *negative* strategy for warding off unjust political combinations. *The Federalist Papers* do display a concern with local communities—namely, the states—but the main thrust here is to argue for the subordination of the states to the national government. Very little is said of the dependence of the national government and national citizenship on the moral resources furnished by local communities. In Smith's writings, on the other hand, we find a fuller account of the importance of preserving vibrant small communities as means for promoting moral and civic virtues that might otherwise be in short supply in mass, commercial societies or "extended republics."

Smith's plan for moderating religious zeal and shaping religious communities toward civic ends does not end with his advocacy of religious freedom and nonestablishment. He also worries, as we have seen, about the excesses of religious enthusiasm, of superstitions that flourish as a consequence of ignorance and credulity, and of the tendency of the austere system left to its own to become "disagreeably rigorous and unsocial."[35] Smith hoped that people would, over time, tend toward what he called "that pure and rational religion, free from every mixture of absurdity, imposture, or fanaticism, such as wise men have in all ages of the world wished to see established."[36] He grants, therefore, that sectarian moral education may stand in some tension with both the private good of individuals and the ethos of liberal democracy.

Smith suggests two remedies for sectarian excess. First, he recommends that free rein be given to all who would undertake gay "publick diversions": painting, poetry, music, dance, drama, and so on. All of these will help "dissipate the melancholy and gloom" of those who might otherwise sink too deep in fire, brimstone, and religious asceticism.[37]

In addition, and perhaps more importantly, Smith sought to promote the social influence of science and philosophy by making the study of these subjects a precondition for admittance to prestigious professions. "Science," says Smith, "is the great antidote to the poison of enthusiasm and superstition; and where all the superior ranks of people were secured from it, the inferior ranks could not be much exposed to it."[38] Educa-

---

[35] Smith, *Wealth of Nations*, vol. 2, V.i.f, p. 767; *ibid.*, vol. 2, II.V.i.g, p. 796.

[36] *Ibid.*, II.V.i.g, p. 793.

[37] *Ibid.*, p. 795.

[38] *Ibid.*, p. 796.

tional requirements for the better-off members of society would thus have cultural "trickle-down" effects for society as a whole, effects which might be augmented once public subsidies for the salaries of clergymen were eliminated. The attraction of a career in the church for the ablest and best-educated people would then decline, and the most eminent men of learning would migrate from the clergy to the universities, helping (Smith might well have expected) to increase the social prestige and influence of universities at the expense of the clergy.[39] And of course, as we have seen, Smith favored public measures to encourage the education of all; for education, he thought, would make everyone less apt to be deluded by superstition, political manipulation, and religious zeal.

Smith saw education—especially science and critical thinking—as a means of elevating and tempering the enthusiastic spirit of popular religion. Education would help defend the Great Society against the sorts of gross delusions and superstitions of religion at its worst, which were epitomized for Smith by the Roman Catholic Church: "the most formidable combination that ever was formed . . . against the liberty, reason, and happiness of mankind."[40]

C. Smith on religious freedom

Smith's is a liberal political science of group life in that he respects the freedom of people to form, join, and leave religious communities without political hindrance. He respects religious freedom without embracing government "neutrality" or laissez faire toward religion, thus avoiding the narrowness of those liberal moral theories that nowadays provide such easy fodder for liberalism's critics. Smith shows that respect for freedom of religious association can be combined with gentle and unobtrusive public policies that shape these associations toward public ends by moderating their potentially illiberal extremes and making them agents of civic education. The lesson for liberals here is that we can respect freedom without leaving the private realm altogether ungoverned: gentle interventions can help insure that private freedom is used in a way that promotes civic education and the public good.

A nervous liberal might still wonder whether Smith's statecraft altogether observes the limits of liberal public authority with respect to religion. After all, while Smith insists that "articles of faith are not within the proper department of a temporal authority," he also says that "public tranquility" and the security of public authority "may frequently depend

---

[39] *Ibid.*, pp. 810–12. I owe this observation to Samuel Fleischacker. One might also worry, of course, that Smith here points (albeit unwittingly) toward today's rather sharp divide (sometimes called a culture war) between university professors and other intellectuals on the one hand, and common people more closely aligned with a popular clergy not associated with elite educational institutions.

[40] Smith, *Wealth of Nations*, vol. 2, V.i.g, pp. 802–3.

upon the doctrines" propagated by the clergy.[41] Is not the latter observation an invitation to dangerous public meddling in the private sphere?

It seems hard to deny, however, that the security of liberal values in a democratic polity depends on the religious and other extra-political convictions of citizens. Liberal citizens must, after all, find space for their political convictions in the context of their moral and philosophical values as a whole. Smith recognizes what some liberals forget: that respect for private freedom does not require that the private realm be sealed off against the deliberate influence of public policies aimed at securing legitimate civic aims.

Smith seems to me absolutely right to recognize that liberalism is about more than merely limiting public authority in the name of freedom. More fundamentally, liberalism must be about constituting a social and political order that is—in both its public and private spheres—capable of sustaining a decent and orderly freedom. This requires going beyond merely observing the bounds of public authority to insure that public values gain the support that they require in all spheres of life.

There will, of course, be limits on what a liberal state can do to bring religious communities into alignment with political imperatives, but it is hard to see how Smith runs afoul of them.[42] He argues for religious nonestablishment and an evenhanded policy of public nonsupport for religion. The freedom to form churches and define dogma is respected. It turns out that these liberal policies will also, Smith believes, generate beneficial changes in the attitudes of religious communities (making them less zealous and more mutually respectful). There is nothing to apologize for if, as a happy side-effect of freedom-respecting policies, private groups become more supportive of liberal virtues.

If Smith supported education in science simply as a way of promoting a particular conception of religious truth, this would be a problem. The public reason for promoting science, philosophy, and education more broadly is, however, to insure a basic level of citizen competence, and to dampen the threats to civil peace posed by enthusiasm, zealotry, and superstition in any and every form. Of course, enthusiastic zeal for superstition is some people's idea of religious truth, but then liberalism is no more compatible with *everyone's* view of religious truth than is any other political theory. Smith's educational policy will not make everyone happy, but it does not depend for its justifiability upon a particular conception of religious truth.[43] His interventions in the religious realm are

---

[41] *Ibid.*, p. 798.

[42] *Ibid.*

[43] This policy is not, of course, neutral with respect to religious beliefs; but then I do not believe that the liberal state should be committed to neutrality, and I argue for this in *Liberal Virtues: Citizenship, Virtue, and Community in Liberal Constitutionalism* (Oxford: Clarendon Press, 1990), pp. 260–63. I discuss these conflicts at greater length in "Liberal Civic Education and Religious Fundamentalism" (*supra* note 5).

indirect, gentle, and guided by public aims and reasons, and thus are entirely legitimate from a liberal point of view.

D. Summary

Commercialism and the modern liberties that it fosters help emancipate people from the restraints of inherited sources of authority, and the relatively fixed expectations of inherited classes and roles. But on Smith's account liberal republics also need to beware the anonymity and extravagance of unbounded individualism. Individual liberation can go too far: the vastness, anonymity, and fluidity of the Great Society makes it a potentially inhospitable environment for the small-scale interactions that remain a crucial component of the moral life. Liberal republics need to temper the internal dynamics of mass commercialism, and furnish partial substitutes for the communal bonds of premodern societies. The Great Society depends upon moral resources which cannot be furnished by institutions fully reflecting the cosmopolitan openness and freedom of that society.

Smith's plan for civic education provides lessons for liberalism today. We can, with Smith, defend the free society without embracing a policy of laissez faire with respect to the civic and moral culture. We should, with Smith, recognize that local communities and other intermediate associations are important indirect instruments of civic education which may, nevertheless, need to be shaped and managed to some degree by public policies designed to encourage them to take forms that are supportive of liberal democracy.

Smith's account is not only vindicated, but also deepened and extended, by more recent social theory and political science. Smith seems to have been right, as we shall see in what follows, to have worried about the slackening of communal bonds, and to have regarded the project of accommodating and shaping new forms of community as a crucial part of a liberal strategy for civic education.

III. CONSTITUTING COMMUNITIES FOR LIBERAL EDUCATION

When does community life promote liberal democracy? Smith suggests one way of answering this question by arguing that public policy should counteract zeal and superstition as attitudes at odds with moderation in the face of diversity. Smith also emphasizes, as we have seen, the moderating effects of the fragmentation and proliferation of religious communities. This latter approach emphasizes the need to influence not the substantive convictions of communities so much as the structure of community life. It is this latter approach that I want to pursue here, for much social science after Smith reaffirms the importance of fostering an overlapping, pluralistic pattern of group memberships and communal allegiances.

Emile Durkheim argued that groups that totally absorb the allegiances of their members destroy the possibility of individual liberty. We should not, therefore, uncritically espouse group-based allegiances or interests, but rather welcome the clash among competing group-based allegiances, and among these allegiances and more-inclusive moral ideals. It is the state, says Durkheim, that protects individual rights, and by so doing safeguards the possibility of defection from groups. The state must

> permeate all those secondary groups of family, trade and profes-
> sional association, Church, regional areas and so on . . . which
> tend . . . to absorb the personality of their members. It must do this
> in order to prevent this absorption and free these individuals, and so
> to remind these partial societies that they are not alone and that there
> is a right that stands above their own rights.[44]

On Durkheim's account, the state safeguards individuals against the domination of particular groups, thereby nurturing their freedom. Groups, in turn, prevent social atomization and individual demoralization, thereby warding off state domination of isolated and weak individuals. Individual liberty thrives in the tension between the state and "secondary groups," therefore; and only by preserving this tension does a social order combat both state and group oppression:

> [I]f that collective force, the State, is to be the liberator of the individ-
> ual, it has itself need of some counterbalance; it must be restrained
> by other collective forces, that is, by . . . secondary groups. . . . [I]t is
> out of this conflict that individual liberties are born.[45]

Durkheim's endorsement of a complex pattern of partial allegiances gains support from the work of post-World War II "mass society" theorists, such as William Kornhauser, who warned that the atrophy of intermediate associations leads to social "atomization" and provides fertile ground for totalitarian political movements. Kornhauser argued that in "mass societies" — societies without layers of crosscutting intermediate groups and associations — both the elites and the masses are "available" for extreme forms of mutual manipulation. Isolated individuals are easily manipulated by opportunistic elites and, because they lack moderat-

---

[44] Emile Durkheim, *Professional Ethics and Civic Morals* (Glencoe, IL: Free Press, 1957), p. 65.

[45] *Ibid.*, pp. 62–63, quoted in William Kornhauser, *The Politics of Mass Society* (Glencoe, IL: Free Press, 1959), p. 79.

ing partial ties to others, they are disposed to form "hyper-attachments" to symbols and leaders.[46] On the other hand, when popular demands can be transmitted very directly to the political center, elites will have little room for maneuvering and will often be forced to respond. In a mass society both the elites and the masses lack the moderating insulation provided by intermediate associations. Such a society is fertile ground for totalitarian political movements. Totalitarian states strive, unsurprisingly, to maintain mass-society conditions: to keep individuals isolated and to prevent the emergence of rival sources of loyalty and power.[47]

A society, on the other hand, with strong layers of associations between the state and individuals is one in which the elites and the masses are insulated from mutual manipulation, and shielded from direct and extreme political demands. Citizens in a pluralistic society will, moreover, tend to form allegiances and attachments to a variety of particular parties, groups, and movements, none of which wholly consumes their loyalties.[48] Political appeals flow toward the center indirectly, fragmented and moderated by associations. Shielded from direct, mass appeals, and the pressures of an unorganized but homogeneous and volatile mass of opinion, political authorities may negotiate with a variety of groups and pressures: [49]

> A plurality of groups that are both independent and non-inclusive not only protects elites and non-elites from one another but does so in a manner that permits liberal democratic control. Liberal democratic control requires that people have *access* to elites, and that they exercise restraint in their participation.[50]

A network of multiple, overlapping memberships—the "cross-cutting solidarities" of a healthy pluralistic society—produces a pattern of complexly divided and partial loyalties, which promotes not only political moderation and stability, but individual liberty as well:

---

[46] Kornhauser, *The Politics of Mass Society*, p. 32, and see, more generally, pp. 30–62.
[47] *Ibid.*, p. 62.
[48] Kornhauser here builds on Durkheim:

> [O]ur political malaise is due to the same cause as our social malaise: that is, to the lack of secondary cadres to interpose between the individual and the State. We have seen that these secondary groups are essential if the State is not to oppress the individual: they are also necessary if the State is to be sufficiently free of the individual. And indeed we can imagine this as suiting both sides; for both have an interest in the two forces not being in immediate contact although they must be linked one with the other. (Durkheim, *Professional Ethics and Civic Morals*, p. 96)

[49] Kornhauser, *The Politics of Mass Society*, pp. 43–49.
[50] *Ibid.*, p. 81. Kornhauser also emphasizes (*ibid.*, pp. 65–66) that citizens actively involved in local group life are less apathetic and more self-confident, as Tocqueville claimed (see *Democracy in America*, passim).

So long as no association claims or receives hegemony over many aspects of its members' lives, its power over the individual will be limited. . . . [T]he authority of a private group can be as oppressive as that of the state.[51]

Freedom-promoting social orders are, it appears, *pluralistic*: societies of partial allegiances in which groups endlessly compete with each other and with the state for the allegiances of individuals, and in which individuals' loyalties are divided among a variety of crosscutting (or only partially overlapping) memberships and affiliations.

Liberalism needs community life, therefore, and it needs community life to be constituted in a certain way. Pluralism is the key. Liberal statecraft should aim for a complex, crosscutting structure of community life in which particular group-based allegiances are tempered by other, competing group allegiances and by a state representing a common, overarching, but partial, point of view that gives everyone something in common. The importance of a pluralistic structure of group life is reaffirmed by Gabriel A. Almond and Sidney Verba, who argue that "pluralism, even if not explicitly political pluralism, may indeed be one of the most important foundations of political democracy."[52]

Partial, overlapping, crosscutting commitments educate toward political moderation in a variety of ways: partly by fostering shifting political coalitions, and with them the habit of flexible cooperation with members of other groups and communities. The fact that allegiances and memberships are partial should also help individuals maintain a critical distance on the demands of any particular group, and, indeed, pluralism should help individuals defect from oppressive group-imposed constraints: defection from a group must be easier when that group represents only a portion of one's allegiances.

Some forms of group life are bound to be pathological from a liberal point of view. These will include "tribalistic" forms of community that entail deep suspicion of outsiders, and totalistic communities that wholly capture the identities of their members, making individual freedom, and cooperation with outsiders, difficult or impossible.

Important contributions to liberal-democratic civic education are made, therefore, not so much by the vigor of associational life per se, but by associational life properly constituted. Groups educate toward moderation, freedom, and political stability when they form complex, pluralistic, crosscutting patterns of overlapping memberships — patterns in which the state overarches all and represents certain common interests. Under

---

[51] Kornhauser, *The Politics of Mass Society*, pp. 80–81.
[52] Gabriel A. Almond and Sidney Verba, *The Civic Culture: Political Attitudes and Democracy in Five Nations* (Princeton: Princeton University Press, 1963), pp. 319–20.

these conditions, local community and group life can be said to foster the liberal-democratic benefits of community without incurring the dangers of group-based oppression, or tribalistic exclusion of outsiders.

IV. LIBERAL CITIZEN VIRTUE AS SOCIAL CAPITAL

I have, so far, focused on arguments for the importance of intermediate associations less well-known than Tocqueville's. Tocqueville adds, however, a dimension to the picture I have sketched that now needs to be recognized. He argued that there is a generalized readiness to associate with others that is augmented through use. "Knowledge of how to combine," says Tocqueville, "is the mother of all other forms of knowledge,"[53] and activity in political associations feeds on and helps encourage activity in civil or extra-political associations, and vice versa:

> Men chance to have a common interest in a certain matter. It may be
> a trading enterprise to direct or an industrial undertaking to bring to
> fruition; those concerned meet and combine; little by little in this way
> they get used to the idea of association.[54]

The experience of cooperation with others breeds familiarity with networks of cooperative people, increases mutual trust, and therefore augments the resources available for further cooperation as new problems arise. James S. Coleman, Robert D. Putnam, and others describe this willingness to cooperate as a vital form of "social capital": a great social resource for handling collective problems, there to be drawn on and indeed augmented as new problems are confronted and new forms of cooperation are needed.[55]

As Smith claimed, great societies need small communities to monitor behavior, enforce social norms, and foster cooperation. Networks of such cooperative communities help generate the resources for new forms of cooperation. In the language of game theory, people constantly confront situations in which everyone would gain by cooperating. In such situations, however, the worst outcome for any individual is to be the one who acts on the expectation that others will cooperate, only to find that they have exploited the situation for their own short-term good. Societies will be better off if people cooperate to solve collective problems, but in the absence of means for enforcing sanctions against defectors, rational self-interest will often counsel noncooperation. Where people lack mutual trust in one another's commitments, cooperation may be impossible.

---

[53] Tocqueville, *Democracy in America*, p. 517.

[54] *Ibid.*, p. 520.

[55] See James S. Coleman, *Foundations of Social Theory* (Cambridge: Harvard University Press, 1990), pp. 300–21; and Robert D. Putnam, *Making Democracy Work: Civic Traditions in Modern Italy* (Princeton: Princeton University Press, 1993), ch. 6.

Behavior can be monitored, norms enforced, and cooperation encouraged more effectively in small groups than in large ones. Consider the "rotating credit associations" which, as Putnam observes, are found on every continent, each consisting of a group of individuals who make regular contributions to a fund which is lent, in whole or in part, to each contributor in turn. The trick, obviously, is to ensure that people keep contributing even after having received a share, so that everyone has a turn to benefit.[56]

As with Smith's sects, the small size of credit associations and their members' frequent interactions make norm enforcement possible. Since there is an obvious short-term payoff to those who would renege after having had their turn, the members of a rotating credit association must be selected with care. A reputation for honesty and reliability is an important qualification, of course, and that reputation may be vouchsafed by previous membership in other such associations. Among the incentives to cooperation, therefore, are the benefits that accrue from a reputation for trustworthiness.

As Smith predicted, membership in associations provides lowly individuals with a public character: a substitute for the more personalized reputations possessed by great individuals. And in societies with dense, overlapping networks of associations, trust can be lent: as Putnam observes, "[s]ocial networks allow trust to become transitive and spread: I trust you, because I trust her and she assures me that she trusts you."[57]

Individuals in cooperative schemes witness the gains of cooperation, and acquire the reputations which make them likely future candidates for more such endeavors. The experience of successful cooperation provides both incentives to, and collective resources for, further cooperation. Credit associations are often found in conjunction with other forms of cooperation such as mutual aid societies. The reason seems to be that "all of these forms of voluntary cooperation seem to be fed by the same underlying stock of social capital," which, at its most fungible, is the generalized readiness to coalesce to form associations prepared to trust, cooperate, and monitor cooperation.[58] The crucial character trait required by cooperative associations, and in turn fostered by them, is not altruism but reciprocity: a willingness to make short-term sacrifices for longer-term payoffs garnered by cooperation.[59]

Groups foster cooperation among members; but maximizing group-specific cooperation should not be our aim, for that could undermine the willingness to cooperate with outsiders. There are trade-offs here. Intra-

---

[56] Putnam, *Making Democracy Work*, pp. 167–68.

[57] *Ibid.*, p. 169.

[58] *Ibid.*

[59] *Ibid.*, pp. 171–72.

group allegiances nurture the close interaction and individualized monitoring needed to enforce group norms, punish defectors, promote cooperation, and assess the reliability of our peers. Leaving people entirely in thrall to group allegiances could, however, undermine new and wider forms of cooperation. So particular group-based allegiances promote the cooperative virtues needed by the larger social order, but they may also stand in some tension with society-wide cooperation.

Here again we can see the advantages of overlapping networks of groups: particular groups will foster cooperativeness among members; but when individuals belong to networks of partially overlapping groups, this should help foster a more generalized attitude of cooperativeness and reciprocity. Putnam's study reaffirms what Durkheim and Kornhauser suggested: healthy structures of group life are ones characterized by rich networks of broad and relatively weak group ties. Under these conditions, particular groups achieve the benefits of cooperation among members, without foreclosing the possibility of new and wider forms of cooperation across group lines. In such a social setting, government rests lightly on citizens because networks of cooperating individuals support collective endeavors and foster mutual trust.

The healthy structure of group life described above implies a corresponding ideal of civic character: one of active participation in a number of overlapping groups, combined with an openness to new groups and wider forms of cooperation. Multiple memberships and an open attitude toward new forms of cooperation would help individuals maintain a critical distance on any particular commitment. The complex structure and open quality of group life should foster personal freedom and toleration for others. Participation in cooperative schemes for mutual advantage should also teach the virtues of self-control and foresight. Where such associations are democratically self-governing, we can expect them to teach other political virtues as well. Eric M. Uslaner suggests that the good citizen can be thought of as the trusting individual, who treats adversaries with civility and respect in order to keep open the possibility of reciprocity and cooperation.[60]

V. SMALL-GROUP COOPERATION AS AN EDUCATION FOR LIBERAL JUSTICE?

One of the most difficult tasks of statecraft is to bridge the gap between the more or less self-interested conduct that individuals seem ready enough to exhibit in market settings, and the more principled and other-regarding behavior that even liberal political theories hope that citizens will at least sometimes exhibit in politics and in other social settings.[61]

---

[60] Eric M. Uslaner, "Trends in Comity over Time" (unpublished manuscript).
[61] I discuss this problem in *Liberal Virtues*, pp. 133–42.

The problem is liable to seem insurmountable if we depict human motivations as divided between narrow self-interest on the one hand, and, on
the other hand, pure forms of moral conduct such as altruism or a commitment to doing the right thing for its own sake without regard to consequences. But just as the division of our social lives into individuals and
the state leaves out those layers of groups and associations that, as we
have seen, are so crucial to moral and political education, so too the stark
bifurcation of human motivations into self-interest and other-regardingness
or public spirit leaves out a category of motives and interests that we have
good reason to regard as crucial to the moral economy of a modern mass
society.

There are, we can now see, a whole set of "cooperative virtues" that
occupy a crucial position intermediate between the noblest forms of self-
sacrifice and the narrowest forms of self-servingness. The "cooperative
virtues" fostered by group life are not simply all-purpose social resources,
but can be important supports for a specifically liberal social order.
Approximating liberal justice in practice may depend not so much on getting individuals to adopt the moral point of view in all its austere
demandingness, but rather on building upon the cooperativeness and
reciprocity exhibited in group life.

Among the citizen virtues on which liberal self-government depends,
according to John Rawls's recent account, are what he describes as the
"cooperative virtues": "the virtue of reasonableness and a sense of fairness, a spirit of compromise and a readiness to meet others halfway, all
of which are connected with the willingness to cooperate with others on
political terms that everyone can publicly accept."[62] The core citizen virtue in Rawls's scheme is reasonableness. Reasonable people are not altru-
ists (or, from a different viewpoint, "suckers") moved by impartially
defined principles irrespective of how others behave, and they are not,
at the other extreme, mere pursuers of rational self-interest. Reasonable
people are willing to "propose principles and standards as fair terms of
cooperation and to abide by them willingly, given the assurance that others will likewise do so."[63] They seek "a social world in which they can
cooperate with others on terms all can accept as free and equal. They
insist that reciprocity should hold within that world so that each benefits
along with the others."[64]

Rawls does not, as one might have supposed, expect people to be educated toward just conduct by philosophical argument or moral suasion

[62] John Rawls, *Political Liberalism* (New York: Columbia University Press, 1993), p. 163.
[63] *Ibid.*, p. 49. There are other aspects of reasonableness for Rawls (see *ibid.*, pp. 81–82),
but they are not germane to my argument.
[64] *Ibid.*, pp. 49–50; see also pp. 16–17; and in Rawls, *A Theory of Justice* (Oxford: Oxford
University Press, 1971), "the basic idea [of reasonableness] is one of reciprocity, a tendency
to answer in kind. . . . [T]his tendency is a deep psychological fact" (p. 494). Reasonable people are what Margaret Levy describes as "contingent consenters," in her important work-
in-progress about the nature of social cooperation, *Contingencies of Consent*.

alone — or even primarily — rather, the experience of cooperation in face-to-face associations plays a crucial role. Good liberal citizens are "ready and willing to do their part" in collective endeavors "provided they have the assurance that others will also do their part." [65] Trust and confidence in our fellow citizens strengthens and grows more complete over the course of time as we observe "other persons with evident intention" striving "to do their part in just or fair arrangements." [66] Successful cooperation breeds, therefore, greater trust and cooperation, and "trust also increases as the basic [political] institutions framed to secure our fundamental interests are more firmly and willingly recognized." [67] The virtues that foster social cooperation are in turn augmented by social cooperation; like Coleman's social capital, these virtues increase with use; as Rawls says, they are part of society's "political capital." [68]

But what sorts of institutions, besides the political process itself, promote the all-important cooperative virtues? In *A Theory of Justice*, Rawls described the "morality of association" as an important preparation for the highest stage of moral development, the "morality of principle." Associations are systems of cooperation organized around shared ideals. Members are taught to take seriously the perspectives of their fellow associates; successful association promotes mutual trust, reliance, and friendship. Associations are especially important educators for social cooperation, because here the ties of friendship and mutual trust are especially intense, Rawls observes, and here too feelings of anger, resentment, and guilt are most likely to be visited upon, or felt by, those who shirk their duties.[69]

Strikingly, the logic of Rawls's account of how the just society might actually be realized is quite similar to accounts emphasizing the "rationality" of cooperation on self-interested grounds. From the perspective of rational self-interest, as we saw above, the reputation for cooperativeness has definite tangible benefits: by cultivating such a reputation, one becomes eligible for participation in other cooperative schemes. But reputation plays a role in Rawls's account as well: virtuous liberal citizens want to be "fully cooperating members of society," and they want to be recognized as such by their fellows; they want, in other words, to realize a certain ideal of citizenship in their conduct and "have it recognized that they realize" this ideal.[70]

The convergence here is striking. "Moralists" such as Rawls hope that citizens come to prize a certain ideal of social life for its own sake: a com-

[65] Rawls, *Political Liberalism*, p. 86.

[66] *Ibid.*

[67] *Ibid.*, p. 163. Experiencing the benefits of cooperation on fair terms aids the transition from a "modus vivendi" to a principled political settlement.

[68] *Ibid.*, p. 157.

[69] Rawls, *A Theory of Justice*, pp. 475, 470.

[70] Rawls, *Political Liberalism*, p. 84.

munity of principle in which citizens act, and are known to act, on fair principles of cooperation. Those who analyze social relations in terms of self-interest and "instrumental" rationality nevertheless converge on a strikingly similar picture of the good society: the very same reputation for fair cooperativeness turns out to be the key to what Tocqueville called "self-interest properly understood."[71]

This convergence is not, in the end, surprising, since in both cases the key set of institutions for *socializing* individual behavior is the network of associations and groups intermediate between individuals and their narrow interests, on the one hand, and the polity as a whole and its very general interests, on the other. Whether one is operating on moralistic or self-interested assumptions, fostering the spirit of cooperation, and the "in-between" virtues of reciprocity, reasonableness, and fairness, turns out to be a crucial element of moral and political education.

VI. CONCLUSION: GROUP DIVERSITY AND LIBERAL STATECRAFT

Liberals often simply ignore the project of political and moral education, perhaps fearing that the very subject brings with it the threat of heavy-handed government interventions. And yet, if Adam Smith did not adopt a "laissez-faire" attitude toward political and moral education, why should we? The health of liberal-democratic political regimes depends upon certain popular virtues and character traits which need to be planned for. Liberalism counsels not the avoidance of civic education, but gentle and (where possible) indirect educative interventions. The arguments surveyed above suggest that liberals should plan for citizen virtue by accommodating and (where possible and necessary) promoting an active and pluralistic pattern of group life.

But why, some will ask, should political observers in America worry about these matters, for surely America remains what Tocqueville observed 150 years ago: a society of "joiners" and active participators, with a vibrant civil society. Unfortunately, this complacency may be misplaced, for America's stock of social capital may be in serious decline. Putnam has recently provided a welter of evidence suggesting that communal activity in America has declined precipitously over the last twenty-five years.[72] Uslaner likewise argues that interpersonal trust was high in the 1960s, but dropped quickly in the mid-1970s, and has since hovered at a level below what is necessary to sustain collective action.[73] Americans may indeed do well, therefore, to think about ways to bolster cooperativeness and community life.

[71] Tocqueville, *Democracy in America*, pp. 525–28.
[72] Robert D. Putnam, "Bowling Alone: Democracy in America at the End of the Twentieth Century," *Journal of Democracy*, vol. 6 (1995), pp. 65–78.
[73] Uslaner, "Trends in Comity over Time."

Beyond specifying the healthy structure of group life, as we have done, we should study the ways that different types of groups foster different sorts of virtues. A fully worked out political science of group life (which I cannot provide here) would provide a taxonomy of groups and the virtues they promote and would say something about the optimal mix. In order to inform statecraft or even substantial policy reform, all of this would need to be supplemented by a critical assessment of present conditions and the social pathologies that most need addressing. It is unlikely that a single society-wide approach would be adequate: what is needed in the great American cities will not likely be altogether appropriate for small towns and rural areas.

Different groups and associations are liable to foster different virtues and values. Public institutions and associations are often expected to be politically accountable, open, and nondiscriminatory, making them capable of promoting some virtues (inclusion, mixing across particularistic group lines, perhaps tolerance) but not others. Fully public institutions must often comply with norms of inclusion. Even where they can exclude those who violate norms, they may have to abide by elaborate requirements of due process, making exclusion and norm-enforcement costly. If individuals cannot be excluded, then it may be hard to enforce demanding forms of self-control and responsibility.

Private institutions may have some great advantages when it comes to promoting certain virtues. Consider the example provided by Mitchell Duneier's *Slim's Table,* which is based on interviews conducted in the Valois Cafe, a haven of order and respectability on the fringe of Chicago ghetto life. The orderly atmosphere of that cafe depends on the readiness of its tough Greek owners to peremptorily evict anyone who violates the expectations of the establishment.[74] The very fact that private communities may expel people (without elaborate due process) makes them capable of enforcing behavioral norms that are not (or no longer) enforced in much of the public realm: in city parks, on the streets, and elsewhere.

Consider another striking example of the moral resources furnished by cooperative private groups. Historian David Beito has recently described the extensive network of mutual aid societies that existed in the United States in the early decades of the twentieth century. Participation in such societies was widespread: in 1920, eighteen million Americans—or 30 percent of all adults over the age of twenty—belonged to fraternal societies.[75] Secret societies like the Masons, Elks, and Odd Fellows could be counted on to provide aid to members in good standing who were in distress, and they built orphanages and homes for elderly members and

[74] Mitchell Duneier, *Slim's Table: Race, Respectability, and Masculinity* (Chicago: University of Chicago Press, 1992), pp. 96–100 and passim.
[75] David Beito, "Mutual Aid for Social Welfare: The Case of American Fraternal Societies," *Critical Review,* vol. 4, no. 4 (1990), p. 711.

their spouses.[76] Fraternal insurance societies played a large social welfare role by offering their members formal insurance policies.[77] Membership in the aid societies was highest among the lowest tiers of wage earners. These societies played a crucial role in resettling the vast wave of immigrants that entered the country around the turn of the century. A 1919 survey of Chicago wage-earning families found that 74.8 percent of the husbands carried life insurance, along with 58.8 percent of the wives and 48.8 percent of the children under age fourteen. Over half the policies carried by husbands were acquired through fraternal orders. Perhaps most startling, the participation rate of black Americans in mutual aid societies was extremely high, rivaling membership in black churches. Black Americans had the *highest* rates of insurance coverage of *any* ethnic group in Chicago in 1919, apparently approaching 95 percent (the widely reported rate of Americans now covered by Social Security).[78]

These fraternal societies practiced exactly the sort of reciprocity that Putnam describes. Consider the remarks of a spokesman for the Modern Woodmen of America (which called its members "Neighbors" and its lodges "camps"):

[A] few dollars given here, a small sum there to help a stricken member back on his feet or keep his protection in force during a crisis in his financial affairs; a sick Neighbor's wheat harvested, his grain hauled to market, his winter's fuel cut or a home built to replace one destroyed by a midnight fire—thus has fraternity been at work among a million members in 14,000 camps.[79]

The mutual aid societies were largely self-managed, and thus they were important political educators, especially among immigrants and the working classes.

The mutual aid societies can be sharply distinguished from later government-sponsored welfare provision by the fact that the aid societies made demands on their members as a condition of participation. Membership was premised on adherence to certain moral standards, and thus, as Beito observes, "[o]ne would be hard pressed to find a fraternal society of any economic class or ethnic group that distributed aid as an unconditional entitlement."[80] Moreover, spokesmen for the fraternal move-

---

[76] *Ibid.*, pp. 712–13.

[77] Before the Depression, fraternal societies dominated the health-insurance market (at least among the working classes). Lodge doctors were hired to care for members for a set fee (*ibid.*, pp. 716–17).

[78] The Illinois Health Insurance Commission estimated in 1919 that 93.5 percent of black families in Chicago had at least one member with life insurance—followed by Bohemians (88.9 percent), Poles (88.4 percent), Irish (88.5 percent), and native whites (85.2 percent). Rates of insurance coverage for blacks were even higher in Philadelphia (*ibid.*, pp. 718–19).

[79] *Ibid.*, p. 713.

[80] *Ibid.*, p. 722.

ment worried precisely that an expanded government role in social welfare would undermine the moral reciprocity on which mutual aid was premised: "The problem of State pensions," they declared, "strikes at the root of national life and character. It destroys the thought of individual responsibility."[81]

Recent social historians have criticized the mutual aid societies for distinguishing between deserving and undeserving poor, and stigmatizing those deemed undeserving. Beito points out that all mutual aid societies of every political stripe imposed morally based restrictions on access to benefits. The socialist Western Miners' Federation, for example, denied benefits to members where "the sickness or accident was caused by intemperance, imprudence or immoral conduct."[82]

Finally, Beito suggests that even where charity organizations and welfare agencies impose behavioral requirements on aid recipients, these will be perceived as less legitimate and credible than norms that emerge from within mutual aid societies. Charity-society admonitions struck a false note, Beito writes,

> not so much in the specific content of the requirements themselves, but because they came from outsiders, most of whom had never been poor. Much like modern welfare-state bureaucrats, early twentieth century charity workers could never truly understand the conditions of the poor nor entirely win their respect. . . . [T]he poor resented and distrusted the impersonal and bureaucratic system that handed them alms.[83]

The rules enforced by mutual aid societies gained their credibility and strength from their nature as horizontally generated and enforced norms. Rules imposed vertically from either charities or state bureaucratic organizations lacked credibility and effectiveness: such rules were not the product of reciprocal mutual commitment, and they were not backed up by the social monitoring of peer groups. Thus, the moral resources and moral education furnished by mutual aid societies stand in sharp contrast with those provided by the welfare state, in which benefits are provided without any behavioral demands (or in which, if behavioral demands are made, they will be ineffective because imposed from the outside). It is crucial, on Beito's account, for aid to spring up from within a moral community, which also generates norms of responsible conduct and means of enforcing these norms.

A crucial task of educational statecraft is to foster a healthy structure and mix of group life. We should, as Tocqueville warned, avoid preempt-

---

[81] *Ibid.*, p. 720.

[82] *Ibid.*, p. 722.

[83] *Ibid.* See also David Beito, "Mutual Aid, State Welfare, and Organized Charity: Fraternal Societies and the 'Deserving' and 'Undeserving' Poor, 1890–1930," *Journal of Policy History*, vol. 5, no. 4 (1993), pp. 419–34, esp. p. 429.

ing associative life by extending centralized political power too far, but that does not mean that we should embrace laissez faire, or that curtailing government is a panacea. Tocqueville himself argued that active citizen participation in political associations complements and encourages active participation in extra-political institutions.[84]

Relatively inclusive political associations can, moreover, help temper the particularism of our narrower and more local affiliations. The two-party system as it has traditionally existed in America, for example, encourages cooperation among disparate interests in broad-based political coalitions. Parties give these coalitions a shared political identity and program that evolves over time, and parties build bridges between local, state, and national institutions and interests.[85] Political parties and other relatively open, inclusive public institutions will play a crucial role, therefore, in fostering broad forms of contact and cooperation across narrower group lines. So public and private groups and associations may have different aptitudes, and neither public nor private associations are panaceas for all that ails us.

Among the tools of community-building and community-shaping that are not much discussed by political scientists are architectural design and urban planning. Christopher Alexander and his associates have argued that today's metropolitan life arrests the development of significantly distinctive subcultures by mixing individuals "irrespective of their life style or culture." Mass societies without opportunities for the development of distinctive subcultures reduce "all life styles to a common denominator" and "[dampen] all significant variety." The appropriate solution is not the creation of insulated ghettoes, but rather a "mosaic of subcultures" supported by some genuine boundedness but not hermetic closure or isolation from outsiders. Alexander and his associates describe ways of "breaking the city" into a "vast mosaic of small and different subcultures," while also encouraging an adequate measure of interaction with outsiders.[86]

Certain virtues are promoted by communities with a geographical, or at least genuinely interactive, basis, and these are not necessarily private. Consider the question of school reform. Many religious schools seem to have an educational advantage because they tap into the right kinds of moral communities—communities of families who genuinely interact with each other. But schools based on choice do not necessarily constitute communities in the relevant sense. While independent private schools may embody certain shared values, they are highly individualis-

---

[84] Tocqueville, *Democracy in America*, pp. 520–22.

[85] See Austin Ranney, "The Political Parties: Reform and Decline," in *The New American Political System*, ed. Anthony King (Washington, DC: American Enterprise Institute, 1980), p. 247.

[86] Christopher Alexander et al., *A Pattern Language: Towns, Buildings, Construction* (New York: Oxford University Press, 1977), pp. 43, 50, and passim.

tic in that the parents who send their children to these schools have no interaction with each other. In fact, Coleman finds that nonreligious private schools have dropout rates that are even higher than those in the public system. Independent private schools seem to lack even the thin forms of community available to public schools, which at least contain students from the same (albeit extensive) geographical area.[87]

Public schools, on the other hand, need not take their bearings solely from the openness and diversity of the Great Society; they need not be "shopping malls." Reformed public schools might develop a focused sense of mission; they might tap into the social capital provided by some neighborhoods or interactive communities of like-minded families; they might even acquire the authority to expel students who do not conform to a school's standards. Paul Hill, Gail Foster, and Tamar Gendler argue that when public schools are not required to serve all the disparate interests of a large school zone, but are allowed to develop a particular educational "focus," they can generate many of the advantages of Catholic schools: a sense of shared purpose, a strong sense of authority within the school, better discipline, and improved academic achievement.[88] The problems of public schooling would seem to have less to do with, as John Chubb and Terry Moe argue, democratic control per se, than with excessive centralization and distance from local interactive communities. Individual choice and market competition are not in themselves educational cure-alls.[89]

It is, likewise, far from obvious that a truly admirable panoply of citizen virtues can be generated solely on the basis of enlightened self-interest, important as this may be. Rotating credit associations and mutual aid groups teach broader and longer-term forms of self-interest along with a number of other important political virtues, but they do not teach all political or moral virtues. They do not, for example, foster beneficence. Beneficence involves, after all, not a series of exchanges for mutual

---

[87] James S. Coleman and Thomas Hoffer, *Public and Private High Schools: The Impact of Communities* (New York: Basic Books, 1987), p. 217.

[88] See Paul T. Hill, Gail E. Foster, and Tamar Gendler, *High Schools with Character* (Santa Monica: Rand, 1990), pp. 15–20, 54–56, and passim. Reform could allow public schools to develop the norms of small societies and the kinds of mechanisms we associate with Catholic schools: uniforms, strict rules about lateness and attendance, and a distinctive sense of mission that is shared by administration, teachers, and students. Of course, the power of teachers' unions is one major obstacle to reform: principals must be freer to select and dismiss staff. Hill et al. suggest that low teacher pay is also a feature of schools with a focused, rather than generalized, sense of mission: it helps insure that teachers share the mission of the school and are not doing the job simply for the money (p. 20). All of this parallels the findings of some important studies of bureaucratic effectiveness; see James Q. Wilson, *Bureaucracy: What Government Agencies Do and Why They Do It* (New York: Basic Books, 1989), esp. pp. 109–10, 366–68.

[89] John E. Chubb and Terry M. Moe, *Politics, Markets, and America's Schools* (Washington, DC: Brookings Institution, 1990).

advantage over time (as modeled by the rotating credit association) but a transfer of resources without the expectation of a return. Acts of beneficence require far-more-substantial moral backup than compliance with schemes of mutual cooperation, in which self-interest may still furnish the basic motive. Beneficence might seem a purely personal virtue, but, as Russell Hardin argues, distributive justice would appear to be a form of beneficence writ large: both involve unreciprocated transfers from the well-off to the less well-off. Both are more difficult to generate than cooperation for mutual advantage.[90]

But how do we foster virtues that go beyond enlightened self-interest, such as beneficence? Religious communities may be especially helpful here. Smith's religious sects may have happy economic and political side-effects, but they are not cooperative schemes for mutual advantage. Religious sects, as Smith described them, promote forms of self-control and discipline more demanding than those promoted by rotating credit associations, and perhaps these are necessary (or at least useful) supports for beneficence and other moral acts which (likewise) must rest on more than considerations of mutual advantage.[91] Tocqueville argued, similarly, that "religious peoples are naturally strong just at the point where democratic peoples are weak," which is to say that religion combats the "inordinate love of material pleasure" that characterizes democratic commercial people.[92]

A political science of group life will acknowledge all of the virtues on which a healthy liberal democracy depends, and attempt to provide for every one. It will not be an exact science or one that permits us to avoid hard moral trade-offs. Local groups may provide moral resources on which liberal democracy depends, but decentralizing authority toward localities, neighborhoods, and particular groups also has its costs. The centralized organizational structures of urban school districts may cause educational pathologies, but these structures also make it possible for public schools to be instruments of integration and inclusion. Localism and particularism have their uses, but they must not be allowed to swallow up an individual's sense of her rights and of the equal political standing of others. In some places, especially rural areas, the educational imperative may still be to encourage the virtues of critical distance on inherited identities. The state plays a legitimate role, as Durkheim argued, in reminding local communities and particular groups that theirs is not the only moral agenda.

---

[90] See the helpful discussion in Russell Hardin, *Morality within the Limits of Reason* (Chicago: University of Chicago Press, 1988), esp. ch. 2.

[91] Of course, one could say that the gains from cooperation are expected to come in the afterlife, and that the cooperative scheme is between sectarians and God.

[92] Tocqueville, *Democracy in America*, pp. 444–45; see also vol. II, Part II, ch. 14.

The liberal political science of group life suggests that we can think more constructively about moral and political education if we think less about the simple and direct means of pedagogy, such as the school curriculum. The very structure of our social lives educates us indirectly, and exerts pervasive influences over our lives. The heavy hand of direct public control may be far from the best way of promoting the character traits and virtues on which our polity depends.

Political Science, Syracuse University

AN AMERICAN CIVIC FORUM: CIVIL SOCIETY BETWEEN MARKET INDIVIDUALS AND THE POLITICAL COMMUNITY

By Benjamin R. Barber

I. Government, the Market, and Civil Society

The polarization of the individual and the community that underlies much of the debate between individualists and communitarians is made possible in part by the literal vanishing of civil society—the domain whose middling terms mediate the stark opposition of state and private sectors and offer women and men a space for activity that is both voluntary and public. Modern democratic ideology and the reality of our political practices sometimes seem to yield only a choice between elephantine and paternalistic government or a radically solipsistic and nearly anarchic private market sector—government gargantuanism or private greed.

Americans do not much like either one. President Clinton's call for national service draws us out of our selfishness without kindling any affection for government. Private markets service our avarice without causing us to like ourselves. The question of how America's decentralized and multi-vocal public can secure a coherent voice in debates over public policy under the conditions precipitated by so hollow and disjunctive a dichotomy is perhaps the most important issue facing both the political theory and social science of democracy and the practice of democratic politics in America today. Two recent stories out of Washington suggest just how grave the situation has become. Health-care reform failed in a paroxysm of mutual recrimination highlighted by the successful campaign of the private sector (well represented in Congress) against a presidential program that seemed to be widely misunderstood. The public at large simply went missing in the debates. Insurance companies, hospitals, doctors, and health-management organizations were heard in private councils and in public. The public was without a voice, and those in search of the public hardly knew where to look: the abyss separating the president and his intended constituents sealed his health plan's doom. Had there been institutions like the "health parliaments" created in Oregon to review the state health plan there, the president's plan might have found greater public understanding and support.

Second, an unrelated but highly pertinent survey taken as health care went under (in September 1994) revealed that only 17 percent of Americans thought their government could solve the problems they faced—down from figures in the sixtieth and seventieth percentiles some years

© 1996 Social Philosophy and Policy Foundation. Printed in the USA.

earlier. This level of cynicism reflects conditions that seem more like a seedbed for revolution than mere alienation, and it provides fodder for the cannons of our multiplying demagogues — people like Ross Perot and Rush Limbaugh who divide the nation into friends and enemies and demonize government and its elected representatives, as if the latter had been parachuted in from outer space. The peculiar logic of "populist" but antidemocratic devices like term limits, supermajorities, and a balanced-budget amendment suggests a public that distrusts not only government but itself, worrying that if left to its own devices it might actually reelect politicians it despises in the regular elections that are a democratic society's natural "term limits" — or that it might make decisions for which it cannot take responsibility.

How did this sorry situation come to pass in a nation that prides itself on its traditions of democracy? How did the classical theory of civil society as articulated in the social contract tradition from John Locke to Jean-Jacques Rousseau and Alexis de Tocqueville get shoved aside in a manner that left postwar social science committed to the bipolar alternatives of radical individualism or coercive communitarianism? I will try presently to answer this question in historical outline, but I want to recognize at the outset that this bipolarity in theory has had disastrous practical consequences. The politically alienated public, equally uncomfortable with what it understands to be a rapacious and unsympathetic government and a fragmented and self-absorbed private sector, finds itself homeless. Although the government is ultimately accountable to the American people, the homeless public confronts it as an almost foreign body: a threatening sphere of quasi-legitimate coercion managed by elected representatives, professional politicians, and bureaucratic managers who have lost much of their authority as authentic voices for the people and the values they supposedly represent.

On the other hand, the private sector, representing the market and constituted by private individuals and corporations, speaks for the public only inasmuch as it aggregates the voices of individuals and companies — private opinions and special interests given a "public" status they do nothing to earn. Not only is the public left voiceless and homeless, but those in government who still try in good faith to receive counsel from the now quite literally phantom public do not really know where to turn, since so-called public opinion polls canvass private prejudice while political parties and assemblies tend to represent special interests and sectarian values and no longer even pretend to seek a larger "national interest." Politicians turn into "professionals" out of touch with their constituencies, while citizens are reduced to whining antagonists of the "professionals" they elect to office — or turn into clients of government services they readily consume without being willing to pay for.

In order to envision a civic entity and imagine (or, as democratic practice, empower) a civic voice to actually speak on its behalf, we need to move beyond the two-celled model of government versus private sector that we have come to rely on. Instead, invoking the traditional language of civil society, we need to begin to think about the actual domains Americans occupy as they go about their daily business as having at least three primary arenas: the government and the private sector to be sure, but also the civil domain: civic space or what was once called "civil society." Civil society, or civic space, occupies the middle ground between government and the private sector. It is the space we occupy when we are engaged neither in government (voting, jury service, paying taxes) nor in commerce (working, producing, shopping, consuming). It is a space defined by such activities as attending church or synagogue, doing community service, participating in a voluntary association, contributing to a charity, assuming responsibility in a parent-teacher association or a neighborhood crime watch or a hospital fund-raising society. Civil society shares with government a sense of publicity and a regard for the general good and the common weal, but unlike government it makes no claims to exercising a monopoly on legitimate coercion. Rather, it is a voluntary and in this sense "private" realm devoted to public goods. It shares with the private sector the gift of liberty: it is voluntary and is constituted by freely associated individuals and groups; but unlike the private sector, it aims at common ground and consensual (that is, integrative and collaborative) modes of action.

Civil society is thus public without being coercive, voluntary without being privatized. It is in this civil domain that such traditional civic institutions as foundations, schools, churches, public-interest organizations, and other voluntary civic associations properly belong. The media too, where they privilege their public responsibilities over their commercial ambitions, are better understood as part of civil society than as part of the private sector. Unhappily, civil society has been eclipsed by bipolarity, and its mediating strengths have been eliminated in favor of the simplistic opposition of state and individual—a regulatory, interventionist government and the free market. Robert Putnam and others have charted this decline in civic and social participation in recent decades. Workaholic men and women newly empowered in the workplace have ever less time for civic or social activity. Everyone worries that voting is down, but participation in everything from parent-teacher associations to bowling leagues is also down by 40 and 50 percent or more, with disastrous consequences for civil society.[1] This leaves Americans with the stark opposition between wholly private commercial activities like shopping and alienating political activities like voting. It forces those wishing to occupy noncoercive civic space back into the private sector where they reappear, quite improperly, as "special-interest" advocates supposedly unmarked

---

[1] See Robert Putnam, "Bowling Alone," *Journal of Democracy*, vol. 6, no. 1 (January 1995), pp. 65–78.

by common concerns or public norms. Environmental associations become "special-interest" pressure groups, and unions become mirror images of employers.

Throughout the first half of the nineteenth century, in Tocqueville's 1830s America and afterward, our society not only reflected but helped codify the three-celled model we have lost in this century. In that era, when (as Tocqueville suggested) liberty was local and civic activity more prevalent, a modest governmental sphere and an unassuming private sector were overshadowed by an extensive civil society tied together by school, church, town, and voluntary associations. Tocqueville used American reality to depict a general theory of democracy:

> Municipal institutions constitute the strength of free nations. Town meetings are to liberty what primary schools are to science; they bring it within the people's reach, they teach men how to use and how to enjoy it. A nation may establish a free government, but without municipal institutions it cannot have the spirit of liberty.[2]

This theory of democracy focused on decentralization and reflected a certain suspicion of all central authority. Hence, the Federalist Constitution and later the Republican Party's federalist statism were by today's benchmark an exercise in civic humility. George Washington governed with an executive staff that numbered only in the dozens, and the states and the people, to whom the Tenth Amendment of the Bill of Rights had left all powers not expressly delegated to the central government by the Constitution, were (as Tocqueville noticed) the real theater for civic action throughout much of the century.

It was only in the late nineteenth century, when individuals who thought of themselves as citizens and groups which were regarded as voluntary associations were supplanted by rapacious corporations legitimized as "legal persons" with limited liability, and in the twentieth century, when voluntary associations began to look more and more like special-interest groups, that market forces began to press in from the private-sector side and encroach on civil society and drive citizens into private markets. For once markets began to expand radically, government responded with an aggressive campaign on behalf of the public weal (but not directly involving the public) against the new monopolies, inadvertently crushing civil society from the state side. Squeezed between the warring realms of the two expanding monopolies, state and corporate, in the course of the years between the two Roosevelts civil society gradually lost its preeminent place in American life. By the time of World War II, civil society had nearly vanished and its civic denizens had been com-

---

[2] Alexis de Tocqueville, *The Spirit of the Laws* (New York: Vintage Books, 1969), vol. 1, ch. 5, p. 63.

pelled to find sanctuary under the feudal tutelage of either big government (their protectors and social servants) or the private sector, where schools, churches, and foundations could assume the identity of corporations and aspire to be no more than special-interest groups formed for the particularistic ends of their members. Whether those ends were, say, market profitability or environmental preservation, was irrelevant, since, by definition all private associations necessarily had private ends. Today there are quite literally no "public spaces" left that are not either commercial (like malls or theme parks) or governmental (a town hall, the Capitol).

Hence, paradoxically, groups organized in defense of the public interest in full employment, dignified work, and a fair distribution of income found themselves cast as mere exemplars of a plundering private-interest association pursuing one more private good. Unions, for example, though concerned with public goods, became the private-sector counterparts of the corporations. When they tried to break the stranglehold of corporations over labor, they were labeled as another special-interest group, no better than those against whom they struck, and perhaps worse (since the companies struck were productive contributors to the wealth of the nation). Environmental groups have undergone the same redefinition more recently. Although pursuing a genuinely public agenda of clean air for all, including the polluters, they have been cast as the polluters' twin — another special-interest group whose interests are to be arbitrated alongside those of toxic-waste dumpers; over time, they have begun to behave that way, hiring lobbyists in Washington to push their own particularistic agendas. Under such conditions, the "public good" could not and did not survive as a reasonable ideal. Its epitaph was written by David Truman, who in his influential 1951 primer *The Governmental Process*, a book that established the dominant paradigm in social science throughout the 1960s and 1970s, summarily wrote that in dealing with the pluralist pressure system of private interests that is America, "we do not need to account for a totally inclusive interest, because one does not exist."[3]

We are left stranded by this melancholy history in an era where civil society is in eclipse and where citizens have neither home for their civic institutions nor voice with which to speak. One can be passively serviced (or passively exploited) by the massive, busybody, bureaucratic state where the word "citizen" has no resonance; or one can sign on to the selfishness and radical individualism of the private sector where the word "citizen" has no resonance. One can be a "citizen," and vote the public scoundrels out of public office, and/or one can be a consumer and exercise one's private rights on behalf of one's private interests: those are the only remaining obligations of the much-diminished office of American citizen.

[3] David Truman, *The Governmental Process* (New York: Viking, 1951), p. 51.

II. CIVIL SOCIETY AND THE PUBLIC VOICE

It is against this background that I want to resuscitate the idea of civil society as a mediating third domain between the overgrown governmental sector and the metastasizing private sector, and thus as a seedbed for the cultivation of citizenship. Critics of big government think that to diminish the encroachments of the state is necessarily to cede power and privilege to the private sector; by the same token, critics of an overly privatized market sector believe that to diminish the corruptions of the private is necessarily to expand government. Anti-statist libertarians and statist communitarians are thus locked in a zero-sum game in which citizens are confronted with a no-win choice between a kind of caricatured Big Brother government that enforces justice but in exchange risks becoming tyrannical, and a kind of caricatured runaway free market that secures liberty but in exchange fosters inequality and social injustice.

Yet democracy is precisely that form of government in which not politicians and bureaucrats but an empowered people use legitimate force to put flesh on the bones of their liberties—and in which liberty carries with it the obligations of social responsibility and citizenship as well as the rights of legal persons. It is that form of government in which rights and responsibilities are two sides of a single civic identity that belongs neither to state bureaucrats nor to private consumers but to citizens alone.

Civil society is the domain of citizens: a mediating domain between private markets and big government. Interposed between the state and the market, it can constrain an obtrusive government without ceding public goods to the private sphere; at the same time, it can dissipate the atmospherics of solitariness and greed that surround markets without suffocating in an energetic big government's exhaust fumes. For *both* government *and* the private sector can be humbled a little by a growing civil society that absorbs some of the public aspirations of government, without casting off its voluntary character as a noncoercive association of equals.

To recreate civil society on this prescription does not necessarily entail a novel civic architecture; rather, it means a reconceptualization and repositioning of institutions already in place. This prescription requires that schools, foundations, community movements, the media, and other civil associations reclaim their public voice and political legitimacy against those who would write them off as hypocritical special interests. It offers the abstract idea of a public voice a palpable geography somewhere other than in the atlas of government, and thus represents a crucial starting-place in answering the question, posed at the outset of this essay, of whether there is a mediating space between the state and the market. Finally, it suggests that through common work, civil society might emerge from the eclipse into which is was propelled, first, by the rapid growth of the private market sector in the 1880s and 1890s (when American corporate energy first exploded), and, second, by the mirror-image expansion of government as it tried to contain the growth of the Gilded Age's predatorily productive monopoly corporations (before World War I) — an expansion that was further augmented by government's attempt to offer social safety-nets for and a contrapuntal balance to a Depression-damaged, corporation-dominated private sector in the period of the New Deal.

It is not enough to offer a theoretical argument on behalf of the notion of civil society as a mediating public space between the community and the individual or between the government and the private sector. It is also necessary to confront the practical implications of a theory which may be adequate but which does not yet have a practice: to take a further step and raise in a concrete fashion the practical question of what it means to speak of and institutionalize a genuinely public voice in American political debate. Where might a president interested in the public view of health care turn? The opinion polls? A television town meeting? Hardly.

As I understand it, the public voice is nothing other than the voice of civil society, the voice of what one might call an American civic forum. That term gets its contemporary resonance from Central and Eastern Europe, where dissidents who wished to speak publicly yet apart from and against government adopted the language of civil society. Vàclav Havel in Czechoslovakia used the civic language to great effect and was rewarded with the presidency of his newly democratized country. In East Germany, a group calling itself "Neues Forum" (New Forum) established a public voice for the dissidents which helped bring down the Communist regime and the Berlin Wall. Ironically, East Europeans thought they were borrowing an American language (and an American practice) of civil society. Perhaps Americans can return the favor by borrowing back the borrowed language.

Giving the public voice a legitimate articulation in an American civic forum is, then, the first priority of anyone who wishes to invest that once sublime title "citizen" with renewed meaning. Too often, however, the meaning of "public" is left indeterminate, a hostage to enthusiastic but ultimately vacant rhetoric. If the idea of a public voice is to be taken seriously as theory or as practice, its characteristics must be clearly rendered. A public voice is not this or that voice, just any voice that happens to address the public—for in this sense all voices seeking to be heard are public. The divisive rant of talk radio is in fact a perfect model of everything that public talk is *not*: people talking without listening, confirming not problematizing dogmas, convicting rather than convincing adversaries, passing along responsibility to others for everything that has gone wrong in their lives. Much of what passes for journalism is in fact mere titillation or dressed-up gossip or polite prejudice. The opinion makers (manipulators) who yell at one another on *Crossfire* demonstrate how long a journey it can be for women and men nurtured in the private sector to find their way to civil society as its measured public voice. Journalist and pundit George Will has ridiculed the idea of a national conversation on the meanings of America proposed by Sheldon Hackney (director of the National Endowment for the Humanities), pointing to the endless talk shows as proof that we are holding more conversations than ever. But whatever else they may be—demagoguery, commerce, entertainment, politics—these media happenings are *not* conversations but their precise contrary.

Among the characteristics that render voice public (and are quite missing in media talk) are the following nine—which, to be sure, stand in a relationship of some tension to one another:

1. *Commonality.* The public voice speaks in terms that evidence and elicit common ground, cooperative strategies, overlapping interests, and a sense of the public weal. This means it must do more than simply aggregate private voices; yet at the same time it must avoid imposing some heteronomous moral that good citizens have not participated in constructing. A common voice is shared by individuals qua individuals (and thus reflects the interests of individuals), but it denotes something they have in common (what defines them as a community).

2. *Deliberativeness.* The public voice is deliberative, which means that it is critically reflective as well as self-aware; it must be able to withstand reiteration, critical cross-examination, and the test of time—which guarantees a certain distance and dispassion and requires a certain provisionality that precludes final closure. Like all deliberative voices, the public voice is dialectical: it transcends contraries without surrendering their distinctiveness (just as a good marriage between strong individual partners makes them one without eliminating their distinctive identities).

3. *Inclusiveness.* The public voice is inclusive, which is to say that its mode is outreaching and multi-vocal. This might seem to contradict the need for commonality; but, rather than denying difference, democratic commonality acknowledges and incorporates it. It does so via sharing rather than through the subordination of the individual by some putatively trans-individual or holistic community. Commonality secured by exclusion, though it can establish a coherent closed community, denies both freedom and equality—essential constitutive elements of any legitimate public voice in a democracy. Multi-vocality and its twin, dissent, are together the real test of inclusiveness. A public voice provides a microphone for those on the margins, those disempowered by the hegemonies of government and the monopolies of the private sector. The debates of the private sector are clublike: discretionary, self-selecting, subject to exclusion. The debates of government, while technically open to all, are too often professional and technocratic and thus in their own way closed. To be part of the voice of civil society is both a right and an obligation, and thus can be denied to no one. Inclusiveness has costs: it can foment anarchy. To achieve multi-vocality without reducing the public voice to a cacophony of special pleadings or irreconcilable interests is a high art

and calls for special civic practices. Common talk that excludes may be unitary and clear, but it is undemocratic and ultimately perilous to individuals. Inclusiveness that results in Babel (or babble) is democratic but unproductive and ultimately perilous to community.

4. *Provisionality.* Because a public that is open and inclusive is itself an evolving political entity, the public voice is always provisional and subject to subsequent emendation, evolution, and even contradiction. Public dialogue is ongoing, and there can be no finality, no terminus, but only a series of provisional resting-points where action becomes possible prior to the initiation of further debate. This is perhaps why Jefferson recommended a little revolution every nineteen or twenty years, and suggested that principles which we have not embraced as our own, generation by generation, lose their legitimacy, however constitutional their origin and however just their substance.[4] This feature of the public voice immunizes it to dogmatism and reflects the essentially tolerant and open-minded spirit of democracy. It explains why no public can be bound by its predecessors or bind its successors, and why each generation must express its own faith in constitutional democracy all over again.

5. *Listening.* The public voice is also a public ear, for the skills of listening are as important to finding common ground as the skills of talking. Private interests can be identified and articulated simply by *speaking* authentically out of one's own needs and wants. Public interests can be identified and articulated only when individuals *listen* to one another — only when they modulate their own voices so that the voices of others can be heard, assimilated, and accommodated, if not fully harmonized. If government opts for "parliaments" where talking (from *parler*) and the differential skills it exhibits are privileged, the civic forum demands an "audioment" where the more egalitarian skills of listening are nurtured. Like Quakers, citizens ought not to fear silence in their civil assemblies. Only when the articulate are silent, are the weak, uncertain voices of the inarticulate and powerless likely to join the conversation and be heard. Listening thus becomes one powerful guarantor of inclusiveness.

6. *Learning.* Just as the public voice requires a public ear, so to participate in public talk is necessarily to learn — to be capable of questioning opinions formerly held and changing positions formerly taken. When talk is merely an exchange of fixed opinions and politics is merely a series of compromises in which positions are arbitrated but never altered, citizenship is impaired. Imagine a *Crossfire* in which one pigheaded pundit declared to another: "I hadn't thought of that! Yes, perhaps I need to review my ideas and reposition myself." Imagine a squawk radio host

---

[4] "The tree of liberty must be refreshed from time to time, with the blood of patriots and tyrants. It is its natural manure" (Thomas Jefferson, Letter to Colonel Smith, November 13, 1787, in *The Life and Selected Writings of Thomas Jefferson*, ed. Adrienne Koch and William Peden [New York: Random House, 1993], p. 403).

confessing to a listener: "I think I understand you [liberals, conservatives, right-to-life partisans, choice partisans] better now. I want to take a few days to really think about what you've said; I may just have to change my mind." Unimaginable? Probably, because talk on the radio is not about learning or changing but about confirming dogmas and reiterating prejudices, closing and sealing the gates of the mind's fort before the enemy (somebody else's ideas) can get inside. Yet polarizing talk is not simply a result of crass broadcast journalism, it is built into the idea that individuals are defined as citizens by their immutable and irreducible interests, and that conversation can do little more than offer an opportunity for the articulation and adjudication of these interests. Learning, on the other hand, entails the mutability of opinion and the susceptibility of viewpoints to modification and growth.

7. *Lateral communication.* The dialogue between government and private-sector voters is most often a vertical conversation between elites and followers, where leaders talk *at* their constituents and occasionally are talked *to* by them. The public voice entails a *lateral* conversation *among* citizens rather than between them and their "leaders." One clear sign of the eclipse of civil society has been the disappearance of those nongovernmental spaces where citizens can talk to one another. Commercial malls and centerless suburbs rob us of our open public squares, what Harry Boyte calls our "free spaces," where we can talk with and listen to one another.[5] The few public institutions left to us are underfunded, overwhelmed, and under siege. In trying to function in an era of antipathy to government, when civil society is no longer recognized, public schools and universities are compelled to sell themselves in the private sector—turning over classrooms to K-III Corporation's sponsors (the current owners of Chris Whittle's Channel One, which brings soft news and ads to twelve thousand American schools) to get desperately needed electronic hardware, or writing single-vendor contracts with corporations like Coca-Cola that have promised institutions like Rutgers University millions of dollars in return for exclusive sales rights and a piece of the university's good name. Churches accommodate themselves to privatization and become instruments of a divisive, extremist politics and of demagogic leaders rather than of ecumenical integration and lateral communication among parishioners. The media are subordinated to commerce and thus privatized, selling gossip and scandal and instant opinion rather than offering an information window on the public world.

A certain kind of logrolling politics can come from vertical elite-to-masses conversation, but the public voice emerges only from lateral conversation; and in the absence of appropriate arenas, the civic forum must discover a new geography for conversation.

[5] See Harry Boyte and Sara Evans, *Free Spaces* (New York: Harper and Row, 1986).

8. Imagination. Public voice is impossible in the absence of imagination, which counts as the single most important mark of the effective citizen. It is through imagination that private interests are stretched and enlarged to encompass the interests of others—through imagination that the wants and needs of others are seen to resemble our own—through imagination that the welfare of the extended communities to which we belong is recognized as the condition for the flourishing of our own interests. What is the bigot other than the man without imagination? The woman unable to see beyond her own color or religion into the kindred soul of a being different but the same? The public voice grows out of imagination and nourishes imagination. It permits a private self to empathize with the interests of others, not as an act of altruism but as a consequence of self-interest imaginatively reconstructed as common interest. It is not an accident that theorists as diverse as Hume and Rousseau saw in imagination and empathy the key to humankind's social skills.

9. Empowerment. Public talk capacitates; for talk that is shared becomes the basis for action, turning talkers into doers. Rights are things we can claim for ourselves against others, and they often entail being left alone. In their "laissez-faire" form, they can mandate *in*action. Responsibilities involve us with others and require that we act along with them. Talk that does not foresee action and thus look forward to consequences is just a game. Nothing that is said really counts. Talk aimed at common work and actions disciplines itself, empowering the talkers to collaborate and deal with conflict, solve problems, secure common goals. If talk is provisional (that is one of its strengths, we have seen), action insists that provisionality yield moments of rest and closure where a decisive action is possible. Thus, the "public" in public talk looks to a world of public action whose ineluctably public consequences are an integral part of what comprises its "publicness." In this respect, public talk stands in sharp contrast to private talk, where nothing common is at stake and where arguments may be pursued endlessly, since nothing turns on their outcome (or even on their having an outcome). But public talk results in action, so that a failure to reach a decision (a nondecision) is itself a kind of action with its own public consequences.

One reason why media talk has perhaps become so irresponsible is that it has been divorced from action. Journalists are merely selling papers, television news departments are selling commercial spots. Anything goes, because nobody is going anywhere. Rush Limbaugh cites unnamed sources that charge President Clinton with murder (supposedly having ordered the death of adversaries in Arkansas), because it is all just talk—funning and fuming to pump up the ratings on which the prices of commercial spots are based. A grand jury indictment on charges of homicide is a rather different matter. Talk concerning action has to be responsible, precisely because it has consequences. Public talk is thus civil society's special form of power: it sets the agenda for common action and provides the language by which a community can pursue its goods — or indict its own failure to pursue goods. Whether it empowers is hence a crucial test of whether talk is genuinely public.

A public voice, then — a voice that is common, deliberative, inclusive, provisional, willing to listen and able to learn, rooted in lateral communication and both founded on and encouraging to imagination, and capable of empowering those who speak — is a voice inflected very differently from either the officially univocal voice of government or the obsessively contrary talk of the private sector's multiple special interests. These nine characteristics, although teased out of the practices of groups seeking to speak publicly, are clearly normative and can be realized in practice only with the help of special institutions designed to foster them. It is here that the real challenge to democratic proponents of civil society is found, since while prospective participants of civil society already nominally belong to the current political system and need only to reposition (and perhaps redefine) themselves to occupy mediating space, the institutions that allow those organizations to nurture an actual public voice with the crucial characteristics enumerated here are for the most part still to be created.

III. ESTABLISHING A CIVIC FORUM

Elsewhere (in my book *Strong Democracy*) I have suggested a series of institutions — including local assemblies, national service, the election of assemblypersons by sortition (by lot, as with jury pools), the civic uses of new technologies, common work, and a number of other innovations — as a starting-place for establishing a stronger form of democracy in a modern society. Such institutions would certainly help revive the idea of civil society and give the American civic forum a place to begin.[6] The notion of a "civic forum" suggests not a single institutional entity at one particular time and place but an umbrella entity that encompasses a variety of civil-society practices, some of which can be legislated by government, some of which require incentives, and some of which can be produced directly by citizens and their associations. The idea reflects the practice of many extant organizations such as American Health Decisions, the Industrial Areas Foundation (from its founder Saul Alinsky to its current heroes like Ernie Cortez), the Oregon Health Parliament, the National Issues Forums of the Kettering Foundation, the Study Circles Movement, policy juries, deliberative video town meetings (see James Fishkin's work, for example),[7] and many other practical and ongoing experiments in delib-

---

[6] See Benjamin R. Barber, *Strong Democracy: Participatory Politics for a New Age* (Berkeley: University of California Press, 1984), ch. 10.

[7] James Fishkin has proposed a form of deliberative television polling that brings together several hundred citizens in a television studio and, over several days of interaction with one another, and with politicians and experts, helps them develop more deliberative

eration and consensus-building among citizens who—without thinking of themselves as constituting a government or public authority—come together around their common aspirations as well as their conflicting interests. For a historical model we might return to the Committees of Correspondence of the Revolutionary War era in America, which gathered citizens together informally in bodies that were neither governmental nor private but which together forged the civic matériel by which the new Republic was first won and then constituted.

One possible centerpiece for a viable civic forum might be a series of video-linked teleconference town meetings. As with New England's "representative" town meetings (where a sample of a large town's population meets to represent the rest of the town), meetings of the civic forum would represent a sampling of institutional citizens of civil society (foundations, schools, voluntary associations, civic groups, social movements) that might change over time. They could be chosen on the basis of rotating principles or even, as many ancient Greek magistrates and juries were, by sortition. Sortition (the lottery) assumes the civic competence of every player in civil society (and in doing so helps forge that competence) and assumes that any particular group of players drawn from civil society's constituents is as likely as any other group to be able to work toward a set of common goods and civic interests. Since Americans regularly turn over life-and-death capital decisions to juries chosen randomly from voter lists, I see no good reason why sortition cannot also be used in other civic domains.

Some will object that the idea of a civic forum is redundant in a bipolar world where government, with its legislatures and representative assemblies, is intended to offer civil society an ear and a voice. Surely democratic government itself offers citizens opportunities for public voice and social organization. In a well-ordered regime, it might actually play such a role; in democratic theory, it is certainly supposed to. But America's political house is in a state of disorder. Both in the United States and elsewhere in the West, people confront their public authorities with a deep suspicion of the professional political classes and a cynicism about the role of government. We have seen the level of trust in government decline to 17 percent, the plummeting voter turnouts, the deep disillusion with government at every level. This has led to a wholesale abdication by citizens of responsibility for what their elected representatives do—a raging "blame-itus" that condemns government and makes litigation a primary mode of interaction with fellow citizens, especially in the litigation-crazed United States, where lawyers have always had too much influence. It is

---

and sophisticated views. In 1994, Channel Four in the United Kingdom successfully broadcast a Fishkin meeting, and PBS is planning a similar experiment for the presidential elections of 1996. For the background, see James Fishkin, *Democracy and Deliberation* (New Haven: Yale University Press, 1991).

as if, even in "functioning democracies," there is a sense of illegitimacy that forces citizens to look elsewhere than to government itself in forging themselves as a public. Here again the Committees of Correspondence seem apt models: for they represented citizens who had quasi-colonial representative institutions of their own which, however, they did not feel belonged to them. They sought a novel form of interaction that acknowledged their commonality but was extra-governmental. The aim in a modern democracy is not, of course, to create an alternative or parallel government, or even an alternative legislative forum, but rather to help citizens and their many voluntary civic institutions find a common voice in which they can speak in turn both to the private sector and to the government. Rather than displace institutions currently speaking for government and the market, a civic forum would add a new layer that might reinvigorate the others and prepare the way for the relegitimation of government. We do not need a third political party but a third sector in which citizens can rediscover their civic competence and repossess the two parties they already have. We do not need a new form of government but citizens willing to take responsibility for the old form of government.

The fact that America is such a vast country and is decentralized economically, geographically, and ethnographically makes conceptualizing a civic forum both more necessary and more challenging than it might be. For while these conditions guarantee diversity and multi-vocality, they would appear to make common ground far more difficult to secure. It was the vast scale and heterogeneity of modern mass societies that created the imperative for representative government in the first place and forced amendments in the direct participatory institutions of earlier township republics and principalities; and it was representative government that, following the iron law of oligarchy, in time distanced citizens from their delegates and compromised the legitimacy of representative democracy. The solution to the problem of mass society grew in time to become the problem. A revitalization of civil society is a way to circumvent the abuses of representation while at the same time refurbishing its legitimacy. A credible public voice gives citizens an alternative mode of expression and weans them from dependency on public-opinion polls and the media, permitting the better angels of their nature (usually muzzled in a privatized, cynical society) to speak freely. The challenge is to find a voice that is sufficiently encompassing to allow almost all of those who occupy civil society to feel that they are represented by it—a voice which still has sufficient coherence and commonality to speak for the citizenry as a whole. Too great an emphasis on representativeness might lead to a civic forum in which everyone feels well-represented but which has nothing coherent, nothing in common to say. Too great an emphasis on commonality and coherence might mean a voice that speaks distinctly and forcefully but that leaves a great many out—above all, those already disenfranchised by conventional power relations in society as it is presently organized.

Back in the early 1950s, as modern positivistic social science established its hegemony in the American academy, many social scientists insisted that public goods and public interests simply could not exist in so large, diversified, and pluralistic a nation, and they developed the theory of a two-celled political system noted above in which there was only a government voice (which was official but not consensual) and a private cacophony of pluralistic voices (in which no commonality at all was detectable). These social scientists were, to be sure, recognizing a new reality: American society had grown to a point where the scale of civil society complicated the task of discovering anything like a public interest or common goods. But the social science they constructed also reinforced the difficulty and seemed to suggest that any pursuit of commonality would be an exercise in futility. Instead, government simply became an arbiter among private interests, while the much-deprecated notion of public interest was defined as little more than the aggregation of those interests. The task today, then, in theory no less than in practice, is to reilluminate public space for a civil society in eclipse. Unless a third way can be found between private markets and coercive government, between anarchistic individualism and dogmatic communitarianism, we seem fated to live out our lives in an era where, in the space where America's public voice should be heard, there will be instead a raucous babble that leaves the nation's civic soul forever mute.

Political Science, Walt Whitman Center for the Culture and Politics of Democracy, Rutgers University

DISTRIBUTIONAL PROBLEMS: THE HOUSEHOLD AND THE STATE

By James S. Coleman

With the development of the division of labor, the household has declined in importance as a unit of economic production. Yet even as the individual wage earner has assumed a central place in modern exchange economies, the household has still been seen as an important unit of distribution, in which wage earners provide for their non-income-producing family members. With the breakdown of the family in recent decades, however, the communal income-sharing function of the family has, in significant part, been taken over by the state.

In this essay, I examine this fundamental change in the structure of production and distribution in modern exchange economies. Going beyond this, I propose a new structure of markets — markets for rights to influence collective decision-making within a society. Such markets, I suggest, would provide a source of income for each member of the society.

I. THE HOUSEHOLD ECONOMY AND THE EXCHANGE ECONOMY

In a society consisting of households producing in a subsistence economy, each household produces most of what it consumes. Throughout history, until about a hundred years ago, this remained the economic structure for most households in even the most economically advanced societies.[1] In such a structure, problems concerning the distribution of economic goods are confined to problems concerning the distribution of the resources (principally land) through which those goods are produced. Any inefficiencies in the functioning of society introduced by imperfect macrosocial institutions are minor in scope, because society consists of many weakly interacting, small social systems, each nearly self-contained.

As subsistence household economies gave way to exchange economies, the principal method of distribution of economic goods that replaced the old system was merely an extension of what had already existed in the economic superstructure that went beyond households: an exchange of wages for labor, and a use of the labor (largely by new corporate actors) to produce goods which were then exchanged for the money that had

[1] It was not until around 1890 that more than half the members of the male labor force in the United States were employed outside agriculture. While agriculture at that time was not the only basis for subsistence households, most agricultural production was subsistence farming.

 © 1996 Social Philosophy and Policy Foundation. Printed in the USA.

been paid in wages. A large interdependent system has replaced the multiple, largely independent, economic systems of each household. Government policies played an increasing role as the single economy replaced the separate ones. Among sociologists it is probably Emile Durkheim who has written most perceptively about this transformation, in his *Division of Labor.*[2] We have experienced this system in large scale only in the past century, however, and have not yet experienced it in full bloom, with full specialization; thus, we do not know whether this double-exchange system — of wages for labor, and consumption goods for wages — is better, in some loosely specified sense, than other possible systems of economic distribution. Nor do we know whether our political institutions, designed for a minimalist role, are appropriate to the vastly more powerful role they now occupy. Marx, writing very early in this transformation, attempted to devise a different system, but one that was doomed to failure through an incorrect conception of the nature of man. By failing to recognize that a socialist system would, like all socioeconomic systems, be populated with rational self-interested persons, Marx created a system that lacked the kind of incentive structures which would motivate productive action.

A major virtue of the double-exchange system is that it retains much of the incentive structure of the household economy. Through the double exchange, consumption goods are obtained by labor, so that consumption depends, at the level of the individual (or the unit within which there is communal consumption), upon production. The system results in the operation of what Adam Smith called the invisible hand, by which (when other conditions are satisfied) the satisfaction of all is increased.

There are, however, subtle differences between the incentive structure of the household economy and the incentives of the employee in the exchange economy. Corporate actors have great difficulty in creating incentives for employees that in fact make wages depend upon production. The sources of this difficulty are several. First, much production is a complex joint-product of the labor of a number of employees. Though corporate actors attempt to establish incentive systems that maintain their employees' productive viability, such attempts are far from successful when the corporate actor is large and its products are the result of complex interactions of employees.

A second source of the difficulty is the fact that corporate actors are involved in several types of markets, only one of which is the labor market. These other markets include the capital market, the raw materials market, the capital equipment market, and the product market. As a consequence of the organization of each of these markets, a corporation can sometimes take from one market and give to another. The most common

[2] Emile Durkheim, *The Division of Labor in Society* [1893], trans. George Simpson (New York: Free Press, 1947).

example is when a corporation passes wage increases given up in labor-management negotiations on to the consumer. This is possible because the power of labor in its market is greater than the power of consumers in theirs.

Because of these possibilities, employees have a second incentive in addition to their incentive to engage in productive labor. They have an incentive to engage in an activity which is socially unproductive: to attempt to capture some of the value that goes to other markets in which the corporate actor is engaged. This can be exemplified by the excess wages, compared to those for comparable occupations in other sectors of the economy, that have traditionally been received by employees of automobile manufacturers in the United States. Corporations which manufacture and sell automobiles have a very dispersed and unorganized set of consumers in their product market, and until recent years have confronted only the weak competition in their product market that often occurs in concentrated industries. However, they have much greater pressure from their well-organized union employees in the labor market. The result has been the manufacturers' ability to "pass through" employee wage increases to consumers.[3] The evidence in this example is strengthened by the fact that in the 1980s and 1990s, since the entry of intense foreign competition in the product market, wages of unionized employees of automobile manufacturers have risen very little.[4]

[3] Another example of the effects of nonproductive activities like wage bargaining in the economy is provided by farmers. Farmers are in a set of markets that have nearly the opposite social structure from that of automobile manufacturers. The suppliers of their inputs (farm-implement manufacturers, chemical companies which manufacture fertilizers and pesticides, and seed suppliers) are much larger and more concentrated than they. Their product markets, in contrast, are as highly competitive as any product market in the economy.

It is true, of course, that farmers confront an inelastic demand, and have an especially large component of random variation in output, due to weather. These conditions, however, are insufficient to account for the especially poor economic position of farmers in modern corporate society, as compared to their position in earlier social systems.

A result is that farmers are in a much worse economic position, relative to others in the economy, than was true before the growth of the corporate economy. While their fathers and grandfathers may have worked harder than their counterparts who were employed at jobs in the city, they nevertheless had leisure, spending Saturdays in the local market-town and relaxing on Sundays. Farmers today, in order to earn a living, work their fields at night by tractor headlights as well as on Saturdays and Sundays; and one or more family members often augment the family income by working at a job in town.

On the side of the farmers' inputs, employees of the corporations that supply them have an incentive to increase their own wages at the expense of prices passed through to farmers. Farmers can increase their income only through increasing their productivity. They are not employees, and their product markets are competitive-auction markets. They are squeezed between an irresistible force and an immovable object. They constitute the principal portion of the economy lying outside the broad segment of the economy populated by corporate actors as employers and natural persons as employees.

[4] Perhaps the best comparison of wages is with other firms in the automobile industry that are parts suppliers to the automobile manufacturers. These firms are generally small and highly competitive, and their principal customers are not consumers, but the large automobile manufacturers. Confronted with this structure, they cannot pass through wage increases to the customer. The result is that their employees—engaged in the same kinds of activities as their counterparts employed by the auto manufacturers, but not covered by

As this example suggests, the structure of the economy results in distributional inequity among different sectors. This is due to the different capability (because of the social structure of the markets in which they are engaged) of different actors to increase their income through nonproductive activity, whether through lobbying in the political arena or through maneuvering in imperfect markets.

Another difference between the incentive structure of the household economy (which I take as the reference point not because of its historical precedence, but because it provides a direct link between productive activity and the consumable goods produced) and the incentive structure of wage employment in the exchange economy lies in the categorical rather than continuous nature of the latter. An employee has a full-time job or is unemployed. While there is sometimes "overtime work" and "part-time work," employment is ordinarily for a fixed period of time, such as a forty-hour week. An employee cannot vary his productivity (and his wage) by the simple device of varying the amount of time he spends working, except for a single all-or-none decision. If demand for a product slackens, the employer cannot, for efficiency reasons, reduce incrementally the time worked and wages earned by each employee. The employer reduces the number of workers, resulting in no change for some and a zero wage for others.

These are some of the differences between the incentives confronting natural persons in an economic system of direct production-consumption — such as occurs in a household subsistence economy — and an economic system based on a division of labor, wage employment of natural persons by corporate actors, and an exchange economy. It is nevertheless true that a major virtue of the double-exchange system (wages for labor, and consumption goods for wages) is that it retains much of the incentive structure of the subsistence economy. The absence of such an incentive structure is not only the source of the failure of Marx's "scientific socialism"; it is also the source of the failure of some large corporations in capitalist economies to maintain competitive viability.

II. Social Change and the Emerging Failure of the Double-Exchange System

There is a fundamental assumption involved in relying on the double-exchange system as a means of distributing consumption goods in a

---

the collective-bargaining agreements which are negotiated corporation-wide for the auto manufacturers — are paid less.

This pattern is not confined to the American domestic automobile industry, but is even more pronounced in Japan. Another illustration of the wage differential is the sale by General Motors in the late 1970s of its Frigidaire subsidiary. The sale was brought about by a two-dollar-an-hour wage differential between Frigidaire workers, covered by the GM–United Auto Workers wage agreements, and the wages of employees of other refrigerator manufacturers, in an industry where the product market was more competitive.

highly interconnected economic system with an extreme division of labor, a system consisting of corporate actors as employers and natural persons as employees. This is the assumption that there is an informal "second round" of distribution beyond the market, via the household and the extended family. The household has been the unit within which wages — extracted by one member, the "wage earner" or "breadwinner," from the new corporate actors through labor—have been redistributed communally for consumption. But the household has fragmented as the family has fragmented. The first fragmentation came as the three-generational economic unit (which may have been in one household or in more than one, but which was largely a single economic unit for purposes of consumption), containing a breadwinner in an income-earning stage of life, gave way to nuclear economic units. The smaller nuclear units which replaced the extended economic unit did not each contain a wage earner: those individuals who were past the income-earning stage of life were without earnings, and those who were dependents, previously tucked away in corners of households, were cast adrift.

The impact of this fragmentation of the extended income-sharing unit was softened (and the fragmentation itself thereby hastened) through the intervention of pensions—both private, financed through one's own earnings at an earlier age, and public, financed through government via taxes on the earnings of all.

The next stage of the decline of the communal income-distribution function of the family arose as the nuclear family itself began to break apart, and as children have come to be produced and raised on a wide scale in households with no wage earner—either through the dissolution of marriage or through the production of children in the absence of marriage. This stage, which began in the last third of the twentieth century, has effectively destroyed a large portion of the family's communal income-sharing function.[5] Figure 1 shows one manifestation of this: the proportion of households without children in the United States from 1870 to 1983.[6] The fraction of the national income distributed to households

---

[5] The extremely high rate of defection of divorced income-earning fathers from payment of alimony is a strong indicator of the fact that income redistribution even to one's own children is ineffective once the household as a living unit is broken. Economists who have examined the effect of marriage dissolution on income available to children have found the effect to be very large.

[6] The data in Figure 1 represent the percentage of households with no children under age eighteen. Data for 1950 through 1980 are from U.S. Bureau of the Census, *Historical Statistics of the United States, Colonial Times to 1970* (Washington, DC: U.S. Government Printing Office, 1975), supplemented by U.S. Bureau of the Census, *Statistical Abstracts of the United States: 1947, 1949, 1984* (Washington, DC: U.S. Government Printing Office, 1947, 1949, 1984). Data for 1930 are from the 1930 census report, using interpolation because figures reported were for children under age twenty-one; see U.S. Bureau of the Census, *Census of Population, 1930* (Washington, DC: U.S. Government Printing Office, 1931). A data point for 1875 was obtained by use of Edward Pryor's analysis of family structure in Bristol, Rhode Island, recalculated using all households as the base; see Edward T. Pryor, Jr.,

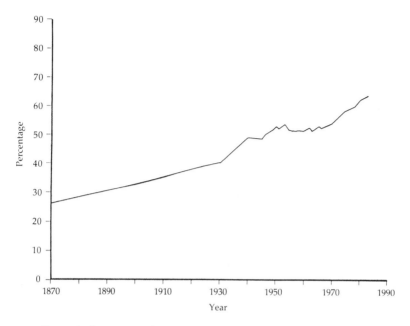

FIGURE 1. Percentage of households without children under eighteen.

with children—and thus the fraction of the society's income available for the raising of children—has declined precipitously as the fraction of households with no children increases.

The actual loss of income available for child-rearing in the United States is suggested by Figure 2, which gives the proportion of persons below the poverty line in 1982.[7] If this fraction were constant over all age-groups, it would indicate that the system of distributing income in the society was age-neutral. If, for example, each household had within it representatives of all age segments of society, in proportion to their total numbers, and if households were the unit of communal distribution, the system would be age-neutral. As Figure 2 indicates, the distribution system is far from age-neutral, with the youngest children the most disadvantaged by the system.

The capability of the double-exchange system to distribute consumption goods depends on an assumption that no longer holds: that households are effective institutions for a second round of distribution beyond

---

"Rhode Island Family Structure, 1875–1960," in *Household and Family in Past Time*, ed. Peter Laslett (Cambridge: Cambridge University Press, 1972), pp. 571–89. In the same volume (p. 80), a sample from Bristol, Rhode Island, is reported as having 13 percent of households without children in 1689.

[7] This figure is reproduced from Samuel Preston, "Children and the Elderly," *Scientific American*, vol. 251, no. 6 (1984), pp. 44–49.

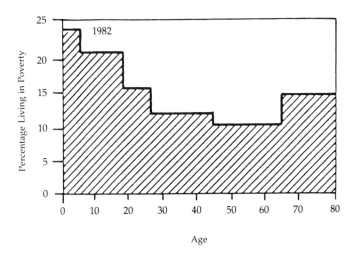

FIGURE 2. Incidence of poverty by age group in the U.S. in 1982.

the market economy. This assumption has been made invalid by the family's decline as a communal unit of income distribution. Exchange economies have always depended on a communal unit, the family, outside the exchange economy, within which income has been distributed approximately on the basis of need, rather than on the basis of contribution.

Thus, as the family is decreasingly capable of redistributing income, the fraction of the population of natural persons who receive income through the distribution system declines. The volume of transfer payments from these persons through government to those who are "dependent" undergoes a continuous increase.

The conclusion that this leads to is straightforward: the double-exchange system is not viable as a distribution system in an economy of abundance when the family no longer serves as a communal distribution unit outside the exchange economy. The money wage paid to employees can be regarded as a drawing right on the aggregate product of all of the society's productive activity; but in an economy of abundance and a society not organized in families, a distribution of these drawing rights through productive work leaves a large fraction of society's members without drawing rights.

Attempts to repair this increasingly large deficiency of the system have been undertaken entirely through a formal second round of distribution after taxation; but this redistribution creates incentives that tend to defeat the first round of distribution through wages for productive activity.[8]

---

[8] For arguments about the importance of these incentives in the United States, see Charles Murray, *Losing Ground* (New York: Basic Books, 1984).

What has not been attempted is a consideration of alternative systems under which these drawing rights might be provided, in such a way that no disincentive to contribute to the aggregate product would be created. To begin with, we may ask how the family, as a communal unit, has solved the problem of disincentives to contribute to its aggregate product. If the family can be seen as the one social unit that has successfully carried out distribution principally on the basis of need, rather than principally on the basis of contribution, then how has it done so? One answer is that it has done so only very imperfectly. There are wives who see their husbands as ne'er-do-wells, and spend their lives struggling to provide an income that the husband will not. There are husbands who see their nonworking wives as sloths, interested only in consuming. Families often have difficulties in inducing their children, employed and living at home, to contribute to the family budget. The extended families of the past often contained an uncle or cousin who was said to spend his life sponging off of his relatives.

Nevertheless, families appear to overcome the disincentive or free-rider problem better than other social units. The means by which they do so appear to be largely social-psychological: the use of stigma to brand noncontributors, and rewards of status and power within the family for those who contribute more than their share.

These are kinds of incentive structures that appear to be effective only in very small social units. In fact, it may be that the size of the unit within which there is communal redistribution on the basis of need has been limited primarily by the size of a unit within which these social-psychological benefits and costs can be effective. This size will of course be larger if the unit within which stigma, reputation, deference, and power are effective is larger.

Yet the social structure of a corporate economy of abundance (a social structure in which persons need one another less, and thus have less opportunity to accumulate social capital) is one in which the size of such social-psychologically effective units is small and becoming smaller. There may be means of reconstituting such groups, whether via the family or via a new institution, thus reviving communal redistribution as a robust complement to primary distribution through the double-exchange economy. Yet apart from scattered and generally short-lived experiments with urban communes by the young, there is little to suggest how such units might be constituted.

The alternative in modern corporate societies with capitalist economies has been for the state to carry out this redistribution through taxation. Taxation for redistribution can be seen (as Arthur Okun has described it)[9] as a second-round redistribution that follows the first-round distribution

[9] Arthur M. Okun, *Equality and Efficiency: The Big Tradeoff* (Washington, DC: Brookings Institution, 1975).

through the market, which allocates wages and other income. Seen in this way, taxation and redistribution implies a set of preferences, on the part of those holding political decision-making rights, for a greater degree of equality than the market, left to function freely, provides.

Okun's description of state-organized taxation and redistribution as a "second-round redistribution" suggests its functional correspondence to the communal redistribution that has traditionally occurred through the family, the household, and the ethnic group. Unlike that redistribution, however, the taxation-fed redistribution organized by the state is one in which the social structure necessary to suppress the disincentive to contribute is missing. This form of second-round redistribution runs into the same incentive barrier to productive activity as has state socialism.

One possible approach to the distribution problem in a double-exchange economy with abundance is to accept that there is a necessity for a second round of distribution, but not of the sort that Okun envisioned. There has always been a second round, in the form of the family. This approach would attempt to bring into being institutions that would have the capacity to produce effective social-psychological incentives of the form that have proven effective in the family: stigma, status, deference, and power.

III. Constitutional Change

Another approach is to turn to the constitutional allocation of rights. As neoclassical economists have made clear, initial endowments determine the final allocation of resources in a perfectly competitive market. The initial endowments with which one enters an economic market of private goods are purely economic. If, however, we extend the conception of a market to include collective decisions within the political system, then the endowments include political rights as well — rights which are in many ways similar to economic resources. The constitution, which provides an "income" of political rights to citizens (just as votes in periodic elections can be seen as an income of political rights), is the instrument through which the "initial endowments" are established. But these endowments are political rights and resources, not directly economic ones.

If all this is so, and if initial endowments determine the final allocation of resources, we must ask why distributional problems cannot be solved by constitutional reallocations of rights. One answer to this question is that this is precisely the stated intent, the ideological underpinning, of socialist revolutions: to reconstitute society in a way that brings about redistribution. The rights that are redistributed are political rights, and the revolutionary goal is to subordinate economic rights, exercised through market transactions, to political rights, exercised by representatives of the people.

Yet this redistribution of rights, suppressing the market, restricting those rights exercised through voluntary transactions, and amplifying those that are exercised through authority, has failed. The amplification of political or authoritative rights, at the expense of rights exercised through a competitive market, drives a social system *away* from a social optimum. Every structural barrier to exchange introduced in the system drives it further from that optimum.

Yet the idea inherent in the socialist revolution—to bring into being a redistribution of economic goods through a redistribution of constitutional rights—is inherently sound. The error lies in increasing the barriers to competitive markets, rather than decreasing them.

Indeed, this error is not confined to socialist states. Democratic constitutions contain some curious elements. The social system is best off, relative to an initial constitutional distribution of rights and resources, if it is what I will call, by analogy to a perfect market, a "perfect social system," with no barriers to convertibility between pairs of resources, no barriers between actors, and sufficient social capital to overcome all free-rider problems.[10]

The decision rules dictated by constitutions, such as the majority rule, are clearly inefficient, and introduce distortions to the outcome that would occur in a perfect system with a consensus decision rule. The more imperfect the social system (including as imperfections the legally imposed barriers to convertibility), the more distortions imposed by social choice governed by decision rules like the majority rule.

Most peculiar of all in the functioning of modern democracies is the use of taxes to impose transfers of income. The necessity for such redistribution is, as a measure of the functioning of the socioeconomic system, a mark of the failure of that system. It is not, of course, a failure of the system in the sense of its productivity, nor is it even a failure of the *economic* system per se. It marks the failure of the whole social system. It can be interpreted as admitting: "We are unable to write a constitution which will allocate rights in such a way that the functioning of the system will give results that we regard as within a tolerable range." Alternatively, it can be interpreted as admitting: "One set of rights, political decision-making rights, represents unlimited power, and whoever holds those rights has unlimited power."

Neither of these interpretations leads to a very sanguine view of the quality of the constitutions of modern democracies. They lead to a view of these constitutions as congeries of rules that have no theoretical justification, or else a justification based on a flawed conception of society. One can ask whether "democratic theory," with its insistence on separa-

[10] For a formal statement of this, see James S. Coleman, *Foundations of Social Theory* (Cambridge: Harvard University Press, 1990), ch. 31.

tion of political and economic resources, might not constitute such a flawed conception. In particular, democratic theory fails to recognize the existence of a new form of actor in society, an actor that has especially strong political interests: the modern corporate actor. The fact that these actors are not endowed with political rights to affect the outcomes of collective decisions does not reduce their interest in doing so. By ignoring the very existence of these new actors in society, democratic theory remains based on a social structure that existed in the eighteenth century, the century in which this theory had its intellectual origins.

There are a number of problems that result from constitutionally created barriers to exchange. One of these is the instability of social choice, when no resources other than partial rights of control of social choices (i.e., other votes, as in logrolling) can be used. Another problem, which exists with or without the instability, is the absence of a process for arriving at the normatively optimal outcome due to the absence of resources with nonconditional value. A third is the problem of enforcement of the barriers separating the different domains of value and power. On both sides of each of these barriers, there are strong interests in transactions that cross the barrier. Enforcement is both costly and imperfect, with a tradeoff between the effectiveness of the barriers and the cost of enforcement.

There are even more fundamental defects, which can be seen in observing the functioning of any such system in a large society with a democratic political system and a market economy. In every such society, there is some degree of convertibility between the political system and the market, in part through circumventing or ignoring constitutional and other legal barriers, and in part through constitutional silence in certain areas. Nevertheless, the general constitutional intent that there be nonconvertibility between "political" and "economic" resources means that the degree and character of convertibility is left to the chance of particular enforcement regimens and particular institutional arrangements. These arrangements may result in outcomes that are far from what might loosely be described as constitutional intent. If constitutional intent were manifested by explicit attention to the degree and means of convertibility between these two sets of resources (and among different "political" resources, which are in general intended to be object-specific), outcomes closer to those constitutionally intended might be achieved.

This issue is particularly important as there come to be shifts in the allocation of rights of control—for example, as there comes to be "collectivization" of activities that were once undertaken individually, or "privatization" of activities that were once undertaken collectively.

One important step toward the construction of a satisfactory political theory was taken by Marx, in seeing that the political and economic systems must be treated together as a single system. If the appropriate conversions between these resources are to occur (rather than the inefficient conversions and the instances of coercion by political rights that now occur), then the two systems must be viewed as a single system. The libertarian concern to exclude any treatment of economic rights and resources in constitutions (beyond the protection of private property, including rights of free acquisition and disposal) is misdirected, for it prevents asking the appropriate question: How should convertibility between economic and political resources take place in order to maximize social efficiency?

There is no justification for keeping separate the domains of political and economic power in the theory that underlies constitutions. The two domains do not stay apart in the social system that functions under a given constitution. If the constitution contains attempts to keep them apart, the system will likely function less well than if their interaction were recognized by the constitution and given institutional support.

What is an alternative to the combination of partly effective barriers to exchange, defective decision rules, and a second-round doctoring up of the results of the distribution of economic resources? To answer that, it is necessary to be clear about just what is the intention behind the political rights, the barriers, the defective decision rules, and the second-round redistribution. The intention appears to be based on the following conception of the functioning of a socioeconomic system:

The economic system should function as freely as possible, without intervention except when it produces results generally agreed to be undesirable.

This is a general expression of liberal political philosophy, though it cannot be regarded as satisfactory even to those who espouse it. The problem, for a libertarian, is in the last phrase, "generally agreed to be undesirable." This phrase allows the camel's nose of collectively held rights under the tent, because it suggests that a society has a right to overturn the outcomes generated by the market system itself.

The obvious alternative to such a makeshift arrangement is one in which barriers to exchanges are wholly eliminated, and in which undesired distributional problems are not patched up after the fact but prevented before the fact through serious attention to the allocation of rights.[11]

Starting afresh, we can begin with the following recognition: All citizens of a society have a certain set of constitutional rights, including par-

[11] I should note that there are suggestions from several points of this idea of eliminating barriers between economic and political resources. In particular, these suggestions may be found in the libertarian branch of the law-and-economics movement, whose theorists have been described as engaged in the effort to "constitutionalize laissez faire." Other law-and-economics theorists have also begun to examine the political-economic interface from this perspective; see, e.g., Richard A. Posner, *The Economic Analysis of Law*, 3d ed. (Boston: Little, Brown, 1986). In what may appear a perverse twist of intellectual paths, this brings the path of such theorists close to that of Marx, who also aimed at a merger of the economic and political systems.

tial control of collective decisions; these rights constitute, in effect, an "income" or endowment of rights over time, as collective actions occur over time; these rights have economic value; and this value could be realized if the political endowments or rights were to become part of a broader market system.

For those endowments to become part of a broader market system, the constitution would have to allow legal convertibility between political and economic resources. This convertibility, in an appropriate institutional structure, would give an income of political rights through the political endowments provided by the constitution; and these rights would have an economic value to their holder — as votes do not, because of the absence of legal convertibility, and because of the defects inherent in a majority decision rule, or in any decision rule other than an auction.

Quite clearly, the citizen's vote *is* a resource that has economic value, although the citizen realizes none of that value under our present system. To see just how that value arises requires looking at a special structural problem that arises in modern society.

IV. Corporate Actors and Natural Persons: Structural Problems

A society composed of a mixture of corporate actors, which hold much of the economic power of the society, and natural persons, who hold most of the constitutionally allocated political rights, contains serious structural problems. The problems lie in the fact that the corporate actors have strong interests in events in the political arena, while natural persons have strong interests in economic resources. Both sides confront difficulties in implementing their interests because of the absence of legal convertibility between the two forms of power.

One might ask if there was a similar problem in the "old" social structure, composed of natural persons and primordial and primordial-derivative corporate actors (that is, families, households, clans, estates, tribes). That structure was one in which *both* political and economic power were held primarily by corporate actors, a condition that would appear to create an even worse problem than the one existing in the new social structure.

But the old structure was different in a fundamental way: the elements making up those old corporate actors were natural persons, not positions. Natural persons were born into those bodies, thus giving them a "birthright" directly derivative from the rights and resources held by the corporate body.

Because persons were born into, and generally remained within, a corporate body of the primordial type in the old social structure, the question of convertibility between political and economic resources did not arise, unless a person was engaged in social mobility. Persons gained their resources through these corporate bodies of which they were the constituent parts, and expressed their political demands through these same corporate bodies (except in the unusual cases of collective action through crowds and mobs).

This structure had its benefits and its costs for persons. The benefits lay in the responsibility that the corporate bodies took, as welfare institutions, for their members. The costs lay in the hierarchy, the rigidity, and the totalitarian character of the structure which enveloped the person. (Modern state socialism reconstitutes in some degree that structure, though based on new corporate actors rather than primordial ones.)

The costs imposed by such a structure on the persons within it are a reminder that to eliminate the defects of the new structure merely by a return to the old, even if that were possible, is no solution. Yet the example of the old structure indicates that there are modes, other than the one we see in liberal democracies, through which an interaction between economic and political resources can take place.

In the new social structure of modern democracies, the lack of convertibility does not prevent economic power from being used to acquire control over political decisions, in the legislative or executive branches of governments; nor does it prevent political power from being used to acquire wealth. Literature on lobbying, campaign financing, and other political activities of corporations attests to the extensive efforts, and considerable success, of corporations in realizing their political interests through use of their economic power. The difference in assets of legislators when they enter office and when they leave office attests to the use of political power to acquire economic power. Nevertheless, the lack of legal convertibility has serious consequences. These can be seen both in the actions of corporate actors realizing their political interests, and in the actions of natural persons realizing their economic interests. I will examine the actions of corporate actors in politics first.

There are two major consequences of the lack of legal convertibility of economic resources for rights of control over governmental actions, and a number of minor consequences. One of the major consequences lies in the fact that the indirect conversions that now occur, through campaign contributions, lobbying expenses, and a variety of other means, may well produce inferior outcomes. For any political decision that is to be made, if each of the two possible outcomes of the decision has a value for the society, then the inability to have that value expressed directly means that the host of indirect conversions that do take place can introduce distortions that lead the outcome with inferior value to dominate.

A second major consequence lies in the fact that control over political decisions is sold at far below its market value. Given that a decision is determined by use of economic resources, the most efficient outcome will occur if it is controlled by the set of actors that will devote the most economic resources to it. However, the exchange that occurs is ordinarily one between corporations (or other corporate actors, such as trade unions; but for expository purposes, I will continue to refer to corporations) and natural persons, such as a few legislators. The different scale of the two actors in the exchanges should be a signal that unless there is a competitive market for exchange of the rights of control over the political actions (which would lead the price actually paid to approximate its economic value to the corporations that value it most highly), the political rights will be sold for far less than their value to corporations. In addition, the legal sanctions against exchange of political and economic rights ("bribery") lead to reduced competition among those holding political rights, resulting in exchanges at far less than the full economic value these rights could command.[12]

For example, consider legislation which would favor the trucking industry at the expense of the railroad industry. The question arises as to which of the two possible outcomes of the legislation will be most socially efficient. Perhaps the best approximation to the correct answer can be seen by auctioning off rights of control over the decision, assuming that whatever actor is successful must pay the full social costs of an adverse outcome (including, for example, welfare costs for employees made redundant) and receives the full social benefits of a beneficial outcome. This assumes, at the extreme, a perfect social system as described earlier, with full social capital to eliminate transaction costs.

The amounts bid in such an auction would very likely be several orders of magnitude greater than the amounts the trucking and railroad industries (both individual corporations and trade associations) now spend to control the outcome for a comparable piece of legislation. This is exemplified by a recent auction of rights to broadcasting frequencies, an auction that earned over two hundred million dollars for the U.S. Treasury.

What now occurs instead of such an auction is mixture of expenditures by corporations and by trade associations in attempting to influence legislators in a variety of ways: through letters and other communications from their constituents, financial contributions to legislators' campaigns, staff aid in writing legislation, and other means. For the side that loses, the expenditures have been wasted; for the side that wins, the gain is many times more valuable than the resources used. As for what happens to those resources, they are nearly all dissipated in the political conflicts preceding the legislative outcome—all the way from election campaigns for the legislators involved, to the contest over the particular legislative action.

---

[12] These legal sanctions are entirely appropriate. The representative is merely an agent for his constituents, and it is *their* votes he is in effect selling (and thus stealing for personal use) when he sells his vote.

V. A New Market for Corporate Actors

If rights to decisions in which corporate actors had an interest were held by citizens, this would create an additional market for a corporation, in addition to the labor, capital, and material markets in which it is involved. The new market could be described as a market in "rights to do business in accord with its interests," rights that are now largely free, except for lobbying costs. This set of rights can be regarded as a factor input for the productive enterprise, similar to its other factor inputs. I will call this its "sovereignty input." Some form of trade association with rights to exclude a corporate actor from the benefits of collective action, or with the right to tax members, would be necessary to overcome the inherent free-rider problems that attend collective decisions.

What would be the value of each collective-decision right? The answer can be approached in this way: Natural persons in society have some interest in the opportunity to earn income through their efforts, an interest that is affected by the opportunity to sell their labor (and thus by the demand for their labor). They also have an interest in the security of satisfying basic needs through resources that are independent of their efforts, i.e., distributed equally. In collective decisions that determined what rights productive enterprises would be required to purchase in order to sell their goods and services, persons would exercise (not sell), through a referendum, their share in the control of these decisions. In turn, the enterprises would, through auctions, establish market prices for these rights, as one of the factor inputs that they would purchase along with labor, materials, and capital. Thus, an equilibrium would be established between two sources of income for natural persons: income acquired through earnings, and thus different for different persons; and income acquired through the sale of citizen rights, equal for all citizens. The equilibrium would arise through increased market value of labor when the marginal value of labor inputs, relative to sovereignty inputs, was high, and through increased market value of sovereignty inputs when the marginal value of those inputs was high. In each case, the reduced income from one or the other of these two sources would lead — through the citizens' preference functions, exercised in a collective decision — to a reduction or an increase in the quantity of sovereignty inputs that corporate actors would need to purchase.

Obviously, the character of this politico-economic structure would require careful design in order to maintain a competitive setting for productive enterprises, an incentive structure for productive labor, and a distribution sufficient for basic needs without taxation. In this system, the only taxation would be taxation of corporate actors by the trade associations formed to acquire rights to control collective decisions.

Such a market merges the political and economic systems, but in a way quite different from that of Marx. Marx was blind to questions of incentives, competition, problems of free riding, and the potential for acquisition of power when political and economic systems are merged. Perhaps because of this, the merging of these systems, in a "planned economy," has come to be associated with authoritarian rule, accumulation of vast power by a few, and the absence of freedom. This need not be so. Once it is recognized that social systems are increasingly coming to consist of a constructed institutional environment, and that primordial social institutions (such as families and households) occupy an increasingly peripheral position in society, it becomes apparent that the society of the future will have both a "planned polity" and a "planned economy." The task is to carry out this design in such a way that natural persons' interests are best realized — including those interests that gave rise to liberal political philosophy in a time when primordial institutions were central, and purposively constructed social organization was in its infancy.

Sociology, University of Chicago

INDEX